BEST AND WORST TRAVELS

By Ramon Carver

Other Books Authored by Ramon Carver

About That trip to New York
About That Trip to Canada

<u>Plays by Ramon Carver</u>

Comfort to Welfare on Interstate 10
Family Album
Ain't Nobody Loves You Like a Mama But Your Mama
Catch as Catch Can
You Can Be A Class Act!
The Land and the River
Texassity
Life & Times (with Rick Smith)

BEST AND WORST TRAVELS

◆

(An Anecdotal Exploration
by an Upper Middle Class Adventurer,
Traveling to Old and New Worlds, Desiring Comfort, Safety,
Good Weather, Good Company, Good Food,
Means of Controlling Heat & Cold,
and Shelter for the Night)

A Travel Anthology by
Ramon Carver

iUniverse, Inc.
New York Lincoln Shanghai

BEST AND WORST TRAVELS
(An Anecdotal Exploration
by an Upper Middle Class Adventurer,
Traveling to Old and New Worlds, Desiring Comfort, Safety,
Good Weather, Good Company, Good Food,
Means of Controlling Heat & Cold,
and Shelter for the Night)

iUniverse books may be ordered through booksellers or by contacting:

iUniverse
2021 Pine Lake Road, Suite 100
Lincoln, NE 68512
www.iuniverse.com
1-800-Authors (1-800-288-4677)

The views expressed in this work are solely those of the author and do not necessarily reflect the views of the publisher, and the publisher hereby disclaims any responsibility for them.

ISBN-13: 978-0-595-42453-5 (pbk)
ISBN-13: 978-0-595-86787-5 (ebk)
ISBN-10: 0-595-42453-8 (pbk)
ISBN-10: 0-595-86787-1 (ebk)

Printed in the United States of America

For Bill Bryson

Contents

Preface

◆

"You have to go there to have been there!"

I have a long-term friend, Mike Boren of Big Bend, Texas, who emailed me recently to say: "I like to read your travel journals. Very informative, but too little blood and guts. No bombings, kidnappings, crocodile attacks. No rape on the beach in Mombassa. Your notion of a bad trip is poor room service or substandard cuisine. Of course, I couldn't really figure your audience."

Well, Mikey, ole buddy, responding to your discriminating criticism, *I'm* the guy I'm writing for. That's what journals are, Mike. And I'm writing for folks who enjoy reading about my good fortune and misfortunes. Particularly middle-aged, upscale middle-class, retirees.

You could say I'm writing for an audience with a sense of humor and people who, like me, want Comfort, Good Weather, Good Company, Good Food, Means of Controlling Heat & Cold, Safety, and Shelter for the Night.

"Ethel, the food and hotels were awful, and we didn't like the people or the places—but we sure did make good time!"

Great expectations when traveling are usually the source of my greatest disappointments. I'm like the guy in a *New Yorker* cartoon studying a brochure telling his travel agent: "I am <u>so</u> looking forward to this. I can't wait to be disappointed."

Actually, I go nuts when someone or something disappoints, and I rejoice when it exceeds expectations. But always, if I can wring a laugh out of a misadventure, I wring it. And I confront my expectations head on.

How does one set up and adjust reasonable travel expectations? The old-fashioned ways:

1. <u>Acquire information</u> in bits and pieces over the course of a lifetime,

2. <u>Save a pot full of money</u>, and then

3. <u>Cross your fingers</u> before and during travel.

<u>Acquire Information</u>: Everybody's attracted to the idea of trips to far away places with strange sounding names as well as places close at hand. That's how we *all* begin our travels for pleasure—with an assumption that a place *might* be a

great destination. But how do we determine if a trip will be right for _us_? Candid travel agents are the best sources. Who else ya gonna trust?

The easiest way to get informed is to listen to traveler's stories or read somebody's personal travel journals. Armchair travel. Doesn't really matter how old the journals are because it's the traveler's experiences you're after, not particulars. All particulars are out-of-date from the moment they're penned.

Centuries of noteworthy writers have kept remarkable journals, and I absolutely recommend reading them as well as those of contemporary blog writers. Every search engine on the net can take you to somebody's first-person account of adventures in the States and abroad, and each blog is biased with op/ed narratives, and the bias is precisely why you'll be reading them.

"You have to be there." is the only accurate way of sharing some adventures/ misadventures: Standing at the ovens at Dachau, cruising the Canals in Burgogne that Thomas Jefferson enjoyed, hiking atop Vesuvius, staring back at the Sphinx while riding a camel, climbing steep steps up and down the Great Wall, you discover there are far more than 1,000 places to visit before you die.

Commercial travel publications cultivate fantasy, not candor. Prospective clients, that is, readers of magazines and tour books, search for authoritative sources of information, but publishers (Travel Czars) are in business to market the industry. It's the _promise of comfort and luxury_ that sells travel like the promise of sex sells sex.

On the upside, they offer directions and maps and useful cultural and historical information to accompany spectacular photography (There is no frigate like a great photograph). But they generally fail to note that their stuff is months old by the time it hits the shelves. In July of this year (any year), one can buy hardback travel books with next year's dates on the cover containing lists of "Best" restaurants, lodgings, etc., even businesses that have gone out of business.

Best source: First hand experiences of travel agents and writers, and acquaintances who have been there. All other sources are risky at best.

Save a Potful of Money: Money is essential. It may not seem so from hearing about historical people who traveled for months at a time, but even cheap travel is expensive. All travel but business travel (an oxymoron) is a luxury, a term Georges Bataille has defined as what we do with energy and funds left over after our material needs are met. If you can't afford to travel today, invest in tomorrow by reading armchair travel journals and prioritize a wish list.

Cross Your Fingers: And hope that you'll have satisfaction. Otherwise, belly up to the bar and adjust your attitude once you arrive on the scene.

Here's where I insert a disclaimer: <u>I'm a traveler who goes places for plea-sure</u>, and I write emphasizing my misadventures because people who invest in budget travel as well as smart luxury travel want to know what can go wrong en route to (and during) their stay in a vacation paradise and what can be done about it. I've experienced virtually every category of "The Worst that can Happen" and "How to Survive Disasters like Theft, Accidents, etc."

And at the risk of seeming disingenuously obvious, here's a primer for first stage travelers: an exhaustive list which covers every possible thing that can happen:

You might end up **Getting Killed or Sick or having an Accident** (It's not likely you'll get wasted in a terrorist attack. Those horrors can happen abroad or at home, but the odds, thank God, are considerable. Getting sick is often avoidable, so don't drink the water, etc.).

Getting Lost (That's the single best reason for going on group tours because if you do get lost, you won't be alone).

It's costly **Wasting Time Finding Places** (That's the other best reason for going with groups; your group leaders have been there before).

Virtually every traveler's guilty of **Not Taking Time to Prepare for the Journey,** and then **Not Taking Time to Reflect During and After your Journey.** And if you really want to regret something, there's **Not Taking Time to Keep a Journal,** like not taking pictures (No matter how inane your reactions may seem when you write, you can always revise).

My worst sin is **Not Taking Time to Nap** (If you don't set a time to nap, you'll nap at all the wrong times). On cruises, I enjoy napping and reading more than eating.

Neglectful: **Not Having Bottled Water** (Always have it or you'll want it).

Criminal: **Not Having Local Currency** (Always have it or you'll need it).

Unbelievable: **Not Having A "No Smoking" Seat if you're a Non-Smoker** (Cough loud and often without complaining and they'll find you a seat elsewhere).

You shouldn't be satisfied **Not Having Great Itineraries** (No rug showrooms, please), **Not Finding Photo Ops** (Evidence to prove you were there), **Not Having Superb Tour Guides** (Tour guides who talk at length while you're left standing in the sun are not superb), **Not Having Interesting Companions** (A great pity), **Not Having Luggage That may be Rolled** (For Transfers, absolutely, with a colorful I.D. attached), and **Not Having Clean Public Toilets** (In some parts of the world, toilets make US Stop & Rob restrooms look good).

You can't travel anywhere without sometimes **Forgetting Things** (You will**),** **Losing Things** (You definitely will, and periodically your luggage), or **Getting robbed** (You will sooner or later, later if you're lucky). You really ought to cultivate a pathological fear that you must not be separated from "items that you must not be separated from." Then trust yourself.

Oh, yeah, did I fail to mention **Getting Bored to Death,** the opposite of **Getting Thrilled Beyond Belief.**

I think that covers absolutely everything that can possibly go awry.

Beauty is in the eye of the camera. Gorgeous photos of far-away places. What greater reason to travel does one need than to go stand at the site of a photo op. It's not just the composition, lines, highlight and shadow, color, balance, and quality of the photographer's art. It's the sheer beauty of the place itself. Go find Beauty! (Everywhere you find the word "Beautiful!" in the text of this book, trust me, I've beheld it!)

I will continue to write about comfort as if it were a highly desirable option because I truly do desire it, and I will neglect writing about Mombassa beach rape, Mikey. (I write about illicit sex on a beach in my Rio journal. Try to find *that* in a travel magazine.)

Introduction

Why have I written this book?

I've been traveling since childhood when my father took me with him to New York, Chicago, Dallas, and elsewhere, and I've developed an appetite for exploration. I eat it with a spoon. Auntie Mame, the world traveler, had a maxim, "Life is a banquet, and most poor bastards are starving to death."

The chapters in this collection occur chronologically from my first larger-than-life cruise to present day. Originally, I thought I might build from the worst at the first of the book and save the best for last. But every trip is the best *and* worst.

I've learned how to anticipate and solve problems as I've grown older and more judicious; hence, the order of journals here. I make scant mention of earlier trips to Europe shepherding college students from one country to the next (the girls seducing waiters during the soup course at dinner, the guys getting stoned at lunch in the Louvre), and trips to New York City with friends and students and any client willing to offset my travel costs. I *do* discuss living in Germany as a US Army serviceman because several of my trips have beginnings in Germany.

I've identified in these journals what I like most (and least) about exploring old and new worlds. I must quickly add that getting there isn't *half* the fun; sometimes it's *none* of the fun. Waiting in airports and schlepping heavy luggage are transfer problems hard to avoid. Who was it that said, "Airports are the eighth circle of Hell."

Travel's not an end in itself. Most tourists view travel as a means to the following ends: They want to

    A. Go somewhere different,

    B. See and do something unusual,

    C. Avoid meeting uninteresting people,

    D. Feel they haven't wasted their time and money because of their own (or somebody else's) poor choices, and

    E. Enjoy themselves.

That's the key. Enjoying <u>oneself</u> [Add excessive exclamation points here]!!!

A modern sage once said, "Never underestimate the value of a one night stand." He wasn't talking about travel, but his sentiment definitely applies to discovering new and old worlds.

This is <u>not</u> a "How To" book. It's a "How I Enjoyed Myself and Sometimes Didn't" guide, 1) alone or with groups, 2) exploring new and old worlds, 3) noting best and worst epiphanies, 4) adapting my attitudes, 5) avoiding disappointments, 6) staying healthy, and 7) appreciating ironies, that is, finding something to laugh about. (Actually, appreciating ironies should top the list.)

Oh, yeah, 8) acknowledging <u>best</u> things that happen as well as worst.

Some of these journals are thank you notes for great times, for example: Years ago, I enjoyed a great Abercrombie & Kent trip to China because it was a great adventure and a great itinerary, and I was part of a great tour group with a great tour director, and we stayed at great hotels (except for a noisy Sheraton in Guilin, China), and we had great weather, and there was great tour management by the A&K tour agency. Seven greats out of seven ain't bad.

Also, on that same trip to China, I didn't get worn out sightseeing or shopping (Shopportunities are tolerable if I'm seeing new things—even trinkets, but it's tiresome to have to wait while the entire herd grazes). I kept my weight down on that trip because I didn't drink or eat too much of anything. And I used preventative medicine from Asperin to Zen to avoid getting sick.

As noted above, dangerous stuff happens to some people while traveling: terrorism, illness, contaminated food or water, crime, crowds, and unfriendly attitudes toward Americans. *And that's just in the States.* Abroad one finds the same dangers.

But stop! If you're afraid to go abroad, just don't go. Your fear of what *might* happen is non-negotiable. Of course, you can reduce your sense of insecurity by

1. Checking current US State Department advisories on the net,

2. Hiring English-speaking guides or drivers in advance or on the scene (and be sure to audition them for about five minutes to insure it's the same English you speak),

3. Learning the local language ("Where's the loo?"),

4. Staying in Western-style luxury hotels eating Western-style food,

5. Traveling with friends,

6. Buying travel insurance, and

7. Just being lucky, prudently avoiding things that can go wrong.

Some of these journals are descriptive narratives, some are editorials, some are old-fashioned daily entries. Some are written as outlines, checklists, summaries, emails, virtual photographs, and some are presented in unconventional formats I think appropriate for the content.

My writing style changes almost as often as modes of conveyance. Clearly I prefer some styles and kinds of conveyances over others for travel. Cruises, for example, are my favorite because meals & lodging are built in.

I learned about half-price the hard way on my first cruise to Alaska on a ship that has since been decommissioned and I hope sunk for a coral reef.

I like high-dollar cruise lines, but not big, glitzy ships that guarantee a good time visiting rip-off islands in the Caribbean at half-price. I've neglected to describe the only trip I took on *Carnival* cruise line, the Wal-Mart of the Waves, or "Kathie Lee's Discount Navy with 13 decks of spring break and a buffet, a floating Marti Gras with bars open 24/7 and wet T-shirt contests by the pool." [From an article by Spud Hilton, *San Francisco Chronicle*, October, 2002].

Please enjoy what I've written—or turn the page.

My very personal thanks to Margaret and Mike Williamson for their photographic expertise. And for their friendship.

Happy trails and bon voyage.

The author's umbrella pointing at crushed rock rubble, the glacier's highway litter.

Alaska

✦

An Ill-fated Cruise
August 23, September 21, 1991

Our travel agent, Diane, said, "You've made a big mistake cashing in those frequent flyer miles for a two-for-one package on Regency Cruise Lines (A defunct cruiseship company not to be confused with Regent Seven Seas Cruises). They don't have a good rep in the biz."

I said something like, "Yeah, well, it can't be the worst cruise we've taken because it's only our first, ha-ha."

She said, "Mark my words, Mr. Ha-ha, it's gonna be a bummer trip, okay?" Diane was one of those painfully blunt folks you meet whom you learn, painfully, to trust. And love. During the last month of her life, she said, "Don't wait for the funeral; come see me now." So we made the four-hour trip and found her lying in bed, propped up on pillows, smiling, and she said, "You know how to make God laugh?"

"How?"

"Tell Him your plans, Mr. Ha-ha."

And it was so. God was roaring when I convinced Barbara, my wife, to take that ill-fated cruise with me on the *Regent Star* to Alaska in the fall of 1991.

<u>The Pre-Cruise</u>

August 23, 24—Seattle To Victoria And Return

We flew directly from Dallas to Seattle's SEATAC airport and stashed our three suitcases in a storage shop, taking only two overnight bags with us for a pre-cruise trip. Then we took a shuttle to Pier 69 where we purchased tickets for Victoria in Canada by Clipper and—while waiting for the departure time—we spent the afternoon strolling through Seattle's Pike Place Fish Market. A fish mar-ket—tourist attraction or not—is a place where they sell fish. I wasn't buying. What are tourists supposed to do with fresh fish?

Keeping on schedule, trying to look like sophisticated travelers, Barbara and I schlepped our luggage aboard the hydrofoil, Victoria Clipper, a catamaran that operates daily from Pier 69, Seattle to Victoria. We sat at a small table quaffing Canadian beer, remarking to one another that it didn't really taste imported. Then we walked stem to stern and watched Seattle slip out of sight. We enjoyed the sunshine and sea spray for the first hour or so. Thereafter, the seas got bumpy, and many folks—not us—got seasick. Messy, those poor sickees staggered around the ship, easily identifiable from their sponged-off shirts & blouses and ashen complexions.

The sun was setting just as we arrived, and the lights outlining the Parliament building blazed on to welcome us. Beautiful! We looked for a taxi, but they all got taken, so we had to walk about a mile to our motel, carrying that heavy, bumpka, bumpka hand luggage (We hadn't sprung for luggage on wheels). With every step—bumpka, bumpka—I thought, "Bummer. Bummer. Bummer."

After checking in, we changed clothes, walked around the harbor and inner city and looked for an inviting restaurant, settling for a crowded touristy pub, the Keg, whose salmon was super.

Afterwards we walked back to the motel, undressed, showered, walked toward the bed, and we were asleep before we hit the sack.

The following morning after breakfast, we hired a "Tally Ho Horse & Carriage," driven by a woman with a mustache who boasted she had been with the company longer than any other carriage driver. That boast proved to be a negative distinction because she was obviously burned out and tired of the job. We enjoyed ourselves, however, and bundled up in heavy, end-of-the-season woolen blankets smelling of horse piss, braving the wind from off Puget Sound, until we started to freeze and asked to cut the trip short. Bummer again.

Afterward, the wind calmed, and we took a free walking tour of the Parliament building, ("Free" doesn't mean that a thing is interesting necessarily, but it's a pretty reliable indicator it's nothing you'd want to pay for). Then we visited the Museum of Natural History with lots of Inuit Indian totem poles and relics (some aboriginal items over 5,000 years old), stuffed animals, and dried vegetation.

Barbara had another serving of salmon for lunch at the Crystal Gardens outdoor restaurant where we watched stony-faced, out-of-shape, old folks at play, lawn bowling. The rules of that game require players not to get excited. The most bored-looking players always win.

That afternoon, we walked through the wonderful old Empress hotel where there was a waiting list for reservations for high tea in the tearoom. We settled for the porch of the hotel where I had a vodka tonic and read a book while Barbara wrote postcards and drank tea, watching the tourists stand on line, waiting to go into the crowded tearoom. [Tea rooms are a universal disappointment if you wait on line for something transcendental to happen. I have found that tea at the Peninsula in Hong Kong, Brown's Hotel in London, and the Plaza in New York tastes pretty much the same. Tea is thin.]

It was chilly, so we got Barbara a good-looking Canadian-made windbreaker for the cruise, and she wore it constantly. Who would have guessed that Alaska would be so cold in August and every other month of the year?

That evening, one of the highlights of the trip—in itself a reason for going to Victoria—was a bus tour to Buchart Gardens, a limestone quarry converted into an imaginative, no, a *remarkable* series of terraces with colorful blooming plants (even in August) and hundreds of varieties of flowers. And fountains.

At last, the bummer curse was broken.

Arriving at the Gardens just about an hour before dusk, the weather was perfect. We enjoyed watching the sun set as we strolled about. Buh-yoo-ti-ful! Then we went to a restaurant on the grounds where we had the best—and most fanciful—dinner that we had the entire trip featuring a salad with greens, mango, shrimp, avocado and edible flowers from the gardens.

Afterwards, we went to the Garden's horticulture desk, learning names of flowers that are edible and flowers to die from. The distinction is significant.

Returning by bus to Victoria, we visited another pub and enjoyed more Canadian beer, then we went to our motel, packed for our return trip to Seattle, and went to bed.

Gonna be a great, great trip.

Early the following morning, refusing to schlep our luggage, we taxied the five long blocks to the Clipper, took another, bumpier boat back to Seattle, and breezed through customs. It seemed that we were returning from abroad.

En Route to Embarkation

Saturday, August 24—Seattle To Anchorage

Seattle was hot and muggy that day. We missed a connection to take a bus tour of the city; so we had to spend an idle afternoon walking around the airport. Finally, at departure time, we boarded the Cowboy Special, or so I called the flight to Anchorage because almost everybody flying resembled farmers and ranchers I've seen in Odessa, Texas. Yo, doaggies.

The weather turned bad, and bouncing around we couldn't see Mt. McKinley when we flew into Anchorage, nor did we ever see it the whole time we were there because of overcast skies. I learned that's a common complaint.

Anchorage in the summer looks like Odessa in the summer but with rain. The driver from the airport to the hotel was an ex-Texan who said he got tired of droughts in Texas so he moved to God's country for the rain. He said, "If rain makes you happy, you'll love Alaska."

We stayed overnight at the Anchorage Sheraton, a dump that has *nothing* to recommend it. Looking out onto the rooftops of Odessa Del Norte, I thought, "If this is God's country, God's a redneck." Lots of tarpaper roofs, lean-tos, and dilapidated buildings in need of repair and paint. They really don't take care of that town. Jeeze!

Sunday, August 25—Anchorage to Whittier

That morning, we walked a few blocks in the drizzle to visit the Museum of Natural History that I recommend highly for superior displays of its collections. Only problem is you have to go to Anchorage to see it.

We returned to the hotel in the rain to await the bus scheduled to transfer us to Whittier. Why didn't the ship dock in Anchorage? Because the tidal basin there (extreme high & low tides) has no place for big ships to dock. So what were we doing in Anchorage? Well, that's how you get to Alaska to transfer to Whittier to embark on cruise ships. You go around your elbow to get to your thumb.

En route to Whittier by bus, we stopped at Portage—or what was left of that town after an earthquake devastated it—and we looked at the Portage Glacier, enormous ice cubes floating in a lake. It was awesome, but we didn't stop and get out of the bus because the driver said we didn't have time. I assumed we would see other glaciers like it, but it was the only one on the entire trip that we got to see up close (except for a fantastic helicopter trip we took in Juneau described below).

The bus continued on the way to Whittier, and the driver slowed down to allow passengers, like voyeurs, to watch salmon spawning themselves to death in a splashing frenzy, churning the waters like you wouldn't believe. Spawning salmon don't look pretty; in fact, their bodies get swollen and muddy brown-colored. I asked the driver to stop and let us take pictures, but he said we didn't have time.

We traveled another mile down the road to a god-forsaken souvenir shop, and the driver announced we would have thirty minutes to stretch our legs. Hell, how long does that take? We stayed in that dive for over 45 minutes wishing we could go back to watch salmon spawn. When we finally reboarded the bus, we discovered there is no highway to Whittier.

We were told (I guess they assumed we already knew) that the only access to the embarkation dock was by train. But we wouldn't be getting off the bus. All twenty busses, in fact, were going to drive up onto the flatbed cars of a train. And that's exactly what happened with remarkable efficiency, all those busses driving up onto flatbed cars. Impressive.

The train started slowly and picked up speed the way trains do, and we rode through a countryside covered with Permafrost. There's nothing pretty about Permafrost. It's about as unattractive as most of West Texas to somebody who's not from West Texas.

Finally, we arrived at the docks, we got off the bus, and we boarded the ship. Hot dog! This is gonna be fantastic, right, Honey?

The Cruise, At Last

A deckhand who couldn't speak English showed us to our cabin, an ugly prison cell with paint peeling off cold metal walls. There was a tiny double bed with a baggy mattress not quite the size of a standard double.

We weren't unhappy. We were madder than Hell, thinking, "We are not gonna be stuck in this shithole for the entire trip!" No way.

I said, "Wait a dadgum minute" to the deckhand. "Our reservations are for Cabin 4 on the Sun Deck, not Cabin 4 on the Promenade Deck."

"Que?" he said.

"And we're supposed to be portside."

"Que?" he said.

I said, "This won't do!"

And he said—as if I didn't know—"No speak English," turned and disappeared.

I looked at Barbara. She wasn't smiling. Her reaction was the same as mine; so I supposed I wasn't overreacting. We were both truly and utterly—inconsolably—pissed.

"Bummer" was back.

I pulled out my well-worn copy of the cruise brochure and went down to the Purser's desk, ready to do battle. It is there that I learned Pursers are not necessarily nice pursons.

I had to stand in a long line with other disenchanted customers, and when it was my turn at the desk, the Purser's assistant told me that no one had ever complained about P4, and she was surprised that my wife and I did not like it. Furthermore, she said virtually every room in the ship was booked.

I said, "Let's check out virtually."

After an interminable wait, she located Cabin 157 on the Main Deck, Starboard side, and she explained that it would cost $175 more than we had already paid. I asked to see her boss, assuming that I would explain I had already paid quite enough, and that we simply would not settle for P4.

It didn't work.

The Boss Purser was a thoroughly nasty, non-negotiable person who said she would tell me only once that if I did not come up with the $175 immediately, I could return to P4 (and the non-negotiable person I had left there), or I had until midnight to leave the ship.

I said, "I want to speak with your boss."

She handed me a card that said "Customer Relations" with a New York phone number on it, and she pointed to a phone on a nearby wall, and said, "You can call my boss on Monday when our New York office is open for business. Or you can leave the ship tonight and return to Anchorage."

Reader, I am sure that, by now, you cannot imagine that Barbara and I are the kind of folks who would be willing to get off a ship in protest. Can't you just see us, two silhouetted ex-passengers standing under a streetlight on that god-for-saken, oil-soaked dock with our overfull suitcases at our sides waiting for a bus on a train flatbed to return while watching the ship sail away.

That ain't us.

I tried using my real ammunition. I said, "Listen. I'm gonna tell *you* only once. If you don't transfer us from P4 to M157 without an additional charge, I'm going to get my wife to talk to you in language only you sailors seem to understand. Okay?"

The Purser took a deep breath and hissed through her teeth: "Which credit card will you be using to charge the $175?"

Without skipping a beat, I said, "Is Mastercard okay?"

She said, "Thank you," and after a meaningful pause and a pronounced hiss, "Ssssssir."

She turned away, processed the card, turned back, and added, "Welcome aboard."

The Purser's assistant assured me I would like M157. "Every guest we've ever had likes M157." (And it was okay. It had two beds, a table, a chair, and it was easily worth the additional $175, but the unexpected charge stuck in my craw.)

We unpacked, then Barbara and I went to dinner at the first seating. We were assigned to a table with eight old farts and two Black women whom nobody wanted to sit near. We seized the opportunity and made the acquaintance of the older woman, a psychologist from L. A., and her daughter, a social worker. They were the only two people on board for the entire trip whom we felt comfortable with aboard that Ship of Fools.

But there was more to come on that first evening aboard.

We saw a performance of shipboard entertainers who presented an original revue, "*Getting to Know You*," introducing the Captain and his staff. I learned from that event that there was nobody on the staff of that tub whom I would probably ever enjoy "getting to know."

The performers looked as if they had been slapped around and shanghaied aboard.

The British Master of Ceremonies for the evening was also the ship's enter-tainment director, a fatuous, leering, unfunny fellow, so I didn't expect entertain-ment aboard ship to be much better than the man in charge, and I was right.

We waited and waited for the ship to sail, and decided to attend a midnight buffet, "Cote D'Azur Night." It was okay, but eating an uninspired cold buffet at midnight is even less exciting than it sounds.

The ship sailed, and we watched land disappear behind us while leaning on the railing, gazing up at a beautiful full moon coming out from behind a cloud. We knew that if the cruise turned out to be disappointing, we would have each other to commiserate with.

We returned to our cabin, noting that it was a cool night, and we probably wouldn't need air conditioning on the trip. It wasn't until the next day we learned there wasn't any A/C. It was broken. We learned why later.

Monday, August 26—At Sea

We slept late and had breakfast delivered to our cabin. Our daily ship's newspaper informed us that we had sailed past College Glacier during the night and that we were currently located in Prince William Sound. I rushed to the porthole and looked out. There was nothing but gloomy fog, and as noted above, on the starboard side, we were staring out to sea.

A defective public address system squawked: "Attent----, Ladies and -- ----- --: When the ship's -- ----- blows for - -- --- -- -, put on you life -- ---- -, and go to your stations. Th--- - --"

We went to our fire drill station, and a crewmember whose English was a tertiary language told us to wait until a ship's officer appeared. When the brass strutted up, one of our group assailed him with news that the gate to the lifeboat at our location had been painted shut. He laughed, tried to open it, failed, and then walked away, swearing at the crewmember whose English was a tertiary language. After that, we were told to return to our cabin.

We selected tours for various ports, a universal ritual that allows all cruise lines to make money without assuming responsibility for land tour agencies' errors and ineptness.

Lunch in the "Cordon Bleu" dining room, then we returned to our cabin where we read and napped, then during the early afternoon, we went to tea (Boring as ever). That evening we attended the Captain's cocktail party and reception, a non-event since the Captain wasn't in attendance. At dinner, Barbara had salmon for a change, and she said she could eat salmon every night. But it didn't appear on the ship's menu again until the last night.

Our travel agent, Diane, had sprung for a bottle of wine, surprising us, and we shared it with our two new best friends.

That night, a storm came up and the ship bobbed about like a cork. I slept through it, but Barbara told me in the morning that she had pitched about all night.

Tuesday, August 27—Sitka

We failed to request breakfast and slept late, so we had to settle for bouillon as punishment, but not before Bouillon Time at 10am. Salty Bouillon's a taste I've never acquired, and it's okay for people in deckchairs in movies, but when it's served cold by a surly waiter, it's not much of a substitute for breakfast.

Most of the wait staff was well mannered, even obsequious, but some were perceptibly resentful. I was told that the crew referred to passengers as "seagulls" because "we screeched at them and shat on them."

But they weren't always civil to one another. That afternoon, we watched a Greek ship's officer yell and use obscene hand signals to direct Philippine crewmen to lower the anchor, a job requiring about twenty men. Don't ask, "How many shanghaied seamen does it take to lower an anchor?"

We disembarked for a visit to Sitka via a tender—a misnomer for a kind of boat that on almost all cruise lines has no more comfort than is required by law.

The village of Sitka has a Russian orthodox church, the only slightly distinctive sight to see aside from a Visitors' Center where local women presented a program of Russian dances. Then we were allowed enough time to shop for souvenirs, but nothing that interested us enough to buy it.

We returned to the ship for dinner and another stage show with the same stalwart entertainers doing *A Broadway Medley* featuring all the show tunes you've ever heard in your life interrupted periodically by the obnoxious M. C.

We retired late and, again, we were rocked to sleep and I slept well.

Wednesday, August 28—Skagway

The steward woke us up earlier than we had asked to be awakened for breakfast because the ship had docked at Skagway, and he said he wanted to finish serving early so he could go ashore. We walked into Skagway, ignored the souvenir shops, then satisfied there was nothing else there to see or do, we returned to sack out for the rest of the morning.

After lunch we took a ride on the White Pass Summit Railroad Lines, a narrow gauge, mountain climbing train (from sea level to 7,000 feet), gold rush territory. We had super weather and a great trip, but like many of the best things in life, it wasn't free and it lasted too long.

An early show featuring a local resident billed as a "jolly balladeer," distracted us while we waited for dinner to be served. After dinner, I and only two other folks watched a Disney movie in the ship's theatre, *White Fang*, an unlikely title for a very entertaining show that had been shot on locale in Skagway.

B. and I stayed awake for a midnight buffet because it was TexMex night. Except for the décor, there wasn't a single TexMex dish served. The menu listed Boston baked beans & franks, rice pudding, and tuna-stuffed bell peppers. It was laughable for everybody who recognized the inappropriate choices for "TexMex" foods.

We read ourselves to sleep. There was another storm at sea during the night, but we didn't know about it till morning.

Thursday, August 29—Juneau *The best and worst day of the cruise*

We arose early, took in a breakfast buffet, and got aboard a smelly tender to go ashore. We shopped around but didn't buy anything.

The Best Part. Around noon, we boarded a bus to transfer to a private heliport where we and two other people boarded a helicopter. I lucked out and got a front seat. Rising up a mountainside, I expected to level off but there was a cliff! It seemed the other side of the mountain had fallen away. A stunning surprise! We could see all twenty-three miles of the Mendenhall Glacier ahead of us. The copter dipped and swooped and landed—Wheeeee!—depositing us on top of the glacier; then, it started up, flew away and left us and passengers from other copters alone on the ice.

There was a profound silence after they flew out of sight. Both Barbara and I gasped as we realized that this was the moment we had come to Alaska for. That moment made all the bummer stuff seem irrelevant and incidental.

Nothing is better than a once-in-a-lifetime excursion. We were walking on the surface of an ages-old frozen river of ice, peering into wells of the purest water, holding hands, ostensibly to keep our balance, but actually to share excitement.

The return trip was also exciting because the weather was changing. The copter was buffeted by wind currents, bouncing and bopping up and down. Eye-popping; the sights were astounding.

Wheeeee!

We had lunch at a fisherman's wharf in Juneau (Barbara had salmon), and we looked out at our great 10-story high passenger ship, safe and snug at anchor.

The Worst Part. All of a sudden, a great wind whipped through town blowing over tables and benches, breaking limbs off trees, and damaging awnings of buildings. Just as suddenly, it stopped blowing on land, but at sea—we watched in horror as our ship was whipped around almost 180 degrees by the wind. Wow.

The ship's horn began to blow short, successive blasts. We assumed it was a distress call because a tugboat sailed out and attached itself to the ship, struggling to pull that sucker back to its original location.

Someone at the restaurant announced that our Captain had issued an emergency call for all passengers to cut short the visit to Juneau and return to the ship because the weather was going to change drastically.

I convinced Barbara to ignore the Captain's orders because each round trip of the tender took thirty minutes and conveyed about fifty passengers at a time to the ship. So we continued shopping and sightseeing for another two hours. And as luck would have it, we returned to the dock and boarded the last tender just as a horrendous rainstorm began.

Seventeen passengers missed the boat and had to be flown at their own expense to join us at the next port.

We learned later that all remaining glacier-bound helicopter flights that had been reserved by other passengers on the ship had been cancelled. We didn't feel lucky; in truth, we felt really bad for the guys who wouldn't know what a once-in-a-lifetime excursion they had missed.

The storm at sea kicked in and continued during the night, but we were having sweet dreams of copters dipping, swooping and diving from one glorious glacier to another.

Friday, August 30—Ketchikan

We awoke to rain and the squawk box: "We regret - --- - - - --- be able to - ----- - in Ketchikan because of --- - ----- - - ---- and rough seas. Please --- - - --- - - --- - - - ----!

Half an hour later, again the squawker: "--- - - ------ --- - - now we -- - --- docking in Ketchi---, you are welcome to go ashore and ---- - - - - --- - -- - - -- on the deck."

At first, it seemed Ketchikan was just another rainy Alaskan hamlet, but by now we didn't want to take these remarkable little towns for granted. Pioneers' settlements, frontier towns. Each has mountains, trees, unique architecture—not often pretty buildings—and boulders and trees and the sea. And rain.

Ketchikan has more rain than any other Alaskan town or any town in the US. It occurred to us that this would be our last stop in Alaska, so we bought cans of—guess what—salmon, different kinds and qualities, and without pausing for a postcard or a sentimental look around, we returned in the rain to the ship and dinner.

We never dried off completely all day.

Saturday, August 31—At Sea

At sea, we kept trying to keep our balance while walking because of choppy waters, the result of leaving the Inside Passage for open seas in a storm in an unseaworthy ship. We walked the decks, we packed suitcases, we ate only at mealtimes, and at the end of the day, we left our luggage outside our door, tagged for SEATAC. Unaccustomed to this conventional luggage procedure, we worried all night that someone might steal it, to no avail, for in the morning the luggage was still outside waiting for sleepy stewards to pick it up.

Sunday, September 21—Vancouver

We returned from stormy seas to sunlight and calm weather in Vancouver, a beautiful docking facility. We spent a lot of time standing on line, processing passports and transfer passes—as if that were the purpose of our travel—and when our transfer to Seattle was announced, we had to leave without looking around Vancouver.

After visiting friends in Seattle, we had no trouble returning home and resuming everyday life. And that's the story of our first cruise. If we ever go to Alaska again, we'll pick our own itinerary, plan well in advance, and take a small boat on the Alaska Marine Highway and/or the Alaska Railroad, traveling light without a tight schedule.

Postscript

About the middle of our voyage, we met a woman aboard ship who confessed that after an initial bout with seasickness, she found her sea legs and spread them for some of the ship's officers and crew.

She told us that one of her officer friends had been stationed on the bridge of the ship, the *Regent Star*, when a local pilot boarded, drunk as a lord, and piloted the ship into an iceberg. That was six weeks before our cruise commenced. She reported that the wreck had damaged some of the engines, disabling the air conditioning system. Aha! That's why it never worked. The remaining engines were used twenty-four hours a day with a three-man team supervising their operation because the cruise line owners refused to take the ship out of commission for repair until the end of the season.

She said our ship had collided with her sister ship earlier that year.

Yikes!

For all the negative events that occurred on the Star, I might have had better feelings about the cruise line if—two weeks after the cruise was over—I had not had a confrontation on the phone with a Customer Relations representative, Ms. Heather Hardy, when I called to ask for a refund of my $175. I dialed the 800 number that the evil Purser had handed me on the day we boarded, and I got a recording telling me to leave my name and number and—if I had a complaint—to put it in writing and send it in.

I decided I would just leave my name and number and wait for a phone call in response.

The next day, I called again. No response.

Two days later, I called again. No response.

Then I decided to use the company's 212 number to the same office. I got an operator who connected me with Customer Relations. I recognized the live voice of the woman who had made the 800 recording, identifying herself as Ms. Hardy. Impatiently, she confessed she had listened to my messages, and she had determined I needed to write out my complaint.

I, Mr. Nice Guy, said that I didn't want to write out a complaint, I simply wanted to know why I wasn't given the rate I thought I was entitled to. Ms. Hardy, the bitch, said she did not intend repeating herself and told me she was going to hang up which she did.

I, Mr. Persistent, called the 800 number back immediately and recorded a message for five minutes, telling her that I refused to A) lose my temper; however, I had no desire to B) write a letter.

She failed to respond that day or the next.

So, I, Mr. Relentless, called the 212 number again and when the operator transferred me to Ms. Hardy, I made the mistake of using her first name to address her.

She took great exception, told me to stop annoying her, and never again to use her first name; then, she slammed down the receiver.

I, Mr. Chauvinist Nuisance, called 212- back immediately and after the customary delayed connection, talked quickly and deliberately, explaining that I fully intended getting an answer from her or from anyone in that office on her level whom she wished to delegate or, if not, then her superior.

"*My* level?" She took a deep, audible breath and said, "How. May. I. Help. You. Sir?"

I said, "Well, as I've explained several times on your voice message machine, I think I was charged $175 more than I should have been on the Promenade Deck even though we got twofers and an early booking rate."

She explained very, very slowly, that passengers who have twofers aren't entitled to a reduced rate for early reservations. The difference, she said, was the same as the amount I paid, $175."

I said, "Oh?"

She said, "Does that answer your question?"

I said, "Well, … Yes, but that doesn't explain your behavior or that of that Purser. Okay? Nor does it make me a satisfied customer. And if I—"

She interrupted my stammer: "Is there anything else I can help you with?"

I said, "Well, yeah. I'm writing a travel book—"

She said, "Why don't you stuff your book up your ass, Sir. Or, as we like to say on my level, 'Fuck you!' Goodbye."

And she hung up.

I was amused and annoyed as I held the telephone receiver in my hand like a plastic chicken, and I thought, "This person is having a bad day, and I'm truly sorry that I'm part of her problem, but she treated me as if I were just another seagull."

The cruise ended for me when I giggled and nested the receiver in its cradle.

Two years later, I was *astonished* to learn that Regent Sea Cruise Lines had declared bankruptcy.

What astonished me was the miracle that allowed that company two years of grace to go out of business.

Emerald Lake is one of the rarest jewels in Canada's Jewel Box lakes.

O Canada

✦

(What You Need to Know Before You Go)
August 14–23, 1992

Prequel

Early in the spring of 1992, Barbara and I decided to travel to Canada because on our trip to Alaska the year before, after spending a weekend in Victoria, we wanted to have a closer look at that country's mountains and lakes. Barbara wanted to see Lake Louise, and I wanted to see the Burgess Shale Fossil beds. When we discovered that the two sites were located within a few kilometers of each other in the Canadian Rockies, we decided that's where we wanted to go. And our daughter wanted to go with us. Fantastic!

So we planned to take the trip to Canada in August of 1992 for two compelling reasons: I would have a week's vacation plus a weekend from teaching, and I would be able to escape West Texas (where we were living at the time) which is hot as Hell in August.

We signed up to go with Tauck Tours, a well-established, upscale packager whose 9-day "Bugaboos by Copter Tour" made me salivate. I had no idea where or what the Bugaboos were, but I had had a taste of copters in Alaska, and I wanted more.

I knew the Bugaboos were located in the remote Rockies, and we would have to fly in a helicopter to get there. We would be isolated for three days in the Bugaboonies. Hot dog!

We invited our daughter, Libba, and son-in-law, Steve, to join us for the trip. But the son-in-law got invited by his father for a week's trip to Cozumel, and Cozumel won out for him. However, our daughter happily agreed to travel with us.

I cannot tell you how delightful it is to vacation with a daughter who's been married awhile. Married daughters have different perspectives from unmarried daughters. If only Canada had been as interesting as I had hoped. Now I understand why their national anthem is "O Canada" as in "Oh. Canada" or "(Yawn) Canada."

I made a payment to Tauck Tours for the entire trip plus insurance, knowing we would have until the due date to change our minds. Finding a tour is easy, but fitting travelers to a timetable can be problematic. It turned out that my daughter couldn't spend the entire nine days with us, only seven because of her work schedule.

So, I made all our flight arrangements, scheduling her return two days ahead of ours. And under normal circumstances, such a two-day adjustment might have worked because I assumed Libba could be easily airlifted from the Bugaboos at the end of the first seven days.

Wrong.

When I called Tauck to ask the customer service rep for special consideration, he said, "Sorry, sweetheart, we can't provide for one person's early return to civilization." He laughed. "Heavens to Betsy. Do you have any idea how much a helicopter flight costs? I'm sorry, but we simply can't allow an early departure from the tour program. I am so so so so sorry."

I said, "But that would mean she can't travel with us."

"Then," the telephone voice said, "it might be best to cancel her trip, Darlin'."

I said, "But that would mean we'd have to cancel *our* trip as well."

And the voice said, "Is that your only option?"

I said, "Yes."

There was a long silence on both ends of the phone, then he said, "Sorry, Sweetheart."

I heaved a great sigh and cancelled our trip with Tauck. It happened that quickly. Cancellation's is just like death except there's no corpse.

But I never for a moment intended to cancel our plans to travel together. I was stuck with a lump sum refunded minus the cost of insurance and three paid-up round-trip airfares on fixed dates to Canada, but I was never daunted (Probably because I don't know the difference between stubbornness and tenacity).

I broke the news to Barbara and Libba, assuring them we could follow another Tauck tour format for a schedule, the "Canadian Rockies Plus Glacier National Park Tour" and drive up to Canada in a rented car, omitting the trip to the Bugaboos. I said, "It'll cost less, and I can handle all the arrangements with no problem."

They believed me, and that made it so.

At the time, I thought traveling with family on a family vacation is more important than the reason for the trip in the first place, and now, that sounds like double-talk.

I had to re-plan the trip in a hurry, and I had no misgivings whatsoever using the Tauck Tour Catalog for a model, adjusting it to suit our means and interests. It was compensation for the lost cost of insurance.

The Tauck plan was relatively easy to modify: We would fly to Calgary, drive south to Montana's *Glacier National Park*, shift gears and head northwest to *Emerald Lake*, switch back northeast to *Jasper*, return Libba to *Calgary*, drive up north to *Edmonton*, and finally return to *Calgary* for our return home. And if you've driven through Canada, you know that one-quarter inch on the map equals about five hundred zillion miles.

Since this was before World Wide Web, I did lots of 800- dialing and waiting on hold for lodging and transportation reservations. I didn't want anybody else on the trip to get blamed for poor choices. And sure enough, that's the way it worked.

"The ~~Tauck~~ [sic] Canadian Rockies Plus Glacier National Park Tour"

Friday, August 14

We flew to Dallas and met Libba arriving from Austin.

[She told us that a friend had dropped her off at the airport, when—uh-oh!—as she was checking in at the ticket counter, she realized she didn't have everything she needed for the trip. She dashed to a pay phone and called her husband at work: "Steve?"

"Yeah?"

"I have thirty minutes. Need birth certificate in the blue basket next to fishbowl."

"Oh, god!"

"I'll be outside American Airlines in the street. Sorry."

"'Sokay, 'sokay." Click.

Steve drove home from work, found the missing document, brought it to her; she made the connection, flew to Dallas and a minor tragedy was averted.]

We settled down on the flight to Calgary, a family reunited, and for entertainment purposes we watched and commented to one another on the behavior of two ancient flight attendants whom we dubbed Ms. Shakey & Ms. Chewgum [Seemed *very* amusing at the time].

Both women appeared to be in their late sixties, and Ms. Shakey had a nervous disorder that my daughter didn't know how to deal with. When she asked Libba what she wanted to drink, Libba said, "Diet 7-Up." The woman had a little spell and shook her head as if alarmed. Libba hastily volunteered, "Okay, then, Sprite's fine."

The attendant said, crossly, "Which one do you want?"

Libba told her. Then we noticed the woman was shaking all the time. When she served food, she shook. When Barbara asked her for water, the water shook.

But when the plane shimmied periodically, Ms. Shakey was a rock. [You had to be there.]

The other woman, Ms. Chewgum, kept her mouth open while masticating. She never stopped chewing, and she never dropped her gum.

They were a comedy duo. We didn't make fun of them to their faces, but we—and other passengers—sure did talk about them. They had to be the two oldest flight attendants we'd ever seen. All they lacked were walkers.

Uh-oh! Bad omen: Upon our arrival at the Calgary airport, we heard our names being called over the public address system. I checked at the baggage counter where an apologetic attendant told me that Barbara's and my luggage had not made the flight to Canada. He assured me that they had been located and put aboard the next flight from Dallas and would be delivered to our lodgings. "So," he said, "Where will you be staying?"

I told him Glacier National Park, Montana, four hours away by car; he blinked, took a deep breath and said, "No problem. We'll do what we always do, hire a taxi to take your bags to you, two hundred and fifty miles away. Or three hundred. What's the damn difference?"

Barbara was not (understatement) pleased; however, Libba told her, "You can wear my clothes." Barbara was not (understatement) mollified.

The line at the Avis car rental counter was fifteen deep; but there was nobody waiting at the Dollar counter. So I rented a car "special" from Dollar for less than I'd been guaranteed at Avis, and then I called the Avis 800 number and canceled my reservation. That's how it's done.

We didn't know when our luggage would catch up with us and, of course, we didn't know that the car we rented was a lemon.

We maneuvered our way out onto the four-laned highway that would take us south to the US border. The lanes diminished from 4- to 3- to 2-lane and the scenery, described in our tour book as "rich farm lands," held no great visual appeal for anyone other than rich farm land owners.

Fortunately, our daughter got on a roll, entertaining us for most of the four-hour drive, singing show tunes, pop songs, risqué lyrics. My grown-up, married daughter. A sheer delight!

Barbara complained that the car shimmied; I said, "I can't feel it."

At the US border, a no-monkey-business guard with a mustache barked at us and briefly detained us. She also had sideburns.

Thirty minutes later we arrived at Many-Glacier Lodge. We had been expecting "old-fashioned," not "primitive." The logs that served as walls inside and outside were quaint but dirty. I mean century-old grimy-dirty.

After dinner and before retiring for bed, I asked at the main desk about our luggage and learned that it hadn't arrived yet.

The weather was hot, in the 90s, and there were no fans, just an occasional gentle breeze. So rather than roast, we kept our windows open all night long, allowing us to hear everyone in the rooms beside us and above us talking and carrying on, keeping us awake and annoyed.

Saturday, August 15—Glacier Park to Waterton National Park

After sleeping in the shirt I had worn the day before, I awoke, wrinkled and still annoyed. Slipping on my trousers and shoes before the girls woke up, I went to the main desk to ask after our luggage.

I was told it hadn't arrived yet, and I was advised to call to check on it.

There were no phones in the rooms, so I had to wait on line for one of three lobby payphones to call the luggage dispatcher in Calgary who informed me that the luggage had just been delivered. I said, "There must be some mistake. Hold on while I check the desk again."

I went to the desk just as the taxi driver walked in with the luggage. He explained that the customs station had closed down at 10 the night before, and he had had to sleep in his cab until they had opened at 7 that morning. I hauled the luggage to our room, arriving just as Barbara and Libba were arising, like baby birds demanding breakfast, asking for their "stuff." Cute.

We took a lake cruise that morning with a tweedy-looking group, then we hiked en masse to another lake where we took another cruise and hiked to a third lake where we watched a tiny speck of a black bear in the distance wandering around, looking for food.

Our young naturalist/tour guide warned us that bears are omnivorous. "That means," he said, "they may eat you in self-defense if they're hungry. But, "he said, "the major problem the National Park Administration faces is keeping forests both wild and safe." He urged us to talk animatedly so as to warn bears and other wild life of our approach. Libba enthusiastically responded, singing aloud, "LA, LA, LA, LA!"

We were uneasy, but we were having great fun. The guide said if a bear should surprise us, we shouldn't look him or her in the eye. We should all lie down and assume a fetal position, and he—the guide—would identify him or her as a brown or black bear.

Libba said, "Who cares? Him? Her? Brown? Black? LA, LA, LA, LA!"

The young naturalist noted that the park had been developed in the early Twentieth Century with trails blazed for upscale travelers who rented horses to traverse from one overnight lodging to another. Nobody much hiked back then. Nowadays, most people hike, so there are only a few of those horse trails still used for horses. We crossed paths once and discovered why the smelly horse trails are maintained apart from the hiking trails.

The weather was delightful; the scenery was awesome; happy moods prevailed, and the three hours passed too quickly.

Returning to the Lodge, we checked out, and I asked the clerk to get us a reservation at the Prince of Wales Lodge in Waterton—a hotel under the same Canadian Pacific management—the clerk called them then told me it was "impossible."

I said, "Oh, bullshit! Sure we can."

We got into the rental car and headed out toward Waterton. By now, I was feeling the car shimmy, but Barbara conceded that it might be her imagination, and I didn't want to mess with her imagination.

En route, we saw some cars ahead of us parked beside the road with people photographing something in a clearing. It turned out to be a small bear eating garbage, an event that thrilled Barbara.

I parked and waited in the car while my wife and daughter got out to view the bear close up. It was a really, really lovely few minutes, watching them watch the bear a distance of about fifty feet.

Libba photographed the bear; he returned to the woods; and they got back into the car, happy and excited. Then, while I drove, Barbara read aloud some descriptive material about bears, and we discovered that those beautiful beasts can charge fifty feet in a few seconds—a sobering thought. What if the bear's mommy had happened along?

"LA, LA, LA, LA!"

We arrived at the Prince of Wales Lodge where the clerk welcomed me with "No problem, we have a room for you."

I said, "And that's how it's done."

He said, "Pardon?"

We drove downhill to the tiny village of Waterton for lunch. No sooner did we arrive than we encountered two enormous mountain goats with tiny kids, walking down the main street, stopping traffic. Then we passed a deer eating grass in the front yard of a house. Barbara said, "Stop!" I stopped and watched as she and Libba clambered out and got as close to the deer as they could.

We'd been married 34 years, and in all that time, I never guessed that some-day Barbara would tell me to stop so she could stalk a baby bear, goats, and a deer. I don't know this woman.

One of the tires on the rental car looked as if it was going flat. So I said, "See? That accounts for the shimmy you felt."

I found a repair garage where—while we ate lunch—a repairman patched the tire.

We shopped for postcards. Libba bought us tickets for a performance of the Jones/Schmidt musical, *I Do! I Do!*, to be presented that evening at the Waterton Opera House.

We went back to the Prince of Wales for a nap, dressed casually for dinner in the dining room, then went to see the show. The theatre was not interesting and the show was a fiasco. The performers had trouble with their zippers during cos-tume changes, and it's hard to watch a show wondering when the actors' clothes are going to drop off next.

At the end of act one, we left. Walking around the little town was much more entertaining. We sat at an outdoor café, drinking beer, listening to a girl guitarist sing sad Sixties protest songs. *"The answer my friend is blowin' in the wind...."*

Returning to our Lodge room, we left our windows open for a breeze as we had the night before, but this time there were no loud noises. Just the echo of that sad girl singing, *"The answer is blowin' in the wind."*

Sunday, August 16—From the Prince of Wales to Yoho National Park

Breakfast, then a walk from the Prince of Wales downhill and around the lake into the village. It was fun. But the return walk, uphill, was difficult for us seriously out-of-shape walkers.

After checking out, we decided not to retrace our routing on the road that had proven uninteresting, so I chose Highway 22 through farming communities. There was moderate Sunday traffic and great weather. I didn't give a thought to the car's continuing shimmy, attributing it to the badly maintained two-lane road. We just kept on driving through those boring flatlands, and occasionally, there would be a sign with typical British reserve promising: "Important Intersection Ahead."

We dodged bike riders who were crazy and/or too assertive for safety, forcing us to look out for them the way we also avoided hitting dear. When we finally connected with Trans-Canadian Highway 1, we discovered it's yet another road full of assertive bikers. Highway 1 had only one harrowing lane with a passing lane leading through the Rockies, across the Continental Divide to our destination for the evening, the wonderful Emerald Lake Lodge.

Although remote parking for guests at the Lodge is inconvenient (we had to wait for the pickup shuttle for about 30 minutes), we were pleased with our cabin whose tiny porch faced Emerald Lake. Beauty, comfort, and great charm, oh, my!

We went for a stroll, sat at an outdoor table beneath an oversized umbrella. Then we got overdressed for dinner at the Lodge dining room. After dinner, we changed into bathing suits and shared a large hot tub with somebody's children. "Little girl, your mother's calling you, and she sounds mad." I have my ways with unaccompanied children.

I inquired at the lodge desk about an advertised trip to the Burgess Shale Area and learned that only 16 persons at a time were ever allowed to make the trip, and only on Mondays and Tuesdays. Furthermore, all of the hikers had been chosen for the next day's trip, and there were only eight slots left for the Tuesday trip. I was told that anyone wanting to go on the Tuesday trip would have to show up at 6:30 a.m. Monday. What?

Libba knew I really wanted to go on this hike, so she volunteered to accompany me and stand on line the following morning.

Returning to our cabin, we decided not to light a fire because it was warmer indoors than out. We sat on the porch overlooking the lake and mountains and watched a glorious, glorious moon rise.

Monday, August 17—Emerald Lake

Libba and I arrived before dawn at the Visitors Station—the sixth and seventh persons to arrive—leaving only one opening in the hiking group. But as we listened to the hikers chat about their adventures, we received the distinct impression that much as we would enjoy seeing the fossils, we would not enjoy the thrill of hiking 10 Ks uphill.

A woman and her friend arrived, distressed that there was only one more slot. "Oh, noooooooooooooooo!"

I took one glance at Libba and determined that if she felt like me, it would be better for us to let them replace us than for us to be designated sissy hikers.

We returned to Emerald Lake, wistful but not truly disappointed. Funny how you can look forward to something for months and then—in a few minutes—realize it's not for you.

After breakfast, the three of us flatlanders took a hike around the lake, and we had a wonderful time.

For lunch, we drove to the village of Field, then to Lake Louise where the crowds were the worst I've ever seen. Never seen anything like it! The impressive view was upstaged by the teeming crowds.

Returning to Emerald Lake's seclusion, I spent some time on the phone rerouting our trip, canceling reservations at Chateau Lake Louise, hoping we'd be able to stay at Jasper Park Lodge where we had reservations beginning the following day.

We napped, rented a canoe and effortlessly (and happily) paddled around the lake. Another short hike, then supper outdoors at the Lodge with birds and squirrels overhead and underfoot. Family fun.

We sat on our porch late into our last night at Emerald Lake. Bliss!

Tuesday, August 18—Emerald Lake to Jasper Park

The weather was excellent, and the sight of mountains and glaciers was inescapably stunning—until zipping along at the speed limit—we got tired of looking at one stunning mountain after another. I wondered aloud, "Why do all these mountains, each one impressive and unique, leave me wanting even more fantastic mountains." I persuaded Libba to take over the driving. For awhile, as a rider, I forced myself to study the mountains, the teacher inside me saying, "Pay attention," but try as I might, I couldn't. I grasped for shapes, highlights, shadows, textures, colors, line, all the details I knew to look for. I started rehearsing a lecture to explain the phenomenon: "It's not enough to dazzle an audience with spectacle; every audience requires action, and even mountains must appear in an arrangement that increases an audience's engagement—or boredom sets in. Zzzzzzzzz."

I dozed, trying to understand what was boring me. I was having a wonderful time with my wife and child. I blamed the speed limit, the sameness of the scenes, the car's shimmy, the steady hum of the tires on the road, the stress of dodging bike riders, and the futile hope of seeing an elk or moose at roadside. Everything contributed to distract me, nothing sustained my interest.

Barbara said she wasn't in the least bored. She was cruising for moose, she said. (Yeah, but I saw her nodding off, too.)

Libba enjoyed herself driving, occasionally noting that "There's something wrong with this odometer and automatic shift, and it's not me." At least I remember her saying that just before I started snoring. I awakened as she pulled off the main highway and stopped in front of the place we had been told about, and we lined up with hundreds of people to take a ride in a gigantic snowmobile up the Athabascar Glacier.

After a thirty-minute wait, we were bussed up the mountain to a point of departure in a specially designed vehicle for conveying tourists like us and a hundred Japanese persons up, up, up onto the glacier. We parked and debarked and walked around, slipping, splashing, and trying to walk upright. It's hard to act blasé while walking on a glacier. Gosh, I love glacier-walking.

Afterwards, we got back on the road, and I thought, "She's right. There *is* something wrong with this automatic shift." I didn't share my thoughts with my passengers, however.

We arrived in Jasper in the early afternoon. I tried unsuccessfully to register a day early at the Jasper Lodge, but we had to settle for an out-of-town cabin at the "Kekarra Lodge" and made the best of the situation.

We drove back into town and sat—at supper—in a restaurant next to a window that allowed us to watch a parade of tourists passing by on the sidewalk, staring at us like it was after curfew. Everyone we saw had nothing to do but walk around aimlessly. Nobody classy-looking or beautiful passed by, just folks wearing warm, colorless, practical clothes.

When we got back into the car, we discovered that the shift was no longer misbehaving, but one of the damned headlights was burned out; so, we returned to the Kekarra Lodge before nightfall, and we sat on a ridge overlooking the confluence of the Miette and Athabascar rivers and watched the sun set. Nice.

After turning in, I slept through a sensational thunder storm that Barbara said sounded like explosions signaling the end of the world.

Wednesday, August 19—Kekarra Lodge to Jasper Park Lodge

In the morning, the ground outside our cabin was littered with branches of trees from the storm.

We checked out after breakfast and went to the Jasper Railroad depot to transfer to a river raft for a whitewater ride down the Athabascar river. It was cool and rainy, but the ride was wonderful five-star fun.

Among our group was a Japanese family whose father said he would never take his six children to the United States I asked why not, and he said it's because he didn't own a handgun. I said, "You're joking." But he wasn't.

Also in the raft was a family of Texans who had moved to Canada to convert Canadians to Christ. I laughed, "There are still a lot of us sinners in Texas." But they weren't amused.

Steering our raft was a former rodeo cowboy with a great sense of humor. The trip was wild and safe, full of screams and laughter. We got drenched from the river and the rain, and we loved it. Later we learned he had a criminal record, but we never learned what crime.

We had a delicious lunch at the Jasper Lodge restaurant; then we checked in at the Lodge desk. As we were unloading our luggage at our cabin, a herd of about twenty elk ambled past, and we stood—awestruck—watching them graze where they shat on the lawn.

Next, we drove several miles to Magligne Lake, stopping en route to let a family of huge mountain goats amble across the road at their own pace. Marvelous!

After refreshments at the lake restaurant, we decided not to take a boat trip around the lake, opting instead to return to the Lodge for supper at one of the Lodge's less elegant cafes (The main restaurant was filled with well-dressed, sophisticated-looking folks; it was the only place on the entire trip where men wore jackets to dinner).

Afterwards, the weather was perfect as we set out for a 2.2 K walk around the lake. Signs warning hikers not to get too close to animals were widely posted.

It was virtually dark by the time we neared the end of the trail, and then, about 500 yards from our cabin—Uh-oh! We almost walked into an enormous flock of Canadian geese napping on the Lodge golf course. One sentinel goose tried to frighten us away, but we were too fascinated to be scared, so we just stared, then skulked around them. Shortly after we passed them, they took off, honking and flapping and beating the air.

It is thrilling to turn a corner of your life and discover a flock of giant wild birds.

We had coffee and dessert in a lounge overlooking the lake at the Lodge, browsed in the shops, then we returned to our cabin to sleep.

Thursday, August 20—Jasper to Calgary via Banff

We arose early, ate breakfast; then, Libba went for a ride on horseback with a group of tourists. Adoring parents that we are, we drove to the end of the trail to photograph her return. She said she had a lovely time.

We checked out after a leisurely morning and ate lunch at a Greek restaurant in town whose food was okay, then we began our return to Calgary, retracing our route past the Columbia Ice fields.

Stopping at Banff, we discovered it's a town full of tourists and shops, pretty but distressingly crowded.

That evening we arrived in Calgary and stopped at a large, uninviting Sheraton hotel whose restaurant had the best food and ambiance and service we had on the entire trip. Go figure!

It was a lovely way to spend our last evening with Libba who had to return to the States the next day. There was a huge Bingo hall lit up like Christmas about two blocks from the hotel, so we drove to it and found it was all lights and no action. Apparently, we were too late for a bingo adventure. So we went to bed.

Friday, August 21—Calgary to Edmonton

I dropped Libba off at the airport at seven a.m. and returned the rental car to the local agency with my list of complaints. The supervisor checked out the I. D. on the car and discovered to her horror that it had been scheduled a month earlier to be pulled off the line. Evidently the vehicle had a long record of complaints, and she said, "There's a notation here that says it must <u>not</u> be driven in the mountains!"

Oh, great!

She apologized profusely, so I couldn't fault her manners, and she upgraded me with a new car and a free rental with no charge for use of the lemon. But apologies don't compensate for life-threatening problems, damn it (Unless, of course, there's no harm done).

I returned to the hotel for breakfast with Barbara and told her that her sensitivity to the car's shimmy was correct. Barbara always enjoys being told she's correct.

We checked out, and Barbara volunteered to drive to Edmonton, our final stop on the trip. The new car was nice, we plugged in a tape describing scenery between Lake Louise and Jasper, and we listened attentively. The landscape, however, was unrelentingly flat and boring, so I dozed off, waking with a start. I said, "There's something wrong with this car. I can feel it."

And I was right that something was indeed amiss; Barbara was driving in a blizzard. In August! (We learned later that it was only the third August blizzard in a hundred years in that part of Canada.) I urged her to pull over and let me drive because she was clearly unnerved with eighteen-wheelers following her too closely on that two-laned highway, but she couldn't find a good place to stop until she finally found a place where we switched, and I got the feel of what it must be like most of the year driving in snowy Canada.

Arriving in Edmonton around 1 PM, we checked into the Fantasyland Hotel at the West Edmonton Mall. Why did we stay at that mall? Because we knew in advance we would never go there again. And we were wowed as most folks are by the enormity of that place.

Objects built by humans can't compare with natural wonders; but architecture like that mall, a place that allows humans to enjoy life indoors during harsh winters, serves a useful as well as economic purpose. The snow outside gave us an idea of the importance of that place in that town—for families especially.

It was circus fun. We strolled around the twenty-four blocks of the first and second floors, then—after an unremarkable dinner—we left the mall and went to town for a theatre "Fringe Festival" performance of a run of the mill revue called *Being Alive*! It begged the question, "Why would they want to be alive!"

We enjoyed coffee and dessert at a coffee shop, returned to our Mall Hotel room, and relaxed by candlelight with wine, soaking in a Jacuzzi before blowing out the candles and climbing into bed.

Sunday, August 23—Edmonton to Calgary to San Angelo

We awoke early, returned to Calgary in 30 degree weather with light snow, and after an excellent lunch at an airport hotel, the Chateau, we went through the security checkpoint just before time to board and—

Suddenly, I realized I hadn't returned my rental car information to the check-in counter. I ran back to the rental car counter, checked in, returned to the Security check point, and Ding-ding-ding-ding-ding!

The overloud gate alarms went off, and I was stopped, thereby blocking the line. The inspecting agent couldn't find the cause while waving his wand all over my body, and he got frustrated, I got frustrated, and nobody waiting on line was sympathetic.

Finally, the agent gave up and allowed me to pass. At the departure gate I found that our plane was oversold, and people were complaining loudly that computer errors had assigned people to wrong seats. It was chaos!

I joined Barbara, we got aboard, and just as we plopped down into our seats, who should welcome us aboard but Ms. Shakey and her buddy, Ms. Chewgum.

The flight back was uneventful, the trip was uneventful, and I concluded that's what trips to Canada are meant to be.

The Sequel

The Worst Things About Our Trip To Canada.

Worrying that our luggage wouldn't catch up with us, Driving through rich farmlands on badly maintained highways for hours on end, Waiting on lines at the US Customs entrance to the States, Driving a lemon, Discovering that Beautiful old log cabin lodges can be unpleasant places, Dodging bicycle riders, Dealing with Crowds, Dealing with my wife and daughter when they got tired and cross, and Finding that even the Rockies become boring after awhile!

The Best Things:

Getting away from home (for awhile), Being with my wife and daughter (most of the time), Looking at the Rocky Mountains (for the first couple hours), Hiking and canoeing and just sitting on our porch at Emerald Lake, Sitting outdoors watching rivers in confluence, and Exploring the West Edmonton Mall.

Unforgettable Stuff

Walking around Emerald Lake with family, Riding in a snowmobile bus on the Athabascar Glacier, Taking a whitewater raft trip with family, Hiking around the lake at Jasper Lodge with family and discovering a flock of Canadian geese, and Adoring my wife and daughter.

These canals and rivers are the same Thomas Jefferson sailed on centuries ago.

Travels in Europe, Six Destinations: Part One:

Bourgogne With French Country Waterways

✦

August 15–21, 1993

Saturday & Sunday, August 14 & 15

We flew from Dallas/Fort Worth to Paris, all four of us, Barbara (my wife) and I and Libba (my daughter), and our favorite (and only) son-in-law, Steve. The flight left us exhausted, but we decided to stroll around the city for awhile, having four or five hours to kill. The walk lasted less than an hour, however, because we were all more interested in resting than in sightseeing. So we went to Hotel Meurice, the place appointed for our meeting with tour representatives of the French Country Waterways staff.

We sat on overstuffed sofas for no longer than it took to doze off, all four of us doubtless looking like dead ones in the dimly-lit reception room off the main lobby of that grand old hotel, but when the staff arrived, we came alive. Voila! We followed her to a van that transferred us to a high-speed train, the TGV, from Paris to Le Creusot near Dijon. From there we rode in a bus to St. Leger-sur-Dheune where the *Horizon II*, our cleverly-designed barge was moored.

Boarding, we met the crew on the Barge at a Champagne Reception and chatted up the other guests, but we weren't impressed with them—at least, not that night. In fact, we received the distinct impression that most of the guests believed as we did that there wouldn't be as many on board as there were, a total of 11 passengers.

The most colorful character aboard was a symphony conductor from San Francisco, a native of Budapest, "Both Buda and Pescht," he said. He wore the same suit and tie every day of the tour because his luggage had gotten lost. The rest of us dressed casually, offering to loan him articles of clothing, but no. He preferred his formal attire even when—after the third day—it began to look frumpy. So, okay, we tried.

Dinner that first evening was delightful! We discovered that there was a procedure to be followed at each dinner: A menu was presented by one of the serving staff describing each of the wines accompanying the meal. When the dinner was over, another staff member described the cheeses being served. The presentations were always well done, and we got accustomed to learning about the wine and cheeses almost as much as we enjoyed consuming those provisions. Every lunch, too, featured presentations of the same victuals. We didn't want to miss a meal or a performance of the staff. Great touch.

Our cabins were not exactly austere in design; neither were they commodious. They were just okay.

Monday, August 16

We cruised on the Canal du Centre. Steve ran laps while some of us walked slowly on paths beside the canal.

We drove through vineyards in the afternoon to Santenay for a cellar tour and tasting at a private vintner. Never did get the name of the wine grower, but the wine was superb.

Returning to the barge, we continued our cruise. Sometimes there were lock-masters, but quite often there was nobody to operate the locks but our crew. It seemed the crew was always working assiduously, cleaning windows, polishing, sometimes painting sides that had been scraped when going through the locks. It was almost painful watching them work while we reclined on chaises. But we managed to keep our heads turned away so as not to embarrass them.

We had an overnight mooring in Chagny. Libba and Steve (hereafter called the "kids") went ashore with some of the barge staff for a pub crawl.

Tuesday, August 17

We cruised to the port city of Chalon-sur-Saone. Hooray! The winds were favorable for Hot Air Ballooning, so that's what we did. "Up, up, and away in our beautiful balloon," we sang, looking down on farmers who waved their fists and cursed us for frightening their cattle.

Barbara and I had some kind of conflict with each other—the substance of that I can't remember—and we had stopped speaking to one another for fear our differences would escalate into a word fight! We didn't want anyone—least of all the kids—to know we weren't on speaking terms, so we acted moderately cordial until the flight was ending.

Uh-oh! As the balloon was descending too quickly, it looked as if we were going to crash into the ground. And that's what happened. I grabbed Barbara, and bang! The balloon basket landed, and we all fell out, rolling on top of one another. Barbara and I were hugging each other for dear life. Then we scrambled up and out of the basket, no harm done, and we were greeted by someone from the balloon rental company who apologized in French (Somehow, when French persons apologize, they seem to be saying sentiments like "If it weren't for you, the accident might not have happened, n'ces pas?") and presented us with certification of our flight by the highly distinguished Montgolfieres Association of France. We were given Montgolfier pins and barets to wear, and the balloon company rep popped a bottle of champagne. We toasted one another, and Barbara and I resumed speaking. We continue speaking to this day.

We had an overnight mooring in Chalon-sur-Saone. The kids went ashore again.

Wednesday, August 18

The morning cruise on the Saone River was at a leisurely pace.

Then in the afternoon we were driven to Beaune to tour the 15th Century Hospice de Beaune, a remarkable museum, and we strolled and shopped and sightsaw. Charming Burgundy capital city.

Overnight, we moored in Seurre. The kids went ashore yet again.

Thursday, August 19

After a morning cruise, we visited a 12th Century abbey and vineyards of the Clos de Vougeot wines. Remarkable artifacts (four 20 foot high presses) used for centuries of winemaking. The vineyards and the winery were owned by monks until the French Revolution, but the chateau and museum are owned by the Confrerie des Chevaliers du Tastevin, and their banquets are held here periodically in the cellars where our winetasting was spread.

In the afternoon we toured the 18th Century Chatteau de Longecourt, a privately-owned home with most of the house occupied by a couple and their children. The chatteau and the children were on display.

Overnight mooring in Longecourt-en-Plaine. The kids went ashore of course.

Friday, August 20

We cruised on the Canal de Bourgogne to Dijon. En route, I decided to bike ahead of the barge, and I started out happily enjoying the bright sun and clear air, singing in French and English. But as the morning continued, I got hot, and the path got dusty, so I sat down to await the arrival of the barge. And I waited and waited. Fearing something might have had happened to the barge or it might have been detoured, I rode back down to a lock that had been closed, and that's where the barge had been stuck until the lock operator could be found. When he arrived, he apologized profusely: "Idiots. If it weren't for your barge, I could be enjoying my nap!"

That afternoon we had a walking tour of Dijon, and we bought samples of various kinds of mustard for gifts to folks back home. [When we presented friends with tiny bottles of mustard, they almost all said the same thing, "Does it have horseradish in it?" And our answer, translated from the French, was "Oui, but of course.] To this day, when I see a bottle of *mutard* on a grocery shelf, I remember that Bourgogne cruise as one of the best family adventures we've ever had.

In the evening all guests went up to the top deck for photographs, and then we enjoyed the Captain's Farewell Dinner.

In addition to our travel on the TGV, we had sailed almost 100 miles, about 20 miles a day. And we consumed dozens of courses of good foods cooked by a Scottish chef. We drank over 20 different wines—not counting Champagnes and aperitifs. And cheeses: over 30.

Sailing on *Horizon II* was idyllic. The weather, the food, the comforts, the pacing. We loved the trip. One of the best ever! One of the best family events imaginable.

Saturday, August 21

We departed the barge after breakfast for an escorted return to Paris via the TGV, arriving around noon where we bid farewell to the kids and rented a car to explore Europe!

There is no prettier city in Europe than Bruges—if what you're looking for's a pretty face.

Travels in Europe, Six Destinations: Part Two:

Bruges, Et. Al.

✦

August 21–26, 1993

Following our return from Dijon to Paris, I rented a Peugeot for a drive with Barbara around Europe like young lovers in a movie. I sang my version of "Love the one you're with especially when the one one's with is the one one loves, Doowah." Barbara rolled her eyes the way she does.

I knew my way around Europe having blazed trails during the two years I was stationed overseas in the US Army. I wanted to visit places that neither Barbara nor I had seen before, so first stop was Luxembourg-ville, capital city of Luxembourg, located in the geographical 'heart of Europe'. A friend of my family, a GI from WWII, had been stationed there just after the Battle of the Bulge and had

34

told us more than one story about the place, but after forty years, it wasn't quite what we expected. There was the old centre with towers, turrets and winding, cobblestone streets declared a World Heritage Site by UNESCO in 1994; but now there is the modern downtown area on the Plâteau du Kirchberg, a monument to contemporary Luxembourg's reputation as a major international financial centre.

We drove through the old city to the classic war memorial, grand and grim, and we located the museum celebrating the Battle of the Bulge. Then we parked and walked around town in the bright sunlight. There were playful statues begging to be photographed and outdoor restaurants. But there was nothing else to compel us to stay there, so we took off for Trier in Germany, not far away.

Why Trier? Because I've never known anyone who went there. And yet it's a 2000-year-old Roman city, the oldest in Germany, home to six Roman emperors. Lots of ruins including the impressive Porta Nigra (the Black Gate), a four-story structure that was once part of the city's walls. The city is located in a valley of the Moselle river, surrounded by forests, vineyards and tiny villages. Shamelessly boasting the birthplace of Karl Marx, it's a university town with about a 100,000 area inhabitants. When we found ourselves in the thick of traffic, we decided to move on down the road, hoping to make Brussels before nightfall.

Brussels is the capital of the Kingdom of Belgium and headquarters of French and Flemish Communities. It's also home of the European Commission and the Council of Ministers of the European Union (EU). Those factors weren't what was luring up to that city, however. We knew it would be a sight to behold, and it was.

As we drove, we weren't speaking to one another, but there was no lingering hostility. We had simply run out of things to say for the moment. Then I started to nod off, Barbara took the wheel, and when I awoke, we had arrived, but we were lost in the outskirts of Brussels. I tried to navigate, but Hell, I couldn't make sense of the map, and perhaps for the first time ever, I understood why Barbara has difficulty navigating.

I wanted to find the Brussels Sheraton where I had reserved a room. The only difficulty getting to the hotel was finding a way to spin out of that circle trap. The Sheraton sign loomed enormously from miles away; all it took to get there was time.

After checking in, we found our way to Royal Square (Place Royale—Koningsplein) and admired the gothic, classic, contemporary, art nouveau, and other styles of architecture that abound there.

But I wanted to see the famous Grote Markt Square with Flemish architectural designs of building and eat dinner in one of the restaurants located there. This historic market square with its splendid storefront guild houses and Town Hall, is truly one of the most beautiful town squares in Europe, and shadows at dusk gave it great charm. Barbara was wowed as we strolled around the Square, lights spilling from restaurants. We made a good choice and enjoyed one of the most delicious dinners we have ever had. Good dinners promote spousal satisfaction.

The next morning, lovey-dovey, we struck out for Bruges, "The Venice of the North." Arriving in the middle of the morning, I drove directly to a hotel where I had reserved a room even before leaving the States. The room was a major disappointment, located on the third floor of an old building that was antiquated and evidently unrestored since the Middle Ages. The mattress was lumpy in the extreme, and the floor was full of splinters. I complained, and the desk clerk refunded my deposit immediately, cheekily assuring me: "Zee room vill be rented by less picky custoomers before zee afternoon ist over."

We reloaded the car and went looking for a decent hotel, expecting the worst, but we found a Novotel with a new and antiseptic room that surprised and delighted us.

The rest of the day was a joy beholding that fairytale village. It seems like a miniature city, but there are reportedly 45,000 inhabitants in the old town. It just *seemed* like a village. A lot of people take day-trips from Brussels to Bruges, and I had been told that most of the tourists' busses would be gone by dinner time, and sure enough, we had the town to ourselves with no difficulty finding a great place for dinner. It was enchanting! I sang to my wife, "When I fell for you, I got a Bruges on my hip." I couldn't improve on that verse, so I nipped it.

Walking around the town, I never ceased to wonder how buildings that look like stage scenery for operettas get maintained in places like Bruges. Somebody makes it happen. That city owes its continued existence to a mixture of good fortune and diplomacy. And enforced zoning. A cosmopolitan attitude has survived from the past to present day because of city stewards who recognize the uniqueness of Bruges, insuring it continues to be one-of-a-kind.

The next morning, after another leisurely stroll, we headed out for Amsterdam's gabled houses and the Rijksmuseum, the Van Gogh Museum, the Stedelijk Museum, the Rembrandt House Museum, and the Anne Frank House. And, of course, that city's red-light district with "coffee shops" selling cannabis. We weren't in the market for either hookers or hashish. We did, however, check out the astounding flower market. Oh, yes.

Amsterdam is the official capital of the Netherlands, founded in the late 12th century as a small fishing village on the banks of the Amstel, and it's now the largest city in the country and its financial and cultural centre. Although it's officially designated the capital of the Netherlands, it is neither the capital of the province in that it's located, North Holland (Haarlem), nor the seat of the government of the Netherlands (The Hague).

China is misnamed the "Bicycle Kingdom." The Netherlands deserves that designation. The population of greater Amsterdam was well over a million when we visited there, and there were at least that many bicycles seeming to come from all directions. If a walker strolls into a whizzing bicycle lane of traffic, the walker is at fault for the collision. Scary.

In the 17th century, a series of concentric, semi-circular canals ("grachten") were built around the older city centre, and they continue to delineate its layout today. Many fine houses and mansions are situated along the canals; most are lived in, others are now offices, and some are public buildings and whorehouses. The brothels can be distinguished at night by glowing red lights and by women posing (and exposing themselves) in the windows. Hard to miss. Barbara rolled her eyes as I sang, "Love the one you're with."

Having satisfied our curiosity by strolling through the Red Light District, arm in arm, Barbara had an accident stepping into a recessed trolley track. We got stuck and almost fell, and it was difficult extricating her foot, and then the shoe. Whew! I thought she had been holding onto me and she thought I had been holding her. The sounds of oncoming trolleys scared us so much it took several Amstel beers to calm us down.

We left Amsterdam the following morning after shopping for antiques and concluding we could find better old furniture in the States than in the countries like Holland where the pieces had originally been built.

Returning to Paris, we decided to spend our last night in a hotel near the airport in order to avoid rising at an impossibly early hour to make a flight connection.

Big, big mistake.

We went to a restaurant close by the hotel and waited for service. And waited. Then, to register our disapproval, we left in a huff. The maitre d' scurried after us, but we said, "Non, non, we awaited too long pour your service, nessy pah?"

At that very moment, Barbara tripped, screamed and fell, breaking her foot. She didn't know the extent of damage to her foot, and she was too embarassed to admit injury and give the maitre d' any satisfaction, so she stood up and (with a little succor from me) limped away. We settled into a booth at our hotel sandwich shoppe, and she said, "It's swelling and it's hurting."

I said, "Let's call for a doctor."

She said, "No, it'll get better. It can't get worse." But it *did* get worse, and she refused to see a doctor, I rolled my eyes, but she refused my ministrations, so she spent a sleepless night, suffering inconsolably.

The next morning, I drove her and the rent car to the airport, parked conveniently, wheeled her to the check-in counter, returned to the car for our luggage, and then I went back to the counter to request a flight upgrade for Barbara's comfort. I completely forgot—

"Oh, my gosh! I'll be right back. I have to return the car to the rental agency."

No prob! In fact, as much as I object to using that universally overused expression, there was absolutely "no problem" discovering the right place to park the car, finding the rental desk, checking in the keys, and returning with time to spare to the airline departure lounge. And American Airlines upgraded us at no charge, bless them.

The upgrade helped Barbara's spirits, but it didn't make the pain go away, and it wasn't until the following day when we got her to a hospital emergency room at home that we learned there's nothing much one can do about a broken foot except take pain medication. So that's what she did, and that's when the trip was officially over.

We had seen and done everything we intended, and we learned that sometimes travel is a pain, literally & figuratively, even when you love the one you're with.

The Danube

♦

From Prague to Vienna to Budapest to Munich
July 31–August 13, 1995

No, the Danube doesn't flow from Prague to Budapest. Nor is Munich on that river.

The first and last segments of our tour were land-based; thereafter, we went by barge. The tour company was "Goahead Vacations," whose clientele is primarily school teachers, so we didn't mind the company, but there were several annoyances on the barge that—We found really—Well, annoying.

July 31 & August 1

We took an overnight flight, one long leg, all the way to Prague. Talk about jet lag.

Arriving, we transferred to our hotel where we were given the rest of the day to recuperate from the flight—more time than we needed. So I strolled around the hotel without seeing much of interest because of our location. Thus uninspired, I sacked out. We enjoyed dinner in the hotel, and then we slept some more.

August 2

Wide awake, we took a city tour and viewed Prague Castle, a beautiful complex of 16th Century palaces and courtyards; St. Vitus Cathedral, gothic and neo-gothic; and Charles Bridge, a 14th Century bridge crowned by statues. The group of teachers (including Barbara) moved too quickly for me, photographing statues, and at one point, I looked around and discovered I was all alone.

I rushed to catch up, but I couldn't find them anywhere. Half an hour later, they found *me* in the middle of Wenceslas Square. I was admonished, "You must stay with the group."

Teachers!

August 3

The next day we went to Prague's Medieval Jewish Quarter and an early 13th Century synagogue located next to the Jewish Cemetery, an astonishingly old and crowded jumble of tombs dating from 1439. There are over 12,000 tombs there, a dozen or so layers deep. Incredible.

That evening we heard Mozart's *Requiem* performed by a large ensemble in a church. It seemed an effortless event to the performers. To us it sounded like Heaven's choir!

August 4

We left Prague today, hundreds of sights unseen, and traveled by bus to Passau, a historic town on the German/Austrian border. While our luggage was being loaded onto the *MS Wolga,* we strolled about, and would you believe, the group lost me again. No matter, we returned to the *Wolga* just as the group was boarding, never having missed us.

The *MS Wolga* was described in the literature we were given as "an intimate ship especially designed to cruise the Danube's waterways. All cabins are on the outside of the ship, affording an ever-changing view of the passing scenery. All have private baths with shower, telephone, air-conditioning, and a radio. The ship is full of amenities from the sun deck and pool to the lounge, beauty shop, and boutique."

That literature omitted other descriptors: "intimate means cramped, private baths means smelling of backed-up sewers; telephone means non working; air conditioning means minimal; radio means broken. Sun deck means not clean; pool means postage-stamp sized; and boutique means always closed.

The crew to a man was surly. We got so that every time we passed a sailor, one of us would begin humming the song, "The Volga Boatman." The cleaning women were unclean; whoo-ee! And the tour director was always happy, smelling of hemp.

Other than that, the ship was serviceable.

August 5

In the morning we cruised through the green and glorious Danube Valley with rolling hills and historic towns and villages, arriving in Vienna mid-morning.

We had a city tour led by a grande dame who was world-weary, and she had obviously not been paid enough to enjoy what she had to say. We rode around in the Ringstrasse, a grand avenue designed by Emperor Franz Joseph to replace

Medieval city walls with Imperial buildings. We passed by the famous operahaus and the Houses of Parliament and City Hall, both parts of a complex of a 19th Century design intended to reflect the history of the city's architectural designs.

What surprised and delighted me most was discovery of the work of a new (to me) architect named Hundertwasser whose ideas and designs were realized in Vienna in a series of wonderful apartments stacked cattywampus on top of one another. "Capricious and bizarre," said our blasé guide.

"Clever and whimsical," I replied.

We also took in the city's parks and statuary; then Barbara and I escaped the group to take a ride on the Riesenrad, a giant Ferris wheel in the city's amusement park, the Prater. One of the most exciting scenes in *The Third Man,* the movie featuring Orson Wells & Joseph Cotton, took place in a car like the one we were riding in.

We returned to the *Wolga,* humming the theme from *Third Man,* and arrived just as the ship was preparing to sail. Clearly, I was not in sync with this group.

August 6

Cruising through Hungary, we saw the region where paprika is grown. The trees and landscape weren't as pretty as that we had passed, but we expected the beauty to return.

Our first Hungarian port of call was Kalocsa whose main street is Istvan Kiralyutca (There will not be a test; so, don't bother to memorize that name) where souvenir shops abound. It's a pretty centuries-old tourist trap.

We were getting to know the teachers aboard, loosening up, most of us drinking schnapps and coining names for the Russians onboard like "Groucho, Dopey, Sleepy, Pitiful and Miserable."

We began to notice that every meal was laced with root vegetables, particularly cabbage in cabbage soup, boiled cabbage, breakfast cabbage—No, there wasn't any breakfast cabbage.

August 7

We woke up in Budapest, majestic and still damaged from the Second World War. Evidently the city fathers are proud of the shell holes, or they don't have enough money to repair the damage, or they just don't care. The town was sad and dingy, but it was also lively with hundreds of people on foot. Not much automobile traffic.

We took an optional city tour led by a woman who was even drearier and wearier than the dowager in Vienna who said, cryptically, "Houses of Parliament.

You must be on right side of bus to see. Too late, we drive past. Now, 13th Century Mattias Cathedral, the only building completely restored from German bombings in war. We do not stop to see because looks like every other Catholic building in world. City across river is Pest, we are in Buda. See Fisherman's Bastion on left side of bus. Too late. Soon we get superb view awaiting from top of Gellert Hill named for saint who was rolled down hill in barrel by Magyar infidels. There is statuary that Russians left behind as unwanted gift. Here is Hero's Square with Millenial Monument marking one-thousandth anniversary of conquest of Hungary. If you enjoy tour, I will be shaking hands when you exit. You may be tipping me. Have a nice day."

Reboarding the *Wolga*, we passed Groucho in a dark hallway whom I addressed in Russian with "*Kak vi pozhivayete?*" (or something phonetic I intended to mean "How are you.") And he, shocked, said, "It was not me! It was not me!" Then he scurried away.

For the rest of the journey Groucho avoided me like the plague. Something I said?

August 8

We didn't sail the next day for Slovakia (Esztergom & Bratislava) because there were rumors of war going on there, and the captain of the *Wolga* candidly told us that the barge's owners instructed him never to risk sinking the *Wolga*. He said, "Ships are expensive and human life is precious."

I asked, "In that order?"

So we spent another day in Budapest, touring to the city park, the Castle, and the Museum of Fine Arts with a collection rich in Old Masters and about 2,000 moderns. There was an entertaining statuary section with a piece entitled "Woman patting her bum."

We went out into the country to a small town where—at a restaurant following dinner—we were serenaded by a bevy of girls in peasant costume singing with the most unpleasant, self-consciously nasal tone I have ever heard—even from people with cleft palate disabilities. Damn! And a guy with his gypsy violin kept coming on to my wife.

Not all local customs are appealing.

August 9

We began our return up river, observing that much of Hungary isn't beautiful. It is only to the East that the woods are well-maintained by Austrians.

The Danube isn't blue, either. It's golden. On more than one occasion, I went up on deck to check out the changing colors of the water reflecting in the sun. And golden is what it was more than any other color.

We stopped at Weissenkirchen, a gorgeous little town with a 15th Century church of Maria Himmelfahrt, and a market place, and the 15th Century Teisenhoferhof history museum.

Charming. Lovely. Beautiful. Heavenly. Jesus, call me home.

August 10

We disembarked at Passau and I left a note in my room for Groucho, "Oh, yes, it *was* you!"

That afternoon in Munich, we explored the Oktoberfest capital of the world. The great beer hall where Hitler got major support is not to be missed, nor is the reconstruction of the Dachau Concentration Camp (or Detention Camp or Murder Camp) where Jews were imprisoned and incinerated during WWII.

I went alone to Dachau, taking a city bus, the direction sign on the front reading, "Dachau." I asked a fellow sitting next to me if this were a commuter bus. He answered me in English, "No, it is a bus not much used by residents of the city. Look around you at all the tourists; you can tell them by the clothes they wear and by the looks on their faces. They've come to see where we are accused of burning their families."

Then he turned away, and so did I.

Getting off the bus, I followed signs to the reconstructed buildings which constitute Dachau. I walked through barracks and on paths and into a building with ovens where bodies had been heedlessly cremated. Then I sat on a bench in the sun, meditating, wondering who had sat there before me. I had my own private thoughts.

I returned to the bus stop and watched a conductor rewind the "Dachau" designation to read, "Munich."

August 11

The next day, Barbara and I went for an early morning stroll to Marienplatz where the town hall is located and we watched the glockenspiel (Mechanical clock) mark the time of day with dancing figures. The Frauenkirche nearby has two towers over 300 feet high and a roof whose tiles are criss-crossed in colorful patterns.

Barbara hadn't wanted to go with me to see Dachau, and as I looked at her enjoying the distinctive features of those wonderful buildings in the Marienplatz, I thought, "This is the Munich she'll remember, and it's just as well."

It was a lovely trip, sailing on the beautiful golden Danube.

The Ultimate Conveyances
(The QE2, The Royal Scotsman,
the Concorde)

✦

An Abercrombie & Kent Adventure
Sept. 21–October 5, 1996

What a glorious title for a tour: *The Ultimate Conveyances.* Irresistible to someone who thinks it's a package deal not likely to be repeated.

I was 63 years old when Diane, our travel agent called to tempt me with the prospect of buying into Abercrombie & Kent's costly package. I was retiring from college teaching that year, and I thought a trip on the QE2 would be a trip to Neverneverland, and—to tell the truth—I was afraid I would never live to see a tour like this again. I was precisely the market A&K was playing to.

So I told Diane to hold on while I conferred with Barbara. I put my hand over the mouthpiece of the phone and asked my wife how she felt about it. Admittedly, she wasn't quite as thrilled as I was, but she moderated her enthusiasm saying, "Well, okay, I guess, but—"

I shouted into the telephone receiver: "Barbara's wild about it, Diane. Hot dog. Hooray!" Whereupon, Barbara took the phone from me and told Diane that she was game to go. That cinched it.

The three conveyances were the refurbished Queen Elizabeth 2, the Royal Scotsman railway train, and British Airways' Concorde. A&K added a penultimate conveyance, a New York limo, to the mix, and I reserved a room at the Marriott Marquis in Times Square for an overnight stay prior to our departure from New York.

Barbara suggested that if I added anything else, it would be prior to my departure from planet Earth!

Saturday, September 21

We left for NYC in the morning, arriving early enough—after checking in—to take in a show at the Minskoff Theatre, *Sunset Boulevard,* a disappointment because the audience was indifferent, and the performance wasn't magic.

"You gotta get a great audience to give a good show."

Sunday, September 22

We went to the Metropolitan Museum for the current Winslow Homer exhibit and lunch in the Met Trustees Dining Room.

That evening we enjoyed a delightful performance at the Shubert of *Big,* the musical adaptation of the Tom Hanks movie. We had a late supper at Joe Allen's on 46th, enjoying the B'way theatre scene.

Monday, September 23

The limo transported us to the dock, we passed through customs, boarded the QE2, went to our stateroom, and Barbara hated the drapes and bedspread. We decided to stay aboard anyway.

There was a cocktail party for the A&K entourage, and we met Carlye Wattis, a widow from Denver, 75 years old. Barbara whispered, "Isn't she a bit long in the tooth to travel alone?" I agreed, confessing that I felt like an ancient mariner at 63. Then and there, that afternoon, we fell in love with Carlye and she fell hard for us. So hard, in fact, that we persuaded the Matre d' in the Queen's Grill to change his immutable table assignments to allow the three of us to sit together at meals for the entire trip. It was a relationship unlike any other we've discovered in our travels, and it might have gone on forever—

But I'm getting ahead of the story.

Tuesday—Friday, September 24–27

Each day was different, but crossing an ocean "On Passage to Southampton" doesn't allow for much sight-seeing except on board or staring at passing ships. So we read books and promenaded from one end of the ship to another and took in lectures and stage shows. The seas were rough from day one, but we never seemed to be bothered bouncing back and forth from wall to wall en route to the Grill. We dressed to the nines and enjoyed the world's second greatest joy, eating at leisure and at length.

We got to know members of our group, disliking our tour director almost at first sight. It was generally conceded that if we had any questions, it might be best to ask them of somebody, anybody, other than Ding-a-ling or his wife, Ding-a-lette. As tour leaders, they were great musicians and enjoyed playing their respective musical instruments for us—even when we were tired of hearing their repertoire.

Time passed slowly and we gained an hour on the ship's clock every day, eliminating jet lag completely. It was a great crossing with nothing for us to do of any consequence but enjoy life. And we did that commendably.

Saturday, September 28

We docked at Southampton, disembarking inefficiently because our A&K tour director hadn't prepared us for luggage chaos. Never saw so many Brits losing their cools, "Blast this!" and "Bloody Hell!" Here a "Jesus!" There a "Crikey!" Everywhere a "God almighty (That was the American contribution to chaos)!"

Finally, we got aboard our bus for a drive to an airport and a flight to the Balmoral Hotel on Princess Street at the foot of Edinburgh Castle.

What a wonderful railway hotel with understated elegance and—even more importantly—a bar that served over 40 single malt whisksys. [To be called a "single malt Scotch whisky (Whiskey is the American spelling of the word), a bottle may contain only malted barley grain distilled at a single distillery.] During our brief stay in the hotel, I tried to discover differences in various tastes from Glenwhatsis to Whatsiddichs, but I couldn't drink enough.

Sunday, September 30

We had a leisurely morning, allowing us to shop and stroll, seizing photo ops of statues at every turn. I had no idea John Calvin was a Scot.

We walked up and around Edinburgh Castle, returning in time to check out and board the Royal Scotsman, departing Waverley Station at 2:15 PM, sharp, to the mournful strains of "Amazing Grace," a tune I genuinely loathe, but I didn't protest because a bagpiper was playing it especially for us—unless there was a funeral going on somewhere in the station. Jaysoos.

We had a suite located near the middle of the train, not far from the dining cars. Poor Carlye was relegated to a single cabin in a car at the tail of the train. It makes good sense to ask for proximity to dining and lounge cars unless one enjoys hiking.

We traveled past moors and lochs until we arrived at Loch Loman, and when we stopped, everyone aboard began humming or whistling that tune. Unfortunately, the drizzle wouldn't stop, so we couldn't go to the water's edge, nor could we make it out very well in the gloom. But gloom's what Scotland has a lot of, so we weren't put off by it.

We continued crossing miles of peat bogs, lochans, boulders, and streams, and we stopped around 9 PM at Spean Bridge where we enjoyed a formal dinner. Afterwards, a fiddle player entertained with traditional music. Fortunately, he didn't play for long, and we retired listening to the train make the strange sounds trains make on sidings at night.

Monday, September 30

Riding the rails of a train in Scotland, when one tries to read the names of towns and lakes and landmarks, words with familiar English language letters are difficult to pronounce. Racing at a top speed of about 30 mph, we strangers on a train made a game of trying to pronounce signs with legends like "Arisaig, Taynuilt, Mmallaig, Bridge of Orchy, Inverawe, and Loch Shiel." The actual pronunciation was anybody's guess, but it was a game suitable for playing with adults whom we were still getting to know. I doubt we could have made a game of making out the sounds of Welsh towns and landmarks—entirely too abstruse. It was an idle pastime until suddenly, we passed a sign that announced "Lockerbie," the site of the great airplane disaster. Strangely, none of our tourguides said anything about it.

We were on a conveyance to nowhere, enjoying ourselves. It was indeed an trip designed to move from point to point with few stops in between.

We arrived at a nowhere town on the coast, Mallaig, and the train stopped for the locomotive to run around to hook onto the other end. After a brief stroll, we reboarded and were served lunch. We rode to the Bridge of Orchy where we visited a smokehous at Inverawe and, shortly after that, a private home where we sampled fish, smoked and sliced, with glasses of wine. Curious event.

That evening we were entertained after a formal dinner by Ding-a-ling & Ding-a-lette playing their musical instruments interminably.

We stayed overnight on a siding at a restored Victorian station at Taynuilt.

Tuesday, October 1

There was a rail strike that caused the train to be rescheduled for the remainder of the journey. Instead of a visit to Lochalsch we were routed to Perth with a visit to Glenturret Distillery and Glamis Castle. The distillery provided the kind of refreshments for that one uses the term "imbibe." When else do you hear that word.

Glamis Castle, the birthplace of H.M. Queen Elizabeth, mother of the present queen, is gloomy in the extreme. The rooms and grounds photograph beautifully, but the public areas that we were allowed to see were enough to convince me that living there was no fun. Glamis is mention in Shakespeare's *Macbeth,* and its use as a metaphor of tragic aspiration is appropriate. Anybody who would live there deserves it. The line of descent of ownership, name by name, was posted prominently on a wall from "Sir John Lyon of Glamis (whom you'll remember was granted the Thaneage of Glamis by King Robert II) in 1382 to the present resident of the castle, Michel Fergus, 18th Earl of Strathmore and Kinghorne (whose signature is "Strathmore and Kinghorne" for short)".

The castle is a great stony curiosity, and a bit of a bloody bore. It may have been the heat and humidity as well as the overcast skies, but that massive temple to British hegemony struck me as almighty stuffy.

That evening, we went to the "Globe Inn," a pub and inn in Dumfries, in continuous operation since 1580 and a favorite haunt of Robert Burns. Word has it that Burns would sleep with lassies in one of the rooms upstairs; so, I asked about the room, and Barbara and I were shown up to where the bed and other accouterments still grace the room.

Downstairs there is a chair to the right of the fireplace where Bobby Burns himself sat, and we were invited to take turns sitting there. I sat, and I didn't have a bona fide psychic experience, but after enjoying a few wee drams of single malt, I swear I felt—That is, I *thought* somebody pinched me. Do you think maybe…. Naw.

I checked my bum when preparing for bed aboard the train, and I discovered—would you believe.—a bright red mark where I had felt the pinch.

Wednesday, October 2

"Maxwelton Braes are bonny…." I had no idea of the meaning of this opening line to the *Ballad of Annie Laurie* by William Douglas of Fingland (who wrote the first version of that famous song) until we arrived at Maxwelton House. I *did* know the tune, however, and I hummed it unceasingly while walking around the grounds of this estate.

Evidently, the daughter of Sir Robert Laurie fell for a lad whom the family disapproved of, so Anna contrived to meet with William somewhere about the Banks and Braes of Maxwelton, where it is presumed she gave him her promise true (Yikes!). The romance didn't work out, but at least the world got a song out of it.

The house has little of architectural interest; however, it was a coy and cozy place for having a spot of tea with biscuits.

Reboarding the train, all of us whistling the tune, we prepared for our farewell dinner, a formal affair featuring Haggis, a dish stuffed with sheep's entrails and other loathsome stuff, but we learned that if we declined it, we would never return to Scotland. So for that reason alone, we ate some and we were certified as worthy foreigners. The evening came to a close as one of our hosts quoted an epigram by Bobby Burns:

"When Death's dark stream I ferry o'er, A time that surely shall come,

In Heav'n itself I'll ask no more, Than a Highland welcome."

And return. So said we all.

Thursday, October 3

Our last day aboard the Royal Scotsman was pleasurable and sunny (for a change). The Scotland we had come to know with its shrouded of mists and overcast skies was suddenly transformed into a bright and shining country. Delightful!

But it was a short morning. The train arrived before noon at the Edinburgh station where we were transferred to the airport for our return trip to London. At Gatwick, we boarded a jet for Dallas—

Wait a minute! This was supposed to be a Concorde flight to JF Kennedy in New York, right? Yeah, well, we determined that if we took that flight, transferring to another New York airport for an additional flight home would take more time. That was the irony: take the Concorde and spend many hours in transfers on the ground, or take the conventional jet back home and save time and grief in airports. It was a no-brainer. Hell, we figured we could take the Concorde at sometime in the future—But no one ever know what the future holds or that there would be no Concorde to fly on unless....

Maybe that remarkable conveyance will be resurrected in the future, and we'll take another trip on remarkable ships on the sea, on land, and in the air.

Hong Kong, Thailand, Malaysia, Singapore

✦

An Asian Nightmare with Yale Exes
February 9–23, 1997

Tuesday, February 9

For the first leg of our trip to China, Thailand, Malaysia, and Singapore with Yale Exes, we traveled from Austin to Los Angeles and checked into the Airport Hilton. We were met by an old friend, Kevin King, who drove us to Santa Monica for a stroll down Third Street and to the Mondrian Hotel for drinks and dinner.

Great first leg of the trip.

Wednesday, February 10

We slept late, then we had lunch with dear friends (I have old friends, dear friends, good friends, and just friends), Todd & Nancy Allen, at an outdoor restaurant in Santa Monica, renewing old acquaintance, but no drinks; the Allens are Christian Scientists.

I haven't the vaguest idea what we did that afternoon, but I remember dinner with Neille de Wulf, a good friend, who gave us a ride with our luggage to the International Airport.

I have friends I haven't used yet.

Barbara and I sat in a crowded departure lounge, waiting to depart on Cathay Air to Hong Kong until 11:45PM. And me without a book to read.

I made a game of surveying the passengers to guess that ones would be traveling with us on that Yale Alumni trip. I spotted several who looked as if they were playing the same game. I counted about ten who looked prosperous, casual, smart, and fun. Only two of those folks turned out to be Yalies.

Satisfactory second leg.

Thursday/Friday, February 11, 12

After crossing the International dateline (a 14½ hour trip) and arriving in Hong Kong at 6:45am, we were the last to get our luggage. If we had been truly prescient, we would have taken that as a bad omen for the entire Asian tour.

Following a bleary early morning 2-hour city tour with an excellent guide, we were transferred to the Grand Hyatt. I left my walking stick on the bus, but I thought, "No big deal." But it was.

The Hotel lobby was garish in the extreme. I thought I'd died and gone to Miami. Our room, however, was terrific. Asian hotel people really know how to do it. We napped then ate lunch in the hotel café where a sparrow had nested high on one of the walls. The bird made endless trips to an exit/entrance above the café doors to the Hotel, and when I asked the white-gloved waiter about the bird, he said birds bring good luck. I asked if the sparrow were house-broken, har-har-har, but the waiter failed to respond. Perhaps he had trouble hearing me, or he couldn't understand my English.

We found our way to the Star Ferry and sailed for Kowloon, passage only 14 cents per person. There we visited the Cultural Arts Museum with several great looking exhibits, but the descriptive information on display was all in Chinese (Hell of a note for a British colony, but perhaps it was because later in that year Hong Kong would revert to China). Then after shopping at a nearby Chinese Arts & Crap store, we returned via Star Ferry to the Hotel loaded down with all the cheap little gewgaws we needed for souvenirs for the entire trip.

Barbara felt that dinner at the Hyatt that evening was the best Chinese food she ever ate, before or since. She hasn't eaten much Chinese since. She says, "You can get enough of a good thing." When I asked our waiter in the large dining room if there were any lucky birds flying about, he didn't hear me, or perhaps it was my English.

Saturday, February 13

We all met and everybody acted nice to us—at first. We had coffee, and they gave us name tags and caps that said YALE on the front. The trip was managed by Thomas Gohagan & Company, Chicago, and fortunately, that gang stayed out of sight during the whole trip.

We toured Aberdeen, the boat city, that smelled to high Heaven. When we finally got back on the bus, I couldn't find my camera, and I hated to think one of those Yalies might have picked it up, but I didn't want to accuse anybody, so I didn't say anything.

We went to the China Club, a restaurant for rich Hong Kong merchants and American movie stars. The art collection was outstanding with several paintings poking fun at Chinese politicians and at mainland Communism.

We had a lecture there from an expert who said there was no telling what would happen to Hong Kong when the Communists reclaimed it from the British. Someone asked, "Won't it be terrible for Hong Kongers to have to be governed by Commies?"

The expert said, "Well, when you consider that the British weren't the best of overlords until the past few years, it's a tossup. If China allows Hong Kong special dispensations, everything will be hunky dory."

Actually, he didn't say "hunky dory," but he did say the Commies had screwed things up so badly after taking Macao over from the French, they'd probably learned to leave well enough alone. And since the Chinese want to take over Taiwan in a peaceful manner someday (or, if that doesn't work, bomb the Hell out of those folks), they'll probably use Hong Kong as a proving ground. "Besides," he said, "If they goose Hong Kong, they may stop laying golden eggs."

Next we went to visit the Tsui private art collection that had a lot of glowing green jade. Jade glows best when illuminated well.

We had lunch at the Pacific Mall's "Tiger Thai" buffet restaurant. I couldn't tell Thai food from Chinese largely because I wasn't yet familiar with Chinese tastes.

Getting back on the bus, the driver handed me my camera and said something like he found it on the floor of the bus. Sure he did.

We returned to the Hotel and took a nap. Then I got a massage by a woman who walked on my back. I said, "What the Sam Hill are you doing up there?"

She said, "You no talk." So I shut up.

That evening, we got overdressed for a cocktail party. Very self-conscious, not knowing anyone.

Sunday, February 14

We took a lecture tour on a bus to a Buddhist temple where the incense was intense. I had my fortune told—I didn't understand a word—but the fortune teller nodded a lot and shook her head only once.

Next stop was a 14-story government housing compound where 8 to 12 folks live in each room with only a hole in the floor in one corner for a toilet where the stuff goes into pipes down the outside of the building, and I asked, "Aren't they afraid the plumbing might freeze in the winter?" Our tour guide said, "Hong

Kong is warm. This is the dead of winter, and it doesn't feel like it's going to freeze, right?"

I was about to respond when suddenly, I shouted out, "Oh, my god! Somebody just picked my pocket. My wallet's gone!"

She said, real softly: "It's in your hand." I apologized, but only because Barbara was embarrassed. By now I had identified myself as someone to avoid. Every poker player knows that when you sit down to play, you look around to see who the mark is. And if you can't find the mark, you're it. I was it.

Later, I went shopping alone to a busy market area of Hong Kong where there were lots of birds and animals for sale. Then I went to a shopping mall that looked like every other mall in the world.

That evening, Barbara and I took a cab to the Pacific Club where they wouldn't admit us at first even though we were international Club Corp members. Finally, they let us in, and I gave Barbara a musical greeting card that played, "You light up my life."

And she gave me one that read, "If you want me to be your Valentine, I will." Are we talkin' great poetry or not?

The food was okay. Then we went back to the mainland on the ferry. Fourteen cents.

Monday, February 15

The next morning, the entourage boarded a plane for Bangkok. When we arrived at the Bangkok airport, we boarded busses for lunch at the Rama Gardens, a kind of dusty outdoor restaurant catering to tourists on the outskirts of Bangkok. We were hungry until somebody said all that dust could be toxic; so everybody pretty much stopped eating after that. Later, we learned there was nothing toxic in that neighborhood. Somebody had just started a rumor.

We retuned to the airport and reboarded the same plane. It had been only a stopover for lunch. We flew directly to Chaing Rai and checked into the Dusit Inn whose rooms needed remodeling big time.

I coughed myself to sleep, the first signs of the dreaded Asian bronchial ailment that affects many tourists, cough, cough. I'm punctuating my retelling of this tale while having coughing fits by inserting cough, cough, in the text so that my readers cough, cough, may percieve how annoying it must have been for my cough, cough, fellow travelers.

Tuesday, February 16

I awoke with cough, cough, a fever. Barbara was very, very sympathetic and volunteered to stay with me rather than tour to the "Golden Triangle," but I told her I could suffer just as easily without her.

She said, "I'll bet that dust really *was* toxic."

When she returned at the end of the day, I was feeling much better, but she was dry-coughing her lungs out. She said the tour went up beyond Chaing Mai to the borders of Myanmar (Burma), Thailand, and Laos, and she'd seen naked little boys swimming out to the boat that she had been crammed into with 10 other passengers. The boys threatened to capsize the boat, but she screamed and they swam away. Then they visited a village where the villagers ate black dogs—not white ones. Go figure. We went to bed, but we were restless all night, alternating coughing fits.

Wednesday, February 17

The next day, coughing big time, we caught a plane back to Bangkok and went directly to visit the Grand Palace and Emerald Buddha, and from there to Wat Po (*Wat* means temple) and the enormous Reclining Buddha, and finally, we were taken to our room in another gorgeous hotel, the Bangkok Sangri-La.

Thursday, February 18

Swilling cough syrup to keep our symptoms repressed, we attended a lecture by a US State Department representative who welcomed us as VIPs to Thailand. Then we took a godawful noisy boat ride on a *klong* (canal) to the home of Jim Thompson, a Yale grad who had become an expat in Thailand, making a bundle of money exporting fabric back to the States. He had mysteriously disappeared into a jungle, and nobody knows what happened to him, but his body was never recovered. Another Yale grad, Bill Klauser, lectured about the house. It wasn't air conditioned, so we just sweated it out, coughing cough, cough, about every 15 seconds.

Returning to the Hotel in a van that we had to ourselves since nobody wanted to share transportation with us, I got a massage by Suzy Wong (that is, a woman who evidently shared the same professional status as Suzy Wong). She volunteered to give me a special massage for 200 dollah. I said, No way; I'm married."

She said, "Fifty."

I said, "Ten."

She said, "You no talk."

Those masseuses sure are thin-skinned.

We got to supper early, but everyone had already taken a seat, and we had to sit at a table by ourselves, cough, cough, coughing endlessly. Does my reader begin to suffer the pains of exclusion as we did then, feeling ostracized because of our hacking coughs? We were cough, cough, twice cursed.

Friday, February 19

We skipped tours today and stayed in our room, hoping we'd get over the crud we'd obviously caught. The Bangkok air and noise pollution was incredible! I ventured out and went to an antique shop and bought a statue of a Thai god or goddess—or it may be an ac/dc god. I couldn't tell from what he/she wears.

Saturday, February 20

We transferred to the Eastern & Oriental Train, making our first stop at the Bridge on the River Quai, a true tourist trap, possibly the worst example of its kind with a tawdry museum.

We enjoyed travel on the train; however, we felt like pariahs, the only folks coughing incessantly. We avoided socializing; but no one made an effort to hang out with us either. Cough, cough, cough, cough, cough, cough, Jesus take me home to heaven!

The train compartment was efficient with a shower—unlike the fabled Orient Express—with very few compromises in design.

Sunday, February 21

We stopped off in Butterworth/Georgetown, Malaysia, and went for a ride on a tri-shaw, that's an open-air, motorized rickshaw, and it was like riding on a power mower needing a tune-up, with dozens of trishaw drivers polluting the air with their exhausts.

We got back onto the train because there wouldn't have been much point in getting off in the middle of Malaysia. There was no practical option.

The food was good, but that night, our coughs were downright consumptive. We cleared out the club car just by making an entrance. We decided to take all our meals in our cabin after that, and no one denied us.

Monday, February 22

Disembarking from the train in Singapore, we had to declare we weren't bringing any chewing gum or drugs into the country. Our coughs may have been communicable, but they weren't illegal like chewing gum.

En route to our hotel, we drove past what has to be the ugliest, most sinister-looking American Consulate in the world. No one would *ever* attempt to attack that massive bunker.

We landed in a beautiful five star hotel, the Regent, where I insisted the Hotel provide me with a doctor—that they did. He cost an arm and a leg, but he gave me some kind of powders that stopped my cough, co—and made me feel good all over, oh, my, recreational drugs.

He assured me that Barbara and I were victims of an Asian curse that afflicts some Westerners, and he said our symptoms would disappear as soon as we left Singapore, probably before our plane landed. (And that's what exactly what happened.)

Barbara wouldn't take any medication because she didn't trust the doctor's easy solicitation, so she didn't regroup as quickly as I did. I had to go to the final cocktail party without her. The gathering was a terribly awkward occasion with old friends and new acquaintances exchanging best wishes, avoiding me totally. I was no longer coughing spastically, but nobody trusted getting near me. Embarrassing. I derived no satisfaction listening to others developing nasty coughs. I was sure we had not spread that cough because we had virtually quarantined ourselves.

God, it's awful to take a trip like that without making social contact (I sincerely hope I've conveying the disappointment and distress we felt).

I left the party early.

Tuesday, February 23

Early in the morning, before the temperature reached 125 degrees F (I'm exaggerating a bit), Barbara and I went for a stroll in a beautiful park with lots of orchids and ferns and trees and birds, and we had a wonderful time, just walking, sweating, knowing we'd have plenty of time to shower before packing our dirty clothes. We had one another's company, and that's all we required (And it was just as well).

We left Singapore (as beautiful a penal colony as I've ever seen) with mountains of gorgeous bougainvillea flowers festooning the roadside to the airport.

We flew to Hong Kong and from there to the States, landed in L. A., and checked back into our favorite hotel, the Airport Hilton. Knowing we would return home the next day, we zonked out.

We had coughed ourselves out.

A remarkably well-preserved author prepares to board a well-preserved Pullman Car.

Pullman Car Vista Canyon

✦

May 4–7, 1997

Trips I've taken by train in Europe and Asia have been comfortable and classy, but a trip that Barbara and I took from Temple, Texas, to St. Louis in a reconditioned Pullman Car was enviably exciting. People are wowed to learn you've been invited as a guest of a train car owner, and that private mode of conveyance is generally regarded highly by all.

The "Vista Canyon" car was owned by our friends, Dale and Fred Springer, and what made it fun was knowing that not many people in the world get invited to travel in a privately-owned antique Pullman with a provenance.

Fred is justly proud of his reconditioned Observation Car with four drawing rooms, one double bedroom, and a lounge car.

History of the Vista Canyon.

My readers may or may not know that on May 12, 1937, the Santa Fe *Super Chief*—an all-Pullman train on the Chicago—Los Angeles route, an upgraded version of the Atchison, Topeka & Santa Fe *Chief*—was America's first diesel-powered lightweight train.

The Vista Canyon (*The very Vista Canyon we traveled in*) was the first of four observation cars designed to serve as the train's last car with a snazzy, classy-looking round-end. In 1956 the round-end on all four of the Santa Fe trains was squared off to allow the cars so they could be hooked at both ends, and that's the way the VC is today, not as snazzy, but still classy.

A number of private owners had sold and resold the Vista Canyon to each other, and Fred bought it in 1994, had it restored and upgraded, and he served as conductor for his family and friends on trips almost everywhere in North America. We were traveling on a historical vehicle.

Text of a letter to us from Fred Springer, April 16, 1997

"The Vista Canyon is currently scheduled to leave Fort Worth at precisely 2:25 PM [We learned that "precisely" is never a precise term because trains run on imprecise schedules, sometime hours behind schedule] on Sunday, May 4, arriving St. Louis, 6:20 AM on Monday, May 5. You have a choice of driving from Salado [where we were living at the time] to Ft. Worth or catching the day coach to Ft. Worth from Temple at 11:25 with stops at McGregor and Cleburn. If you take the Temple option, you will have to purchase tickets on the train after you've called Amtrak in Austin (512-476-5690) [a number that revealed a folksy male ticket sales person who inquired about our health and welfare] for coach seat reservations, one-way, as we expect to return you to Temple at the end of our trip when we'll be connected to the tail end of the *Texas Eagle* [Notice: there's no mention of whiplash] leaving St. Louis at 12:15 AM on Wednesday, May 7, arriving Ft. Worth 4:12 PM and Temple 7:12 PM [Not one of those scheduled times was correct, but we amused each other guessing the delay times]. Oh, by the way, Amtrak may be shut down if the Congress does not approve funding by May 10, so the *Texas Eagle* may shut down earlier, leaving us stranded in St. Louis. I'm writing this two weeks in advance of our trip because I felt I needed to give you some time for advance planning."

The Trip—A Synopsis

The trip came off without a hitch because of Fred's meticulous planning and because nothing went amiss. We arrived five hours late, but hey, we had no other plans.

Dale did all the cooking in her kitchen aboard the train, and she cooked and bounced from wall to wall when the train was in motion. What an artist!

To own and operate a car, it takes a dauntless couple like the Springers—as well as an engineer that Fred employed—to troubleshoot and negotiate with railroad union employees, Amtrak and otherwise.

As planned, we slept aboard and stayed overnight in St. Louis at the terminal there. We visited museums and a friend; then we turned around and came back. The trip was of a short and enjoyable duration.

The ride was smooth everywhere there was a smooth stretch of tracks. We learned railway lore about train travel we had never thought to ask. Fred enjoys talking about trains and his and Dale's travels by rail all over the world, and he almost made train travel seem like the kind of thing we might want to do, go shopping for a sleeper car—almost.

At the conclusion of the trip when we pulled into temple, I promised myself I'd go for a long ride someday on Amtrak. How was I to know I'd get what I wished for?

Keystone, Colorado

◆

A Summer Vacation
July 7–23, 1997

Nothing much happened in Keystone that summer until suddenly, something great happened. My readers may be aware of a novel by Joseph Heller entitled, *Something Happened!*, a long narrative during which nothing happens until about page 100,000 when something shocking happens. That, in brief, is what you'll discover below.

Monday, July 7.

Barbara and Libba and I arrived at Keystone, CO, and settled in "Keekorak," the house we had rented from a fellow Yale alumnus for the summer. It was better by far than we expected, located on a river with a walking trail.

Tuesday, July 8.

We shopped for groceries and foam pillows, clothes hangers, etc. Amazing how much time's required to settle into a place that doesn't have stuff we're accustomed to.

Wednesday, July 9.

Shopped at factory outlet shops. Why? Because they're there. Dinner at Keystone's Der Fondle Chessel, a good restaurant at the top of a 40 minute gondola ride. Libba had a bad night with an ear ache.

Thursday, July 10.

Arose early, visited a doctor who advised Libba her ear ache would go away. It did, but other ailments attributable to high altitude made her feel depressed. That evening Barbara and I celebrated our 38th anniversary with an amble down the walking trail together.

Friday, July 11.

B & L watched a Yoga video and then went hiking on the trail by the river while I spent the day doing errands. Dinner that night at Ski Tip Ranch, another good restaurant. Libba still feeling poorly.

Saturday, July 12.

Attended an arts and crap fair. They're never, never worth the time. Libba was diagnosed by a local physician as having Strep Throat.

Sunday, July 13.

Tried to follow a slow-paced Tai Chi video, but got bored and gave up. Spent the afternoon and early evening in Breckenridge, and ate supper at the Blue River Bistro, good enough for only one visit.

Monday, July 14.

Libba was better, so she and I went for an escorted Jeep ride over mountain back roads, then I spent 70 bucks for a pizza for the three of us. It was just okay.

Tuesday, July 15.

While the girls did Yoga, I bicycled to the post office, huffing and puffing uphill, coasting downhill, both ways. Later, we went walking together on and off the trail, a great pleasure.

Wednesday, July 16.

Suddenly, I Became a Hero.

After we had a yawner of a day, we were bussed with about 100 tourists out into the countryside for a hayride (sans hay). We boarded long wagons pulled by huge dray horses to a picnic spot in the mountains.

Very poor chuck wagon supper. Then on our return to the departure area, while we were being transferring from the wagon to a bus, the horses bolted. Damn!

A woman seated next to me with a 5-month-old baby in her arms started to fall out of the wagon, and I threw my arms around her and the baby, catching them just in time. The mother was embarrassed and shaken up, and she failed to say, "Thanks."

I thought, "My one big chance in life to be a big hero and nobody thanks me but that's okay."

When we reboarded the bus for our return trip, passengers who had witnessed the event burst into applause and said nice things to me. Now, *that* was the great thing that happened.

At bed time, just before I fell asleep, Barbara whispered in my ear: "You're *my* hero!" I agreed.

Thursday, July 17.

Another big event. We went sailing in the afternoon, hiring a boat and sailor to steer us, zigzagging way out onto Dillon Lake. The sky was clear, then it suddenly became overcast, and then Bam! The wind kicked in, the rain drenched us, and suddenly we were in a squall, hanging onto the sides of the boat for dear life. Libba and I enjoyed ourselves thoroughly, thinking it was part of the show. Barbara didn't like it a bit. Libba said, when we returned to shore, "Can we go again?"

The sailor said, "You have no idea how close a call that was."

You can be a hero one day, and the next you can almost get killed and not learn about it until after the danger's past.

Friday, July 18.

Libba's last day with us.

We drove through Loveland Pass, through snow, and arrived in Denver around noon where we dropped Libba off at a friend's home (She had arranged to have lunch with her friend and family and a transfer to the airport). We hugged goodbye and acted brave, but driving away was a letdown for us. We enjoy our visits and travels with her so much.

Then, as planned, we had lunch with the daughter of Carlye Wattis, the friend whom we had met on our trip to Scotland and who had died unexpectedly of a botched operation earlier in the year. Ann, the daughter, gave us a gift her mother had left for us: Tickets to a performance of *Madame Butterfly* at Colorado's Central City Opera House.

Carlye, Barbara and I had made plans to attend a performance together, but Ann told us Carlye had handed her the tickets just before she went to the hospital. She had feared the worst.

We drove back to Keystone in a heavy rain lasting all afternoon.

Saturday, July 19.

The *Butterfly* matinee was super. Afterwards, we returned to Keekorak and began work on a picture puzzle. I had resolved that I would never do a picture puzzle, never, never, never. But it was something to do.

Sunday, July 20.

Having spent a week one previous summer in Aspen, attending concerts, we decided to drive over to Copper Mountain and Vail to check out those resorts. Supper at Vail's Ore House was good, and then we returned to Keystone to read the N.Y.Times.

Monday, July 21

Stayed at home during the day doing nothing.

Tuesday, July 22

Rain. Then a good dinner at Swan Mountain Inn.

Wednesday, July 23.

We took one last stroll on the trail, then we drove back home. Nothing much had happened during our stay in Keekorak, except for that one shining chance I got to rise to hero status. And the one near death boat ride. Unforgettable! That made it a great summer.

Barbados to Brazil

♦

A Silversea Cruise
October 26–November 15, 1997

We sailed on the Silver Cloud for our second cruise ship trip because Silver Seas Cruise Lines was recommended by readers of *Conde Nast* magazine as the best cruise line of its kind in the world (and that was at a time I believed those 100 Best ratings were accurate indicators of magazine readers' opinions; I no longer find their rating system valid. It's too subjective and can't be validated.), and because we thought a leisurely trip to South America would have an exotic itinerary. It wasn't exotic exactly, but it was an interesting itinerary. Same thing, I guess.

The ship was sensational, and there were few big disappointments, but the little disappointments were a bitch.

Sunday, October 26, 1997

It took us fourteen hours from 6:30 AM when we arose to travel from Salado, TX, to Bridgetown, Barbados, arriving at 9:30 PM. Total travel time, 7 hours. Total transfer time 7 hours.

To appreciate Barbados, you really have to know who Claudette Colbert was. More about her below.

The first person we met in the badly-illuminated airport was a five-hundred pound female gorilla-porter who pushed our luggage through customs.

"Well!" I said, brightly: "Do you enjoy your work, sweating in this 100 degree hot weather and talking with loquacious tourists?"

She fixed me with a baleful stare and spoke in a Bajan patois I couldn't comprehend, but I guessed she was saying, "Welcome to Barbados, the tropical island of enchantment," or, perhaps she said, "Knock off the small talk, buddy, I'm not getting paid to entertain your ass."

She connected with a taxi driver, saying "Take these nice people to their hotel," or she may have said, "These two fools talk too much. Take 'em for a ride."

Which is precisely what he did, driving wildly over every pot hole en route to the Hilton where—upon arriving—I understood him to say, "You owe me forty American dollars, not the twenty you just handed me." Actually, he was saying, "Give me twenty bucks more, or you won't get your luggage, and I'll beat the hell out of you, understand?"

I looked to the bellman for help translating his precise meaning, and the bellman smiled and said something like: "Give the driver the money, or they'll find your bodies washed up on the beach tomorrow morning."

I responded by telling the taxi driver, "You can't intimidate me, Mister!"

Actually, I said, "Do you promise to give us our luggage if I tip you twenty more dollars, right?"

He growled, and I took that to mean "Yes, thank you."

We checked in, I tipped the bellman excessively, we registered as Hilton frequent guests, and that was the last time we have stayed in a Hilton. There was no elevator, so we walked up three flights to our room, looked around and noted with dismay the filthy bedspread, the television set that had no picture but seemed to be blaring a song called "Beavis & Butthead," and a grumbling air conditioning system that would not budge from 84 degrees Fahrenheit.

The filthy bedspread we threw into a corner of the room.

The TV—we discovered—was actually the sound from an adjoining room, a problem that resolved itself around midnight when our neighbor turned it off.

But it was the a/c we called to complain about. I spoke sternly: "You've got to do something to cool down this room, and I mean now!"

The desk clerk said—as far as I could understand—"Yes, sir, immediately."

Or she may have said, "Suck it in, Sweetheart, you're gonna sweat all night." because that's what we did.

Monday, October 27

The next day, before Barbara awoke, I went for an truly delightful walk around the hotel grounds, discovering a wonderful beach, ruins of an old fort and a military cemetery. I was appalled to see what I thought were rats—which turned out to be mongooses—they only look like rats—but actually they're an animal imported by landowners centuries ago from India to kill snakes in sugar cane fields that they did then, but now, of course, the mongooses can't be eradicated.

Barbara and I dressed and paid 75 dollars for a breakfast special buffet of mangos, papayas, guavas, with accompaniments of flies and bullfinches in the open air hotel restaurant. (All Bajan restaurants are open air, allowing birds to fly about freely.)

Afterwards, our hostess smiled and asked if we had enjoyed our breakfast, and I said "It cost too much and you've got to do something about those damn birds."

She responded with: "Wonderful. Have a good day. See you soon."

We checked out of the Hilton immediately and transferred bag and baggage to the Cobblers Cove hotel where we were warmly received, given a lovely suite of rooms, and provided with a driver named Adrian who took us for a tour of the entire island including mahogany trees, west coast boulders, and the former Claudette Colbert's house. He said, "She was a famous movie star, but now she's dead, you know? She was on the National Historical Museum board, you know? The library board, and the art museum board, and if she hadn't lived here, you know, there wouldn't have been a historical museum, library or art museum, you know?"

That night, after dinner watching the birds table-hop—literally—at the hotel's 4-star restaurant, we retired to our room where we were lulled to sleep by the incessant sound of ocean waves and "whistling frogs" who, when mating, sound a lot like the two-toned sirens of European ambulances. Too-too, Too-too, Too-too, into the night.

Tuesday, October 28

For breakfast the next day, I had fried flying fish, scrambled eggs, and Barbara ate something that gave her red blotches on her neck. Bullfinches & crows kept trying to join us at the table.

Later, a bird I did not recognize—by this time I was coining names for them, Billy Bob Crow and Bubba Bullfinch—flew over Barbara and dropped a welcome gift of bird byproduct on her shoulder. (Splat!) Barbara was glad she hadn't been hit by one of the coconuts that fall periodically from the palms. (Thunk!)

Our driver, Adrian, took us to the ambitious but austere National Art Museum (Yawn) that Claudette Colbert had helped build, you know, then to the well-designed National Historical Museum, then a thoroughly uninteresting downtown department store where he dropped us for a lunch—popular with locals—of peas and rice and chicken. It was okay, I guess.

Afterwards we took a tour of a Bajan rum distillery and tasted a thimble full of raw white rum that had never seen the inside of a cask (It's bottled as soon as it's processed), and a tiny sip of aged rum. The difference in taste is like gasoline from brandy.

That evening, the owners of the hotel threw a cocktail party for all their guests (and birds) followed by a barbecue dinner that was classy, poolside, but that really wasn't very good because the sauce was too bland. We were informed by two Brits from the Isle of Wight: "Americans don't enjoy spicy foods."

Wednesday, October 29

The next day, Barbara's blotches were little changed, so she took some antihistamine drugs, and we went for a tour of Barbados's marvelous Forest Gardens.

Then Adrian took us to the so-called "castle" of Sam Lord, the 18th Century pirate king, where we had some unspicy native vegeburgers for lunch. We decided not to stay over for a special dinner around the actual table in the castle where Prince Andrew dined with Claudette Colbert, you know, because the cost of the dinner was $230 per plate.

Instead, we went to the Sandy Lane five-star hotel outdoor restaurant that evening where Queen Elizabeth once lunched with Claudette Colbert, you know—and we had a marvelous dinner, the only one devoid of bullfinches & crows because they had put up mesh screens to keep out the birds.

Barbara's blotches—It's a miracle!—disappeared overnight. Maybe she's allergic to bird byproduct.

Thursday, October 30

The following morning, I went swimming in the Atlantic with my shoes on to avoid cutting up my feet on the coral reef offshore. We breakfasted on the patio with Billy Bob and Bubba, after which we told them goodbye, packed, checked out, and taxied to the dock where the Silver Cloud was anchored.

Our taxi driver said something I understood to mean "You folks come back to see us again, you hear?" but that Barbara understood as "Is $5 all you're gonna tip me, sucker?"

The Bajan phase of our adventure was history, forever.

The bright and shining Silver Cloud was no disappointment.

The Silver Cloud

Our suite (and veranda) aboard the ship was great. By evening we had discovered ten things we liked best about the ship.

First, no birds and no avian residue.

Second, we had a deliciously private verandah to our suite, located on the port side of the ship that means that—since we would be sailing southwards—no intense west afternoon sun, only blissful sea breezes when there was good weather. And we had good weather every day.

Third, the service was categorically superb. No tipping was allowed, so the waiters and housekeepers didn't work at being nice; they just were nice and skilled and efficient and—always—friendly, with 24 hour room service. The glass and brass and marble was spit polished. All staff and crew were dressed impeccably and behaved as if they were proud of the ship. And all mistakes were rectified immediately, but nobody made any mistakes that we noticed.

Fourth, the food was either superior or good, never bad. And the dining room & cafe and bars aboard ship were never crowded—even with near-capacity. Every dinner lasted at least three hours.

Fifth, the medical staff was cheerful and accommodating when I caught a cold. The French doctor was so handsome that Barbara went gaga when he chatted her up, and Annie, the nurse, gave my backside some magic bullet shots I probably didn't need, but I was feeling better in no time.

Sixth, the ship's land tour staff tried to please us, but they weren't the best organized outfit aboard. Transfers from boat to shore and tours on busses are evidently not easy to do right. We enjoyed only one of the tours, and it was the self-guided one we didn't pay for.

Seventh, the passengers aboard ship were easy to talk with. At every meal, we sat with different people, some unique, all of them cordial. Most were cruise ship refugees (And by that I mean the main topic of conversation was usually an evaluation of the virtues of Crystal cruise ships over Seaborne or Silversea over Cunard). The QE2 was usually described as a disappointing ship that—one Brit said—ought to be put down forthwith. One night we sat with Lord and Lady Bellinger—You'll remember, of course, he was lord mayor of London in 1966. His wife said she much admired "Margaret" (meaning Margaret Thatcher, not Princess Margaret) but despised Thatcher's son, Mark, who lives in Houston—"a perfect boor."

Another night we sat with an Egyptian couple who are actually French but whose residence is in London where they had met Princess Di on three social occasions before, of course, her untimely death. We met two Philippine doctors from Odessa, Texas. We met so many gracious people that we never missed Bubba and Billy Bob.

Eighth, the entertainment quality was uneven but energetic. The costumes were pathetic. The performers tried a bit too hard to please, but I expected more and better. And the smarmy cruise director was simply too cheerful and artificial to appreciate. I avoided him.

Ninth, the captain, an Italian, was cordial and always obliging, welcoming us aboard, glad-handing at high tea, and showing off his bridge.

Tenth, there was a wonderful feeling of going nowhere fast aboard a smooth-sailing ship on calm waters; good weather and good sailing.

So. Where did we go? Nowhere much. We were at sea for the first day of the trip.

Friday, October 31

As noted above, simply going out onto our verandah and reading while sipping room service drinks was like dying and going to Heaven.

Saturday, November 1

Our first stop was Devils' Islands, that's plural.

Apparently, there are three islands in French Guyana that were used for the infamous prison. We walked all around the central island for about 3 hours and visited the ruins there as well as a museum and—Incredible, but true—a hotel full of tourists.

Barbara almost got hit by birdshit, (Splat) *and* a falling coconut (Thunk).

One of the islands was used for isolation purposes when it was a prison, and the other—where Papillion and Jack Hughes lived (or was his name Drey-fus?)—anyway, the island where special troublemakers were confined—was and still is virtually inaccessible. The currents are so strong and the shore is so steep, there is no place to dock boats. The sharks still swim close to shore, remembering that the butcher shop was located at a site where they used to dump blood and carcasses into the sea.

Although the islands were originally stripped of vegetation, the French planted tropical fruit and palms, and today, the place looks like an idyllic movie set. Really, it's very pretty for a prison.

We returned to the ship and set sail for what was listed on our itinerary as the "Breves Narrows" and that turned out to be located over 500 nautical miles into the mouth of the Amazon river.

Saturday, October 31.

We crossed the equator at Macapa and entered the Amazon. Wow! We could see land at least fifty miles away on both sides of the ship. Then the distance began to narrow until—on several occasions—we were within a hundred yards of the shore on each side, looking down onto some overgrown waterfront property managed by people willing to live in the jungle—not natives, they live in the interior—just poor people who take what they can get.

We must have seen over 200 dugouts with men, women, and children, waving, paddling close as they dared to the ship, most of them wearing tee-shirts, some (we were told) with designer labels.

Knowing you're sailing on the Amazon River is an awesome experience; however, 500 miles is only a fraction of the area covered by the river and its hundreds of territorials.

It took two days to go into the Amazon and return to the Atlantic. We had hoped to see some pink dolphins called "bocas" that inhabit the river. (There's an old legend that says that pink dolphins turn into young men at night and swim ashore where they succeed in making some of the local girls pregnant. Children who are born of the union of boca and virgin are called sons of bocas or SOBs).

Sunday, November 2

The next stop was Fortelesa, a lackluster skyscraper city of two million Brazillians. Barbara and I had never heard of it before. Or since.

Our bus tour took us for a visit to the ugliest cathedral I've ever seen. It looks like a stack of great, gray concrete bunkers shipped over from Omaha Beach. The next stop was an old prison converted to stalls where local merchants sell fabrics like lace and placemats. None of the tourists in our group bought any of that antimacassar stuff. The last bus stop was a fish market with fantastic looking fish, none of whom we could take home with us.

The most generous thing we could say about Fortelesa was that our curiosity was absolutely and completely satisfied.

Monday, November 3

Salvador was our next stop, another big coastal city with nothing of great interest to us. We visited a baroque cathedral with carved wood covered with gold leaf. Children outside the church begged for money, vendors relentlessly pursued us, and street performers knocked themselves out doing uncoordinated voodoo dances accompanied by loud boomboxes.

Then there was a cocktail party at a local museum that exhibited costly antiques and artifacts, and again, we watched dancers in costumes do what looked like wild voodoo ritual dances until they stumbled, exhausted, from the stage.

Then we reboarded the bus and returned to the ship.

Tuesday and Wednesday, November 4 & 5

At sea. We continued to enjoy our veranda and each other.

Thursday, November 6

The next morning, sailing into Rio was exciting. That beautiful coastline was as breathtaking to us as it must have been to the first explorers and developers of that city.

We packed our luggage, then sat on our verandah for a last half hour, prepared to disembark, knowing the next three days would be the final phase of our adventure.

<u>Rio de Janeiro</u>

Nobody much spoke English in Rio. And we couldn't keep track of time because our guidebooks said not to wear watches in public for fear they would be ripped off. Culture shock.

Our first impressions were strongly negative. We felt we had walked into a surreal third world. And that was just getting off the ship at the dock.

It cost $80 for the taxi to the Sheraton Hotel in Rio. Damn! We got a shabby room at the Sheraton, and we changed rooms the following day. Funny how a bad hotel room costing an arm and a leg can make a person feel resentful.

The hotel's beach was remarkable with hundreds of children playing in the rip tide and diving off a massive boulder located out in the bay. I walked along the beach wearing shoes because there was trash and broken bottles and unspeakable stuff everywhere. Brazilians have apparently been told not to bother using trash cans—because there weren't any.

All of a sudden, I just about stumbled over a couple copulating.

She was very, very pregnant, and he was on top of her, humping and holding a soccer ball under one arm as he did the dirty deed. I said, "Oh, excuse me," and turned away, doing my best to act as if that's the kind of thing one sees every day, walking away without changing my pace, leaving them alone.

Farther down the beach, I encountered a tour agent who said she had met an eight-year-old hooker the day before. I said, "Welcome to Paradise."

She said, "Brazil is really a beautiful place, you just have to look for it, you know, like everywhere?"

I said, "I agree, but sometimes beauty is harder to see for all the distractions."

We met some courteous hotel staff, we had Brazilian beer, and our attitudes began to change. Rio didn't, we did. We went for a taxi ride and the driver almost ran over a guy wearing a catheter, carrying his half-filled bottle of urine while crossing a heavily crowded street on Cococabana beach. I asked Barbara, "Is that guy carrying what I think he's carrying?"

Barbara said, "Gulp."

I looked up to Corcovada mountain where the Christ with his arms out-stretched seems to be saying, "Rio, What am I gonna do with you?"

We took the concierge's advice that evening and went to a restaurant named "Satyricon" whose name had nothing to do with the excellent dinner we were served, and then we went to a nearby slummy-looking night club that had another improbable name, "Platforma", and witnessed the most lavish, spectacular costume show I have ever seen—featuring gorgeous costumes from Rio's annual Carneval. The music was loud and Latin, and the dancing was exceedingly amateurish, but it was a great show.

Friday, November 7.

The next day, we went—reluctantly—to the H. Sterns factory, an extremely aggressive jewelry store where you're assured you won't be pressured into buying something you don't want, and then you get pressured big time. We walked though a shop where jewelry is cut and finished, and we spent most of our time trying to shake off salespersons who acted resentful that we weren't interested in buying anything.

We visited a badly maintained—but beautiful, nonetheless—botanical park, and afterwards we traveled for about an hour on a bus to reach South America's largest shopping mall. It's so large that a monorail is required to get from one extreme location to another.

The mall has nothing to recommend it. We had hoped to find some folk art and crafts, especially Christmas decorations, but virtually everything Christmassy for sale was made in China.

We were failures as tourists; we didn't buy anything, but we ate Brazilian food & drank Brazilian wine on our last night at Rio's Sheraton.

Saturday, November 8

The following day we hired a taxi driver who said that a new law had been passed in Rio requiring permits for handguns. He said he was a little nervous because he had carried one in his glove compartment for over twenty years, and he feels naked without it. I joked and said, "You feel naked now?"

He said, "No, I decided to keep my gun in the car. You never know."

We toured the city's beautiful but decaying Santa Theresa district and visited the Villa Lobos Museum where one of my favorite composers had lived; then the National Opera Cafe for lunch—a dark and dismal dinery—and then, the National Art Museum—with half of the exhibits not open for viewing and the other half filled with copies of old Greek & Roman stuff, just not very interesting.

The best museum on our whirlwind tour of Rio was the Carmen Miranda Memorial Museum with lots of her extravagant dresses and headgear and photographs with a museum staff that was proud of her and their tiny museum.

En route to the airport that evening, we drove on a highway located near thousands of poorly constructed shanties where the poor lived. Our English-speaking driver was unsympathetic. He said, "They've all got electricity and television sets, and the government can't get them to move because they're afraid they'll lose their welfare checks. They do nothing but make babies, and they've got all the missionaries from the States they can handle." I didn't respond, and after a minute, he said, "And they're almost all niggers."

He waited, and I waited, and finally I said, "You know, this is the first time on this trip I've wished our driver couldn't speak English." He never said another word.

Our plane to the States departed Rio at 8:45 that evening with an uninteresting four-hour layover in Sao Paulo.

Sunday, November 9

We arrived home around 2 PM the following day having driven in our car from Austin to Salado.

Oh, shit! At, home, while unloading our luggage, I discovered I had picked up a suitcase in Austin that looked like one of Barbara's but that wasn't. So, we got back in the car, drove back to Austin, exchanged suitcases, and returned to Salado by 5 PM, collapsing by 5:01 PM. The only one significant inconvenience was the mistake I made with our luggage.

Would we do it again? The ship, yes; the tour, no; Barbados, gosh, no.

These rocks are the remains of Sacsayhuaman, (easily pronounced *Sexy woman*).

Machu Picchu & Patagonia

♦

A Jointly Sponsored Tour
January 15–February 2, 1998

In January of 1998, I joined a tour to Machu Picchu and Patagonia sponsored by the American Geographical Society, The Metropolitan Museum of Art, and The National Trust for Historic Preservation.

Transportation involved 12 planes, several buses, and a ship through Magellan's Strait and around the Horn, winding through the fiords and around the cordilleras of South America.

I enjoyed the folks who took the tour; however, I didn't much care for the people representing the company that managed the tour (Raymond & Whitcomb).

Diversions off the beaten path (that is, restaurant dinners, home tours, and lots of folk music groups) were highlights calculated to appeal to big time spenders, but it was the wild and wooly countries of South America that charmed my socks off.

A Pre-Cruise Odyssey to Machu Picchu, January 15–21.

First stop was Lima, Peru, where I enjoyed staying at the Ora Verde Hotel overnight and tours of a private "Inca Gold Museum" (Priceless pre-Columbian golden treasures displayed badly; I've seen better-looking garage sales), a Pre-Columbian Art Museum (Boring but beautiful), and the Peruvian National Art Museum (Superb presentation of a knockout collection). You ain't seen pre-Columbian until you've been to Peru.

VIA—the Peruvian National Airlines—squeezed us in the tightest seats and rows imaginable for a flight to Cuzco, whose Old Town is the most visited spot on the South American continent. The city is also located at one of the highest elevations in the continent. Three (a pretty high percentage) of our tour group were not able to handle the altitude and had to return to Lima with nose bleeds and racing heart beats.

The group stayed at the five star Hotel Libertador, located directly across the street from the Santo Domingo Monastery, whose curious combination of both Inca & Spanish architecture makes it unique. Earthquakes have reduced many Spanish buildings and Inca temples to rubble (That is, temples altered by the Spanish conquerors), but Inca constructions continue to stand. (Why? See below.)

We toured the massive remains of an Incan fortress, Sacsayhuaman [pronounced: "Sexywoman"] whose great boulders are evidence of the grand scale hallmark of Incan architecture. We also traveled to Incan Ruins at Tambomachay, Keno, and Puca Pucara, clambering up great temple steps to marvel at those incredibly grand projects in the steps of centuries of travelers.

In the village of Pisac, old as the Incas, we walked from stall to stall at a Sunday Market, studying foodstuffs, artifacts, and clothing on sale. Unaffectedly primitive, the people are unspoiled by tourism. The women wore traditional bowler hats and multicolored shawls and dresses with hairstyles identifying them as unmarried or married or widowed, available or unavailable. We Spoiled Tourists traveled to the Urumbamba Valley & Ollantaytambo Inca Fortress for a tour of a private farmhouse, "Huayoccari" (not your backwoodsy farmhouse but a country club hideaway), followed by lunch on the grounds.

The last day of our visit to Peru was a pilgrimage to Machu Picchu, the best reason for traveling to that country full of good reasons. Early that day, we boarded a train that switched back and forth and then up and down the sharp mountainsides. We rode through the jungle, occasionally viewing a trail that we might have taken if we had hiked to the Machu Picchu Ruins.

Upon arrival, we were transferred to a bus that zigzagged up to the Ruins nearly invisible from below, tucked away on a small hilltop between two Andean peaks, only 7,000 feet above sea level. As the bus bumped, our guide reviewed the basics: The site had lain hidden to all but a few peasants for hundreds of years, never discovered by the Spanish or mentioned in their chronicles, nor recorded in annals written by pre-Colonial cultures of Peru. In 1911, A Yale professor of archeology, Hiram Bingham, discovered the Ruins buried beneath dense undergrowth. The land has since been reclaimed from the forest.

We arrived at the entrance to the grounds, and I paid a small fee to have "Machu Picchu" stamped into my passport.

Anticipation carried us around and through the outbuildings that serve as a kind of melodramatic passage from the new world to the old. And then, there it was, exactly like the photographs but in glorious 3-D. Manicured, neat and tidy, there was no evidence on the grounds of tourists who had come before us. Could it be that Disneyland maintenance had beat us to the spot?

The first sight of Machu Picchu is magical with temples, fields, terraces, and baths appearing as an elegant green paradise carved into natural surroundings. There are three areas—agricultural, urban, and religious—and structures are arranged so that their functions match their surroundings. The agricultural terracing and aqueducts are located on natural slopes; low areas contain buildings occupied by farmers and teachers; and areas that served religious purposes occupy the crest of the hill, overlooking the Urubamba Valley, thousands of feet below.

The view from the Funerary Rock Hut offers a dramatic overview of the Ruins. From here we could see the start of the Inca trail, spotted from the train as noted above, a well-developed if treacherous foot trail connecting Cusco with Machu Picchu. We learned that at the end of each day a small herd of llamas enters Machu Picchu from the terraces near the Funerary Rock Hut to graze on the grass (keeping it mowed).

A Royal Tomb is located underneath the circular Temple of the Sun, a cave-like area containing ceremonial niches and an Inca cross (no relationship to a Christian cross), carved at one wall. The cross resembles a series of steps, and represents the three levels of existence in the world of the Inca: the snake (the underworld or death), the jaguar (the present, human life), and the condor (the celestial/spiritual plane of the gods). To the left of the Royal Tomb there is a series of 16 ceremonial baths linked by an aqueduct system. And at the top of this system is the watershed hut.

The Royal Tomb has been the site of excavations of more than 100 skeletal remains. 80 percent of whom were women. This fact, among others, leads scholars to surmise that Machu Picchu was inhabited primarily by high priests and chosen women. But don't let me confuse fact with surmise. *The true purpose of Machu Pichu has never been conclusively determined.*

Up a steep set of stairs on the far side of the quarry is a four-sided Sacred Plaza surrounded by the Temple of Three Windows (named for three identical, trapezoidal windows that open into the main plaza), a small room called the Sacristy (containing a polished stone bench and several carved niches in the wall, presumably for religious objects), and the Principal Temple with large stone blocks polished smooth and joined perfectly (a remarkable engineering feat accomplished by the Inca who used no mortar to hold their walls in place, relying upon precisely-cut stones, geometry, and female and male joints in the corners and foundations). The Inca's best-built structures have survived the passing of centuries, even multiple earthquakes as noted above, without damage. Amazingly, not even credit cards can be forced to fit between most of the perfectly joined stones.

At the top of a final set of stairs is the centerpiece of Machu Picchu, *Intiwatana* or the "hitching post of the sun," a carved rock pillar whose four corners are oriented toward the four cardinal points. The Inca were accomplished astronomers as well as architects, and presumably used the angles of the pillar to predict the solstices. The sun exerted a crucial influence on agriculture, and therefore the well-being of the whole society. There are people today who feel that Machu Picchu is one of the Earth's magnetic focal points with an inherent spiritual or metaphysical power.

Here is where I hoped for a spiritual or psychic experience; here is also where I was disappointed. The pillar was imposing, but I was expecting too much. I truly believe that when one *expects* mystery, it's elusive at best.

"The time has come for me to take pen in hand and report the great things there are to tell of Peru." These were the words of the Spanish Chronicler Pedro Cieza de Leon, writing to King Philip II of Spain in 1558. The amazing omission in his report is mention of Machu Picchu. It is entirely likely that he never saw the site, arguably the most impressive and spectacular accomplishment of the Inca Empire.

My account in no way accurately describes Ruins that beguiled me but that failed to pull me into its mystique. We left before the groundskeepers and llamas arrived to restore the grounds to their pristine beauty, an act that ostensibly pre-pares the Ruins for tourists but that also seems like a ritual suitable for welcoming the return of the original priests and virgins. Perhaps their ghosts arrived after we left.

PATAGONIA PASSAGE, January 22–February 2

Returning to Lima where the roofs of buildings are flat because it seldom rains, we joined the tourists who would go with us to Patagonia, and we toured the Santa Rita Winery where we got the kind of cordial reception one longs for when traveling in foreign lands.

In Santiago (Chile) we stayed at the Hyatt Regency Hotel, toured the Cousino Palace and the Bellas Artes Museum, then I struck off by myself for a walking tour of the huge National Railroad Museum (absolutely worth the visit for a rail-road buff).

After a flight to windy Punta Arenas, Chile, we saw the Strait of Magellan for the first time and boarded the *Hanseatic* (an icebreaker designed for explorers rather than cruise ship passengers, hence a bit short on glamour), sailing from Patagonia. First stop, Tierra del Fuego, an archipelago consisting of one large island, five medium-sized islands, and great rocks too small to be called islands, separated by inlets and channels. We were promised rainfall that we didn't get, but we got great windstorms.

A small town, Puerto Natales, is located not far from the Ultima Esperanza ("Last Hope") fjord in the north, so-named by its discoverer, Juan de Ladrillero, who, in 1557, was desperately trying to find the western exit of the maze that is the Strait of Magellan. Fortunately for him and his crew, he succeeded, and the town became Chile's cattle-raising and exporting center in Patagonia until late in the 20th Century. By the time we visited, it had become little more than a jump-ing off place for tourists.

Docking at Puerto Natales we traveled by bus for a rough two-hour ride to or "Torres del Paine" National Park, an area almost completely deserted with knotty Magellanic trees rising from a level of 200 meters to 3050 meters. Great Condors dip and swoop over this impressive mountain range with its improbable shear, steep granite towers (Horns or "Cuernos") that make the Paine Grande a photo-genic wonderland.

Returning to the ship and setting sail, we passed through Cabo Froward (South America's southernmost land mass), the dangerous crossroads of the Magellan Strait known as one of the largest maritime cemeteries of the world. Early the next morning, we lined up at a great distance from the Kirke Narrows, a 50 yard passageway in the Strait of Magellan, and on a signal from a boat stationed at the site, we raced at full-speed to pass through the Narrows. Evidently the passage opens and remains open for a short period. We watched it close up behind us, leaving us inside the Cordilleras surrounding the Darwin & Beagle Channel and the Tierra del Fuego Archipelago.

We boarded Zodiacs and sailed to the Bay of Mountains Glacier where we hoped to see penguins, but there were none. "Awww," resonated from all the Zodiacs when we were told there would be no penguins. Awww.

The next morning, we sailed through the Drake Passage around Cape Horn, an event that was every bit as stormy as we were promised it might be. I and about five other intrepid passengers went down to breakfast and watched tables and chairs slide across the messroom as the storm intensified. Suddenly, a stack of dishes flew into the air like a batch of china frizbies followed by the entire buffet set out for breakfast. In no time we were knee-deep in Weaties and milk and scrambled eggs and muffins. Small wonder they call it a mess.

Fortunately, I've earned my sea legs, and I was more thrilled than frightened. It took the remainder of the day for the ship to return to smooth sailing before my sickly fellow passengers emerged from their cabins.

At Puerto Williams (Chile), the Museum of the "Southernmost Town in The World" was our next stop. Not much to look at.

Next, we visited a museum at Ushuaia (Argentina), "The End of the World Museum," but it wasn't much either. For all the claims these rival nations made, the sites are significant only by virtue of their botton-of-the-New-Worldness.

In Ushuaia, we debarked and flew to Buenos Aires and transferred to the Caesar Park Hotel (quite comfortable) not far from the Bellas Artes Museum. Like the rest of Buenos Aires, the Museum is more European than Spanish with 32 exhibit halls, state of the art technology, and works by Europeans Goya, Renoir, Van Gogh, and Rodin.

The Plaza de Mayo is the city center (the city, in fact, was literally built around it), and some of Argentina's most important historical events took place there. Evita Peron sang, "Don't Cry for Me, Argentina." [or she would have if she had known the lyrics]. Today the Plaza probably owes most of its notoriety to the "Madres de la Plaza de Mayo," the women who still show up in the square seeking information on the deseparecidos, their loved ones who were kidnapped during the "Dirty War."

We took a tour of the city, stopping at La Boca, a section of town near the port where there's an assortment of houses made of wood and metal painted bright primary colors. Thence to Ricoleta Cemetery (with tombs of old Argentinian families including the grave of Eva Peron), and the Teatro Colon Opera (one of the world's premier opera houses with 3,500 seats, having hosted Maria Callas, Toscanini, Stravinsky, and even Caruso).

At dinner that same evening, there was a demonstration of tango dancers, not an amateur bone in their lithe and sensual bodies.

The highlight of the visit to Argentina was a flight to Iguassu Falls, a stunning sight and an engineering accomplishment with steps descending into the falls and frightening, furry little raccoon-like creatures called "Coatis" running around everywhere.

The trip concluded with a visit to an estancia (ranch) on the Pampas with a barbecue and a show featuring gauchos on horseback. For a Texan, this ranch visit wasn't the special event it may have seemed to others on the tour.

The return to the States by air took more time than I anticipated, and I had jet lag—even though I lost no more than a couple hours in transit.

Bright sunlight, clear mountain air, what else do you need in summer? Rain?

Highlands, North Carolina

✦

Another Summer Vacation
Summer, 1998

We stayed for one summer at Highlands, a little town in North Carolina's hills (the highest elevations east of the Mississippi), but all I recall are the lazy days, one following another uneventfully. I never thought I would recount what happened (or what didn't much happen) in Highlands, so I didn't keep a journal, but I have one bright and shimmering memory of a special trip when Barbara, Libba, and I drove from Highlands to Winston-Salem. It was there that I had taught English for a year in 1961 to indifferent but charming students at an all-girls college. Returning to visit this town and school, showing Libba where we lived during the year before she was conceived, was a pleasant and nostalgic non-event. The memories of the time we had spent in that place were faded and fragmented, but we walked to the Old Salem campus and looked for the building where Barbara and I had lived for a year. It had been razed. And there was no historical marker to note that's where the Carver's lived on campus.

That night, the three of us stayed overnight at a Salem hotel that housed a café that had obviously been named the Carver Café in our honor, but there was no one around to assure us that was true.

Next day, we continued on the road to the coast. We toured the Tryon Palace and Gardens in New Bern, an elegant Georgian-style mansion that had served as both home of Royal Governor William Tryon and the capital of the Colony of North Carolina during the 18th-Century, furnished with an outstanding collection of antiques and art. And we listened to well-trained docents in costume tell us what had happened in that venerable old statehouse, and then we moved on.

The highlight of the trip was a climb up to the Wilber and Orville Wright Monument at Kitty Hawk, located on windswept dunes, covered with various kinds of grasses. The museum located there was crowded and filled with artifacts (a replica of the first Wright airplane), and there was a lecturer, but it had a sterile atmosphere with lots of stuff on display that mostly looked like stuff, so we got back in the car and drove away.

Libba and I walked up to the marble monument to the Wright Brothers flight, located about a mile away, while Barbara stayed in the car. It was great exploring together that great windy, tribute to the Wright Brothers. But it was the concept that left me awestruck. I continue to wonder who the individual was who caused that memorial to happen. Somebody's notion resulted in a wonderful monument.

On the way back to Highlands, we stopped at Roanoke, NC, where a historical play was in rehearsal. We walked up and into the outdoor theatre and watched scenes being staged. Having directed outdoor drama myself, I knew how to appreciate the work that that theatrical production required. But *The Lost Colony,* the subject of the play, was not actually so remarkable an event as is the annual celebration of that event. Again, I marveled at the notion of a celebratory drama that someone had wrestled into being. Yes, some group had made it happen, but it was an idea sparked by one individual, the guy who started it all, that impressed me most.

From there we returned to Highlands and a pleasurable summer hiatus in those North Carolina mountains.

Ask me what I did that summer? Hell, I don't remember. What does that say about Highlands. And me.

The John Steinbeck museum is an unexpected joy! Artifacts: Books & movies abound.

California Dreaming

✦

Postcards from the State on the Edge of the World March 25–28, 1999

Early in the spring of 1999, Barbara and I decided to check out California's west coast between San Francisco & Los Angeles. We wanted to see that area of the country, stay in some extremely Comfortable (with a capital "C") lodgings, eat some extraordinary food, and return home able to say, "You really don't want to miss...."

So you'll find italicized comments in the text below, the kind I might have written on postcards—if I had sent postcards.

With help from our trusty travel agent, Diane, I lined up a rental car and arranged for stays at Big Sur, Pebble Beach, and Santa Monica, at places we had heard about: Carmel, the Pacific coast, the Hearst Castle in San Simeon, the Steinbeck Museum at Salinas, and the Getty Museum in Los Angeles. *Looking forward to this adventure.*

And so, on Thursday, March 25th, we flew from Austin to San Francisco where we rented a car from Avis, a white Buick, easy to enjoy. *Not a care in the world.*

The drive down to Big Sur on old US Highway 1 took a couple of hours under cloudy skies with great waves pounding the shoreline, really exciting, and we listened to a portion of an audio book version of George Stephanopoulos' tattle-tale, <u>All Too Human</u>, deciding that the author was definitively self-aggrandizing. *US Highway 1 is a beautiful and remarkable engineering achievement.*

We arrived in Big Sur (that is actually a neighborhood rather than a city, stretching for miles) at the much overrated Post Ranch Inn where we stayed three nights in a "Tree house" overlooking the Pacific. The Inn is a pricey, self-congratulatory resort (Stephanopoulos would have loved it) whose architecture was at best arbitrary with sharp triangular corners, handmade furnishings, and curious décor. We had to park about two hundred feet from our cabin and take a shuttle because the management doesn't want guests' cars to crowd the narrow paths and damage the landscaping (that was both natural-looking and cleverly designed to look natural). *Stay there for one night just to have stayed there one night.*

At dinner that first evening at the lodge restaurant, we decided that the handmade silverware and plates were hard to use and impossibly unconventional in design—arbitrary, like the architecture. The food and service were okay. *Don't eat there.*

The weather was superb for the entire weekend, and we spent the next day travelling to and visiting Hearst Castle near San Simeon. Docents were academically informative, but the visit was expensive. *If you like castles, this is an Americanized castle.*

The Cavalier Restaurant in San Simeon saw us coming and jacked up the price for lunch—or it seemed so. *Don't go there, but there didn't seem to be any place else to go.*

Returning, the coast road going north was not nearly so interesting as the trip south had been earlier that same day. The Santa Maria mountains, the Pacific, the two-lane highway with little traffic, and the weather were awesome. *Traverse that highway at your own risk and only in good weather.*

We returned to Big Sur and ate a world class dinner at the Ventana Inn Restaurant—across the highway from our lodging. *If ever you're in Big Sur, you don't*

want to miss dinner at the Ventana Inn Restaurant if it's still under the same man-
agement and if the same chefs & service personnel are employed there.

We spent the next day in downtown Carmel looking for a parking place. We ate lunch at a touristy café, shopped briefly on Ocean Drive, drove to a wonderfully landscaped mall, and ended the day with dinner in an above average restaurant, the Rio Grill, that I liked and Barbara didn't. *Former mayor of Carmel, Clint Eastwood, was nowhere in sight.*

On our last morning at the Post Ranch, we checked out early and drove to Salinas to enjoy the Steinbeck library & museum, a well-conceived and executed showplace *The Steinbeck Library is an outstanding destination, don't miss it!*

We returned to Carmel and traveled south on the "Seventeen Mile Road," driving around the coast and through neighborhoods with great houses and stunning trees for scenery, but it was about 15 miles too long. That evening we checked into the Pebble Beach Inn at Spanish Bay for one night. The dinner at the hotel's crowded Roy's Grill was good, *but don't go out of your way.*

Checking out the following morning, we began a five-hour trek via Highway 101 to Santa Barbara, listening to the remainder of the Stephanopoulos tape. Barbara nodded off, and I envied her.

Nothing much remarkable about US 101 or the Stephanopoulos tape.

We had decided to take the last leg of our trip on the Amtrak "San Diegan" because our train buff friend, Fred Springer, said we shouldn't miss seeing the ocean from San Louis Obispo to L. A. Unfortunately, repair work on the track from SJO to Santa Barbara was not completed, so we were told only an Amtrak bus was available. That didn't sound like much fun to me, so I opted to begin the train ride at Santa Barbara. We got a bargain holiday price for "Custom" 1st class seat reservations, but I thought to myself, "Wait a minute, this will be the first bargain we've found in California." *There are no bargains in California.*

I picked up our tickets at a temporary Amtrak trailer house where the clerk told me, with regret, that the first part of that trip would have to be on bus to the town of Oxnard.

I said, "Shit!"

She said, "That's what everybody says, but the tracks aren't repaired yet."

I said, "Well, okay, we've turned in our rental car, so please tell me the bus won't be crowded."

She said, "There's hardly anybody going on the bus."

I said, "Small wonder."

Barbara and I checked our two large suitcases at the Ryder rental truck that was being used for temporary storage purposes, and we watched a skinhead muscleman throw our luggage aboard. Then we waited for the bus that—you've guessed it—was quite crowded. We had to sit in separate seats (that was okay by me since Barbara was livid), and the seats were narrow, and snarling California traffic was slow, and I was pissed—all the way to Oxnard. The bus got back onto Highway 101, and we traveled bumper to bumper looking down onto the coastal road about 500 yards parallel with the highway, watching tourists cruising at about thirty miles an hour, exceeding our speed by—oh, say, thirty miles an hour. Then, at Oxnard, the train was waiting for us, and I watched our luggage disappear into a car two cars behind ours. *We were not having a wonderful time.*

We boarded the train and were directed to the custom-seating, 1st class car, where a smiling attendant welcomed us warmly and explained that the air conditioning was not working on the rear of the car or the right side of the front end, so would we kindly crowd together at the left side of the front end. And sit facing the rear. Barbara and I sat in separate seats, stealing glances at each other, mostly rolling our eyes.

I thought, "What else can go wrong?" I soon revised that question to "What next?"

The attendant announced that she would serve cranberry juice to us shortly—that she did, apologizing that "the two toilets in this car don't function properly sometimes." She said we were welcome to use the one that was working in the next car.

The windows were dirty, but I thought, "At least we'll be able to see the coast," that—you'll remember—was the original reason for the trip by train. I soon learned that the ride from Oxnard to L. A. was all inland, and for four hours, we watched rock formations, tunnels, newly planted crops, virtually unbroken stretches of suburbs, and all manner of trailer houses: double wide, single shotgun, and an occasional roofless tornado-damaged trailer park.

An announcer screamed the names of stations over the PA system, and we first class travelers were pacified with cranberry juice as promised, as well as peanuts & pretzels, cookies, and finally, California wine. I asked for and got a second glass of wine.

We pulled into the station at Los Angeles where our luggage was efficiently and promptly transferred to the baggage claim room. It came up out of the carousel into the baggage room about 40 long minutes after we arrived. A guy who looked like Stephen King double-checked our claim tickets.

A former student and friend met us at the baggage room and transferred us to the Shutters hotel on Santa Monica beach that was expensive but okay. *Don't stay there either*. But dinner in the hotel that night was wonderful. In fact, it was unforgettable because I had too much to drink.

The next day, after recovering from my hangover, we took a taxi to the Getty Museum whose lower entrance has all the character of a theme park. Our hour-long wait on line and then aboard the tram up the mountain side didn't prepare us for the great pleasure of arriving at the Museum complex. We immediately joined an architecture tour in progress and learned that Richard Meier, the architect, and the Museum's director (somebody whose name I can't remember), had created a grand scale masterpiece that is much more impressive than I expected it to be. We loved the surprise vistas, the gardens, the attention to detail. The art exhibits were only okay. *Don't miss it*.

That evening we flew home direct from LAX to Austin, and I reflected that one has to visit a place at least once to learn how to get around; that's how a person can best determine whether it's worth another trip. *Unless, of course, one reads postcards in a reliable journal by someone who's been there*.

We don't plan to make a second trip retracing our tracks, but I'm glad we did it once. *You might want to pass on this trip or just do it in three days*.

Norsemen were successful invaders because they were successful ship designers & builders.

A Cruise to Scandinavia & St. Petersburg

◆

Baltic Highlights and Shadows
June 15–July 2, 1999

We flew from Austin to DFW to London Gatwick, no problem that sleep couldn't cure.

Our travel agent arranged for a private car, Gatwick to Mayfair (The trip took too long, our driver was late picking us up, we got lost en route, and the car was dirty, but we slept most of the way).

Overnight at the posh Connought Hotel, lovely suite, lovely dinner, lovely stroll, lovely sleep.

Next day, we shopped, visited museums, and in the evening, saw *Julius Caesar* at Shakespeare's Old Globe Theatre (after a detour from the West End Gielgud Theatre formerly known as the Globe. Our cab driver refused to charge us for going out of the way).

Next day, we taxied to the Tower of London during a rainstorm where we were transferred by tender to the Seabourn *Pride*. There was great delay and confusion, but we liked the ship a lot.

That evening, we disembarked to see *Whistle Down the Wind*, a so-so musical by Lloyd Webber.

Next day, sunny weather allowed us to visit St. Katherine's Dock near the pier where the ship was berthed. Later in the afternoon, we sailed away under London's Tower Bridge as "Hail Britannia" was played by the ship musicians and traffic stopped and the bridge raised to let us pass through, really exciting.

We cruised down the Thames past the new Greenwich Millennium Dome and out into the North Sea.

Great cruise, great weather, great food, good company, good cabin, excellent service, super lectures, ho-hum entertainment, poor-to-superb land tours; start to finish, the ship was terrific, and the cruise was as peaceful and unaffecting as the countries we visited. No wonder folks don't get excited visiting those countries.

1st stop, via the North Sea (a pussycat sea), Oslo, Norway, we toured a "World War II Resistance Museum" on a rainy day, not an impressive display. Then we visited the Kon Tiki Boat Museum and Viking Ship Museum, authentic but not imposing presentations.

2nd stop, via the Kattegat (rough sailing) to Helsingborg, Sweden. What's another word for unexciting.

3rd stop, via the Baltic Sea (calm and untroubled) Visby, Gotland—an island off Sweden—with lots of poppies & "blue weeds", limestone, ruins. Forgettable. Ask anybody who's ever been there if they remember anything much about it.

4th stop, Stockholm, Sweden, a visit to the Town Hall where the Nobel Prize Dinners are served, a big hall that was no big deal; then, at last: We were *greatly* impressed by the "Vasa" ship and its museum, remarkable, really remarkable.

Not so interesting was a tour to the Miles Sculpture Studio & Museum, but it was a lovely summer day. Then a shopping stop at the NK Department Store, pricey (because of exchange rates) where I bought a CD of an opera by ABBA with music I grew to enjoy, but with a text I could never appreciate. It was in Swedish.

5th stop, via the Gulf of Finland (very tame), Helsinki, Finland. By now I was no longer expecting to see something as special as the Vasa. We toured a ruined fortress in the morning and an architect's studio and private art collection in the afternoon, each simply another stop en route.

That evening, bright daylight at 10 PM, Land Ho: Mother Russia on the Port Side. Now, *that* was visceral, even a little scary.

6th stop, via the Neva River, St. Petersburg, Russia. St. Petersburg commands attention. We docked and listened to a welcoming concert by a scraggly, ragtag orchestra on the dock playing Russian tunes, then brightly, "New York, New York", "Mack the Knife," and a really pitiful version of the "Star Spangled Banner."

Customs officials who were almost as self-important-seeming as some US customs agents we've met checked us off the ship and back on for all tours including the trip to a hot as Hell Hermitage Museum, where our visit lasted two hours, timed to the minute (with only 20 minutes allowed in the impressionist paintings rooms).

We were locked <u>out</u>side of the Hermitage's gold exhibit—the only air conditioned room we visited in S. P.—where we waited 20 minutes, and then we were locked <u>in</u>side for 30 minutes.

That afternoon, I went alone to a pitiful excuse for a department store, and I changed money at a bank where two guards carrying rifles and wearing bulletproof vests and gunbelts, stared me down as I asked for $20 worth of Rubles that, of course, are worth nothing outside Russia.

"Unbelievably hot" was what attending a reception was in a private palace without an air circulation or cooling system, all the male tourists wearing tuxes, sweating excessively while violinists played Mozart too slowly. We could not wait for the overrated event to end so we could rip off our clothes on the bus back to the ship.

The next day, a tour in the rain to the Peterhof Castle was uncomfortably warm and wet, but the rooms and fountains were imposing. Later, we learned that some tourists had been mobbed by young punks in the same park we had ambled about in.

The real low point for us, was a visit to three churches, one that has a big dome, one where all the czars of Russia are buried with their families, and another Eastern Orthodox church where we watched worshippers kiss icons and quarrel with one another. I prayed: Please, God, no more fortresses, churches, department stores, or guides who lecture captive audiences with the same jokes yesterday's guides used.

The final tour in St. Petersburg exceeded our expectations absolutely; it was worth the trip to Russia: Tea with an ill-at-ease young woman in her small apartment. We were actually allowed to talk with this young Russian who spoke freely and critically of Russia and her life as a professional who gets paid $100 each month as a surgeon in a hospital, requiring her to moonlight as an acupuncturist and massage therapist in order to make a decent living. She was also paid to allow tourists to visit her apartment where she lived with her boyfriend, and her mother and her mother's boyfriend, in two rooms barely large enough for double beds.

What she said seemed honest and hopeless and dreary, but she (and we) found it amusing when we began responding to her broken English with a kind of pigeon English.

The cookies she served us were store-bought and stale, but the home-made rhubarb preserves were delicious. It was the visit that was the treat.

We were charmed and touched by this frightened young woman. I tried to email our thanks, but we never heard from her again.

7th Stop, after leaving St. Petersburg, we went ashore at Taillin, Estonia, a medieval old town, with an old tour guide who required us to go with her through another damn church, fortress, and department store.

8th stop, after a day at sea (the Baltic), we arrived at Copenhagen, Denmark, where we disembarked, and toured streets and canals and parks on our own. A nice overnight stay in the Angleterre Hotel, then a taxi to the airport, a definitive Danish pastry to remember before catching the plane, then a slow-paced return from a slightly interesting two-week visit to seven (Count 'em) gloomy countries. Maybe I expected too much.

Two Cities, Philidelphia & Washington, best and worst of America in the United States.

Philadelphia & Washington

✦

Self-Touring
August 6–8 1999

Friday, August 6

See America first! Or soon as you can.

Notably Philadelphia & Washington.

In August of 1999, I decided to check out Philadelphia because a former student of mine, Eric Henry, was conducting a workshop in a Bucks County town nearby. I attended and enjoyed his workshop on the subject of coaching teachers, and then he and I took a short train ride to Philadelphia

After checking into our respective hotel rooms, we went immediately to the Visitors' Center in the Old City, pride of the National Park Service, and I admired it for several reasons: Information, Courtesy, Availability of Guides, and Exhibits.

After an orientation, we took a "Tipplers' Tour" of the old city with a thoroughly professional quartet of singers. Following that, we strolled down the lane where Ben Franklin had his shops. Then we enjoyed supper at the City Tavern enjoying duck, greens, and grits.

That evening we moved from location to location outdoors in the old city watching what was billed as an "Unforgettable" Sound and Light show depicting the heroes of the American Revolution with special reference to Pennsylvania. The unforgettable part was how poor the show was. Sound & Light shows universally are pretty boring. The only memorable segment was a big finish with loud patriotic music coming from trees and bushes surrounding the audience.

Not good enough.

Saturday, August 7

The following morning we went early to the Visitors' Center to sign up for free tours. The tickets go quickly for set times during the day.

Our first stop was Carpenters Hall, built in 1770, a handsome building where delegates to the First Continental Congress met in September, 1774, to air their grievances against King George III. During the Revolutionary War the Hall served as a hospital and an arsenal for American forces. The building is still owned and maintained by the Carpenters' Union.

Next stop was Independence Hall, formerly the State House of Pennsylvania. You don't get to go through all the rooms, just the two main ones. There's a large entrance foyer and beyond that, the rooms where the Second Continental Congress (and subsequent assemblies) hammered out both the Declaration of Independence and the Constitution. It was inescapably exhilarating.

We had a short but outstanding tour of the First Bank of the US, the Second Bank of the US, and Congress Hall, conducted by a Park Ranger who knew how to expertly play the role of Witness to History. His performance was followed by a less-than-dynamic Park Ranger leading us on a less-than-fantastic tour of the Dolly Todd (Madison) House and Bishop White house.

We saw a colossal IMAX show about the founding and development of Philadelphia. Very impressive. And at the end of the day when we said goodbye to one another, our patriotic ardor had maxed out, but we had enjoyed each other's company and the occasion to see Philadelphia.

Then he flew home and I took a train to Washington, phase two of a pilgrimage I hadn't expected to be as absorbing as it was.

Sunday, August 8

Visiting the new Franklin Delano Roosevelt Memorial, I was disappointed at the scale of walls and the mixed-bag statuary. The stunted height of four compartment walls makes everything seem less than fully realized. Designed by Lawrence Halprin, the memorial incorporates the work of prominent American artists Leonard Baskin, Robert Graham, Thomas Hardy, and George Segal, as well as master stonecarver John Benson. The most imposing statue of Roosevelt by Neil Estern is a cloying representation by inclusion of FDR's dog, Fala. And whereas several of the statues have tragic character, they appear competitive in design and all invite comparison.

Legend has it that Roosevelt asked that he not have a memorial created to honor him; the source of the legend wasn't Roosevelt, rather someone who quoted him. It was my feeling after seeing this regrettably disoriented showcase of slogans and images, that FDR might have said he didn't want a memorial sensing that any tribute to his greatness with the Lincoln & Jefferson memorials located nearby would have to seem better in concept and design—or appear worse.

Sure enough, it's worse. Perhaps the trees and landscaping newly-planted will enhance the scene. I dearly hope so.

The location for the FDR Memorial is not in the mainstream of Washington, so I had to take a taxi to my next stop. I had never visited the Holocaust Museum because I expected it to be tomblike and depressing. And the only reason I made it a point to stop there was because one of my former students had a significant job on the staff. And wouldn't you know, it was her day off.

So I took the self-tour and was handed a booklet that allowed me to follow the path through the museum of one of the children whose lives were commemorated there. From one room to the next I traced the events that led from the child's birth to death with artifacts as evidence that the child had been slaughtered with thousands of other Jews.

At the end of the tour, there is a chapel that caught me unawares, a place to meditate. Without thinking, I threw the booklet into a collection bin nearby. It didn't seem an inappropriate gesture at the moment, but seconds later it hit me, and I broke into tears. I don't think the juxtaposition of the chapel near that bin was designed to have that effect, but it did to me.

I had to sit down awhile.

Then I visited the Freer & Sackler Museums located nearby. Never having been to those museums, they were an unexpected treasure chest of paintings. Reader, put them on your list.

Next, the National Gallery with a show featuring the work of Mary Cassatt.

Late in the day, I walked past the White House and observed new roadblocks designed to keep the street clear of traffic, serving as an obstacle course for terrorists.

I got my luggage and took off from the newly remodeled Reagan Airport Terminal, flying non stop to the new Austin Terminal.

Barbara was there to greet me. I told her about Philadelphia and Washington and historical stuff—and then we talked of matters at home, the stuff of life.

Talk about Globalization: McNuggets delivered by Ronald McChina on wheels.

China

✦

An Abercrombie & Kent Tour
September 10–26, 1999

In brief, on my trip to China with the Abercrombie & Kent tour company, I was a tourist—not a bona fide explorer—and it was an expensive seventeen days; however, I can't imagine receiving more bang for my buck

By the end of my trip I had taken about a thousand 3-D photographs that I winnowed down to 180. Stereo photos are much better than conventional pictures at capturing the look of where one has been, because 3-D establishes spatial dimensions.

But pictures aren't words. And that's what this journal is.

September 10, 11, 12

I crossed the date line to Hong Kong. Having been there before with Yale Exes, I appreciated comparing that trip, lodging in the Hong Kong's Grand Hyatt, with staying at the Mandarin Oriental, on this trip.

Our tour director Devin Gwie, picked me up at the new Hong Kong Chek Lap Kok airport, and as I was checking in at the hotel, uh-oh, I couldn't find my passport. I told Devin that the last time I had seen it was in the airport when I showed it to him. Without another word, he left to return to the airport, and one hour later, he came back with the passport in hand (where he kept it for the entire tour).

After sacking out for several hours after the long flight from the US, I awoke and joined the A&K group. Activities during the first two days were undemanding; we weren't even required to stay awake on a bus ride around the city, a Peak Tram funicular ride to Victoria Park, and an Aberdeen Sampan ride. It was in Aberdeen that I had lost a camera on my first trip to Hong Kong, and again I lost a camera, an inexpensive disposable one, but I had no desire to report a second loss to Devin. I was setting a record losing cameras, and I decided to keep it a private one.

The group was a small one (22). We were given admonitions by Chairman Devin that he intended to be amusing.

"Some tourist restaurants are called killing fields. We won't be eating there."

"Everything green for sale in China is called Jade."

"Remember, to the Chinese, all you whites look alike."

"Beware bogus 3-week old antiques made of permastone."

"Chinese pickpockets and con artists look just like you, only Chinese."

"Some friendly natives are butterflies (Hookers) or dragonflies (Male hustlers)."

"Some quilts have bugs that enjoy chewing up clothes in your suitcase."

"Smoking or non-smoking rooms are rooms with or without ashtrays."

"Plaster replicas of terra cotta warriors, if left out in the rain, turn Caucasian."

"I'll never serve rice to you because you'll say I'm stuffing you with cheap carbohydrates."

"Public bathrooms are generally free of flies because flies can't stand the smell."

"Don't order Evian water because the bottles are filled in China not France."

"Some airlines have total disregard of passengers—unlike airlines in the States, right?"

"Flight Schedules are like lotteries; first prize is a seat."

"Some busses were built in the Ming dynasty."

"Don't be a souvenir coolie; wait to buy stuff at the end of the tour."

"Oh, yeah. Have a good trip."

September 13

From Hong Kong, we flew to Guilin (Gway-lin), landing at night. We didn't see what it looked like until the following morning. The Sheraton was a big disappointment after Hong Kong. It was designated 5 star by the People's Republic of China, but it was a 1 ½ star in my book. Would the rest of our lodgings be this poor? Nope, it was the worst.

September 14

Morning light through a dirty window didn't dismay me when I beheld my first sight of Old China, a hazy copper Sun climbing above the limestone mountains just beyond the Li river. Wow! They were the same mountains I had seen in Chinese art for years, and they weren't exaggerated. The mountains actually look like hazy, giant ant hills.

We (and well over a thousand other tourists each day) sailed on private and unpretentious boats down the river, viewing the ancient limestone formations and getting to know one another. It became clear to me that these folks would be fun to hang out with. And they were.

Lunch aboard boat was okay. Food on the tour was super every now and again, never terrible, mostly Chinese. Seldom Western.

That afternoon at Fubo Hill, we visited a cave with some thousand year old Buddhas and inscriptions carved in the rocks.

September 15

First thing the next morning, I rode in a Pedicab (a kind of bicycle rickshaw built for two—plus the driver) dodging bicycle traffic, viewing Tai Chi exercisers, and avoiding open manholes. We watched workers laboring 24 hours each day to meet a deadline of October 1st of that year to finish construction projects all over town (and all over China for that matter) in time to celebrate the 50th anniversary of Communist rule in that country. I had not planned for the trip to occur at that time, but I was glad to be in China at a time the government was sprucing the place up.

September 16

Boarding a bus to the airport the next morning, our local tour guide (not to be confused with out tour director, Devin) informed us that China is a socialistic/capitalistic country but that really doesn't matter because to quote former Premiere Deng Xiaoping, "Whether a cat is black or white doesn't matter, it's still a cat."

She said Deng Xiaoping may have had a more positive impact on this century than anybody else because in the 15 years following the death of Mao, he turned a totalitarian state into the second biggest economy in the world. He established varying degrees of economic and personal freedom. It was he who limited the number of children the urban Chinese could have to only one, but that was to help the rest get rich. He said, "Somebody has to get rich first, otherwise we'll all remain poor together."

It must be said that he was also complicit in the 1989 Tiananmen Square killings of somewhere between 500 and 2,000 activists following an order for martial law issued by Premier Li Peng that resulted in the killing confrontation. Li is reputedly considered by most Chinese to have "bloody hands."

Editorializing, it's noteworthy that killing by Chinese leaders has always been an option. Mao killed over 35,000,000. Chiang Kai Shek killed over 10,000,000 when he blew up dams killing innocents and antagonists alike.

In Russia, Stalin killed over 60,000,000, and the German government in this century alone killed unaccountable numbers; so the Chinese rank only third in the world as mass murderers. And governments of Japan and other Asian countries have done some big killing.

The guide shrugged his shoulders and said with a straight face: "The world is a killing field periodically."

Learning about political mass murders while traveling in China was like putting pieces of puzzles together, replacing pieces that used to fit snugly.

All our Chinese tour guides were members of CITS (Chinese Information & Tourist Service), and they were guarded in their comments about politics. They were also like tour guides everywhere in the world, generally lacking in star quality. Our tour guide in Shanghai, however, was dynamic and personable. So let's segue to him.

September 17

We flew on big airbuses every time we went from one city to the next, and they were all new. I was greatly impressed by the newness but not the no-monkey-business, in-your-face efficiency of flight attendants. One hastily offered me a choice between rice or ooh-duh. I said, "What?"

She said, "Ooh-duh."

I said, "What's ooh-duh?" She handed me noodles without comment.

But I could read her mind, "Die, Yankee Infidel!"

Our Shanghai tour guide, Yuan Zu Kang, greeted us when we arrived and talked animatedly as we drove on a super highway that had been opened for travel *only the day before*. Very attractive highways with ferns planted in boxes on the roadsides.

Our Shanghai Garden hotel, located a stone's throw away from the building where Nixon & Mao signed the '72 treaty, was a luxury palace, managed by a Japanese company.

September 18, 19

During the next two days, we visited a Buddhist temple whose relics had been saved during the infamous Cultural Revolution when mobs followed Chairman Mao's dictum to destroy artifacts of historical China. The temple warders had saved the relics by pasting Mao's picture on the front of the display case containing the Buddha, scaring away the teenage mobs.

The Cultural Revolution, 1964–76 was an insane Chinese historical period. Young Chinese were encouraged to inform on their parents, destroy antiques & architecture, and kill or exile intellectuals, scholars, and teachers. In effect, their aim was to throw out four "old things," traditions, culture, customs, habits. It's a miracle that the nation ever recovered, and it's remarkable that as many old things survived as we were able to view.

Yuan also took us to the Chinese Market and the Yuyuan Garden (16th century Ming Dynasty architecture), and the excellent Shanghai Museum. Then we drove past new buildings at Pudong, a nine year old development built on an island across from the Bund on the Huangpu river, stunning to behold! Towers there, skyscrapers, are a showplace for Chinese contemporary architectural design that resembles Emerald City illustrations in old *Wizard of Oz* books.

We had lunch at a hotel that purported to be Nixon's residence during his stay in China. The food was okay.

That evening we watched an overlong acrobatic show with superior performers who deserved a better technical production staff than they got. I was distressed after the show to learn that all the restrooms in the building had been locked up; so, I learned how to maneuver in the restroom of a bus while driving in heavy traffic. Talk about acrobatics.

Next day, we traveled to Suzhou to check out the charming "Fisherman's Gardens" as well as the Embroidery Institute that barely held my attention but fascinated many of the shoppers in our group.

A short trip by boat down the 6th Century Grand Canal wasn't short enough. It had the character of a Grand Sewer.

On the up side of the Suzhou bus trip, Yuan told us about growing up during the Cultural Revolution and his life since then. He was relatively candid and, unlike our other guides, he didn't pull punches, nor did he denigrate his country.

That evening, I skipped a bus tour of the Bund at night, opting for a delicious dinner at an East Indian restaurant with three of four young members of our group whom I called "The Young and Restless." On other nights, as odd man out, I enjoyed the company of another foursome.

September 20

The following morning I avoided a shopping trip to a rug dealer and rejoined the tour in time for transfer by plane to Wuhan where we took a five hour bus ride (interminable, but the scenery was unique and conversation on the bus was lively) to Yichang where, late at night, we boarded the East Queen, our Yangzee riverboat.

First impression: The Yangzee is a muddy fast-flowing (8 knots) river; I don't want to fall into that sucker.

September 21

I was awakened early the next morning and told that this would be our only opportunity to see the enormous new dam site under construction at Gezhouba. A TV video I had purchased in the States had better views of the dam than I saw in that early morning light and haze, but it was exciting to be where the world's biggest dam was being constructed. But what if it breaks and millions of Chinese get drowned? Considering the number of lives the Yangzee claims periodically, it's a calculated risk on a grand scale.

Later that morning we passed through the first of the three famous Yangzee Gorges, Xiling. It's tall, but I expected awesome. The other two gorges, Wu and Qutang, impressed me more, especially when I learned that the 4,000 year old body of a prehistoric man with burial artifacts had been discovered in a mountain at the confluence of two rivers. That site will be flooded when the new dam goes into operation as will all the low-lying villages on the Yangzee's banks. The Gorges will be diminished considerably.

We disembarked for a trip up the Shenong River Gorge, rowed by villagers who sang for us. These incredibly thin and wiry boat men pulled and punted us upstream against the tide.

We got back aboard the East Queen, sailed awhile, then stopped ashore again to visit a tiny village that was—hard to believe—over three thousand years old. There's something disconcerting about standing on a path that has lasted that long, knowing in a few years it's going underwater forever.

September 22

The next day was uneventful, and we enjoyed cruising upriver watching the shore turn from rocks to bamboo forests to farmland to mud flats with staircases leading up to villages and towns.

That evening after dark, we docked and walked the streets of a poorly lighted, dirty town, Shibaozhai, with commerce of all kinds on each side of the main street; foods, videos, hardware, massages, brothels, all kinds of commerce. The tour guides didn't attempt to hide from us the poverty that exists in villages in China.

The visit provoked the usual "They're poor but happy" comments from some folks, as well as "Yeah, and we're not their keepers" from others. It's been my experience on tours abroad that when confronted with poverty, most tourists who can afford expensive travel react with superficial comments no matter how deeply they feel because poverty isn't something it's easy to extemporize about. Mostly that night there was judicious silence.

September 23

Next day, docking and driving to Chonging (G.I. pronunciation: Chungking, thus the popular brand of Chinese food in the US), we discovered one of China's largest cities that had been almost completely rebuilt since WW2. On a visit to the poorly-maintained General Stillwell Museum, we saw lots of photos of Mao sharing smiles with Stilwell & Chaing Kai-shek. Provocative.

We visited an artists' colony, and I admired the bus driver's skill driving through tight alleys but I was not interested in the resident artists' politically correct art works. We saw more political art that day than at any other time while we were in China.

We visited the city zoo and photographed a playful panda who concluded his act by turning upstage and defecating downstage.

The rest of the day was spent flying to Xian (She-ann). Travel from one city to another seems to take at least a day; 5 days out of 17 were primarily travel days.

Xian is sensational. We visited the south entrance to the city wall and the New Shaanxi Museum whose artifacts were superbly presented. We spent a meditative hour at the Drum & Bell Tower garden with a Pagoda. We had a retail sales opportunity at a jade factory and silk manufacturing plant. Then we drove out to the site of the Great Tomb and viewed the famous Terra Cotta Warriors & Horses of the Qin (Chin, for whom China is named) Dynasty. We joined thousands of other tourists surveying three pits, watching excavations still in progress. Dynamite!

That evening, I skipped a Las Vegas style performance of the local Tang Dynasty Theatre in order to call my wife and daughter in the states. Instant phone connections help to make such calls a joy! I learned that my daughter—pregnant with in vitro twins due in October—was bearing up bravely.

As we left Xian for the airport with a police car blowing its siren (Chinese driving habits are incredible heart-stoppers), we stopped at a new museum, the Yang Ling Mausoleum of the Han Dynasty, not yet finished nor open to the public. The Curator walked us into a workroom few people ever see. All around us were terra cotta artifacts, mostly two foot high anatomically correct soldiers, encrusted with mud, centuries old, being restored painstakingly. Boxes and plastic tubs and table tops were filled to overflowing with arms & legs & torsos. I might have acquired a rare tiny foot souvenir if I had simply reached into an open drawer. But it was like walking through a dusty holy of holys, examining religious relics, and we were expected to regard the artifacts as treasures not meant for private ownership.

We also toured nearby digs and peered down at thousands more of the Tang Dynasty Soldiers in a pit four stories below us without a guard rail to lean on. Death defying! It was one of the most dazzling experiences I've ever had in my life, just being permitted to be there.

That same afternoon, after landing in Beijing (Beijing is Mandarin spelling, the Pin-Yin form; Peking is Setzuan, the Wade-Giles form), I was greatly impressed by a clear blue sky (after having been forewarned that smog in that city is incredibly bad), and I learned that all polluting industry had been shut down to insure that the 50th anniversary celebration of communism in the People's Republic of China on October 1, would be smog-free.

After we checked into the Palace, a luxury hotel with upscale shops, I went to an enormous mall downtown where I got my film developed and shopped for souvenirs.

September 24

The following morning we had another police escort, and we sped to the Great Wall, 70 miles north of Beijing. There's no way to describe the impact of seeing the awesome Great Wall for the first time. And climbing up and down steep or shallow steps without a railing intensifies the experience. (A portion of the original old Wall remains, composed of rock, dirt, and sticky rice soup. We were told sticky rice binds the entire wall together.)

I was amused to learn it's possible to place long distance calls to the States or anywhere else from a booth on the Wall; several of our group did just that, to tell friends & relatives where they were standing. On our approach up towards the Wall, relentless venders thrust sales objects upon us, and then, after we said No a thousand times they called after us, "I will remember you." It was an obvious sales ploy, so I picked up on it, and on the way downhill, before they could start their sales pitches, I pointed to each of them in turn and said, "I remember you." That simple greeting broke 'em up, and they laughed and acted like old buddies. I had great fun at the Great Wall.

Then, back in Beijing, we came to Tiananmen Square.

We walked around alone by ourselves on that largest square in the world (with room for 500,000 people) for almost an hour, and I took pictures of sinister-looking stick-figure guards, kite-flyers, Chinese parents with their only child in tow, a soldier hand in hand with his little boy smiling proudly for a photograph

There were workmen planting flowerpots strategically around the square preparing for the big celebration.

Just before I returned to our prearranged meeting place, I saw a man and woman sitting on the ground with no one else within 30 yards of them. The woman was crying, the man comforting her with his arm around her shoulders. For a moment, I wondered if that were the place where the student stood down the tank in May of 1989.

I learned later I was wrong.

We got back aboard the bus and asked our director and guide to tell us what really happened on June 5, 1989. They gave us what seemed to be the party line, "500 to 1,000 students and non-students impaled themselves on soldiers bayonets." I guess if I were a tour guide talking with a bunch of tourists whom I would never meet again, among whom one might be an informer, I'd have trod the party line.

That evening we attended a Chinese Opera performance that bored virtually everybody on the tour. Because I have a background in drama (I've even been a member of a Chinese Opera production staff before), I appreciated what they were doing.

September 25

We took a bus trip to the Summer Palace in the rain. It was more crowded than the Great Wall had been. Not much ambience with all the crowds.

Returning, we stopped for another retail sales opportunity at a Cloisonné factory, then lunch at a Russian hotel, then a stroll through the grounds of the Temple of Heaven.

We had reached the final stages of a tour, taking in the sights as sights—not as places where events happened. The thrill was gone.

On a return trip to the mall for my photographs, I inserted my debit card in an ATM that swallowed it in one gulp with what sounded like a belch.

September 26

Next morning, the Forbidden City. I was knocked out by that magnificent, enormous palace, sealed off like a high-dollar tourist theme park. It was probably more like a prison than a palace for its inhabitants. I was impressed that one of the buildings is still used as a testing center where all persons who receive a Ph. D. in China must answer philosophic questions. Funny, a hall where autocratic rule once prevailed is haunted by the ghost of Confucius.

Afterwards, we visited a "Friendship Store" where English is reduced to "You like? You buy?"

Dinner that evening was at the China Club—not nearly so highbrow as the Hong Kong China Club. But it was a pleasant end to a wonderful trip, and saying goodbye wasn't easy to my peers and to China.

A Conclusion

Throughout my trip to China, I couldn't escape a nagging, guilty feeling that—although I was a paying guest—I was being regarded as a snooper/peeker. It was a parallel universe I didn't know anything about, and it is dynamic. One of the tour guides called it the "Bicycle Kingdom," but he was clearly a believer in China's bright future.

After thinking about it, I truly believe Nixon was right (and astute) when he wrote in the October, '67, issue of *Foreign Affairs*: "Taking the long view, we simply cannot afford to leave China forever outside the family of nations, there to nurture its fantasies, cherish its hates and threaten its neighbors. There is no place on this small planet for a billion of its potentially most able people to live in angry isolation."

China's not the kind of vacation spot one thinks of on a list with Cancun or the Caribbean. In fact, people I talk with generally say they imagine it's a grim, decaying country like Russia. Well, that's not what I saw. I've been to St. Petersburg, and I've been to Shanghai, and there's no comparison.

Do I want go back ever again? To Russia, not on a bet. To China, sure.

Surprise & delight: From the mountains in Texas you can see the desert & Rio Grande.

Big Bend National Park

◆

Friends in Hot Places
January 15–17, 2000

I really have a problem traveling in hot climates, so I had never imagined I'd visit Big Bend National Park in Texas. But that was before I was invited by friends for a short & sweet visit during winter. I gave the trip more plusses (+) than minuses (-).

January 15

The best travel arrangements I could make were not as the crow flies. To reach the Park I had to drive from home in Salado to the airport in Austin (one hour), fly west to El Paso (two hours—rather than ten hours by car), and then zig in a rental car back in the direction I had zagged from (five hours that seemed like ten hours). Took about as much time as it takes to fly to Europe. Negative reaction -.

By the time I reached Marfa, I breezed through ignoring the art museum they boast of, stopped in Marathon at the hotel where a bison's head is ensconced over the lobby mantle, and then resumed driving south to Big Bend. The only part of the entire trip on the road I enjoyed was the drive from Marathon to the Park entrance, looking at curious foothills unlike any I've ever seen. That was a plus +.

Then I had to slow down to a 45 mph speed limit for the drive from the Park entrance to "Panther Junction" where the Park Ranger station is located and where I met my host, my friend and former student, Mike Boren, Executive Director of the Park's Natural History Association. Mike and Terry, his wife, had invited me to stay in their home for a weekend, and that's where I shared their company with a one pound African Gray Parrot, Oscar, Terry's pet, who stared me down, confronting an intruder with his unblinking reptilian eyes, whistling shrilly and calling me, "Buckaroo." The bird was intimidating, but staying with the Borens was another plus +.

That evening at Terlingua, home of the annual Texas Chili Cookoff, we listened to a one man band at the Starlight Theatre/bar (mostly bar) and enjoyed Mexican beer and dinner and introductions to local characters, many of whom could win prizes like strangest or weirdest or just bizarrest. +

Returning to the Boren's home, the three of us entertained the bird awhile, then went to bed.

January 16

The following morning, a Sunday, Mike piled survival gear in his vintage pickup truck, and Terry prepared food and gallons of water for Mike and me to take on a trip through the desert. En route, he pointed out low-lying clouds of carbon nitrate in the distance, partially obscuring the view of Mexico's Sierra del Carbon limestone cliffs, 8,000 feet high. "Visibility Impairment" is what it's officially called, caused by smoke from two coal-fired electric power plants south of the border. And where do they buy the coal that blackens the sky? From Texas, of course. Texas gets a minus -.

All that smog seemed miles away. Where we stood was clear as glass, and I said, "I can't imagine a more beautiful location with these remarkable big ass mountain ranges surrounding us." Plus, plus, plus +++.

We took off. The weather was cool, but the winter sun's rays stabbed my chest through the windshield as we rode for miles and miles, occasionally speeding up to 15 mph on the worst back roads and trails I've ever seen. I asked Mike if he had ever broken an axle before, and he said no, but I kept thinking, "Today he's gonna break an axle." But he didn't, amazingly. +.

I enjoyed the rough and rocky trip through the Black Gap on the misnamed River Road, and I had only two moments when I got frightened. One was when I realized with a start that if we ever truly needed all the survival stuff he had brought along, we would be in a life or death situation. But then I looked over at Mike and my confidence returned. He told me that if we developed motor trouble, "Not to worry. We won't be able to walk for more than nine miles without water in the heat of the sun—even in winter—without perishing. And," he said, "fat, out-of-shape dudes like us probably wouldn't make it five miles." I wasn't reassured -.

The second fright occurred when we rounded a bend and began traveling on a narrow valley road with sinister vegetation on either side. Mike said, "This is a good site for an ambush," and he pointed to graves at a cemetery where bodies had been laid out on the impenetrable ground, covered with rocks, and with crosses of wood fashioned for grave markers. Cacti were growing up through the stones on some of the graves. Bizarre! + -.

Mike stopped, got out of the truck, took with him a trenching spade and a roll of toilet paper, and went out of sight behind a dune. When he returned, he explained that because he's an ecologist, he had been obliged to dig a hole to bury his shit rather than leave it to dry and become a permanent part of the arid landscape.

I said, "You plant a cactus with it?"

He wasn't amused.

We stopped to look at the Rio Grande flowing past, shallow & wide. Then we viewed the entrance to a mercury mine shaft at a great distance. Lastly, driving past an RV camp, we decided not to check out a swimming hole where tourists swim naked. The prospect of watching RV owners and their families swim in the nude was not a turn-on for me. -.

We drove back to the Borens' home, exhilarated after having driven through a vast, awe-inspiring, primeval Hell of clay and sand and tuff and lava and rocks and boulders and mountains. A great adventure. And not everybody who visits the region gets to explore with a professional guide. + + +

That evening we drove up into the awesome Chisos mountains to view the sunset. The further and higher we went, the more vegetation appeared until we arrived in a great forested Basin and drove around for a great view of Casa Grande, spectacular. Then we drove past the cabins and RV locations (not spectacular) to the dining room at the Chisos Lodge where the food was okay. +

Back at the Borens', I slept well. +

January 17

After Mike left the house for work, I packed up and gave Terry a lift to her work station near Mike's. En route, we visited Mike's office again, and I said, "You guys are reason enough for a trip to Big Bend." I hugged them both and embarrassed us all. +

Returning the way I had come, I thought, "I've been here and I know where it is, and I'll never come back (Unless I have to, of course), but I've got unforgettable memories of the river road, the graves, the Rio Grande, the Lodge, Terry's bird, and the Boren's hospitality and a buncha big ass rocks." Plus, plus, plus + + +

And throw in a few more plusses +++++

Closest animal God ever got to creating an all-weather means of transportation.

Egypt

◆

An Abercrombie & Kent Tour
February 24–March 9, 2000

For two weeks I traveled to Egypt via air, bus, taxi, van, horse-drawn buggy, cruise ship, felucca (sail boat) and camel (a dromedary).

Friends and acquaintances ask, "Did you have a good time?"

What am I gonna say, "No?"

So I've prepared a Q&A scenario to insure that everyone gets the same answers. And to show that my answers are unique, I've included the results of an informal Q&A survey I took of my fellow passengers addressing fifty or so questions I raised.

Q: What did you like best?

The best thing was the Abercrombie and Kent tour group I was with, (None of whom I had met before the tour began), 13 people who were compatible and comfortable with each other (Dick & Vivian, Mary & Jodelle, Man Kong & Susan, Wally & Pat, Inge & Marc, Paul and Gretchen, and me). And we unanimously felt that our professional tour guide, Aki Allam, an Egyptologist and world class performer, was also one of the best things that happened to us. Nobody does what Aki does better. We had great, great fun together

Q: What were your top ten favorites?
With only one dissenting vote for each of the following items, we were all blown away by 1) the amazing Antiquities Museum in Cairo featuring the lavish contents of King Tut's tomb. (Tut's mummy inside a sarcophagus is located in his actual tomb), 2) the massive and awe-inspiring three pyramids and sphinx at Giza (free of scaffolding for the first time in ten years), and 3) the exquisite, colorful tomb of Queen Nefertari located in the Valley of the Queens. We also enjoyed 4) a party we threw for ourselves. And if the above had been all that happened to please us, that would have been enough, but there were other special items and events we liked very much. 5) Most of the group liked the weather because it was cool and breezy and dry, and we were inspired by 6) the Temples at Luxor and 7) Karnac, 8) the Museum at Luxor, 9) the Temple of Abu Simbel, and 10) the Giza Sound & Light Show (that I skipped because I didn't like the S&L show I endured at the Luxor Temple that a British tourist described to me aptly as "simply rubbish").

Q: What did you NOT like?

1. The Al-Gezira Sheraton Hotel in Cairo is a mismanaged, inhospitable dump that even the Fodor tour book says should be viewed only as a back-up option when other hotels are full. Our entire group was in agreement that we did not like the staff, the rooms, or the furniture—so what else does a hotel have to offer.

2. What else didn't we like? a) an amateur belly dance show aboard ship, b) a rug factory featuring preteen boys & girls slaving away at looms, c) all public restrooms (I discovered only one clean one during the entire two weeks), d) And most of us didn't enjoy a jewelry store visit that allowed some shoppers to purchase "cartuches" (Gold-plated souvenir jewelry personalized with one's name in hieroglyphics).

3. We outsnobbed French tourists aboard ship who smoked constantly as if it were a cultural thing to do.

4.   And we found annoying the relentlessly aggressive, souvenir-hawking vendors at every historical site and in Cairo's Bazaar of Khan El-Kalili (where I got hopelessly lost—more about that later).

Q: Then you didn't really have a good time, did you?

Oh, yes, I did. Old Egypt is stunning. And even New Egypt is Old. Remarkable things happened to offset the annoying things. But one gets the feeling everything must have gone to hell after the Romans got driven out, leaving the field to early Coptic Christians who mutilated the faces and genitalia of statues and the carvings on tombs and walls of temples. And witch worshippers gouged holes in the monuments believing the crumbly sandstone to have magic properties. And the desert scorched everything, and sand buried the country for centuries. And soldiers who were charged with guarding the graves of kings and pharaohs robbed them of all their trappings just as most archeologists continue to do today, systematically "saving" treasures to be filed in storage rooms. And local and international politicians have helped themselves, looting Egypt's treasures with impunity for centuries.

(It's pitiful while walking through the mummy room at the Cairo Museum looking at Rameses II's arms that seem be trying to burst free from the winding cloth. One can almost hear him saying, "If I were alive, I'd kill you sons of bitches.")

Q: So why'd you go to Egypt? And all those places you go?

Remember how you always wanted your teacher to say to you, "Now, that's a good question?"

Q: Yeah?

Well, that's not a good question because it doesn't have an answer. So, of course, I'll try. One friend said to me in jest, "Are you taking all these trips because you've got some terminal disease you don't want to talk about?"

I acted shocked as if she'd discovered the truth, and for a moment she went ashen.

So I immediately told her Life is always terminal, and I travel because I feel I'd better take the time now when I'm feeling great, before my diminishing faculties get the better of me, and my eyes go bad, and my hearing fails, and yadayada. I assured her I'm having a great time at a good time in my life. I'm not one of those people who thinks there's gonna be a better time later on, and this time the time was now and Egypt was the place.

Q: But was this really a good time to go, so soon after that tourist massacre at Queen Hatshepsut's Temple back in '97.

Well, judging by the sold out hotels, and the number of armed military on the streets on guard and in patrols, I'd say yes. Egypt is doing a thriving business. I couldn't imagine larger crowds. I asked our hotel concierge if it would be safe to stroll around the Al-Gezira island, and he said yes, and I said then if it's so safe, why are guards stationed every 100 yards, and he said "To insure your safety, sir." The word tourists hear most often is "Welcome."

Q: So really, why'd you go there?

Because as our tour guide, Aki, said, "The ancient gods called us back." I truly believe there's some truth in that. But it doesn't make for a verifiable answer.

Q: Why did others in your group travel to Egypt?

Here are some of their answers in earnest and some in jest:

"Because I can afford to, and this is how I spend my money."

"I like to escape from loneliness."

"To learn new stuff. Some people buy stuff, I like to learn stuff."

"I want to return to the roots of my roots."

"I need to see the genuine article. Las Vegas is all ersatz."

"I like to satisfy my curiosity."

"We all get stimulated by the media to travel."

"Specific spatial dimensions are important to me."

"I like to get away from home, and then go back home."

"I like to meet people, not stupid people; civil people."

"Hell, I'm happy I just stumbled and found myself here."

Q: I'll bet some of those answers are yours, right?

Some.

Q: So after you decided to go, did your read up on Egypt?

Yes, but it was all hieroglyphics to me—until I walked up to an ancient wall and pressed my fingers gently into the bas-reliefs and leaned forward so that my eyes could examine tiny detail and then backed way up to see and appreciate the scale of great and massive architecture. Wow. I said, "Wow." a lot.

Q: Did you know in advance where you were going, precisely?

Sure, the A&K catalog called it the "Pharaohs and Pyramids" tour and promised cities and villages, archeological digs, a cruise down the Nile, land arrangements including all lodgings, food, group transfers, bottles of mineral water, sightseeing (including entrance fees), airfares within Egypt, services of a professional Egyptologist, handling of two bags per person, and all gratuities—except to the Egyptologist. A&K is a well-organized, well-managed, superior organization.

Q: What wasn't included?

Laundry, insurance, excess baggage fees, phone charges, cost of passport & visa, airfares to and from Egypt, all beverages except water, and sightseeing not included in the itinerary (like the visit to Nefertari's tomb).

Q: Were you provided with a study guide?

Yes, but like the texts that college teachers make you buy, it wasn't followed by the lecturer (Thank goodness). But it did provide insights like "By the time the country was eventually invaded, Egypt was so strongly developed that is was able to absorb the conquering peoples, who then became part of Egyptian culture." And it discussed the evolution of the burial process that ultimately resulted in mummification procedures.

We learned from our tour guide that all vital organs were removed, and the brain was sucked out of the head by inserting metal straws through the nose of the deceased. Gag.

Q: Did you learn what the pyramids are doing in Egypt?

From the first "step pyramid" at Saqqara (designed by Imhotep, architect to King Zoser), they were designed to house the tombs of royalty. Zoser's pyramid (c., 2780 B. C.) was the first stone building ever constructed with the first columns and the first curved wall. Amazing. I was enormously wowed viewing that great first pyramid up close.

Cheops' Great Pyramid—the only surviving of the seven wonders of the ancient Greek world—was even more impressive because it's so tall and imposing, with two million, three hundred thousand blocks of granite—each one taller than me.

And construction required no slave labor, only the voluntary work of devoted followers (100,000 or so for each monthly shift) who believed like all advocates of religion universally, "If I scratch my god-king's back, he'll scratch mine."

Q: Did you meet any ancient gods personally?

No, Silly, but their images are everywhere in the ruins where they were worshipped:

Amun Ra—The falcon-headed god of life, always wears two feathers on his headdress. You get so you can recognize him.

Anubis—The god (who also has a falcon's head) of tombs & mummies.

Aten—The solar disc god whom Amenhotep IV called the one true god. Now, there's an interesting Pharoah.

Bes—The dwarf god of fun (my kind of guy) who chases away skies of gray.

Hathor—The goddess of love & happiness with a cow's head (or ears). Go figure.

Horus—The son of Isis & Osiris, god of honesty & justice, anointed by Anubis to avenge his father's death at the hands of Seth. Get ready for a story.

Isis—The goddess of wifely love and devotion, mother of Horus.

Khunum—The ram-headed god of creativity who created man.

Osiris—A mummy-wrapped god with crown, scepter, and flail, supreme judge of the dead.

Seth—A bad guy, with a snout & long ears, and here's the story: He was the murderer of his brother Osiris whom he cut up into 14 pieces. After Isis rescued all but the 14th piece (that contained Osiris' penis), she fashioned one for him out of clay. Osiris came back to life, sustained an erection, impregnated Isis (who had become a falcon for that special event), and then, exhausted, expired forever (and smoked a cigarette, doubtless). Talk about great and improbable fiction. And that's just a few of the Egyptian gods.

Q: Did you "walk like an Egyptian?"

You mean with my shoulders facing in one direction and my head and feet facing another? Sure, and I said unto all my followers, "Walk this way."

Q: Okay, so really, why did the artists and artisans represent figures like that?

The best explanation I could get from anyone is they viewed figures from all sides and painted the perspectives in only two dimensions. Except for statuary, almost all representations show heads & feet in profile. And it's no problem, I mean, after you've assimilated a woman's head with cow's ears, everything looks conventional

Q: What about modern Egypt?

It's unique, but it pales by comparison with ancient Egypt.

About 64,000.000 people live there. Only 100 or so Jews remain in the country A few (10 percent of the population) are Coptic Christian, the rest Sunni (Not Shiite) Muslim (They don't like being called Mohammedan), all of whom speak Arabic, almost all living on less than 4 percent of the land (only that bordering the Nile), surrounded by the Sahara that is all rock and powdery sand where nothing grows much. But look out, the developers are coming.

Tourism is Egypt's second largest industry after Oil. And it's kind of interesting when asked by vendors "Where you from?" to note that they pretend they can't guess Americans from Italians from Germans from French.

Q: So did you record your impressions in a daily journal?

Yes, but I'm not about to share all my journal entries.

Q: Why not?

Because I like to be honest when writing a paper folks might read—but not candid—and because some stuff I wrote is boring, and all you want to hear is the good stuff.

Q: Oh, please.

Nope. All I'm transcribing here is dynamite stuff I hope might interest you. And if it doesn't, don't read it. Here's where it begins:

February 24, 25, 26, Thursday through Saturday

1. My good friend, Paul Boston, volunteered to drive me to the Austin airport.

2. In Chicago, I couldn't find a money exchange easily in O'Hare Airport, but the AAmerican Admiral's club is a comfortable place to relax between flights (and my frequent flyer upgrade to Business Class allows me to use that club).

3. The Zurich Airport is exactly like other busy airports except they can't seem to stop rebuilding it, and Swissair Coach Class is like American Business Class except the seats are smaller (and for a fat person, that's significant).

4. The oily tour agent who met us on arrival at Cairo turned out to be the bullshitter I guessed him to be.

5. A warm hotel room with no air moving is unpleasant, but a reluctant desk clerk who promises to do something about it and never delivers is downright vexatious. It's hard for one to sleep in an overwarm room with an unresolved conflict occupying one's thoughts.

6. A trip to the Cairo Museum requires patience, standing on line, going through metal-detectors, but the payoff is great. A remarkable collection is on display and no telling what they keep in the closet. The presentation is unimaginative and the lighting is awful, but the treasures are incredible. Wandered around for 4 hours, wondering why I felt so exhausted with a back and legs aching. They're building a new Cairo Museum.

7. A person may be called the hotel's masseur, but that doesn't necessarily mean he knows how to give a good massage.

8. A French dinner at Justine's is enough to make anyone forgive a taxi driver who took 45 minutes to find the place even though it was within 10 minutes walking distance from my hotel.

9. Random thoughts: The Nile is wider'n a mile. A felucca in harbor is safe and beautiful, but that's not what feluccas are for. I hope those ugly looking guns carried by the police and military aren't loaded. Egyptian's car horns are shrill and the drivers use them frequently and aggressively. Arabic men look swarthy and macho, but they kiss each other on the cheeks and hold hands and lock arms; a sight that requires adjusting my thinking.

February 27, Sunday

1. Meeting our Egyptologist/Tour Guide, we determine we're in great hands immediately, and thank Allah, we're right. He can perform a monolog, tell jokes, use American lingo, and act academic and entertaining all at once. Touring with him through the Cairo museum makes the place light up and shine.

2. I was stunned watching workmen and women carrying buckets of cement on their heads, laying tiles on the banks of the Nile, wearing billowing galabeos (An Arabic mode of dress). I thought, "These are the people who built the pyramids."

3. At dinner, hosted by A&K, I'm seated next to and across from Republicans who cannot imagine why I, a Democrat, can possibly object to their cracks about the Clintons and Gore. I almost say, "But you can't blame a guy like Clinton when all he wanted was a great blow job." I realize I am going to have to adjust my attitude considerably since they're probably all Republicans, and they just might be nice people as well. Two sleeping tablets helped me forget them.

4. A visit via bus from Cairo to Mereruka's Mastaba (a tomb of a nobleman superbly decorated with scenes from daily life including force-feeding geese to get paté, and a circumcision in progress). And a visit to Teti's Pyramid (a crawlspace passageway leading to a sarcophagus under a ceiling decorated with stars) is a great way to get close to history, nose pressed to the walls of those ancient rooms. Zoser's step pyramid complex is impressive to behold; and it makes a great backdrop for a group photo of tourists.

5. Lunch at the Mena House Restaurant followed by a drive around the Giza Pyramids, Solar Boat, and Sphinx is thrilling. Even seeing Cheops' Pyramid doesn't help one to believe it; it's so monumentally huge. It was disconcerting when the police rousted hundreds of tour-ists—including us—out of the area, closing early to set up for the evening's sound and light show, by blasting us out with foghorns and broadcasting what sounded like threats. And all those guys carrying guns. Damn.

6. But then, the big event, the life-changing event: For 5 pounds (about $2), I rode a camel, a smelly, slobbering, ungainly beast whose hump I straddled, clutching the saddle joystick for dear life, led by a blasé 12-year old lad who asks if I'm French. I say, "Oui." He responds by saying "Your camel's name is Michael Jackson." I say, "Sacre Bleu." He says, "You wanna buy a scarab brooch?" The camel trips and lurches, and I almost fall to my death 10 feet below. "Merci, non," I mutter. After 5 minutes, he parks the beast in a pool of stale urine, smiles and says, "Have a good day, Froggy."

7. Shopping in a jewelry store with tourists bent on buying expensive sou-venirs was soooooo boring for most of our group until one of our mem-bers, Wally, turned to a hovering clerk who kept offering him help and said, "Listen, Buddy. Watch me, but don't talk to me, ok?" The clerk got the message. We learn that "La, Shukran" means "No, thank you (Get lost.)"

8. That evening, after a so-so supper at the hotel, I collapse in bed, packed up for travel at daybreak to Luxor where our ship awaits.

February 29, Leap Year, Monday

1. After early morning air travel, we tour Luxor immediately, visiting Thebes where an enormous fallen statue of Rameses II is Ozymandisian.

2. The Temple at Karnak is a sight to behold with statuary to touch and our superlative tour guide telling stories about ancient kings and queens and the making of the film, Agatha Christie's *Death on the Nile*. What an incredible ruin Karnak's temple is. A study in Egyptian royal oneups-manship between royal descendents to Egypt's throne.

3. Then, a visit to the Temple at Luxor, and I recognized patterns and rhythms in the art and architecture of the ancients and realized I'm beginning to understand that culture.

4. We were transferred to the Sun Boat III, an A&K-owned boat, that I didn't like at first but that grew on me. I had no complaints about bugs or cleanliness and housekeeping, but I think the décor is somebody's wife's cousin's idea. As the cruise progresses, I grew to appreciate the staff, and I'm disappointed in myself for being hypercritical. Well, I'm not really disappointed or hypercritical, but I tell folks I am.

5. We visited the Luxor Museum, a beautiful and imaginatively designed space for artifacts as art objects. Simply stunning. Really.

March 1, Tuesday

1. We sailed on the Nile up river to Lower Egypt (North) from Upper Egypt (South), and I had a great morning, schmoozing with our fast-bonding group, strolling on deck, enjoying the cool weather, watching police streaking past riding motorboats like cowboys while farmers plow their acreage using water buffaloes. Their families live with them in mud huts in an area of the country where it never rains (or the huts would collapse).

2. In many ways, Egypt is a primitive country ruled by local customs. On an afternoon trip to Hathor's Temple, our bus is included in a convoy of showoff police, brandishing weapons at the head and tail of the convoy. The Temple visit isn't nearly as exciting, but our tour guide told us the spellbinding legend of Isis & Osiris, death, resurrection, sex, and eternal life. Wow.

3. A cocktail party permanently alienated us from the French tourists on board who enjoy smoking.

4. I enjoyed dinner with two Brits, Brian & Elizabeth, who dissed Maggie Thatcher and Tony Blair, The IRA, Americans who support the IRA, Aussies, et. al. I thoroughly enjoyed listening to them carry on.

March 2, Wednesday

1. On the sun deck, I enjoyed chatting with my new friends.

2. The ship returned to Luxor, and I went for a stroll in the sun with cool breezes to the Winter Palace Hotel where I had tea with a few of the gang.

3. Then I strolled back to the ship at a leisurely pace—in the sun—and would you believe I began to feel the effects of being exposed to the Egyptian sun and dry heat all day long, and I almost passed out.

4. After putting up a front at suppertime, I spent a sleepless night with a burning face heating up the pillows. Around 3 AM, I stupidly self-medicated and screwed up all my systems so that when we arose early the following morning, I was a loonybird.

March 3, Thursday

1. We stood on line at a ticket booth at 6 AM to insure that we would be among the 150 people permitted to enter the Tomb of Nefertari, then we went to Tut's Tomb, Rameses II's Tomb, and somebody else's tomb with cool weather outdoors, and warm, stuffy tomb air indoors. I thought, "I'm gonna be sick, but it's bad form to upchuck in tombs," so I just didn't. Restraint is what I've got in amounts equal to my chutzpah.

2. A visit to Nefertari's tomb was everything my travel agent promised it would be, a reason for making the trip. The colors, the designs, the care and maintenance devoted to that tomb is superior to all others.

3. By 9 AM, the sun god was a killer, so I stayed in the air-conditioned bus while my groupsters visited the Temple of Queen Hatshepsut where the German tourists got murdered. Yes, security was tight, and I felt safe enough to lie down on the back seat of the bus where I had a dream of an uprising with soldiers shooting terrorists, vendors squawking and tourists screaming with explosions borrowed from movies I've seen with Bruce Willis. And just as the flames were enveloping the bus, I awoke and realized the air-conditioning had gone off. So I went for a visit to the oldest toilet in the civilized world where even Rameses would have puked his guts out and then, returning to the bus, I decided not to share my hallucinations with my comrades until this writing.

4. Then we stopped at the remarkable tomb of Ramose, a high-level official, where the artwork is unique and unfinished, with sketches and

chalk snaplines indicating artists' concepts. Children were selling dirty, ratty dolls to tourists, and I was easily able to resist buying one.

5. We returned to the ship, dusty and exhausted, where I showered and sacked out for the rest of the day. That evening, I had pretty much regained my health, but the management, assuming I had a case of mummy tummy, insisted I eat rice soup. I said okay, ate the stuff, and then bloated beyond belief like a Thanksgiving day parade balloon, I went to bed.

March 4, Friday

1. I arose after my first good night's sleep, ate a hearty breakfast, then wearing sunblock and a hat we went for a tour to the Esme Temple and bought galebeas to wear for the party scheduled in the evening.

2. We sailed to Edfu where I shared a horse-drawn buggy with Aki, and we toured the Temple of Horus where the grounds were being renovated and great tractors were moving earth & dust, and we got an idea of what it's like to be in an Egyptian dust storm during the months of March & April, incredible.

3. The costume dinner party was fun because we guests all looked like failed Arabians. Sailors danced to frenzied Nubian music, and we had a good time looking on.

March 5, Saturday

1. After cruising down to upper Egypt all night in our flat-bottomed boat (unshaken by wakes of passing ships), we docked at Kom Ombo where the temple was located no more than a hundred yards from the boat. By now, every temple looked like every other temple, but this one was a twofer, with places to worship the cow god and the croc god. There is a gigantic bas-relief on the side of the building where Roman designs and customs are in evidence.

2. Sailing to Aswan, we watched the shoreline change from vegetation with date palms to desert and mud houses painted gaily denoting newlyweds.

3. In Aswan, we took a bus to the island of Agilika and visited the Philae temple, moved lock, stock, and barrel from another elevation (underwa-

ter at present), a remarkable accomplishment, and we danced with children visiting the island. Marvelous.

4.   Then we sailed around the Nile in Aswan, tacking to and fro, in a felucca, a blissful experience, watching the boatswain dance about, steering the boat in good winds. ("Boatswain?" Okay, he was both the captain and crew of that little sailboat, and he put on a great show.)

5.   That evening, the entire American and British contingent aboard celebrated in two of our number's palatial suite. I performed a satirical piece written expressly for the occasion, and Aki regaled us with stories about other tour groups he has shepherded. That evening, we were all gods and royalty, and we couldn't tell the difference. What a lovely group of people.

6.   A belly dancer performed after dinner, but nobody much liked her show.

March 6, Sunday

1.   We transferred to the airport for a trip to Abu Simbel where we visited the monolithic statues fronting the temples of Rameses II and Nefertari, excavated and moved to a higher location at great expense to save the structures from being inundated by Lake Nasser when the Aswan High Dam was built. For me, the latter day rescue upstaged the original design and construction of the temples. Lovely place for a picnic. But we returned to eat our picnic lunches in the airport hoping to be first on line for the return flight. We waited and waited and our patience wore thin.

2.   By the time we returned to Aswan for a trip to the High Dam Memorial, a tribute to the Russian engineers who built the thing, we weren't particularly interested in it. I couldn't help but feel that the temples and tombs of ancient Egypt were engineering miracles; whereas, the High Dam and other modern achievements were simply successful political maneuvers.

3.   Several members of the group and I took tea at the Cataract Hotel where scenes from Death on the Nile were filmed. Terribly civilizing experience, don't you know.

4. We visited the new Nubian Museum where the landscaping is as imaginative as the Museum's interior. Wandering through the rooms, I kept thinking, "I've heard of Nubian slaves, but why have I never heard of the Nubians as a civilization before now." The museum is the answer; the Egyptian government has attempted to make up for neglect of study of those people.

5. After a smashing farewell dinner aboard ship, I watched a closed circuit showing of *Death on the Nile* while reclining in bed. What an improbable adventure that script is. Christie's story was possibly undone in the editing.

March 7, Monday

1. We had a delayed departure at the airport, but our spirits didn't flag, and we returned to Cairo by 12:30 PM. Our reception at the Sheraton was just as bad as it had been before except this time, we were told to wait in our overwarm rooms until our luggage was delivered, but it wasn't delivered for over an hour, and the air conditioning repairman was not forthcoming, and so I disobeyed instructions and went down to the café where our oily tour rep was eating dinner, scarfing his food with his head down in his plate. I asked him why the delay and he said something like, "Oh, everybody wanted to change beds from what I had expected, and the bellmen'll get around to sending up the bags later." I chastised him for not telling us that we might as well leave our rooms in order to eat lunch since he was obviously enjoying his lunch. Funny how one callused person in a badly managed hotel can piss one off royally.

2. We all rested after the 3 PM lunch, feeling the day had been wasted. But we used the time to regroup at 9 o'clock that evening, and I met for dinner with two of our departing comrades. It was a sentimental and fond farewell.

March 8, Tuesday

1. Those of us remaining in Cairo visited a Coptic Christian church reputed to be built over a cave where the Holy Family stayed after they fled to Egypt following the birth of Jesus. Then to a synagogue located at the site where Moses was discovered in the bulrushes. And then we visited a mosque and the Anderson Museum where old furniture and

early household items are displayed. Then a trip to the Citadel and the Mohammed Ali Mosque.

2. Afterwards, a visit to the Cairo Souk (Market place) and lunch at the Kahn al-Khalili restaurant. We agreed to shop for 45 minutes and then return to the restaurant, but I started wandering around the crowded souk and got lost dodging traffic, ratty cats, toothless and uncared for children, and contentious crowds surging in one direction then another then another. That bazaar is bazarre. It was as near to Mayhem as I have ever experienced. I was 20 minutes late returning. Aki was waiting for me and escorted me back to the bus urging me to push and shove as needed. So I started saying, "Excuse me, please." in German as I elbowed my way through the crowd, until one guy said, "You goddamn Germans always run roughshod over everybody." I said, "Es tut mir leit, Sweetheart."

3. Returning to the hotel, I reported the a/c wasn't working again, and 30 minutes later I called yet again. A building superintendent came up and held his hand over the vent and said, "Yes, it's not working. I'll fix it." Then he looked expectantly at me, and I recognized he was either coming on to me or simply, wordlessly, requesting a tip. I thought, "I'll be damned if I'll let him bully me. This is probably a scam anyway, so I turned away and said, "Thanks for taking care of it." I heard the door close behind him, and I thought, "That takes care of that." and sure enough, within 10 minutes the a/c began to blow cool air. And I thought, "Ha. I didn't tip him. My integrity is intact."

4. That evening I attended a performance of a visiting Flamenco dance troupe at the Cairo Opera House but left at intermission because only the last 64 bars before the end of the first act were exciting, and I said to myself: "I am not about to wait forever until I get another exciting 64 bars."

5. I enjoyed strolling alone (except for the entire army) in the dark back to the hotel where I had a late supper. I went to bed, pleased to find the a/c still working until about 1 AM when it stopped and never came on again. I was roasting in Hell, but Ha. My integrity remained intact.

March 9, Wednesday

1. I arose around 4:15 AM, packed and dressed for the ride to the airport at 5:30 and my plane's departure at 7. I joined some of our group for the bus ride, and we said our farewells at the airport. The Swissair flight to Zurich didn't take long, and I wangled a seat without a seat mate on the AAmerican return trip to the States, and the flight attendant was kind enough to give me a bottle of good French wine when I told her I really liked it. Little perks like that really enhance a good trip, and I believe they can help save a bad one.

2. Barbara picked me up in Austin, and we drove home, arriving around midnight.

I slept late the following morning, awoke, and the trip was over. It was as if I had dreamed it all, a sweet, sweet dream.

I want Mont St. Michel to be on my list of places to return someday.

The Dordogne

◆

From Bordeaux to Normandy with Yale Exes
June 27–July 6, 2000

A Yale Alumni flyer advertising a trip to "The Dordogne and the West Coast of France" reached out of our mailbox and grabbed me ("A new concept in cruising awaits you....").

Barbara was not grabbed, and I couldn't persuade her to go along, so I made a reservation for myself in February of 2000 aboard the Panorama. Wow. A Yacht-cruise™ promising a "personalized travel experience" and a "custom-tailored itinerary that includes undiscovered and unspoiled places." Irresistible.

The flyer featured photographs of Mont St. Michel at low tide, a cave painting at Lascaux, and a map outlining travel by motorcoach & ship from Bordeaux around in the Atlantic to Caudebec, France.

It seemed like the kind of trip I might never be able to take again, and I was pleased when a letter came promptly from Joan Kneeland (Assistant Director for Education of the Association of Yale Alumni), acknowledging receipt of my deposit with the assurance that I would receive confirmation shortly from Travel Dynamics, Inc.

I was eventually disappointed as a direct result of believing a trip could be as good as that flyer's authors described it. Following sensational trips to China and Egypt, my expectations for this trip to prehistoric France were too high. The odds caught up with me. It wasn't a bad trip. *Some* things were great.

I was thrilled every time the ship hoisted its sails (over 50 feet high).

I was astonished [repeat *astonished.*]by cave paintings and carvings done by Cro-Magnon Man (male or female) over twelve hundred years ago.

I enjoyed a few outstanding lunches and dinners at French provincial restaurants (but the meals aboard ship were no better than good).

I was blown away by the craggy coastlines at Belle-Ile (where Monet & Sara Bernhardt hung out—but not at the same times).

I was greatly awed by Mont St. Michel's remarkable architecture.

I was moved to tears at the American Cemetery near Omaha Beach.

And I appreciated the efficiency of the management, except I chafed every time changes were made in the itinerary, and I was told "You must be flexible." Hell, Flexible is my middle name. Inconstant was theirs.

Hanging out with participants was one of the most satisfying aspects of the trip even though the flyer didn't promise camaraderie. That seems curious in retrospect because bonding with fellow passengers is one of the best things that can happen on a trip. I didn't dislike anyone. And we had an excellent lecturer.

The choices of ports of call had only one minor drawback: travel by bus to sites with local guides droning on and on as they almost always do. Tour guides are notoriously poor the world over, and our guides were polite but not aware of their lack of skill with English as a second language. There was only one outstanding guide on the entire trip whose comments about Rouen were entertaining, concise, instructive, and aloof (I can appreciate aloof).

The ship was cleaned daily, the crew was amiable, and the sailing—even in rough seas—was great. But it had been launched in '94 and was overdue for reconditioning. The hull needed painting, the carpet and drapes needed replacing, and much of the woodwork needed serious repair.

The weather was wonderful with only two rainy days, and the scenery was gorgeous. Ironically, the back roads in France (That is, the ones we traveled on much of the time) are engineered efficiently without charm—unlike the farm to market roads in countries where the roads snake and bend around old farms and land-marks. Only in touristy "old towns" were the streets paved to follow odd twists and turns. Roads we traveled—even those with room for only one tourist bus on each side—didn't show evidence of centuries of use. It was as if some French tourism agency had come along and straightened them out for the busses. Super-highways were every bit as boring as American interstates. None of this, of course, was mentioned in the flyer.

When the trip was over, like everything else in life, I forgot and forgave events that were forgettable and forgivable.

So much for an overall critique; here's what went right or wrong.

On **June 21, 2000**, during the week before I departed, I got a call from Amer-ican Airlines telling me my flight to France had been canceled for fear of an impending strike by Paris air controllers. My travel agent rerouted me to Frank-furt with an Air France flight to Paris followed by another Air France flight to Bordeaux. She urged me to check this flight plan by calling her number the next day.

The next day, Thursday, I called to learn that Frankfurt was still a "go" but Air France was canceled; so, the agent put me on an early flight that hadn't yet been canceled and promised that Air France would convert my 2nd flight to a train transfer, Nice to Bordeaux.

On Saturday, just before leaving for the airport, the agent said, "Tomorrow you're gonna fly from Austin to Newark to Chicago and then to Paris."

I said, "What."

And she said, "First Class, okay?"

I said, "If it doesn't cost me extra."

She said, "No, sir, you're a valued customer, and I just looked at the history of your arrangements for this flight, and you deserve a break today."

And that's what happened on Sunday when I got to the Newark air-port—except that they put me on an earlier flight to Chicago because I arrived early at the airport.

Flexible.

Incidentally, my Saturday flight from Austin to Newark was changed to LaGuardia via Houston when I arrived early at the airport, and the Agent guaran-teed me I could get a first class seat on that flight; whereas she couldn't promise me a first class seat on the flight I had been scheduled to take.

What's the difference in flexible and ridiculous?

I began the trip on Sunday, and on **Monday, June 27**, I arrived and, sure enough, the strike was on. The airport had closed up except for a few flights like mine.

The AA Arrivals Admirals Club welcomed me with a shower, water, and breakfast snack and a charming French receptionist who indicated I was the only passenger who had used that facility that day. But I dawdled and missed my train connection.

I spent an hour and a half on line exchanging my original rail ticket for another one to Bordeaux. Then I missed that train connection because my watch stopped unaccountably, and I got the time wrong.

Then the worst thing happened: My third ticket required me to schlep my bags (Heavy luggage doesn't weigh a thing—unless one has to schlep it oneself, and that's the strongest argument I can proffer for packing light) through the corridors of the Paris Metro from one station (up and down flights of stairs) to another, to a terminal where I had to stand on line again to exchange my transfer for yet another missed train.

Oh, no. I learned *that* train had been sold out (but it was a milk train anyway), and I had to exchange for an express train that departed one hour later. As a consequence, I rode four hours to Bordeaux and discovered there was no one to meet me at the station. I looked around and remember what Rick Steves, the travel guide had written: "Bordeaux must mean 'boredom' in some ancient language. If I were offered a free trip to that town, I'd stay home and clean the fridge."

I asked for a taxi transfer from Bordeaux to my destination, the Chateaux de Puy Robert in Bontignac Lescaux (French for "Bumfucque") that—I was told—would cost $240. Damn.

Two hours later, after arriving at the Chateaux, my driver—who reminded me of Inspector Clouseau in the Pink Panther films—argued that he deserved more than $240. I said "Mai non." that is French for Bullshit. The Chateaux management told him he had been amply paid. [I was reimbursed in that amount by the Yale Alumni offices at the close of the trip.]

I ate a salad, drank a glass of wine, and went to bed in an excellent bedchambre on the second floor behind one of the Chateaux turrets.

Tuesday, June 27, I awoke in time to eat breakfast and board the bus for trips to three caves, all filled with (Gol-ly.) stunning artifacts: Lascaux II (An excellent reproduction of the famous 12th Century cave interior), Bara-Bahau, and Les Eyzies.

We had lunch and returned to the Chateaux for a swim. An al fresco reception followed, and then I had one of the most congenial dinners I can remember during the entire trip.

Wednesday, June 28, our bus tour guide (an anthropologist) argued with our Yale Faculty Lecturer (an art historian) that Cro-Magnon men and women did not live deep inside caves except possibly at the entrances to caves that provided "shelter." So the issue arose: When is a shelter a cave and a cave a shelter? The anthropologist was an informed person, but she was also sternly authoritarian, and she pissed some of us off.

We visited two more caves, Cap Blanc where great horses were carved in caves/shelters and Rouffignac, where we rode an electric train for a great distance underground to view awesome primitive drawings on the ceiling of the cave. We also walked through a museum that blew me away because in China I had viewed 4,000 year old terra cotta statues, in Egypt 7,000 year old bas relief, and now in France I was looking at 30,000 year old tools and weapons.

Prehistoric makes Precolumbian look post modern.

Thursday, June 29, we checked out of the Chateau and traveled to St. Emilion for wine-tasting at a local winery and a walk around town. Then on to Verdom [not Verdun] to embark on the Panorama and a speech from the ship's first officer, a Greek, who was so young he giggled uncontrollably welcoming us aboard the ship whose name he pronounced "PanORaMA." We were briefed by the tour director to dispose of toilet paper in waste baskets located beside the toilets. But what world traveler doesn't already know that.

Our beds would be made daily, but sheets would not be changed during our stay.

We were told to attend briefings every day before dinner at which time the next day's schedule would be read aloud to us, and each instruction would be repeated. Each instruction would be repeated. The same schedule would be printed and placed on our beds each evening, then the same schedule that had been read aloud and printed would be placed on our beds each evening. Redundant. Redundant.

Hey, I'm just a flexible passenger here.

Five minutes into the briefing, I realized I would need to adjust my attitude after listening to the tour director—which I had to do—on a daily basis.

After drinks and dinner, I retired to my cabin (that might best be described as monastic), and the ship departed for our first night at sea.

Friday, June 30, we docked in La Rochelle where the Germans had built massive concrete submarine shelters during WWII, ugly as sin.

We bussed to town for a walkabout, returned to the Pan<u>ora</u>ma for lunch, and then I went back to town to shop for gifts for my infant grandtwins.

That evening, we had a semi-formal reception, and we met the captain (for the first and last time), followed by dinner. The wines were an indifferent French white and red. Very French.

Saturday, July 1, we took a tender to Belle Ile and drove around to view that island's massive coastal rocks, then we walked around town. The weather was stormy that afternoon, so the captain hoisted sails to help stabilize the ship. My cabin was in the bow, and the waves splashed against my porthole, but no mal de mer. Just bumpy boat.

Sunday, July 2, rainy weather in Morlaix where we visited two museums and two churches, St. Thegonnec and Guimilliau with competing "Calvarys." I learned that a Calvary is an outdoor icon (or series of statues) depicting scenes from the life and crucifixion of Christ.

That evening we had a Greek supper cooked by the two American chefs hired for the cruise. The food aboard ship was always ample and never bad.

Monday, July 3, we drove by bus to Mont St. Michel, the world's first theme park—only the roller coaster was missing. Designed as a tourist attraction for religious pilgrimages, the place continues to be undeniably grand, even with all the commercial trappings that surround the church. I suppose Mont St. Michel was about as close as I ever got to a genuinely "spiritual" moment on the trip, but the crowds and the uneven stairs made concentration difficult. The tide was receding as we watched, and we learned that it goes out for miles and then comes rushing back ashore "like horses galloping." I would like to return there someday and stay in one of the 4-star hotels and eat in a 4-star restaurant at that multi-star church.

Later in the day, on our return to St. Malo, I went browsing and bought another set of outfits for my grandtwins and a trinket for my wife.

The ship left the dock and while others were dutifully attending briefing, I walked the deck and watched the captain negotiate the locks and hoist the sails that blew us out to sea.

Tuesday, July 4th, we took a 1½ hour trip to the Bayeux Tapestry Museum to view what must be the most theatrically-presented historical artifact in the Western World as well as the most egregiously opportunistic retail sales facility I've ever seen.

The museum was crowded with "Geriatric Americans and silly schoolchildren" I overheard a young Englishman complain. And the visit was a hurried, noisy affair.

We visited another Romanesque-gothic-Norman church, another forgettable edifice.

I advise my readers to avoid that museum and church.

Soon after lunch we arrived at "Gold Beach," site of British landings on D-Day, June 6, 1944. We visited a hodge-podge museum featuring WWII military artifacts and uniforms and watched a short film and slide show and then bought postcards. I thought, "This sure isn't much of a July 4th celebration."

But that was before we went to the American Cemetery where over 10,000 young men and women, average age: 25, are buried.

I was moved to tears. A fellow tourist asked why was I crying? Was there someone I was related to buried there? I said yes, and I meant, "Yes, Americans like me."

Our bus passed by vast and ghostly Omaha beach. Nothing sentimental was said; neither was any acknowledgment made. Just a ride down that beach on a bus. That was enough.

Our last stop was the church at Ste. Mere Eglise where a paratrooper (a dummy) hangs from the roof by his parachute, memorializing an event that happened there on D-Day.

That evening, I called Barbara to update her with my current travel plans. Then, back on the boat, we were served an American picnic dinner with sensational fried chicken. It was my last supper aboard the PanORaMA.

I reflected that there is no evidence of battles or bloodshed on Utah and Omaha beaches, nor at any other historical site we visited where armies have clashed for thousands of years. Only commemorative plaques and graves and—of course—the stories we retell.

It's good to visit those places and retell those stories. Otherwise, one would never know what happened.

Wednesday, July 5, I disembarked and we headed for Rouen. The tour guide was excellent.

I said farewell, left the group on a taxi to the train station, took an express train to Paris, another taxi to the airport Sheraton (imaginative in design), and slept for 10 hours.

On **Thursday, July 6**, I walked for about 5 minutes from the hotel to the American departure desk, checked in, and the plane left around 10:30 am. During the flight, I watched 3 complete movies and began organizing notes for this narrative.

A Yale Alumni flyer advertising a trip to "The Dordogne and the West Coast of France" reached out of our mailbox and grabbed me ("A new concept in cruising awaits you....").

<u>*Two Weeks Split Between Scotland and Italy*</u>

PART I:

Scotland; the Hebridean Princess

◆

April 4–10, 2000

The Hebrides is generally regarded as the islands and inlets located on the West Coast of Scotland in the Sea of Hebrides as well as the Inner and Outer Hebrides bays, firths and sounds and lochs too numerous to mention.

The Scots gave the land and seas of the Hebrides untranslatable and unpronounceable Gaelic names; and that's just as well because after only one trip to that desolate seacoast, this author is convinced only reclusive native Scots can live for long in Kilmartin, Craighouse on Jura, Scalasaig and other tiny seaport towns with naught to do but await the next ragin' sea storm and consume whisky by the "wee dram" (A metaphorical measurement ranging from a splash to a tidal wave).

I imagine folks who live in the hard-bitten Hebrides must have an absolutely insatiable need for isolation. And there is no position this writer can take to recommend going there except going aboard a classy ship like the Hebridean Princess (Pronounced HEB-ri-DEE-un prin-CESS).

Barbara and I were the only Americans aboard the cruise itinerary we selected, a short 5-day adventure in inactivity, and we liked the ship, we liked the Brits and Scots we met (Except for a woman we dubbed Mrs. Bucket because she outdid the pretentious TV character), and we liked the gardens on shore, the colors of grays, greens, and blues in the sky and landscape, and the unlikely sunny weather we encountered one memorable day out of five.

The question we were asked most often (at least a dozen times) by our shipmates was "How did you two Americans learn about this cruise?" that we interpreted as a polite way of saying, "What are you intrepid foreigners doing here?" We spoke the same language, approximately; however I noted a propensity for some Brits to use "one" as the subject of their sentences, and I picked up on the habit because one truly wants to fit in, right? We were treated by all passengers and crew as cordially and ceremonially as one treats uninvited guests, and we had a jolly good time, don't you know.

Usually, when one travels on a cruise ship, one meets mostly one's American peers. But on the PrinCESS, one was able to talk with natives. One developed an affection for several of the couples who talked about their countrymen candidly, describing Brits to Americans. For the most part, we had great handshake conversations, asking for their feelings about their government and responding to their curiosity about Bill Clinton and Hillary. "The Blairs and Clintons are a bit too chummy, don't you think?"

So why did we decide on that particular ship and cruise?

Well, some years ago, in a conversation with passengers at dinner on another cruise ship, we were playing a one-upmanship game I call "Cruise ship Refugees." Everyone was comparing Silversea with Seabourn with Cunard lines, and someone said, "Well, all ships pale by comparison with the Hebridean Princess, of course." Silence. Nobody wanted to be the first to say, "Huh? Whuts that?" Until one (I was the one) casually asked, "Huh? Whuts a HEBriDEan PRINcess?" HA. I called the guy's bluff.

He folded: "Uh, well, I think it's one of those ships that sail up in the highlands of Scotland. Please pass the fruit jelly, okay?"

That nudge was all one needed to seek and find the specs on this trump card mystery ship. And after sending an inquiry to the ship line, one began receiving brochures with fees listed in English pounds rather than dollars, and one decided the ship was too rich for one's blood. Then, this year's brochure offered sampler cruises of shorter than customary duration at early season dates and rates, and so, one decided to check it out.

Now, when one plays "Refugee," one will be able to wait till just the right moment, then throw in one's wild card, and when called out, one will say, "Yeah, it was okay. We hadda good time, you betcha." And only when pressed will one admit that "Hell, it really don't matter none. A cruise is only as good as your attitude and expectations, right?"

And that's where this report begins on day one:

Tuesday, April 4, 2000

Paul Boston (friend and comrade) arrived at our house to ride with us to Austin where he would repeat his past kindness, returning our van to Salado. We left Salado on time, but 15 minutes out of town, I discovered I had left my ubiquitous blue jacket at home.

We returned (15 minutes) to get the jacket because I have nothing else ubiquitous to wear, and after another 15 minutes on the road we caught up to the point where we'd turned off, 45 minutes behind schedule. Not to worry. I always pad my schedule by an hour.

And the airplane was late leaving, so no problem.

En route, Austin to Chicago, thence to Heathrow, I reflected that modern travel consists of riding to an airport in a car, stepping into a magic time machine, sitting in an air-pressurized tunnel-like structure for hours, and then climbing out of the tunnel, depressurized, into another world. I can understand the time differential, but I suspect proprieties in different countries are controlled by politicians, priests, businessmen, and others who have a vested interested in preserving our differences. Won't it be grand when American TV finally sets the standards of cultural behaviors all over the world? Oh, my.

Wednesday, April 5

We arrived on schedule at LHR (Heathrow), and we transferred to the Sheraton Skyline Heathrow hotel via taxi for an overnight. Why that Sheraton? Because an airlines reservation agent said in passing that she enjoyed her stay there. Yeah, well, I don't know what (or who) she enjoyed, but that 2nd class Sheraton had nothing to recommend it except frequent flyer mile credits. I hate bad, overpriced hotels. But I must note that it was almost worth staying there after meeting a gracious and generous room service waiter named Archie who gave us a free half bottle of Piemonte Barbera red that (in addition to the Melatonin and Ambian I took) helped induce sleep.

Scheduling a rest stop on the day we arrive allows us to catch up on all the sleep we've lost while preparing to travel. It also allows us to sleep through the jet lag interval. Okay, it's a wasted day, but I've slept through so many theatrical shows scheduled for the day of our arrivals, I'd rather waste time than money.

Thursday, April 6

Around noon, we fled the hotel via taxi back to the world's largest maze, Heathrow, walked from the entrance where the taxi driver dropped us because he misunderstood us (His English was broken beyond repair), and we finally met a reception agent who steered us to a check-in counter and the gate to our flight to Glasgow that I mispronounced "Gasglow" to the gate attendant who corrected me gently and said, "Americans make that mistake somehow."

Arriving late (because our plane was an hour late departing from LHR) at GLASgow in the early afternoon, we were asked to be patient and wait because our ship's bus (Motor coach, rather) had gone on to pick up other passengers at the railroad station. We were patient for a goddamned hour, and then a young lad (whose Scottish brogue was so thick the Brits waiting with us couldn't understand him) came to announce the return of the motor coach that transferred us to Oban, arriving at that not remarkable port city just before dark. We sailed almost immediately with a piper on land playing some mournful tune (*Amazing Grace* again, doubtless), sorry to see us sail away.

At dinner that evening we learned that all couples had been assigned to separate tables, and all singles were seated at two large 8-tops for the entire trip. Fortunately, the couples at tables near us were friendly and communicative, and we truly enjoyed their company every morning, noon, and night.

We sacked out in a pretty stateroom with an enormous bathroom and slept well.

Friday, April 7

I awoke early and walked around the entire ship in a brisk 15 minutes. I discovered we had docked overnight at an extremely hostile-looking landscape, Coabh Haven (but I never heard the name pronounced aloud, probably because it was misspelled. Who would have known the correct spelling.).

I had breakfast of porridge (oatmeal) with a wee dram (best oatmeal I've ever eaten), a poached egg, and Cumberland sausage that tasted almost like eggs & sausage at home—but different. I watched a good-natured Scot (Ian Merry, seated with his pleasant wife, Joan) eat kippers; Jesus. Fish for breakfast.

There was a fire drill, then the tender left for shore, and I visited a remarkable garden with flowers blooming extravagantly, Arduaine Gardens, product of over a century of caretakers.

The ship's tender gave us a rocky ride returning to the PrinCESS; I almost threw up.

After lunch and a change of location, Barbara and I went ashore and strolled around a village on an old canal tow path in the drizzling rain, sharing a sagging brolley (an umbrella).

We turned back and—with our spirits high but our clothes considerably dampened—we sailed in the tender back to the ship on a calm sea.

The Captain's champagne reception was cordial that evening, dinner was smashing, and the port wine was passable at a gathering after dinner.

Bedtime around tennish.

Saturday, April 8

We ate, read, napped, and then I discovered while strolling on the shore at Crinan that morning, there's not much to look at; nor, in the afternoon, at Craighouse on Jura—except for a visit to Jura's single-malt whisky distillery where we tasted the required wee dram, a taste, a mere taste, and returned to the PrinCESS in one of the ship's small speedboats; "That'll blow y'r ears back."

On the aft deck I enjoyed a visit with Cowan & Wenda Bradley, a mixed marriage, he's a Kiwi (New Zealander), and she's a Brit, both personable blokes. Also enjoyed meeting other fellow travelers costumed like extras in old Hitchcock movies, bundled up in tweeds, smiling, eager to chat.

We napped, dined, and then after dinner, appreciated conversation in the ship's lounge where we attended an event emceed by a clever ship's officer and tasted three more rounds of whisky.

We went to ten around beddish.

Sunday, April 9

I was up and about by 7am, chatting up Brits, assimilating the language, on the partially enclosed promenade deck. Thence to breakfast. Afterwards, whilst leaning at the rail, I looked out at a barren, uninviting mountainscape and a castle surrounded by hundreds of bloody caravans (house-trailers). Couldn't appreciate the castle for the crowds of caravans.

Some of the Brits said they had expected Barbara and me to be extroverts. It turned out they were more interested in talking with us than we had expected them to be. And they were candid describing their attitudes toward other Brits.

A Yorkshire lad was defensive, saying he's not as roughhewn as York farmers are thought to be; a Surrey matron boasted about her B&B; a Lancaster homeowner talked about the sheer fun of spending weekends aboard his barge sailing on canals with his wife, docking "pubside." They all seemed amused when they spoke of America as one of their "former colonies."

I went ashore to what must be one of the most barren beaches on Earth and walked on "shingles" or big, round rip-rack rocks. It was a clear, beautiful day, and I enjoyed being alone enormously. But I continued to marvel at the choices of islander Scots who live alone almost all the bloody time.

Barbara joined me for a visit to the Colonsby House Gardens, a private estate with an old garden not well-maintained because only a governmental agency could afford to employ the small army of garden keepers who would be required to keep it up nowadays. The surrounding Colonsby countryside was wild and woolly with hundreds of sheep, and our driver—an amateur archeologist who said he enjoyed hearing himself blather—pointed out locations of ancient battles, unusual geological formations, and religious relics. We, too, enjoyed his blather.

We reboarded the ship, napped, dressed for a formal final dinner, enjoyed a wee dram at the Captain's final reception, liked the dinner—even the Haggis served up ceremonially—but we skipped out on the farewell party in the ship's lounge located above us, as rowdy an affair as we could ever expect to overhear. Instead of partying, we packed our luggage, drank a final wee dram, and went to bed around ten.

Monday, April 10

I arose early and paid up at the purser's. We ate breakfast, and after docking, left the ship to board a bus bound for GLASgow, leaving Oban behind forever.

Yes, we enjoyed sailing nowhere, doing nothing, but we missed whatever it is that lures British tourists to return for yet another cruise aboard the PrinCESS. I had read that there is supposed to be less rain in April than any other time during the year, but it rained all but one day. The hills we saw weren't exactly awesome. Take away the rain and sea and castles and gardens, and moldy charm, and the Hebrides looks just like West Texas. Well, a little.

The point is we all develop strong affection and attachments for the worlds we're accustomed to seeing, right? The B&B woman in tweeds from Surrey told me only a barbarian could fail to see the beauty of that barren countryside (originally settled by barbarians). All I saw recalled for me a line from one of Dylan Thomas' poems describing a Welsh town as a "backwater of life." We had enjoyed a trip years ago to the mainland of Scotland, but this part of Scotland seems unbelievably cold and wet and grim. For me, the pleasure was in sailing on a handsome vessel, meeting people who made the trip well worth doing—once.

Two people whom we particularly liked were the Bradleys. After we arrived from GLASgow at Heathrow, they insisted on taking us in their car to Gatwick where the next leg of our journey was to begin. Then, en route, they called the hotel where we planned to stay, got directions, and delivered us to the front door. What superior people.

Our hotel that evening was Langshott Manor, located about 20 minutes from Gatwick. It's a handsome treasure of a Tudor manor and maintained to a fault. I had selected it because of its proximity to Gatwick, and both Barbara and I were impressed with the service, our room and four-poster, drinks in the morning room, dinner in the dining room, coffee in the library, and a walk in the 3-acre garden. The only disappointment was having to leave early the next morning to catch a plane for Italy. As disappointments go, not a serious one.

Two Weeks Split Between Scotland and Italy:

PART II:

Lake Bellaggio and Villa D'Este

✦

April 11–18, 2000

Tuesday April 11

At 6 am, Barbara and I took a complimentary taxi ride provided by the Langshott Manor to Gatwick for a British Airways flight to Milan scheduled to leave at 8:45 am. The plane was late, and we arrived at Milan's Malpensa Airport around noon and met a long-term friend, Joyce Mayer whom we had known for over thirty years in San Angelo, Texas.

Old friends are the best for all the obvious reasons, but Joyce isn't old and neither were we when we talked and laughed with her about old times. For the week we were reunited, we told jokes only an adolescent would find amusing; we sang hymns, bawdy songs, and show tunes; we gossiped and commiserated because Barbara and I both had loved Joyce's husband, Bob, a guy who died too soon.

I rented a car, a stick shift Opel, small but as large as I dared drive on mountainous Italian roads. We got lost even before we reached Milan, but after an overlong but happy drive, we checked into hotel Principe de Savoia, an elegant old landmark, had a snack at the bar, napped, dressed, and took a taxi to a La Scala opera performance of *Ariadne Auf Naxos*, a singspiel snooze by Richard Strauss. It was great fun hearing and seeing a show we had never witnessed before (nor shall we ever again), enjoying the singers vocal pyrotechnics and the lush orchestral score; never for a moment understanding anything the actors were doing or saying—except for the scene when the girl masquerading as a guy puts the make on another girl. Woah, that got our attention.

At intermission, the three of us compared stories we had made up for ourselves in order to calculate what was happening onstage, and it was as if we had attended three different shows. All three of us, however, had been watching the reactions of that audience of (mostly) impeccably dressed women, sophisticated looking men, and disdainful student ushers, all of them Italians listening to lyrics in German. Incongruous was how it seemed (and bizarre was what it was) when—at the final curtain—those who didn't grab their coats and leave the Theatre running, applauded wildly. I wasn't quite sure who won the game, Italians or Germans.

After the performance we had dinner at a restaurant in the same building, crowded with opera goers in large and small groups. We enjoyed watching what amounted to a post opera performance featuring a cast of café characters, and we made up stories of that improvised opera's action.

Wednesday, April 12

We arose early, shopped in the Milan Gallery (the world's first giant shopping mall), strolled around the plaza in front of the Dome, and then returned to check out of the hotel, driving to Lake Como via the autostrada (Italian for interstate highway).

We discovered that the Hotel d'Este is located—not in the town of Como, but—in Cernobbio on Lake Como. The Hotel—a palace—had the quality of a kingdom unto itself, a city-state. And from the moment we arrived, we felt welcomed to an extraordinary 16th Century castle, not too ornate, not too plain, just exquisite.

We were shown to our suite (two bedrooms, two baths, and a drawing room) by one of the hotel's registration clerks who enjoyed the reactions of Barbara and Joyce, walking around the suite with their eyes wide open, awestruck, while I stood by watching with a sly Cheshire cat smile on my face, unaffected, blasé. Yeah, sure.

When the clerk left the room, I opened French doors to discover a terrace, and we marveled at the view of the lake, the grounds, and the hotel. I'm sure there are no better rooms (#133, #134) in the entire hotel, and we celebrated our good fortune by sitting around a table, consuming tangerines from a silver fruit bowl.

"Wait a minute," Barbara said (and for a second I thought she was going to eat the last tangerine), "Why are we here in this suite? How did it happen? What on Earth did you <u>do</u>."

"Well," I said, "You're right. And I've waited to tell you till now."

Then I confessed that I had sent a fax to the Villa d'Este Reservations Manager requesting accommodations for Dr. Carver, the travel writer. I wrote that Dr. Carver might write an article about the Villa d'Este, and he would appreciate any courtesy that could be extended to him and his guests; and I signed the fax, "M. Pemberton" (Barbara's maiden name and my nom de plume).

The Manager responded by asking M. Pemberton to fax copies of Dr. Carver's business cards to her office for verification.

I copied my union membership card for the National Writers Guild as well as my Austin Writers Guild membership card and sent a fax.

The Manager thanked M. Pemberton and graciously reduced the price of the rooms by 20 percent, a significant amount even with off-season rates. They gave me no indication, however, that we would be ensconced in what appeared to be the best rooms in the Hotel.

I looked at Barbara and Joyce as they rolled their eyes at one another, and I asked them, "Well?"

After a moment, Barbara said, "This room will do nicely."

Joyce said, "You betcha."

And Barbara handed me a reward, the last tangerine.

We unpacked and then went for a walk, and what a walk. The grounds and gardens of the Hotel are sensational. There is a great hybrid Sycamore tree (a Plane tree) commanding the grounds, and fountains and a faux fortress, and flowers and walkways and statuary and orange trees with fruit; everything one could want in a palatial setting. We walked alongside the "water chain" (a series of waterfalls) that paralleled a path from the Hercules monument at the top of a hill to the Nymphaeum at the bottom. But it wasn't the *things* that made the place seem so grand; it's the way it has been designed, engineered, and—of course—maintained for centuries. Glorious, just glorious.

And the company of Barbara and Joyce was wonderful.

Dinner that evening at the Hotel Grill was also wonderful, a stroll around the lighted grounds was wonderful, and finally going to bed, sleeping between freshly pressed linen sheets was wonderful.

Yowza.

Thursday, April 13

We drove (and it took all three of us to spot the road signs) from Cerobbio to Laveno, took a ferry and transferred to the Isola Bella Palazzo and Gardens on Lake Maggiore. Wow. The beauty of the place was more impressive than its history (with the bed Napoleon slept in).

The trip took over twelve hours on the road and the ferry (counting the time we spent seeing the sights), and even after rain set in, we had a great time.

Returning to our gorgeous suite at the Hotel, we called for room service, ate dinner (not remarkable), and went to bed early. Ah, those sheets. I told Barbara I could get accustomed to sleeping on linen sheets.

She said, "Don't."

Friday, April 14

I arose, ate breakfast, and went for a massage that was only okay.

We received a friendly fax from our daughter, Libba, assuring us all was well on the home front. I went down to the fax office on the ground floor and used a computer with an Italian language keyboard and typed up a response that couldn't be transmitted because (we learned later that) Libba's dog, Sugar, had destroyed the fax connection. So I called and read the fax aloud to her over the phone, and she and I and Barbara chatted briefly. With cell phones in use nowadays, it seems I'm writing about the Dark Ages in Communication when I recorded this information.

While I was waiting in the Hotel lobby for access to the computer, I watched new arrivals to the Hotel sitting or standing uncomfortably, apprehensive. It was like watching a slow parade of movie extras acting miscast, conscious of the eyes of onlookers (like me), and I thought, "Of course. That's how one behaves if one feels one doesn't truly belong in the lobby of one of the most discriminating hotels in the world."

I guessed that everyone I could see was confirmed upper middle class, like the BBD&O conventioneers and Japanese businesspersons, because I doubt that the Hotel's old rich patrons would ever hang around that crowd in the lobby. The Americans, Germans, and Japanese couples were wearing new, upscale clothes, (and all their tennis shoes were brand spanking new and white). There were a few Italians and virtually no French or Spanish tourists (One of the staff told me: "They don't come to Italy, and we don't go to France or Spain.").

The staff, for the most part, are faultlessly gracious. They don't always do what they say they will ("Immediately, Dr. Carver, your car will be ready," means "I may forget to send for your car, but when you come to the entrance and ask for it one more time, I'll get it and apologize profusely. Scusé."), and some requests don't get filled because it don't seem logical to them for someone to prefer a foam over a down pillow. In any event, they were a cut above most staff, multilingual and hospitable.

Barbara wanted pizza for lunch, and Joyce, seated in a gilded armchair, imitating Marie Antoinette said, "Let her eat pizza." The hotel doesn't serve stuff like that, so we went to find any parking space near any pizzeria, but we could find only one, and it was miles from the pizza parlor. Regrettably, the pizza was only okay.

We drove up a road parallel with the lake's edge between grand and medium-grand villas, and we never saw a vacancy sign once. (Well, of course not. Advertisements in that neighborhood would have been bad form.) We returned to the Hotel, and I was amazed at how much damage those two women could do to one little hotel gift shop. I bought a tie on sale for less than $100,000.

That evening, we ate dinner in the Empire Room of the Hotel and enjoyed the pacing of the food service, like a carefully orchestrated ballet, oh, my.

Suddenly, we heard from one end of the room, about 40 Japanese tourists singing and clapping, "Happy Birthday to you." They were very loud.

From the other end of the room, the entrance, I heard a cry of outrage and watched the hotel manager screaming at the matre d' something to the effect of "That's not the kinda thing we let people do here." The Matre d' protested, and the manager screamed, "Basta." and walked off in a huff. Managers behaving badly.

After eating more than a sufficiency at dinner, Barbara and Joyce and I decided—in lieu of running 10 laps—we would go for a walk outdoors. We stepped outside in the drizzling cold and after taking about 10 steps, we returned, went up to our rooms, and conversed for hours in a bold attempt to use up calories.

[Simple pleasures: I think I enjoyed the linen sheets and hand towels more than anything else in our quarters at the Villa d'Este, and I really liked the distinctive art objects and antiques, the curious night light in the bathroom, the heated towel racks, Bulgari brand bath products, the fresh flowers, fruit. My sense of well-being increased exponentially.]

Saturday, April 15

We opted for a drive, lakeside, to Bellagio on a twisted, cliffside mountain road. Even with detours, the trip didn't take more than 45 minutes, and we parked where we had been advised, all the way around the town in front of the Hotel Du Lac, avoiding hundreds of remote parking spaces elsewhere. Shopping in the rain, we didn't find many exclusive stores; the town seemed like a charming strip mall. Commerce is commerce.

We ate a good lunch at a lakeside hotel, and then we returned to Como (a travel & shopping excursion lasting only 4 frigging hours) and the Villa d'Este.

I dropped the girls off at the Hotel and went back into town looking for a children's shop, seeking something Italian for our grandtwins. I turned down a narrow road with ancient-looking walls on both sides and drove and drove and the walls got narrower and narrower until I looked ahead and thought to myself,

"This Opel's not gonna make it through the eye of that needle." So I started backing down the twisting roadway and made virtually no progress, straightening up, backing, driving forward, straightening—Until a woman emerged from a nearby house, smiling, and told me in incomprehensible Italian (but meaningful gestures) to continue forward where I would eventually find a turnaround. I gratzied her, sucked in my viscera, and started forward again, just missing scraping the sides of the car. Eventually I found a driveway to turn around in and started back down, slowly, painstakingly, until I got out of that tight alley and forced myself to relax parts of my body that don't customarily tighten up. I drove back to the hotel, resolved not to embarrass myself by confessing my error of judgment over dinner.

We ate at the Grill, one of our favorite places, and afterwards, strolling beside the lake, I watched a well-dressed young woman emerge from a water taxi, fall off the dock, pick herself up out of the water, and shoulders high, her blouse sticking to her skin, march into the hotel, refusing all help from bystanders, looking like Sophia Loren in *Marriage Italian Style*. Ah, those Italian women.

After my afternoon's adventure in the narrow alley noted above, I reflected that we learn a lot about the lives of natives of countries from their roads. Even more than we can learn from personal interaction. When foreign visitors come to our town in Texas, I generally act like a chamber of commerce representative and extol the virtues of my environs—except to those persons whom I know intimately and trust absolutely. Travelers really don't learn much conversing with strangers. Why not? Because strangers are strange, and "the kindness of strangers" is risky. But driving through—and looking at—roads and houses, one may study the work of architects, artists, politicians, and—especially—engineers. We enter their minds as we ride through countrysides and cities. We marvel at centuries-old paths, ancient and modern highways, the turns and dips and surfaces and road signage (Oh, for better universal road signage.) to determines directions taken. I learn more from driving around in strange countries than I ever learn from translations of conversations with natives. And roads don't lie.

Sunday, April 16

This was our last day in Italy, so we drove to Lugano, Switzerland (only 40 minutes by autostrada), for a brief visit to a modern art gallery (Ho-hum) and the Hotel Splendide for a buffet lunch (Splendid.).

The daily rain set in as we returned, but it was a gentle sprinkle, very Swiss misty.

At the Hotel, we napped, packed, then went downstairs for tea accompanied by a quartet (two strings, a guitar, and an accordion) playing waltzes and polkas, repeating all the repeats, heavy on the accordion. We left at intermission.

Dinner that evening in the Verandah Dining Room, seated next to a window overlooking the lake (with the giant Plane tree illuminated brilliantly) was great because of the company, but the food was only so-so. We returned to the suite, finished packing, and went to bed early.

Monday, April 17

We arose at 6am, ate breakfast at 7, departed at 8, arrived at Malpensa Airport at 9:30, discovered how to return and park the damned rental car by noon, and got a VAT return credit on our Visa card (a simple transaction; the long wait on line is the hard part). We ate pizza at an efficient buffet, but it was only okay.

We said goodbye to Joyce who returned directly to the States, and we boarded a BA plane bound for Gatwick where we transferred via express train to London and the 22 Jermyn St. Hotel, touted as an exceptional family-owned small hotel. It <u>was</u>, and we were well treated. We had an excellent supper at Fortnam & Mason's, and I went to a West End show by Alan Ayckbourn, *Comic Potential*, with an outstanding female performer, Jamie Dee, a good supporting cast, but a ragbag script.

On my return to Jermyn Street, I had to walk past hundreds of hyperactive teenagers at Piccadilly Circus; it was an effing circus.

Tuesday, April 18

The noise from early morning traffic woke us up, and I learned why we had each been give two soft pillows; one was to cover your head.

Room service breakfast was entirely too expensive (50 bucks for rolls, coffee, & juice for two. The British exchange rate was low, but that breakfast was exorbitantly extortionate (and if there wasn't such a word as extortionate before, there is now).

The Hotel staff was extremely helpful loading our stuff (that is stuffing our load) into a waiting taxi. We transferred to Victoria Station, driving past Buckingham Palace where a new building is being erected to handle crowds who will tour the Palace when it opens all year round as a tourist attraction after the Queen moves out to Windsor Castle. Traffic came to a standstill, and we had plenty of time to sit and watch people watch each other stuck in gridlock. When we finally arrived at the American Airlines desk at Victoria Station, we were able to check our luggage through and catch the Gatwick express. No problem.

Riding on the train past institutional housing whose only interesting facets were the Dickensian chimneys, I imagined the rooms must be tiny and crowded with furniture and stressed-out occupants.

Ah, for the grace and elegance of an Italian villa where we all might live out our lives.

Croatia, Slovenia, Venice, Berlin

✦

All Over the Map
June 24–July 5, 2000

Late in June, a cruise on a yacht, the M/V Monet, in the Adriatic (looking at a map of Italy, it's the sea on Italy's left coast) seemed like a great idea whose time had come. Unfortunately, the cruise line wasn't quite ready for the idea.

My luggage got lost on the way over (when I detoured for an overnight at Zagreb just to check it out) and again on my return home (going through Zurich where the airport continued undergoing repairs). Lost suitcases aren't nearly as difficult to acknowledge as unsympathetic agents are, even though they're employed to deal with the public. Europe is all bureaucrats; Americans can't begin to compete with them.

The Zagreb taxi driver tried to overcharge me, but my hotel doorman wouldn't let him. I am certain over half the taxi drivers I've had in my travels have screwed me. They take one look at me, and I can see "You're screwed." in their eyes.

The Sheraton in Zagreb was okay, but don't go out of your way to stay there.

The Croatian tour was run by "Elegant Cruises & Tours, Inc." Sounds like a poor English translation of a great notion, and it should have tipped me off. The entire cruise was run by folks who thought Americans would be willing to return to Croatia ten years after the war that had destroyed their greatest industry, tourism. Regrettably, I was the only person aboard who bought that sales pitch. The other eight passengers were—in one way or another—visiting because they had family or friends in Croatia. Wait a minute, there were only nine of us? Yep, on a ship that could have accommodated well over a hundred? Yup. It was an adventure on the S. S. Edsel.

It could have been a better trip if the cabins had been cleaner, the food service classier, and the management a whole lot more sophisticated. The ship's tour director (His name was Bozho, pronounced "Bozo," believe it.) and the ship's captain had been officers in the Croatian navy during the war, and they were accustomed to handling military troops. But they weren't ready for international guests.

They used English expressions that were condescending at best, "Dear Ladies and Gentlemens, you will now go to the dining room where you will be dining. I will not be telling you again." That got old fast.

Our fire drill lasted less than thirty seconds. We reported to assigned stations where a sailor said, "Do not panic. Have a nice day."

Aboard ship without my suitcase, I had to wear the same clothes for the first couple of days at sea, but it wasn't a fashion-conscious bunch of passengers. In fact, we all looked as socially mismatched as our clothes. The rich ones looked poor, and the poor ones looked overdressed. The crew looked sharper than we did. But that was just appearances.

We sailed from Dubrovnik to Sibenik (She-BIN-Ik) where we saw the Krka Waterfall (a tropical garden stretching for miles) and the Sibenik Cathedral. Yawn. I yawned most of the trip, but that was only most of it. Blasé is not what I am when I'm stunned by beauty or greatness.

Our English-speaking land tour guides were pretty uninspiring, and more than once I wondered what the Hell I was doing in Croatia.

We sailed through the Kornati Archipelago (An inside passage, islands without vegetation) to Opatija crossing the border into Slovenia for a horse show at the Lipica Stud Farm (where the Lippizzaner Horses are bred) and the Postojna Cave (where we rode on an underground train with hundreds of tourists for around twelve miles and walked through fascinating limestone caves). Thence to Pula and its amphitheatre that originally seated 22,000.

From there we sailed across to Venice, Italy, for a walking tour of St. Mark's and the Square, and we cruised in a gondola through the canals for 45 minutes (Our gondolier kept his eye on his watch). Venice was too crowded to enjoy. It was my third trip to Venice, and it seemed just as crowded (and as beautiful) as ever.

About thirty Englishmen and women boarded at Venice for the return trip to Dubrovnik, and we sailed to Split (for a visit to Emperor Vespasianus' Gladiators' arena and Diocletian's 3rd Century Palace, a distinctive ruin).

Then to Korcula that is _the_ place to visit. A castle, a cathedral, a clear and beautiful waterfront with cottages, a café with a singing Croatian male quartet, great weather, and charm—lotsa charm. I recommend a stay in Korcula. I walked around the pier visiting Marco Polo's house just before we sailed, and I was truly disappointed we couldn't stay longer.

On our final day, arriving in Dubrovnik, we had a city tour.

Dubie's a beautiful and formidable fortress. I can't help but think the founding fathers of that city knew that someday it would be a great vacation spot. I really liked Dubrovnik, but I was happy the only Americans I saw there were service men and women, on passes from a battleship anchored in the harbor, no Yankee tourists.

The next morning I abandoned ship and took the only daily flight to Zurich and Berlin.

For what it's worth, I recommend visits to Dubrovnik & Korcula; they're easy to like and easy to pronounce. But magic portals just didn't open for me elsewhere in Croatia and Slovenia.

But Berlin was welcoming. Wilkommen.

Second only to China and Egypt, I like Germany most (probably because I was stationed there from 1958–60, learning enough of the language to get by, and I feel comfortable traveling around on my own). Berlin I like best of all, not for any easily identified reason—just an appreciation of a place that continues to exist after a century of world wars, a cold war, and an unending war for its own survival. One can't walk around Berlin without sensing its extraordinary and disturbing history. Knowing it's the capital of Europe's strongest and richest country makes it awesome.

Back in 1958, I made my first trip to Berlin, riding on an overnight train whose windows had been shuttered for fear passengers might glimpse East Germany en route. I visited the city just before the Wall went up, and I toured the Russian zone. It was as grim as it was reported to be, and I have photographs to prove it. This time when I visited, years after the Wall had been torn down, I spent most of my time in the rebuilt Eastern part of the unified Berlin. There are big city poverty pockets, but Berlin ain't what it was back in the 50s.

I stayed in the Four Seasons Hotel, one of the best in the world, with a view of the English and German churches at Gendarmarkt Square. I walked all over town, up and down Unter den Linden, and I walked so much I hurt my right leg, ankle, and foot, and my left foot complained, too. But that didn't stop me or slow me down. I went to every museum and restaurant and theatre I could crowd into my time there.

The hotel is remarkable and so is its restaurant. The food and the service is great. Courtesy prevails at the Four Seasons: the concierge, the wait staff, the chambermaid, everybody. What a pleasure.

My first evening in Berlin, I attended a performance of *The Magic Flute* at the Komische Oper. The voices were great but the production values were pitiful. I left at intermission.

I ate dinner at Borchardt, a *schnitzel* (that was an okay *schnitzel*, but I'm sure it was an off day or they wouldn't have earned an international reputation).

The next day, I went on a pilgrimage to the Brecht-Weigel Museum located in an apartment in the house where one of my favorite playwrights and his actress wife lived. I was one of only two people allowed at a time in the apartment, and I was permitted by a generous lecturer to look at artifacts to my heart's content. Then I went to a nearby cemetery where the Brechts are buried. That evening, I ate supper at a bar where Brecht used to hang out, and I went to a performance at the theatre where he and his wife produced shows, The Berliner Ensemble, and I heard a program of Brecht/Weill songs.

Next day, I went to the slapdash Museum at Checkpoint Charlie, crowded with artifacts from the Cold War, and I marveled at the record of escape attempts made by East Berliners and the curious and desperate devices they used.

That evening, I ate a sensational dinner at the Vau restaurant where I told my waitress I'm a writer who keeps a travel journal. Immediately, the wife of the chef/owner appeared and presented me with a brochure of PR for Vau. I told her I didn't need promo, I planned to write Vau a rave. So here.

I crashed a performance of the Berliner Philharmonic for the second half of that evening's program. Superb. Then coffee at an outdoor café.

Next day, I walked through the Berlin Cathedral, a Protestant memorial to Huguenot refugees, with statues of Luther and his buddies. Then the Schinkel Museum a few blocks away. Quite accidentally, I happened on a midday organ recital attended by a small number of music lovers in nearby St. Hedwig's Catholic Church. I walked through—slowly and painfully on my sore feet—the Pergamon Museum on Museum Island. Then lunch at the 12 Apostles Pizza Palace, fast and cheap.

I went to the much balleyhooed Potzdammer Platz and saw an animated IMAX film with roller coaster footage. Even though it was just animated, I got sick to my stomach watching that 3-D flick. Dinner that evening at the Dressler Restaurant on Unter den Linden was very good.

Next day, I took a train to Potsdam and the Sanssouci Park that is a crowded, amiable place to walk if you don't mind pea gravel. My feet hurt so much, however, I gave up and took a taxi to the Schloss Cecilienhof (the site of the Potsdam Conference after WWII) and had a delightful lunch in the restaurant there, sitting where Stalin and Truman and Atlee might have sat.

I took in an off-the-wall theatrical event that evening, Chamaleon. Sometimes avant garde means a thing is boring as well as new.

Next day, I went shopping at the KaDaWe department store for gifts for my grandchildren. And later, my last evening, I ate the best dinner I can remember ever eating at a restaurant, alone, served by an impeccable staff at L'Etoile in the Adlon Hotel, overlooking the Brandenburg Gate. Then I went to a big Las Vegas type revue celebrating Berlin with more than three hundred in the cast, and more than three thousand in the house. Show Biz, but good.

I've got to go back to Berlin someday, one of the few places that I'd like to go back to again and again and again.

The Terra Cotta Warriors are only a few of the wonders to be discovered in Xian.

Xian, China

♦

Two Weeks with Global Volunteers
October 14–30, 2000

"Honk If You Love Traffic."

An Essay on Traffic in Xian—You have to see it to believe how terrifying it is to some of us Western Devils (Well, maybe not Italian drivers), either riding as passengers in a vehicle or trying to cross a street.

[How's that for an opening paragraph to segue into a journal describing my three-week trip to China, teaching Conversational English under the auspices of Global Volunteers, a not-for-profit service organization whose purpose is to serve the needs of people the world over (in Xian, teaching children and adults conversational English).]

This trip was my third to China, pleasurable and productive. To continue on the subject of Xian Traffic—]

Every time I set out to jaywalk or cross streets at corners, I thought, "My mother wouldn't want me to cross without holding onto her hand." Like a child, I was scared I'd get killed—except that little Chinese children wander across busy streets without even looking. Schoolchildren and mothers with babes in arms provide safe shields for foreigners like me. On more than one occasion I sidled up next to a defenseless-looking woman as if I were helping her to cross the street.

The Chinese seem to take chaotic traffic conditions for granted. Pedestrians wear their famous inscrutable masks, and no matter how close they come to getting clobbered or getting honked at, they act oblivious, as if the truck that screeches to a halt within one foot of them is supposed to stop precisely there. Stopping is something traffic doesn't do often—unless there's a jam—and then drivers just keep moving forward, changing lanes, bumper to bumper, clutching and accelerating at the same time, varoom, varoom, king of the road.

One death-defying taxi driver who drove me from one side of Xian to another turned into oncoming traffic at every intersection, driving up onto sidewalks, just barely steering clear of trees and human obstacles, zig-zagging from gutter to corner to center line, defying confrontational vehicles, pedestrians, and destiny, blasting his horn, laughing uncontrollably at accidents.

He drove over a car fender lying in the middle of the street and laughed as the fender gouged out the undersides of his car. Then a woman passenger stepped out of a stopped taxi ahead of my driver and started to cross in front of her own car when suddenly, her taxi driver inadvertently stepped on the gas and almost ran her down. She screamed at him, smashed her purse on the hood of the car, crossed to the curb, glared back, screamed again, and walked away. My driver almost died laughing, "Yuk, yuk, snigger, har-har, hotdog." (He might not have said "Hot dog." but it sounded like it.)

When I was told it takes a calendar year for drivers to qualify for their licenses, I said, "Yeah, license to kill." Ba-dump-bump.

Every imaginable form of conveyance uses the streets, primarily bicycles. Hand-drawn carts with sections of twenty-foot-long rebar. Honey wagons—sloshing their cargo—dodge in and out of traffic, challenging trucks, tractors, taxis, horse & buggies, and pedicabs for road-warrior supremacy.

On average, every third day I saw a wreck that had just recently occurred. Once, my driver swerved sharply to avoid hitting a bicycle lying on the street with the front tire still spinning. He never looked back. And, as he sped on, I looked back—but couldn't see anything—through the dirty rear window. I really think the driver kept going to avert a pileup because all the cars around us also kept going full speed ahead.

One might suppose Chinese drivers don't value the lives of others highly, but one might also conclude they value their own lives even more highly. I think the truth is my original point: Xian drivers are neither prudent nor careful, and pedestrians are either lucky or not. I lived to tell the tale, but my reader will note that Traffic in Xian became a preoccupation with me as I drafted the journal that follows.

October 15, 2000

When I sat down at a word processor on the second day after I arrived in Xian to type up my personal observations, I discovered—quite by accident—that another traveler had already typed up and saved to disk her impressions. On impulse, I copied her reactions in one column (with her kind permission) and compared my comments to hers in a second column for three pages. It was as if she and I were reacting to two Chinas at once (Incidentally, I've changed her name to Yadayada to protect her privacy).

YADAYADA'S FIRST IMPRESSIONS

"All the Global Volunteers met at the airport baggage counter after arriving in Xian and took good care of one another. Outside we met Ann Marett and Tammy Huang, who had a van waiting to take us to our hotel. We had about an hour ride to The Orient Hotel. On our way we passed many farms and noticed drying corn on the roof tops. From the plane I had thought they were bright yellow tiles. We saw children on bicycles or walking, as it was lunch break at school. There were many kinds of cars and trucks on the roads and the bikes had their own lane, but every lane had bikes.

"As we entered urban areas, I noticed a beautiful Public Library on the right side of the road. Then lo and behold, right in front of me, there it was the Bell Tower, just as I had seen it in the video *The Silk Road*. It always thrills me to see in person something I read about or saw in a movie. I can't wait to visit it and go to the top.

"We arrived at our hotel and were assigned rooms and roommates. I was pleasantly surprised with my accommodations. We had lunch and later dinner in a private dining room in the hotel. The food was superb. Some of us tried eating with our chopsticks. They slowed me down but somehow did not stop me from overeating tofu, eggplant, rice, soup and fruit. Then we shared stories about ourselves. I felt great being part of such an intelligent, warm friendly group as this is my first experience traveling alone. I felt comfortable with all my teammates and enjoyed learning of their lives, lifestyles and philosophies.

"I was a little saddened to go back to my room so early, but I was sleepy and it was only 8 P.M. Then Edith knocked on my door and asked if I wanted to take a walk. Wow. It felt so good to walk and stretch my legs after that long plane ride.

"There was oodles of traffic, bicycles, horns honking and noise. We carefully crossed the street to beautifully arranged fruit stands and fruit baskets. We saw many eateries, where people were eating both inside and outside. We saw people cleaning and preparing vegetables. We saw what looked like a candy store at the end of the block. We walked back toward the hotel and found a camera shop and a laundry.

"We were looking for an Internet Café but did not find one, and we concluded we had been looking in the wrong direction. Walking was exhilarating, but you must watch your step, especially in the evenings as much of the sidewalks were beautifully paved but some areas were muddy and chopped up. I had a great night's sleep and I hope everyone else did too."

RAMON'S FIRST IMPRESSIONS. Let's get real.

It was a dark and chilly night when I stepped off the plane into rainy Xian. I was stopped at Customs because I hadn't filled out an arrival card; so I waited among the herd of fellow travelers for my turn—until I realized I was getting pushed to the end of the line because it's a custom for everybody to get ahead of everybody else. I adapted to custom and fought my way to the luggage carousel, and from there I met John An, an obliging 27-year-old native and one-man welcoming party.

We took a mud-splattered cab in the blinding rain to the hotel and chatted all the way. At the time, I thought, "If John's English proficiency is anything like the way my students might handle English, I'll have a great time." (Little did I know he was one of the best ESL speakers I would meet).

I couldn't see much of anything outside the window because the road was dismally unlighted, and the truck and bicycle traffic (at 10 pm) was intense. The mud splashed on the windshield in layers. I rocked and rolled as the driver braked and accelerated the engine again and again. John and I talked as if it were a conventional cab ride although I kept involuntarily punctuating my comments with gasps and yelps, reacting to traffic. It was like riding in an out-of-control amusement park time machine for an hour.

We finally arrived at the Orient Hotel, a second-class establishment, but to be fair, it was clean and bugfree, the hot water was hot, and the elevator was great. The thermostat was inoperable, however, and there was no Kleenex. I had expected worse; I would have liked better.

I met Ann and Carolyn, our sponsors, who took me to my room and made sure I understood how to unlock an unconventional door lock.

I had asked for a single with a king bed, and what I got was double beds (No problem, I used the second bed as a sorting table). There was a desk, a TV, a closet for midgets, and two hot water decanters for tea. The sheets were changed only when I left instructions, but the room was cleaned daily to my satisfaction.

There are only two English-speaking channels on Xian TV, and theirprogramming was weird with updated news reports mixed with C-Span along with Voice of America, situation comedies, and old nature shows.

I awoke the next day after sleeping well (no jet lag). The view from my room on the 14th floor (of a 20-floor building) looked like cold fog soup.

After breakfast I met my cohorts, liked 'em, and went to an Introduction to China class. Then a Chinese language class, learning necessary expressions.

I got my teaching assignment, and curiously enough, I felt an excitement which had been evading me. Just the idea of a real school with real kids gave me a buzz. On Tuesday, I would begin teaching English at the Shaanxi Foreign Languages Academy. Sounded like a peach of an assignment. It wasn't peachy. But it wasn't anything I regretted.

After an unimaginative lunch at the hotel, I went for a walk down streets with another teacher and through alleys. Alleys? Don't ask why; we just found ourselves walking in mud puddles through a back alley which never seemed to end. Then we went into an arcade that was full of junk stuff (not junk souvenir stuff, just everyday cheapo stuff).

Returning, the GV staff took our pictures (so that they would be able to identify our bodies, we joked), and we met individually with staff and faculty who prepped us for teaching assignments. Ann tried to help me with a lesson plan, but I discovered our "plans" consisted of whatever we devised (except for those few teachers who were restricted to textbook lesson sessions).

That evening, dinner at the misnamed "Medical Palace" restaurant was okay. For the first time it occurred to me that we would be fed Chinese every noon and night. Where was my head.

I waited on line to use the hotel's one internet connection, then I went to bed at eight. The business office called around ten to say there was no longer a line at the computer. I said, "Very amusing," dropped back to sleep and slept well.

The next day, we were given brief training sessions to prepare us for living and teaching in China. I can't imagine any bases that weren't covered from the getgo by the GV staff in Xian. Ann was the organizer, Carolyn was supervisor, and Tammy (wife of John An) served as a translator and facilitator—all super sensitive to criticism, however. I realized right away that these managers would not be the kind of folks one might be candid with. They were defensive, so I soft-pedaled my criticism. In truth, however, the three-week's project couldn't have been better planned or managed; and—by the end of our stay—I'm sure the consensus of all participants was positive. But it's sometimes hard to work with thin-skinned, anal supervisors.

Rather than present journal entries on a day-to-day basis: I've crunched my activities and opinions together under various headings:

TEACHING IN CHINA

My job most nearly resembled the role and function of a substitute teacher in classrooms universally—with a difference. We had neither lesson plans nor supervision inside the classroom. Very few of the students' real teachers stayed with us (because—we assumed—they didn't want to be shown up for deficient conversational skills. Most Chinese teachers of English I met were unintelligible).

For three weeks, I succeeded in keeping the attention of my students using performance skills, drilling them on pronunciation, and talking about my family, home and the States. When dealing with high school/college age kids, I noted they have the same interests and boredom thresholds as teenagers the world over. They gobbled up stories and songs, and their eyes glazed over when I got descriptive—except when I required them to pronounce what I was saying.

The students' attitudes were affectionate, never antagonistic, at least that's how I interpreted their behavior. Only a few students slept through class or misbehaved, but buzz-buzz-buzz, they all chattered and whispered to each other without cease, constantly helping each other understand what I was saying. There was a sibilant continuum of sound throughout each class period, distracting but not a serious problem.

Frankly, teaching students in a Chinese private school whose academic standards were quite low made me feel underutilized. But I got a genuine sense of usefulness during my first week, sharing my pronunciation, because their teachers' conversational skills were so woefully lacking. Very few students were easy to understand. Hell, most students were absolutely incomprehensible; they knew ABC, 123, and Do-ray-me (the song), but they could not converse (no oral skills).

Chalk dust was a *big* problem, curiously enough, making breathing difficult and snow-whitening our clothes.

Classrooms and dormitories had no decorations whatsoever; they were grim and depressing.

The 90 minute length of the class period was stressful. I had to stretch 30 minutes' worth of information to 90.

A LESSON PLAN: I devised a basic plan that I used in every class I taught for the first time—repeating everything aloud. On second encounters I had to wing it.

1. I introduced myself using my name in Chinese & English.

2. I assigned English names to all students, A-Z.

3. I got them to sing the ABC song, both Chinese & English versions.

4. I performed a song of my own: "You got to get good folks out front in the house...."

5. I used maps of China & US to identify places.

6. I taught them to sing, "Red River Valley," with difficult sounds V, R, Th, L.

7. I played a "How old am I?" Guessing Game.

8. I showed them pictures of grandchildren and family and required them to ask questions that I answered, and then I got them to repeat my answers aloud.

9. I got them to sing all the songs they had ever learned in Chinese & English.

10. I got them to sing "The Star Spangled Banner." Softly.

WHAT ELSE DID I DO AS A GLOBAL VOLUNTEER INSTRUCTOR?

On two occasions I chatted with small groups of graduate school students at the Institute of Finance & Economics.

And during my last week, I transferred from the Foreign Languages Academy to a Small Business Administration startup ("Incubation") agency, "Software Park Development Center," coaching adults on pronunciation and vernacular speech. I was assigned a cubicle and computer with access to the internet and email, so I felt real grownup. I helped Chen Hui edit a translation of a speech he was to give before a Belgian delegation of businessmen.

WHAT DID I DO AS A TOURIST?

The greatest pleasure of traveling alone is being alone. To quote a forgotten source: "A degree of loneliness sharpens the perceptions wonderfully whilst traveling."

One of the best aspects of my three-week stay in Xian was leisure time for shopping, sight-seeing, and assimilating the local tourist scene. I shopped alone in two large department stores, visited the Shaanxi Historical Museum (because I wanted to see the artifacts at my own pace), and I visited the Little Wild Goose Pagoda (Both the Museum & Pagoda were on my itinerary when I visited Xian on the A&K Tour). I also returned to the Han Dynasty Yang Ling Mausoleum (Much improved and developed since my earlier visit, but no gift shop for souvenirs).

I decided not to return to the Terracotta Warriors museum & digs because I couldn't arrange to get any closer to the objects than tourists customarily do; I wanted an in-your-face private tour, but I couldn't arrange it during this trip. Maybe next time.

My favorite stops were the Muslim Bazaar and Great Mosque (with beautiful Chinese architecture), the "Banpo Village" (The 6,000 year old poorly lighted—but unique—remains of an early settlement in China), and the Taxing-shan Buddhist Temple (I visited that beauty twice).

I also checked out an outdoor pageant pavilion (with a boring costume parade and 15 minute Chinese Opera performance).

Other places and events in Xian that interested me:

1. The Forest of Tablets (Steles) at the Provincial Museum with enormous statuary and flat-faced stones with calligraphic inscriptions (Confucius' Analects, for example)

2. A rummage sale at the Taoist Monastery & Temple of the Eight Immortals

3. A highly-theatrical performance of a Las Vegas type spectacular show featuring dances & instrumental solos replete with costumes, scenery, and lighting.—show-busy but not unimpressive

4. A Tai Chi lesson, slow (like Chinese water torture) and painful

5. A surprise fireworks display—big deal.—viewed from my hotel window

6. A stroll on top of the city wall from the South Gate

ENCOUNTERS WITH REAL PEOPLE:

I had four people-to-people encounters I truly liked:

1. Dormitory visits with small groups of students, listening to them fire questions at me and sing popular songs (some in English), and watching then lean forward eagerly listening to me respond.

2. A visit to a nameless farm town where the farmers live in concrete and tile houses without any heating or cooling systems, their children showing off for our tour group without a care in the world.

3. Three encounters at the Institute for Finance & Economics graduate school with both male and female students in small groups, discussing personal impressions of our respective countries.

4. A home visit with a Chinese family for a dumpling dinner. Here's the report I prepared for inclusion in the team's daily journal:

<u>Wednesday, October 25, 2000, a Journal Entry</u>

After breakfast with the Gang of Ten, Edith Lockard (my team-teaching mate at The Foreign Languages Academy) and I left the hotel for our customary suicide ride to school where we each taught two 90-minute sessions. The school secretary took pictures of me in action, so, of course I overacted enormously and acted thrilled when I persuaded a student to change her pronunciation of the word "noodah" to "noodles." It's noodles, not noodah, okay? I'm sure she was singing to herself: "I say noodah; and you say noodle—"

Returning to the hotel, I joined the ladies who lunch, and we sloppily slurped noodah without butter—no big deal for folks who don't eat butter on their noodah.

That evening we had dinner with Edith and Warren Lowe, hosted by Zheng Jun (President of the Foreign Language Assn.) at the home of one of his friends. The friend was introduced as "The Boss," a contractor with a big smile who makes millions of yuan annually, therefore, middle-class status. He and his smiling wife, daughter, and son, taught us to make dumplings, sitting around their dinner table.

166   BEST AND WORST TRAVELS

How To Make Chinese Dumplings

First they covered the table with a thin sheet of plastic (The Chinese cover their tables—even their table clothes—with ultra thin, slippery, obnoxious plastic), then they brought in dumpling dough the size of a loaf of American white bread.

The boss's daughter cut a section of the dough, stretched it into a rope, and pinched off tiny pieces. Then she rolled each piece into a little pancake, and we each plopped dollops of a pork and veggie mix (prepared by the boss' wife) into the center of the pancake and sealed each dumpling for eternity. We made over two hundred during the next hour, chatting with one another incomprehensibly, smiling and laughing through a great language barrier.

The smiling boss' wife cooked the two thousand dumplings in a hot water pot, and served them in several bowls with instructions for us to dip them into our saucers containing rice vinegar, soy sauce, and oil.

Edith, Warren and I took our first bites of those little suckers, fearing the worst. But what happened was we started looking at each other as if this stuff was really, really good. Damn. Even without butter.

I must have eaten two hundred thousand dumplings before I finally fell over on the floor, stuffed. I had to be coaxed to eat another two million.

Warren said he was only going to eat four, but he ate twelve, and he might have eaten more but he embarrassed himself with his lack of chopstick proficiency. Then the soup was served, the same water the dumplings were boiled in, and it was just terrible. It tasted like water used to boil dumplings in. Naturally, we didn't say anything tacky about the soup—not just to be polite—but because the dumplings were so unforgettably delicious, their taste offset our disappointment with the soup.

Sheng Jun said to our smiling hosts, "Well, we've eaten your food, and now it's time to go. Goodbye," about as unceremonious an exit as I have ever witnessed.

Our hosts posed for pictures, then we literally tripped down four flights of stairs in the semi-dark, boarded our van, and returned to our quarters—never having enjoyed dumplings so much as we did last night.

A LECTURE BY A CHINESE DOCTOR OF HOMEOPATHIC MEDICINE:

We had a lecture by a Chinese doctor, Dr. Zhang Lian Chen who, accompanied by his wife, explained that the Chinese believe in four means of treating illness: Medicinal Herbs, Physical Massage, Acupuncture, and Qi Jong (kee shong). He said with concentration, he could induce a flow of "chi" (energy) allowing him to heal physical ailments through massage therapy. When he asked for volunteers, I allowed him to demonstrate his skill on me in front of the other GVs, working on my neck and shoulders. I felt both pain and pleasure.

I made an appointment with him; he failed to show up; but he sent his wife (his "associate") who did a pretty thorough job on me; afterwards, however, I felt more pain than pleasure in my lower back, and it took me about a week to recuperate.

I was amused and annoyed when she was working on my back with one hand and holding her cell phone to talk with the other, briefly.

I feel that my disappointment was a result of having been setup to expect a psychic flow of "chi." I was then—and am now—skeptical.

A LECTURE ON CHINESE CUSTOMS:

I enjoyed a lecture by Professor Xu, former head of the English Department at Northwest China University who characterized himself and his countrymen as being modest (and proud of it) and industrious (but not ambitious). He said the Chinese are like a hot water flask, cold on the outside, but hot inside.

On marriage & family, he said the one child per family rule applies only to city dwellers, not farmers and not minorities. The idea of three and four Chinese generations of families living under the same roof no longer applies widely. Children still feel they should take care of their elders, but the formalities in those relationships are gone. Kids no longer kow-tow, and elders no longer reward good behavior with money. There is no social security program in place in China, so people without personal savings become impoverished in old age. The divorce rate in China has increased to 40 percent.

On behaviors, there is no "ladies first" tradition in China, no hugging, and no familiarity with persons of the opposite sex in public. The Chinese have borrowed our Labor Day, also use of the term "Bye-bye," and asking for doggie bags at restaurants. Very few wives take their husbands family name after marriage; and children sometimes take their mothers' last names if they're ashamed of their fathers.

A LECTURE ON CHINESE EDUCATION:

Mr. Zheng Jun, director of the school where I taught, said every year in "Black July," all middle school students compete in tests to be admitted to state colleges. Those who fail the test (at least half of those taking it) may continue studying in a private school toward a diploma available for "self-taught" students. A third kind of diploma may be earned by taking tests through TV instruction.

All children in China are required to advance to 9th grade status, even farmers' children. At any time, children may be sent to state-run boarding schools when their fathers say, "There's room for only one emperor in this family."

[Most students studying English are taught textbook language without being instructed by native speakers of English. That would sound deplorable and ridiculous—except, of course, that's how foreign languages are taught in the States more often than not.

The major problem I had with students was determining how much English they were able to comprehend because I could seldom tell from their speech; and yet, when I would glance over their notebooks and dictionaries, I could tell they had studied both vocabulary and syntax. Usage was their downfall, and their instructors were, evidentially, little help.]

FOODS & RESTAURANTS:

All our breakfasts were held in our hotel's unceremonial breakfast room where most tour groups seemed to converge (and where there were several nationalities and groups like American Elderhostel).

Lunch was generally served in a smaller dining room in the hotel, but we often walked to nearby restaurants.

For dinners, we walked or taxied to specialty restaurants (For example, a dinner theatre specializing in 17 kinds of dumplings and, onstage, dancing girls) for dumplings, chow mien, a Mongolian hot pot, Muslin noodles & beef, a Hunan menu, and dinners with a wide variety of dishes.

The excitement of eating out was increased exponentially by traffic confrontations en route.

PREPARATION REQUIRED FOR GOING ON SIGHT-SEEING TRIPS:

Every time I left the hotel to go for a walk or to see sites, I organized stuff that I expected to need (or find useful) in pockets. I was amazed that I felt I usually needed 15 things:

Left pants pocket: Wash&Dri packets, Kleenex, Room Key, Safe Deposit Key
Right pants pocket: Purel hand sanitizer, Eyedrops, Coughdrops, Loose change
Shirt pocket: Butter packet, Sweetener packet

Left jacket pocket: Camera, Extra film canisters, Address list in both English & Chinese with Hotel return address (Very important)

Right jacket pocket: Small bottle of drinking water

WALKING AROUND XIAN (OR ANYWHERE ELSE) BY ONESELF:

On tours with conventional tour groups, many participants say they feel they've been herded through historical sites with time constraints imposed by a group leader. I think that—even when a person has only one partner—time spent at a site is determined the same way, by hanging out for as long as the other fellow wants to and splitting the difference.

When I return to places where I was herded on a time schedule the first time, I realize—more often than not while setting my own pace—that there's only so much to see and do. And only those objects that compel my attention (for whatever reason) slow my pace. Funny, but when I see something for a second time by myself, I go faster—unless it's something I want to study seriously or just soak up.

THE WEATHER IN XIAN:

After two weeks of polluted smog and cold drizzling rain, the sun broke through on Sunday, Oct. 29, and continued for a few days, revealing dust and mud caked on virtually everything. The entire city looked grim, grimy, and gloomy.

In China, very few coal-burning furnaces have scrubbers, so coal smoke and diesel exhaust hang in the air, mixed with dust and fog. Xian is not pretty. You can't see the architecture for the dirty buildings. And the smell of automobiles in traffic is toxic. It's hard to appreciate beauty with noxious distractions.

I had planned to use this quote in my journal, "Once you've seen the sun rise on the other side of the world, it never looks the same again," but I never saw the sun rise. I just saw it glow, sometimes.

NOISES AND SMELLS:

The constant blaring of automobile horns (that mostly seem to be calibrated to produce angry, earsplitting, screaming sounds) is scary and sounds like two Chinese persons arguing, shouting at one another. The dirty pea soup fog that permeates the streets has enough smells to wrinkle the nose of a hardened world traveler: predominantly car exhaust but also urine, meats, cologne, dust, and pungent veggies. Air soup.

FINALLY: WHAT DO I THINK ABOUT GLOBAL VOLUNTEER'S PROGRAM IN CHINA?

When one considers that by the year 2010, the Chinese language will be spoken by over half the population of the world, it's clear that the Chinese need to learn English because we English-speakers have no plans to learn Chinese.

In classes, when students asked me, "What do Americans think of us?" I could only answer, "They don't think of you at all—except as a possible threat. You're a giant, and everybody's afraid of giants. But when you look at me and my comrades, you see that we're human beings just like you. If Americans could see you as I do, they'd probably like what they see."

When I ask then what they know of the States and our people, they don't know Texas from New York, and they can't hear southern from northern dialects. They're virtually clueless; and that kind of scares me because they know our language and how our respective governments feel, but they don't know us.

Every Chinese school child, by the age 9, has begun to study English with teachers of reading and writing—but not speaking. Instruction in conversational English is important, clearly, but I am extremely doubtful the 3 hours I spent (on average) with classes was useful. Even when you add up all the hours volunteered by GV teachers over a year's time, it ain't much. I think the chief purpose GVs serve in China is attitudinal.

I felt that our students considered us to be Americans who care about them. That's spreading global good will—and it's important that we represent our country in a positive way—even though I don't think we make a really significant difference in their language skills.

I'm convinced Chinese instructors of English need intensive instruction in oral skills. This GV program attracts participants who want to travel to a foreign land and do some good. An intensive course in English for Chinese teachers would do even more good. Sure, every little bit helps, but a very little bit is all this program can do—like a sparrow chipping away for all eternity at one brick on the great wall of China (to coin a Confucian-sounding phrase).

I also believe with one of the participants, "If you don't think something's possible, okay; just stay out of the way of the ones who do."

The Panama Canal

✦

A Virtual Photograph Album
November 9–19, 2000

A Google Earth photograph of the entire Panama Canal might make a great picture, but what the canal looks like isn't as important as what it is: An ingenious engineering miracle.

Nothing I can say about the Canal will do it justice; however, that won't stop me trying to convey some of the awe I felt when Barbara and I passed through the Canal on a cruise in 2000.

>Open the virtual photo album here.<

Picture the sleepy, nonplused faces of Ramon & Barbara arising at 3:10 AM on **Thursday, November 9**, departing Salado at 4:15 am, arriving at the Austin airport at 5:20 AM with the same early-morning-uncomprehending, nonplused faces. (We never travel anywhere on an airplane or any other mode of conveyance that early in the morning, so what were we doing up at 3:10? The Princess Cruise Transportation Department had issued us "Take it or leave it" tickets less than one week prior to departure, and we had been persuaded by the cruise company they would take care of us. Right.)

Picture Barbara and Ramon checking in at the Delta Airlines departure gate by 6 am, still in a state of nonplusment.

But wait. Check out the looks on their faces at 6:30 when the gate attendant announces that the flight has been canceled. What....

This next picture is blurred because it's Ramon walking quickly to the Delta ticket counter, where he exchanges Delta tickets for American Airlines tickets, rerouting us through Dallas to our destination, Puerto Rico. Behind Ramon on line, note the 100 or so passengers who didn't walk as quickly as Ramon.

Here's a lonely-looking shot of Ramon waiting at a carousel for luggage he had checked in at Delta to be returned to him following the new issuance of tickets requiring him to take the suitcases to the AA desk where Barbara stands on line, waiting for seat assignments.

171

This is Ramon—with a chagrined (no longer nonplused) look on his face—joining Barbara who is now plussed off, at the AA desk. They discover they have narrowly missed the AA flight because Delta took 30 minutes to return the luggage.

Ah, but here's a photograph of the kindly AA desk agent who rebooked R&B on yet another flight, on American, adjusting the connection for a later flight from Dallas to Puerto Rico.

The look on Barbara's face saying, "Whatever."

Here's Ramon and Barbara, arriving at DFW AA gate C20, with a two hour wait between planes. Ramon has taken off his new shoes because they're killing him. He is sockfooted, walking around in the crowded terminal, seeking a store selling shoes. Only three people in the entire crowded airport notice he is sockfooted.

Here's a shot of a Ramon entering a golf shop at DFW's "E" terminal (located about two miles away from the "C" Terminal, accessible only by taxi since the entrance to the "C" tram is being rebuilt). It's one hour later, and Ramon is buying a pair of size 10 sandals (a half size too small)—the only men's footwear on sale at the Airport.

Another blurry shot of Ramon racing—tripping and bruising his toes in the ill-fitting sandals—back to the AA gate with only 30 minutes to spare before flight time.

But look. This is another kindly gate agent who—Hooray.—upgrades Ramon & Barbara to first class for the trip to Puerto Rico ostensibly because Ramon's a "Gold Card AA Member," but actually because the gate agent is a truly kind person.

This is the appeased (and pleased) look on Barbara's face as she sits next to her hero, enjoying first class seats, for the 4 1/2 hour flight to PR. [Good food is always important to Ramon; therefore, it is not unimportant to note that on that PR flight, Ramon enjoyed possibly the best airplane entree, "Shrimp Fritters," he's ever eaten aboard an aircraft.]

Arriving in Puerto Rico 15 hours after beginning the trip, here's Barbara and Ramon being transferred to the ship on a bus—crowded to the max—giggling uncontrollably because they're crammed into low-rider bus seats and can barely see out the window. They know that the only memory they will probably ever have of Puerto Rico will be the upper parts of buildings they pass in the night. And the driver is obviously trying to hit every pothole in Puerto Rico. They might as well laugh themselves silly.

Ohhhhh. This is their first view of the enormous Princess *Sun* at the PR dock, Ahhhhh., garlanded with lights. Note the smiles on the faces of all the low-riders on the bus. This was the best sight they had seen all day long.

Here's Ramon & Barbara, five minutes later, smile-less, standing on line at the terminal with hundreds of other grumpy late arrivals, waiting, waiting, waiting to flash passports and cruise tickets.

The passengers: Most of the women have big hair done up real good, and most of the men are wearing goofy smiles. Everybody's wearing outfits they think everybody else will be wearing. Ramon & Barbara roll their eyes as they form their first impressions of fellow passengers.

This shot was snapped one hour later: Barbara and Ramon embracing Barbara's cousin, Mary Lou & her husband, Jim Wagner, the two reasons the Carvers had been persuaded to sail on the *Sun* through the Panama Canal.

That same evening: the two couples sitting together at a Welcome Aboard show featuring a hyper-frenetic tour director, followed by a thoroughly obnoxious comedian poking fun at Bill & Hillary. Oh, shit. It's gonna be a long, awful trip.

A dress code prevails at dinners when passengers are told that there will be formal, informal, or casual nights with never a ratty-looking night, only ratty-looking breakfasts and lunches. Get a shot of that woman who has either disregarded or doesn't understand "casual attire" sitting at our table wearing a sequined T-shirt on the first formal night; then on a casual night check out her long dress with big bazoom cleavage. You can't see her knee hitting mine by accident under the table. (Get ready, Reader, or you won't be prepared for some risqué reading in a few pages …)

There she goes: seeking and finding another table and somebody else's knees to knock on. She's one of only a handful of aging passengers who look as if they might be sexually active. None look to be on the prowl. In fact, they mostly look as if they've settled into something more comfortable than classy.

What difference does all this make to Ramon, himself an aging, overweight globetrotter? None at all. In fact, he is perfectly disguised among the other dowdy dressers. [American tourists have no monopoly on bad taste or fat bad dressers. And would you believe. The ship's stores don't sell large or extra-large clothes, only small and medium-sized.] On ships and in public places the world over, we all study each other and wonder why the other guys are wearing funny-looking outfits and why good-looking wives allow them to get away with it.

Okay. Here we are the next day, **Friday, November 10**, arriving in St. Thomas, A Third World Retail Sales Opportunity, and the first in an unbroken chain of "Outstretched Palm Islands." The international greeting is "You gonna tip me, Mon?" There are beggars waiting for handouts on the streets and tourists waiting on lines at open air jewelry stores.

That's Barbara and me riding over speed bumps in an open-air, careening sight-seeing shuttle bus through hills and woods to the end of the line, a crowded beach.

Then B&R deciding they've seen better beaches elsewhere, thus choosing to remain aboard the bumpy bus, returning to the ship, cutting a swath through thousands of shoppers who pour out of four more cruise ships who've just docked in this overrated port on the same day.

A note about crowd manners: They're bad.

Most passengers are pushy and oblivious of other passengers, particularly at entrances, exits, in passing, at buffets, on elevators, in restrooms, and on vehicles (Have I left out anyplace?) Sometimes, the only way to make headway is to stand perfectly still so that the opposing stream of traffic clears a path for you, uncertain of the action you may be taking.

Some travelers have foreheads that glow, "Mentally Challenged."

Also note: When a crowd discovers something they want to stare at—like a screaming sick person being evacuated from the ship—they lean over railings like seabirds perched on the bleached bones of a beached whale, causing the ship to tilt.

Skip to the same evening where back aboard ship, you see R&B attending a welcoming cocktail party hosted by our tour organizers, then the Captain's reception (minus the Captain who was otherwise occupied), followed by a first-sitting dinner.

Later, look at all the sun-burned passengers sitting in the ship's theatre, watching a well-choreographed song and dance show featuring old show tunes. (That puzzled look on Ramon's face means he's wondering if anything other than goldie oldies will be performed at ship shows for the duration of the trip. Of course not, Ramon. Every performance is calculated to appeal to the over-sixty crowds aboard ship who want old tunes they can hum.)

Next day, **November 11th, Saturday**, picture an island (I had never heard of), Dominica. And see, there's Ramon and Jim Wagner getting into a crowded van, bouncing over the driver's favorite speedbumps, to a dirty little beach where, hot and sweaty, Ramon and Jim and about twenty other campers set sail and discover that sitting and paddling a badly-designed and leaky kayak is a pain in the ass and thigh muscles and back muscles and toes bruised and blistered.

Lookathere. Ramon bails out and boards the junker that follows the kayakers, gloating while the others paddle bravely, painfully on to the appointed shore where they snorkel and Ramon watches.

One hour later, this is Ramon returning with his new friends to the original shore, boarding the crowded van, and bouncing back—without missing one of the already cited potholes and speedbumps—to the ship.

Wait a minute. What's Ramon doing, entering the ship's spa to get a pedicure in hopes of easing the pain from wearing the foot killing shoes noted above? The pedicure and foot massage doesn't do much for the blisters and bruises, but the pedicure person accidentally drops Ramon's foot down between her legs three times. Gosh. (Neither Ramon nor the Reader of this report was expecting that little bonus anecdote. Right? Ramon has been asked by some of my readers with prurient interests to jazz up his reports with gratuitous sexual escapades. Imagine a fat, old man writing stories about libidinous misadventures. I don't think so.)

Returning to the mini-suite, Ramon finds Barbara worn to a frazzle, after a harrowing trip over rocky terrain to a major sight seeker's disappointment, "Dominica's Famous Emerald Pool," a scam. The exertion has reportedly caused her cousin's heart to fibrillate. Picture the two women fearing they would never make it back to the ship.

Are we having fun yet? Do we enjoy "adventure" cruise land options? No and no.

Visualize R&B resolutely napping in order to recover from their exertions in time to eat dinner, attend a show, and commiserate with cousins.

On **Sunday, November 12**, picture the enormous ship—a massive hotel afloat—docking at Barbados, that sweaty little island that R&B had visited years ago and that they had no desire to visit again, sharing restaurant meals with scrawny birds at open air tables.

Here's B&R, leisurely strolling on the ship's promenade, eating mediocre pizza midship, then in their cabin, napping, then enjoying an afternoon snack in a public room, then taking another nap, then writing a journal entry and posting an email, then having drinks with the Wagners, then eating dinner, then attending a show full of familiar French songs, yawn, then a snack, finally to bed, worn out.

[Indolence. That's what a cruise to nowhere is—with ports of call for shopping and sightseeing to break the blissful monotony. At this point, I could introduce an argument on behalf of the poor and indigent of the world and say rich folks cruise and poor folks lose. The only problem with that argument is neither rich nor poor sail on cruise ships. Only the middle class cruises. The non-middle-class reader may want to skip the following few paragraphs if not truly interested in cruises and ships.

Reader, you will never run into Princess Margaret on a cruise ship for two reasons: 1) She wouldn't be caught dead on one, and 2) she *is* dead. I knew you were middle-class or you wouldn't be reading these paragraphs …

To date, Barbara and I have sailed on two large ships, three medium-sized ships, one small ship, one yacht, two flatbed ferries, two barges, and an icebreaker. The passengers have all been middle-class and/or nouveau riche. The old rich own their ships, and they sail whenever and wherever they please—unless they want to economize incognito.]

<u>An interpolation: What do middle-class cruise passengers expect?</u>

1. *Accommodations* are very important. The advantage of unpacking only one time in only one location while traveling is one of the most compelling aspects of cruising.

    Some folks want inexpensive rooms because they'd rather spend their money on other priorities. Barbara and I want a cabin we can enjoy hiding out in with a verandah on port side (A verandah is an important feature in warm weather, inconsequential in cold climates.)

    Other cabin features we appreciated on the *Sun*: The acoustical sound insulation in walls between cabins was excellent. The phone systems were relatively sophisticated. We had a queen-sized bed, a drawing room area, marble tile in both the shower, toilet, and entrance areas and ceilings. We asked for and got free fruit bowls daily. Very agreeable.

2. *Food* is next in importance (How else is it possible to stay fat). And food service. The *Sun*'s dining room food is good, but their evening service is professional, personal, and presentation is superior. Lunch service gets a mixed review after having to ask one's waiter to be sure hot food is served hot.

    The ship's pizza parlor, snack bar and room service food is satisfactory, but again, the service is excellent.

    But here's a big common complaint: Unlike expensive ships (that don't keep tabs on consumption of booze and other bottled drinks), behemoths like the *Princess Sun* charge for everything but juices, coffee and tea—even soft drinks and bottled water—plus gratuities. What a nuisance.

3.   *Everything else available on a ship* is optional.

Like most cruise ships for pleasure-seekers, the Princess has karaoke, singles & couples bars and both disco & musical ensembles. There are exercise rooms, swimming pools in calm seas, hot tubs, sunning decks—even a deck where women may go braless. Also massage and beauty parlor facilities where they push items you don't need. "Art auctions" are a rip-off, with auctioneers urging passengers to buy art for absurd "investment purposes." And a closet-sized "Business Center" where you pay a fee to use a computer terminal. Gambling room action requires no class, only cash. Also Big-time Bingo. The photo shop displays thousands of processed smiling faces, usually flattering.

There's no charge for use of a paneled library, a game room, and a theatre for movies, stage shows and lectures by classy lecturers.

The Pursers aboard most ships are the bosses. It's not unusual to see ten people lined up at the 30 ft long purser's desk where two resentful-looking pursers chant, "It is not possible" or "We are so sorry, but it cannot be helped." They are masters of condescending indifference and arrogance. Mothers, don't let your children grow up to be pursers.

What else is worth noting? Floral arrangements on the ship are sensational.

A Reality Check.

Picture Ramon & Barbara, on **Sunday, November 13th**, at sea for the entire day, making the following idle observations for inclusion in this journal:

1.   Most of the world's infirm are on this ship. The *Sun* has more wheelchairs & walkers than children aboard; of course, most kids are in school in November, thank goodness.

2.   There's a scandalously obese women who rides around the ship on her 3-wheeled trike, her ass spilling out over the sides of her seat like a pendulous saddlebag.

3. Ka-boom. Was that the sound of thunder or the growl of an extinct vol-
    cano threatening adventures we haven't bargained for. Fooey, it was just
    thunder.

4. At lunch, I found the table manners of a guy sitting across from me at
    another table hard to ignore. His "Aruba" tank top didn't bother me; it
    was his wet bushy beard, chest hair and armpits. And he kept scratching
    his body parts. And then he sneezed and used a table napkin to wipe his
    nose. Then he cleaned his nails (Tell me when you've had enough), and
    then—Enough. Not all passengers have class.

5. By now, I've had plenty of chances to chat up folks on the trip, and
    everybody I've met acts likable. "Where're y'all from?" Appearances
    aren't misleading however; most look uncomfortable in their travel
    clothes. "We can't wear shorts in the dining room tonight." But they're
    as congenial a homogeneous crowd as I could ever hope to meet on an
    elevator. "Will you push 9 for me? I'm wet as a duck." Lots of friends
    traveling with friends. A few lonely couples. And as the trip progresses,
    most (like me) seem progressively willing to talk with strangers (like
    me), but I have no reason to believe I'm meeting princes and potentates;
    rather, it's like visiting with Cousin Beau and Aunt Estelle following the
    funeral. "Eddie never looked better in that casket."

On **November 14th, Monday**, picture Aruba—not quite as junky as the
other two islands we've visited, all owned and operated by the rich and populated
by the poor to exploit the middle-class.

Here's Jim and Ramon descending 150 feet below sea level for a thirty minute
submarine ride, viewing a desertscape with cactus-looking coral and colorful fish
swimming about, directionless.

Then, returning to the pier, see Jim and Ramon shop (without buying anything) in crowded strip malls, then back to the ship, to lunch, to nap, to read, to
write, to eat dinner, and to sleep—no productivity.

"When are we gonna get to the Panama Canal, Daddy?"

Patience, kiddo.

November 15th, Tuesday, we arrive at Cartegna, Columbia, and watch for a
half hour a series of maneuvers on a dock the length of two football stadiums.
First a view of the empty pier, then longshoremen, then police with a drug-sniff-
ing dog, then 50+ busses with yellow-shirted drivers and tour guides, then—in
this setting—ten dark-skinned dancing girls in native costumes, arms akimbo,

flailing, flouncing their hips with bare-chested boys moving—quick tempo—in an ambitiously choreographed series of primitive dances calculated to make a missionary blanch. Funny what choreographers can get away with in the name of "Native dances".

In the meantime, dock bureaucrats and tourists from the boat move onto the dock, a mass of humanity that completely disappears after thirty minutes, gone on tours and to shopping centers.

See Barbara and Ramon opt for a taxi ride to Old Town Aruba where they are set upon by hundreds of souvenir salespersons, more relentless than all the merchants of China and Egypt put together. After Ramon receives several friendly pats on his backside, he takes his billfold out of his back pocket and carries it—fearing the pats were preliminary to getting his pockets picked.

Watch R&B return to the ship, buying Colombian coffee at a dockside souvenir shop, then an inexpensive costume jewelry purchase, a Pre-Columbian broach.

Then lunch, nap, tea, email, drinks en suite, a formal diner, then a show, then back to sea.

"Any signs of Panama yet?"

Yes, there it is, **November 16, Wednesday**, at 6 am, a view of the Atlantic breakwater entrance to the Panama Canal.

One hour later, visualize the ship—guided by trains on either side of the ship—entering the three Gatun (the name of the village displaced when the Canal was built) locks, keeping the enormous *Sun* centered—rising to the level of the man-made Gatun lake, 85 feet above sea level.

First impressions: Not much to look at, but knowing thousands of workers died from disease and accidents while building the Canal, one can't escape feeling this place—like the Great Wall of China and the Giza Pyramids—is full of ghosts.

Watch the ship cruising through a dense tropical rain forest (The rain falling sporadically) while passengers look at trees that don't seem so tall from the 14th deck of a floating hotel.

Okay, the big questions everybody asks: Why was the canal built utilizing the great dammed-up river lake above the center of the country? Why didn't the engineers just cut a path through the rain forest without going up 85 feet? After all, the two oceans have the same sea levels.

And the answer is the two oceans don't have the same *tides.*

Ahhhhhh, that would mean if the two seas were connected at this point, the canal would be a great tidal basin, flooding one moment, drying up the next, virtually unnavigable.

But why go up 85 feet? Because the Lake makes it possible for gravity to control the rise and fall of water in the locks. Panama has well over 100 inches of rainfall each year, a more-than-adequate supply to keep the lake full—for so long as the rain forest isn't destroyed by private or national interests. [I hate to just slip a hit of ecological disaster into this narrative, but saving that rainforest is absolutely vital.]

Any other questions? Well, here are the answers:

The cost of one-way transit for the *Sun* Princess through the Canal was about $174,000.

The capacity of the Canal's locks is 1,000 ft long by 110 feet wide (beam). (The Princess *Sun* is 857' long and 106' wide, leaving 2' on either side. Whew, what a squeak.) Ship builders the world over continue to design large ships to these dimensions in the event that someday they might want to pass through that Canal.

The locks gates are made of steel, hollow and sealed on the inside to insure buoyancy, 7 feet thick, 47–82 feet high, and 60 feet wide.

It's particularly impressive watching the ship rising and lowering at about 1 inch per second, like a cork bobbing, secured only by the lines held taut by the trains at each side.

More virtual pictures: Watch the Natives and canal workers wave and salute as the ship passes though the locks. Waving back always generates smiles. Even for folks who don't feel like smiling.

Nine hours later, after descending through Pedro Miguel locks and the Miraflores locks, the ship passes within view of low tide mudflats under the "Bridge of the Americas" spanning the western breakwater and sails out into the pacific, leaving Panama City unexplored behind us (Evidentially, relations between Panamanians & Americans are still strained).

The Pacific looks just like the Atlantic.

Exhausted after all that Canal crossing, watch B&R nap, eat dinner, enjoy a movie, and return to their cabin to claim a "Certificate of Passage through the Panama Canal" made out to "Fill in the blank."

Observations about the sea: Great bodies of water are both awesome and scary, really scary. Like a window in a skyscraper, one could easily jump over the railing, into the sea and disappear from sight—by accident (risking the lives of your rescuers) or by design—with only the wake of the ship leading back to the jump site—*IF* anyone witnessed the jump. A splash or shout for help would go unnoticed, and a rough sea or night would hide the ship's wake. Someone would have to see you fall, and scream: "Stop! Man overboard!" and hope that someone who knows how to stop a ship is listening. On an ocean, one is in persistent peril. Of course, so is one in traffic on land.

Our lives are always in peril.

Thursday, November 17th, a ship at sea is a great place to be. This is a cruise ship, not an old-fashioned, purposeful ocean liner. The *Sun* isn't supposed to go somewhere. It's supposed to be a place to lie back and chill out, something I don't do well, but I try. Some folks can enjoy lying around the ship's pools, frying in the sun like puffy bacon strips.

This ship has plenty of deck chairs, many made of wood (Unlike the QE2 that has cheap plastic deck chairs), a lot of promenade space, and a wonderful play area for children, and a small "Cyberspace" game room for kids.

The ship's itinerary: This behemoth docks only at ports that are big enough and deep enough to accommodate dockside landing; we don't use tenders because it would probably take forever to unload the thousands of passengers aboard.

This ship docks only at sleazy islands with trashy public beaches full of oily-looking, black volcanic sand and overgrown weeds. Why do travel magazines lie about the beauty of these islands? I don't know; they may be writing about someplace else. Probably Princess Margaret's private island.

The weather is perfect; it's too hot and too steamy for me, but that's the way many people like their islands.

People aboard ship: On the first night of the cruise, one of our dinner table party volunteered, "Israelis are fascists; they were taught by masters." Furthermore, he said, "All the troubles of the world can be attributed to fundamentalist religious beliefs. I'm a United Methodist, and no, we're not fundamentalists." And that was just the salvo he fired over the bow on the first night we met him.

On the last day of the voyage, I watched a couple, oversized, both wearing souvenir caps; she looked like a ruined maiden with bad hair who had been rescued from a pirate party boat, the "Cholly Roger (Bermuda Registry)," wearing a T-shirt with a great panda bear on the front, and he looked like a lumbering, lovable Disney bear. They were happy with each other. And I was happy for them, but I had no desire to hang out with them.

Picture Ramon & Barbara arriving at Costa Rica (a Banana Republica) debarking the ship on **Sunday, November 19th**, at 9:30 in the morning, riding over Costa Rican roads in a filthy jam-packed bus (Important. Respectable tour companies simply don't squeeze their passengers into dirty busses.). I think we got what we paid for.

Watch our two protagonists, arriving at the San Jose airport two hours later, standing on line another hour, eating a ten dollar fried cheese sandwich (The only choice was fried or not fried) at the Airport tourist canteen.

Barbara and Ramon are neither commiserating nor speaking to each other until—Watch the smug smiles light up their faces after Ramon persuades a gate agent to upgrade them, gratis, to 1st class for the trip to Atlanta. Hot dog. Rejoice. Rejoice.

Ramon, you sly boots, you've done it again.

Wait a minute. Costa Rica, flying east to Atlanta; then, west to Austin? Yep. Remember the Princess Transportation "Take it or Leave it" ticket arrangements? Fantastic. First class.

Finally, following the transfer from Atlanta to Austin (after a two-hour delay trying to phone friends in Atlanta), study the nonplused faces of Ramon and Barbara at 1:30 AM as they schlep their luggage (overstuffed with coffee beans) into the trunk of their van.

The ride home to Salado is uneventful and—even with road repairs in progress—it wasn't bumpy.

Final photograph: Sunset on a cold and rainy day after a week of rainy days, but no matter, it's Texas, and it's home.

From both Portland, OR, or Portland, ME, Amtrak is a punishing way to travel.

Amtrak Misadventures:

Part I,

Boston to Temple

✦

August 15–20, 2000

Bottom Line: Don't go anywhere by Amtrak unless you get a reduced rate as I did.

Or unless it's a short distance, and you're taking your 8 year-old grandson for a birthday trip just so he'll know what a train is.

Okay. I took a trip on Amtrak returning from a visit with friends in Maine. I wanted to see if I would enjoy Amtrak as an adventure/transportation option like a cruise ship (All trains and ships have in common is waking up the following morning somewhere else).

I took the trip for pleasure, but the trip I took wasn't.

The trip began on August 15, 2000, when I flew from Killeen, Texas, to Portland, Maine, where I rented a car to visit with long-term friends, Joyce Mayer and her family, in Camden/Rockport. The next day I drove to Boothbay/Southport for a great overnight visit with friends.

Then I drove 3 hours to Boston, turned in the rental car, taxied to the depot, and began my journey of a million miles. The trip to Maine by air had been okay, the rental car was no problem, and I made the connection in Boston easily with directions the friends gave me.

I boarded three trains—one after another—on the four-day trip: The Shoreliner (Boston overnight to Washington, DC), The Cardinal (DC to Chicago), and the Texas Eagle (Chicago overnight to Temple with a stopover in Dallas). They were all late departing and arriving.

In Washington I had breakfast and a visit a friend & former student. In Chicago I spent the day with another friend & former student. In Dallas, I had dinner with friends & former students.

What I enjoyed most was sleeping with the train rocking me to sleep each night. I liked riding with my feet propped up, looking out the window at the world passing by. And I particularly enjoyed time I spent alone. It's no problem being alone when one knows there will be someone waiting for you at the end of a trip.

But that's it. If my reader wants a happy ending, stop here.

All aboard.

The Dining Car

I met some interesting multicultural personalities in the dining car, and I appreciated every new encounter. That's one of the best things that happened on the trip, sharing tables and meeting weirdoes at mealtime on a train

We were served poor food on plasticized paper plates (usually with paper napkins and plastic utensils set out on worn plastic tablecloths), and indifferent service. Each dining car was run like a fiefdom by a lord of the manor and his union members. The ones who weren't hostile were downright surly. I learned early that if you don't sit where the manager tells you, he threatens you'll have to wait for a later seating—and he means it.

On my first meal in the Shoreliner dining car, I was told to sit at a table where I had to ride backwards, facing suitcases and some stacked paper bags in the seat opposite me. Every time they'd fall out into the aisle, someone would amble over and restack them without apology. That Dining Car doubled as a storage room.

Overstuffed seats in the dining booths on all the trains were comfortable but in need of repair. Even the duct tape patching the cover of seats was worn thin.

The only upscale item on the table was Equal sweetener. The only upscale item on all the trains I rode was Equal sweetener.

The Lounge Car

"Lounge Car" is a euphemism for refugee camp.

Seats are designed for occupants to spin around, blocking the aisle, creating a hazardous thoroughfare.

Many Lounge Car passengers wear curious hairstyles Easter Egg colors. There are all manner of pierced body parts. The rule governing costuming is simply "Dress Down, But Wear Shoes." ("And don't forget to bring a skuzzy, dirty quilt or blanket so that when snoozing, the blanket can flood into the aisle and trip folks walking through the car.")

There is a café located on the lower deck of the Lounge Car on all trains with tables and bossy, humorless attendants selling Pepsi, candy and chips, etc. The Café floor is always littered with trash.

So What's to See?

Amtrak's motto could be "See Ugly America Onboard as well as Outside the Train."

Folks who live beside train tracks don't spend much on landscaping. Therefore, railroad track real estate isn't very scenic. Sure, there are beautiful natural wonders like trees and mountains and sunsets for passengers to look at, particularly in unlikely places like West Virginia, but single- and double-wide trailers and derelict shacks are everywhere, relieved only by the backsides of badly-maintained buildings.

Alongside tracks in Texas, a defoliation chemical had been used to kill weeds that might come in proximity with the tracks. There was evidence of brush fires, probably caused by dead undergrowth. Dead trees looked like they might burn crisply if set afire in the drought-plagued countrysides.

The worst blight on the landscape I ever saw was—no contest—the jail at Texarkana, Texas, where barbed- and razor-wire is wrapped around the ugliest ramshackle building in the world. I thought, "Don't ever screw up, or they might incarcerate you here, watching trains pass by."

The First Class Sleepers

For the first leg of the trip I bought a ticket for a "Viewliner Sleeper;" that's a small 1st class sleeper with two seats facing each other, converting to upper and lower singles. There's room to stand up, but if you share the room with someone, one of you will have to keep getting out of the way.

As anyone who has ever traveled on a train sleeper will tell you, there is no way to change clothes standing up on a bunk bed.

There is a covered toilet and sink with a mirror built in, but you have to kneel on the toilet cover to use the sink & mirror if the bed hasn't been converted to a seat after breakfast by the attendant (and it isn't converted until you ask the attendant and he acts like he's doing you a big favor).

Oh yeah, once the seats have been converted into a lower bed, access to the toilet is extremely difficult.

Dressing in the morning, I amused myself flopping about on my butt, my knees, my back, and my side. But then I stopped laughing and started saying "Shit." Repeatedly, excessively.

Incidentally, if you require space for a suitcase, you discover it must be squeezed into the postage stamp floor space in front of the toilet (leaving you no place to stand to pee) or strapped to the wall, inaccessible.

For the second portion of the trip, I paid for a First Class Sleeper with a couch, easy chair and fold-away table. A sink and mirror is easily available—except when the lower berth is down. Two adults (or one adult and two children, or four children, fighting) might find this arrangement fun—but not for long.

Get this: The toilet enclosure serves as a shower stall with instructions to "Sit on the tiny toilet when showering. Hold the shower head in one hand. Press the start button. Be prepared for 100 degree F water to spray over you and the toilet for 30 seconds. Push the button again for additional 30 second spray bursts." Can my reader guess how long it takes before the cold water in the hose becomes scaldingly hot?

There are no instructions when low water pressure causes the water to dribble, but you learn quickly that you have to hold the button pushed with your wrist while your hand holds the shower head, and the other hand scrubs your body, and you keep bouncing against the wall. And you keep thinking, "Surely, there is a better engineering solution to this. I emerged from this plastic toilet/shower chamber with the curious sensation of having returned from a space exploration.

[A public shower stall on the level below was much larger, located in a room big enough for wheelchair access, and it was disgustingly dirty. There is a public toilet with receptacles larger than the tiny private bowls. And dirtier.]

There are tiny towels for use drying off your body. There are no bath-sized towels.

I called for the attendant to come make up my bed.

I called again 10 minutes later.

I waited until she appeared, apologizing that she has more work to do than she can possibly do, and she likes passengers who understand that her salary isn't enough to support her family. She finished pulling out the couch seat, converting it to a double bed for midgets, turning down the threadbare sheet and smoothing a blue blanket (that had probably never seen the inside of a washing machine), and plumping plumped the pillow she assured me: "You gon' like this."

I did not respond.

I requested a bottle of water, and she returned a half hour later with two bottles, assuring me I'm a passenger who understands how difficult her job is, etc.

I locked her out, and she and other staff went into the unoccupied cabin next door where they laughed loudly, keeping me awake. I rapped soundly on the wall to let them know I could hear them: Rap-rap-rap-rap-rap.

I expected silence, but after a brief pause, there was a burst of maniacal laughter as several people rapped back: Brrrrap-rap-rap-rap-rap-rap-rap-rap.

I gnashed my teeth and discovered that gnashing in time with the clickity-clack (Don't fight back) covered the sound of their voices—if not the variety of squeaks and squawks of the misaligned doors and parts of cabinets. Also, my imagination kept me awake wondering where weird sounds were coming from.

Next thing I know, I'm waking up the following morning.

After a layover, en route from Washington, we got sidetracked by a freight train. Then another freight train. Then another freight train passed us by. We were three hours late when we arrived.

So why do freight trains get priority? Easy, freight train companies own the rails.

Later that day, our departure out of Chicago was delayed an hour when freight cars were hooked onto the tail end of the Texas Eagle, making us a slow passenger/freight train.

On the third portion of the trip, I got a slightly better first class compartment, designed to allow me to sit in the easy chair facing forward rather than backwards.

When the attendant made up the bed for the evening, she reversed the wafer-thin mattress so that my head would be located just under the air vent. I turned the mattress around, facing the window, and the noise of the train increased, but it was either noise or air blast.

That night, doors between cars opened and slammed shut; 1,000 car freight trains passed by whooshing; every cabinet and door hinge in the cabin twittered; it was an inharmonic, cacophonic symphony. Squeak-squeak, clickity-clack, gnash-gnash, take me home to Jesus.

The following day, I got off the Texas Eagle at Dallas for a short visit, slept overnight at the Hyatt Reunion Hotel (very nice.), then reboarded the same train headed south, two-hours late, but this time in coach. The air-conditioning had gone off in the first coach I entered, so I found a seat in the next car on the port side where I wouldn't be spotlighted by the Sun. An attendant passed by and asked if I wanted one of the dirty little pillows she carried. I said no, thank you, so she gave me one anyway.

I reclined—three inches at most.

The ceiling tiles had duct tape peeling off.

My foot rest was broken and duct-taped to the foot rest next to mine.

Even though the seats were roomier than airplane seats, I can't sleep on my back, and the fetal position simply doesn't work sideways on seats designed for back-sleepers.

All those poor folks who went without a first class sleeper had suffered for thousands of miles.

I had been lucky, and I just didn't know it.

Finally: I have been told Amtrak serves an important purpose, allowing folks to choose between various modes of transportation; however, first class travel by rail is not cheap, and coach class for any length of time is pure torture. Nobody I talked with aboard any of the trains was happy about the trip. And there was no evidence of good quality in any area of service or equipment on the trains.

I concluded that the management obviously feels passengers or employees will abuse or steal anything of high quality. And that attitude argues that if passengers were confronted with quality, they wouldn't know it.

A Recommendation: I strongly recommend that private freight train company managers replace Amtrak management and be required to operate passenger trains efficiently.

Furthermore, I believe all management should ride their own trains periodically.

But what do I know?

Amtrak Misadventures:

Part II,

Seattle to Temple

♦

January 9–14, 2001

Same Bottom Line: Don't go by Amtrak unless you're an inveterate train buff. Or unless you have a high pain threshold. Or you get another special reduced rate. Or unless you just wanna see if I'm making a big deal out of nothing.

So Why did I take A Second Trip on Amtrak?

I complained to Amtrak about the first trip, and I was rewarded with an invitation to take another trip courtesy of Amtrak. How else does one cash in a "Transportation Certificate" but to use it for the only purpose negotiable?

January's a slow month, and it seemed a good idea at the time to explore the US West Coast, riding down from Seattle to L. A. on the Coast Starlight and across from L. A. to Temple, Texas, on the Texas Eagle.

Prelude

After flying from Killeen, Texas, to Seattle, Washington, I stayed at the Olympic Four Seasons hotel, enjoying the luxury of a classy lodging (at a special January rate).

I called Barbara to say, "I'm using my cell phone, and it's not costing anything more than the basic phone rate, so won't it be nice staying in contact as I travel?"

She said, "Real nice."

A few blocks from the hotel is the Seattle Art Museum where I went to see a John Singer Sargent exhibit—important paintings and sketches.

And then I rode a monorail through a stunningly beautiful, awesome architectural palace designed by Frank Gehry at the foot of Seattle's Space Needle. The building houses the EMP, or "Experience Music Project" (a curious euphemism for the world's biggest Rock & Roll museum).

I viewed the building from the top of the Space Needle, and then, walking around the front, back, and sides reverentially, I kept saying to myself: "Wow. What a wonderful building."

A couple of years before, I had visited Gehry's Guggenheim Museum designed for Bilboa, Spain, similar in style, and I found both trips akin to a spiritual pilgrimage.

But the interior was something else—a cacophonic Babel. I tried appreciating Jimi Hendrick's literal and metaphorical mutilation of musical instruments (a fragment of one of the guitars he busted was on display). All I could think was "Gilbert & Sullivan makes sense to me; this doesn't."

My judgment: the building was awesome; the EMP was awful.

The "Coast Starlight"

Thursday morning, January 10, 2001, I boarded the Coast Starlight and immediately noted a difference in the trains I had traveled on this past summer.

The first class deluxe compartment I occupied wasn't located on the coastal side of the southbound trip, but there wasn't really all that much coast to see, and I was usually in the dining car anyway when we passed by the ocean or sound or mud flats or scenic spots.

I called Barbara on my cell phone to tell her I had recharged the battery for the trip. Then I settled back and as before, I particularly enjoyed the time en route reflecting, meditating, planning, budgeting (Budgeting? Yep.), and reading. And I particularly enjoyed sleeping.

It was a kind of spiritual retreat. Even preparing budgets is spiritual when there are no time or space constraints.

But unexpectedly, miles and miles down the track, at midnight on Thursday, I awoke, and—sensing something strange about to happen—I pulled the curtains of my windows back to discover a movie-setting landscape of bright moonlight with inches of snow covering everything, day at night.

And then suddenly. A massive mountain loomed. For an instant it appeared to be the Mother of all Mountains. Straight up. Out of nowhere. Mystical. Incredible. How'd they do that.

I learned later I had discovered Mt. Shasta dressed with snow & a full moon, a special showing for me alone.

Quite often during the 4-day trip I felt I was seeing unique things out that window, specially planned for me. And I really didn't regret—when surprised by beauty—that I didn't have anyone to share my reaction with. Quite often, I said aloud: "Ohmygosh, lookit that." and "Whadaya think of that."

Barbara would surely have enjoyed the view, but the room simply wasn't big enough for the two of us. Neither of us likes crowding, and when traveling by American trains, two's a crowd.

The room was markedly cleaner and better maintained than any of the other compartments I had ridden in, but there was a strong draft of air moving through the vent above the mirror and sink—very difficult for combing hair, making my challenge to fix my face and hair even more difficult than usual. The toilet was upgraded to flush itself when the lid was closed. That upgrade prevented pushing the shower button by mistake when seeking to flush. The mattress was lumpy, and that made me grumpy.

The First Class Lounge and Diner

I met some interesting folks at a "wine tasting" in the first class Lounge on Thursday and in the dining car, and I enjoyed talking with everyone I met. There were no strangers on that train.

The seats in the Lounge were too narrow for my butt (and most of the fat butts of folks I met), but the place was clean, and nothing was patched with duct tape.

Regrettably, the Lounge windows were the dirtiest of anywhere on the train. A sad irony.

The diner was institutional, but there were tablecloths and cloth napkins, stainless utensils, glass dishes, and the food was good at dinners; just okay at breakfasts & lunches.

I called Barbara to tell her about Mt. Shasta, the wine tasting, good food, and she was receptive if not thrilled I called.

Abysmal Service Personnel

Trains seem to attract service employees who have personal grudges. Not so much on the Coast Starlight where everyone was upbeat except for the woman who was in charge of my sleeper car; let's call her Deborah because that's her name, and I called her D. A. for Dumb Ass because that's what she was.

Some service personnel have a look that says "eager to please." D. A. didn't even have a "willing to accommodate" look. Instead, she had that "I'm too busy for you" look that I remembered from attendants on the earlier trip from Maine. Her eyes never met mine. She sighed aloud and excessively. She wasn't getting paid to smile. Was she part of my problems? Did her attitude affect my attitude? Did it affect her tip? Guess.

By the time I reached L. A., I was happy that, except for physical discomfort, I can recommend First Class on the Coast Starlight. But without comfort, whadaya got? First class? No.

Complaining Aboard the Texas Eagle

At the L. A. station, the Coast Starlight was only a few minutes late, and the Eagle was only one platform away. An attendant stopped me as I walked in the direction of the station. "Wait a minute. You coach or sleeper?"

I said, "Sleeper. Where is it?"

She sighed excessively, looked away, and said, "You just walked past it, fool."

I returned to the entrance of the sleeper, stepped aboard, and a service person interrupted a conversation he was having with a coworker and said, "Wait right there. Let me see your ticket."

He took my ticket. "You coach or sleeper?"

I said, "Sleeper. Is this some kind of test I have to pass?"

He studied my ticket, tore it out of the booklet, handed the receipt back to me, and said, "Okay," then resumed his conversation with the coworker.

I waited a few seconds then interrupted, "I'm in B. Where's B?"

He stopped talking, paused a moment, then turned around, smiled unbelievably, flashing his teeth, and said, "You need help? Lemme take that bag. You just follow me, okay?"

He took my bag, turned, and led the way to my compartment.

The door to B had fallen off the track.

"I gotta fix that door."

I said, "I don't want a broken door compartment."

He said, "All the others are taken. You can go sit in coach."

I smiled, showing my teeth, and said, "Not after paying for this first class ticket. Fix the door, and I'll stay here."

He set to work, fixed it, and said, "You see?" He pulled the curtain aside revealing the already-made bed.

I squeezed past and said, "Thank you. It's hot in here."

He said, "You can adjust that knob over there."

The knob came off in my hand.

He said, "Uh-oh. I'll have to report that to [somebody whose name I didn't get] when we get to Chicago. My name is Tony [a name I did get]. You have a good night's sleep."

I said, "Don't go yet, it's too hot in here."

He said, "I'll go see about it." Then he left for about 30 minutes.

I rang his bell. He reappeared. I said, "Well? I'm still hot."

He said, "It'll be all right. It's coolin' down in coach. Give it some time. I'll see you tomorrow. It'll be all right." Then he left.

I dressed for bed and moved my suitcase across to a chair, discovering that the bunk blanket was soiled.

I rang the bell. I waited.

I rang again. I waited.

I rang again. Damn.

He never came back, so I went to sleep under a dirty blanket as the train began moving. The air conditioner began to cool things down to a comfortable temperature, and I cooled down, too, and went to sleep. It was too late at night to call Barbara.

The Following Morning ...

The following morning I arose, showered in the space toilet/shower, dressed, and gosh, somehow I spilled a cup of Diet Pepsi on the soiled blanket. I called Tony, he appeared, I told him, "I spilled Pepsi on the blanket."

He said, "That's okay, it was about time to wash it anyway."

I said, "You think?"

He said "You want me to put your bed back up?"

I said, "You want me to ask you to do it, don't you? You want me to ask for everything, right?"

He said, "I'll fix it while you're eating breakfast."

I went to breakfast.

A nice waitperson asked, "You coach or sleeper?"

"Sleeper."

"Sign here, okay?"

I signed, ordered food, chatted with a woman seated next to me who revealed that she's an antique dealer and her son deals drugs. What should she do for him?

I said report him to the police. She stopped talking with me.

Across from us was a young teenaged mother with her 4 year-old boy and 2 year-old girl, returning from the coast to Texas where—the boy blabbed—"Our other daddy lives." The teenaged mother said, "You're in a sleeper? Wow. We're bustin' our asses in coach."

I ate and returned to my compartment and attempted to close the sliding door without knocking it off the track. It fell off anyway.

I called Tony. He fixed it without a word.

That afternoon …

I read. I napped. I went to lunch, crossing through the observation car where not one person resembled the image used so frequently in advertising Amtrak, the happy 1940s family of mother, father, and young son pointing and smiling at something outside the window. All I could see were weirdoes.

At lunch I sat next to a California girl who was moving from L. A. "because the people there are so insensitive" to Dallas "where everybody's laid back and friendly."

Oh, yeah.

Across the table from us was a big (400 lbs.) train buff wearing an engineer's cap explaining that his daughter is a Union Pacific brakeman.

I ate while he talked about his thankless grandchildren. And the California girl raved about Dallas-friendly men.

I somehow managed to finish eating and leave their company without revealing anything about myself, my interests, or my attitude. They were the entertainers; I was the audience.

I returned to my compartment, called for Tony who came to fix the door.

I napped, read, and wrote. The highlight of the afternoon was a fifteen minute rest stop in El Paso when we got to walk outside and look through chain link fences at Mexicans looking back at us.

I called Barbara. She said she was amazed the battery on my phone had lasted so long. I said I'd call her again for so long as there was battery power. Then I got back aboard.

All during the day, various attendants & conductors used the loud speaker system to announce nonevents ("This is Tony saying let me know if there's anything I can do after I come back from my break."), to urge caution when walking ("Do not—repeat not—be walking barefoot, okay?"), to threaten smokers ("You'll be put off the train if we catch you smoking."), and to promise that the dining room would be open soon (or "is open now," or "will be closed in a few minutes"). Once they started using the microphone, they couldn't stop repeating themselves and correcting some of their mistakes as they made them. And then they repeated themselves.

At lunch, I had watched about twelve of the train staff sitting together as a party, laughing loudly and carrying on. Acting like it was a reunion. They enjoyed themselves more than we enjoyed them.

At supper ...

At supper I was seated with two likeable gay guys who travel annually by train to Disney World because planes give Robert headaches. They talked about Raymond Carver, the "fabulous" short story writer, and they sounded like scholars. I was impressed with their learning until later when I discovered a current Time magazine article was the source of all their information. It's curious how informed a person can sound after reading a news magazine.

When I returned to my compartment, the door had slipped off the track, but this time I simply forced it into a position where I could lock it for the night.

That Night ...

That night I slept soundly until we arrived at San Antonio around 4 a.m., and our train's coach and sleeper was switched to another engine. There was a *wham* as the engine backed into our cars and I was almost thrown out of bed.

Then another *wham* (Obviously, the coupling had not worked).

Then a *wham-wham*, another and another series of *whams*, for a total of five successive *whammies*, all missing the mark until—after a pause—**Whammomomomomo**.

Evidently, that did it.

The Morning After ...

The morning after, I slept till 8. Then another busy day aboard the Texas Eagle.

The weather was great; no rain, few clouds, cool, comfortable. Every day had been gorgeous.

I called Barbara who said that getting calls from me every hour or so was almost like having me at home during the whole trip. What a nice thing to say.

Rounding the corner upon our arrival at Temple, my destination, I was standing with my back to the window at my toilet when Tony appeared and said, "You go ahead and finish what you're doin'. I fixed that door. I'm taking your bag down."

It was the first time he didn't ask me to ask him.

As the train jerked to a stop, he set the bag down on the ground and stuck out his hand to shake hands. I shook it, and he stuck it out to shake again.

No, actually, his meaning was clear so I gave him this tip: "Never wear white shoes after Labor Day."

No, I tipped him. Cash. But not much.

Barbara and Dale & Fred Springer, were waiting and took my picture standing against the train with a grimy "Amtrak" legend for a background.

Okay, I enjoyed the trip as I knew I would. But mainly because I enjoyed myself.

"You can't go home again" originated after someone attended a 50 year class reunion.

Tampa, Florida

◆

My 50th High School Class Reunion
March 21–23, 2001

I flew to Tampa, Florida, for my 50th Reunion at H. B. Plant High School on Friday, March 21[st,] 2001.

The first encounter I had with a former classmate occurred as I was schlepping my suitcase into the Ybor City Hilton, the designated reunion headquarters. A voice behind me called out, "Ramon?" I turned, recognized an old man and opened my arms to welcome, "Fred." The old man made a face and said, "No, it's Paul." He stuck out a hand, and I quickly converted my affectionate hug into a manly handshake.

And that's pretty much how the rest of the weekend went, meeting and mistaking old folks for teenagers I had known. There were about 150 who graduated in our class, and only 60 (plus some spouses) attended the Reunion. Everyone was cordial, and there was not one unpleasant memory rehashed (partly because memory is declining), not one recrimination, and—regrettably—not one glorious recollection of a great moment in time.

On the next morning, we strolled through the halls of our alma mater, and I was greatly dismayed to view changes caused by poor maintenance, poor remodeling concepts, and a prevailing institutional look. Paint colors were grim, poor choices, and sunlight had been shut out of hallways to provide for new classrooms where tall windows had been. Of all the events I attended during that 50th anniversary weekend, the school tour was the most disappointing. I had looked forward to the stroll through scenes of my adolescent triumphs and despairs. And they simply weren't there anymore.

I chatted up a school secretary and asked whatever happened to our "permanent records?" I said, "All the good and bad things teachers said they were going to keep on file here forever?"

And she laughed and said, "Those records are lost forever."

Only one of my old friends was in attendance, George Hearne, a university president and graduate of Yale. I thoroughly enjoyed hanging out with him. And when we parted on Saturday night, knowing we might not ever run into each other again, George hugged me and I bear hugged him back. It was the nearest thing to a thrill all weekend.

Prior to my departure for Tampa, I had called several classmates in hopes of seeing them at the reunion.

My closest high school buddy, Marvin Solomon (and his wife Karen) was out of town attending somebody's bar mitzvah in NYC. I said to him, "Missing a 50th class reunion is irresponsible."

Mary Ann McDonald Martindale said—when I phoned her a week beforehand—she might come, but she didn't. John Crider didn't return my call and also didn't come to town, and—because I always measure everybody's expectations by my own—I wondered why two of my dearest old friends didn't come to see me. Me, not the rest of those folks. Hell, reunions are simply a pretext for renewing desirable old acquaintances.

Gloria Saffron (nee Cermak), Patsy Garcia Kendall, Jennette Jones Walton, Beverly Dasher Ennis Johnson, Ruth Ann Deckard Ross, Carol Peebles Brooks, were no-shows I would really have enjoyed chatting with. Instead, I listened to a lot of people talk about sad lives and great misfortunes. Sonovabitch husbands who walked out on 'em. Gays who died of AIDS.

And I listened to a caustic bitch who had a little thrombosis while I was talking with her. I felt no triumph listening to her babble, neither did I feel any pity for her; she had been too mean to too many folks in high school. I just listened to her stuff like "I never got along with anybody in high school because everybody was so stupid."

There was a guy dressed like a GQ dropout with his 4th trophy wife.

And there was a couple who asked if my relationship with Jesus is the joy of my life.

I tried not to stare at a woman with a face lift who looked 30 years older than the rest of us.

Or stare at the football hero whose wife does all the talking for him.

I was particularly impressed with the world class smile of a guy I remembered as a laid-back teenager who's a judge now in North Florida.

I admired 70 year old Cheerleaders who could still hop to "Two bits, four bits, six bits, a dollar; Everybody for Plant High, stand up and holler." Had great conversations with an interesting Swarthmore graduate married to an Episcopal priest/sailboat enthusiast. Enjoyed talking with an entrepreneur who had persuaded the Super Bowl administration to bring the big game to Tampa twice, and his brother who generously donated brass paperweight souvenirs for all attending the reunion.

I chatted up a sexy blonde/brunette with long, long hair, thinning perceptibly. And I enjoyed renewing acquaintance with a college publicist whom I remembered for his temper tantrums in elementary school.

There were several girls-who-slept-around-in-high-school who married well and didn't look like whores.

In fact, most folks in attendance had turned out well after half a century. No Nobel prize winners, though. There were lots of ghosts: folks who had died leaving fond or pitiable memories; an athlete who died young; one who died in prison; another from drinking too much; and another, a war hero, who had gone to fight and died in Korea while the most of us went to college.

At the Yacht Club party on Saturday night, the MC for the evening, Larry Stagg, asked me to perform for the assembled crowd. He introduced me as the most talented performer ever to graduate from Plant High School. Bullshit, but I didn't object.

I got a perfunctory round of applause and waited for this classroom of unruly alumni to get quiet.

And I waited.

And at just the right moment, I began reading the monolog I had prepared:

"People take high school or college diplomas for granted—unless they never got one. My mother and father never graduated from high school; so my dad giggled like a kid when he told me—after the graduation ceremony—"I am so proud of you, son."

Then, in 1955, when he was more than ten years younger than most of us here are today, he had a stroke. And he lived twenty-five years after that, a very angry man at first, until he resigned himself to having only two words that he could say with any spontaneity, and those words were "pretty day" and "God Damn."

Mother said, "I wish he wouldn't say that. Nobody has to take the Lord's name in vain. But," she said, "That's all the poor man can say." No, it wasn't.

He could say, "Okay," or "Pretty day, okay?" Or when he got excited or confused, he'd say, "Pretty day, God Damn."

On the afternoon I came home with my diploma from Yale, I gave it to him to look at and I said, "This is a return on you investment in my education, and he studied it and said, "Pretty day," and he tried to say—I am <u>sure</u> he tried to say, "I am so proud of you, son," but he stopped after several attempts to form the words, and put the diploma down and turned away. I remember feeling cheated at that moment on two counts because I wanted him to say it, but I couldn't. say, "That's what you want to say, isn' t it?"

I didn't want to sound sentimental and stupid.

He didn't want pity, and he wasn't ever helpless. There were just some things he couldn't do very well. Like walk straight. And he had always been right handed, but he was never able to use it again after the stroke, and his left hand—he called his left hand, "It." "It" gave him fits. It did everything all wrong; not him, it. But he'd laugh at himself. My father had a great, robust laugh. He never lost that.

My folks didn't get along because he did things she didn't want him doing. They lived here in Tampa, 2425 Prospect Road, and she'd get so angry when he insisted on painting the outside of their stucco house—every other year. Don't ask why. I don't know. Because he never tried to explain. He just said he was going to do it, and God Damn it, he did it. And every two years—it would take about two years to finish—he'd call me and expect me to understand what he meant when he'd say, "Pretty day."

Mama didn't want him using the phone: "He gets everything so dirty. He got stucco paint on the buffet. On the sidewalk. On the azaleas."

But when she'd leave the house, the phone would ring, and he'd crash into the desk, grab the phone and answer, and take notes that none of us could read.

And that's what happened the day after I gave him my diploma to look at.

I had gone out of the house with mother, he was there all alone, the phone rang, he answered, "Yes." And someone was calling for me and left a number, and he painstakingly wrote down each number slowly using "it." Then, he hung up the phone and discovered he had used the backside of my diploma for scratch paper. So he tried to erase it, and he smeared the face of the diploma, and I found him when I came home, just standing there in a state of shock. He wouldn't look at me. He held up the diploma and said, "God Damn, okay?"

And I looked at it. I remember it was late that afternoon. And thank goodness I had the presence of mind to tell him it didn't matter. Really. After all, until then it was just another diploma, but now—and forever—it would be mine and his. And he got this look on his face. And giggled like a little boy.

And the next day, I took it to a frame shop, and that's how I got 'em to frame it. You can't tell that it's smudged and dirty—unless you pick it up and look at it.

And every time I do, it's that same afternoon, and I remember the little boy look on his face."

Applause, applause. They appreciated it.

On the way out the Yacht Club door, somebody said, "We thought H. B. Plant was a little microcosm, right?"

And I said, "Yeah, we thought it was real life, but it wasn't. High school is life without a permanent record."

And the other guy said, "Wait a minute. You mean they didn't keep our permanent records?"

And I said, "Nope."

He said, "Well, I'll be damned," and walked away.

Fifty years from now....

Provence

✦

Nice to Aix with the University of Tennessee
April 23–May 3, 2001

Barbara and I traveled to Provence with a tour group sponsored by her alma mater, the University of Tennessee, and we expected Provence to be more than it is.

We stayed the first night in Nice to recuperate from jet lag (and because I always like to add a day onto the beginning and ends of trips in case there's an airline foul-up like a delayed departure or transfer), but overnight in Nice taking the recommendation of an airline flight attendant to stay at an inexpensive hotel on the Boulevard was a mistake. The room smelled of flight attendants' cigarettes. We asked to be moved to another room, and that one smelled of cigars. We had to open the window because there was no air conditioning, and the late night traffic noises and smells of Diesel fuel made sleeping difficult.

We also made a poor choice for dinner at a highly recommended restaurant, the Boccaccio: "Fruit of the Sea" looked good as a menu item, and the massive serving dish packed with ice chips looked absolutely great with cold shrimp, crab, oysters, lobster, sea urchin, and conch, but—regrettably—it wasn't cooked or seasoned in any of the ways we're accustomed to eating shellfish. I tasted everything but the spiney sea urchin. The oysters stayed with me for days.

So far, so bad.

On the following morning, we joined our tour group, University of Tennessee Exes, for a bus ride to Aix en Provence where we would be staying for a week. En route, we sat in the front row of the bus, but there wasn't much to see on that super privatized tollway, just international interstate highway terrain.

The four-star Aquabella Hotel in Aix deserves mention only because it's where we stayed, but our room was unremarkable, the housekeeping was perfunctory, the hotel's food and service was unimaginative, and front desk personnel were indifferent. I wonder why some folks think the French don't give a merde.

(I protest, dear reader, I'm not a snob. I'm simply a sucker for great hospitality and service. Less than satisfactory is not satisfying.)

We truly wanted to love Provence. We had looked forward to visiting Provence for years. We were underwhelmed by it for reasons noted above and below.

We traveled to historical sites like Avignon (with its Popes' Palace, a 14th Century peculiarity) and Arles (with Roman ruins and gypsies perched atop walls like buzzards) and Le Baux, but only Le Baux is a knockout, located on a mountain top, with super-extraordinary views.

We enjoyed a boat trip through the Fjordland Francais, the Calanques near Cassis, a nature preserve of inlets and gorgeous blue water.

Bus trips, even on busses that allow room for couples to occupy seats in separate rows, are still trips on busses. And Motor Coach parking lots are smelly hangouts for those massive motorized dinosaurs. A limo would have been much nicer; of course, but we weren't interested in seeing Provence paying limo prices.

A visit to Vincent Van Gogh's asylum at St. Remy, crowded with tourists, was bizarre. The blue irises he painted were still there, and the fields had horizons I recognized, but viewing the world from the tiny chamber where he stayed was eerie. I felt like an intruder holding an admission ticket.

As we left the Asylum, the tour guide had the bus driver play "Starry, starry night" on the bus speaker system. "Starry, starry night/Paint your palette blue and gray,/Look out on a summer's day...." And the chorus: "Now I understand what you tried to say to me,/How you suffered for your sanity,/How you tried to set them free./They did not listen, they're not listening still./Perhaps they never will."

Very, very sad and the most bittersweet moment of the entire trip.

The weather was grand almost every day—except for pollen from Plane trees (Sycamores) at Pont du Gard that produced severe allergic reactions, causing many of us to weep copiously.

The tour director and U.T. faculty (This tour was, after all, a bone fide study trip) were excellent, Claude Blanc and Pamela Morton, sophisticated, amusing, and personable. And the students (our fellow tourists) were cordial and colorful, mostly Southerners with pronounced dialects and drawls.

Barbara and I were given Certificates of Achievement for participating in the tour, and we were ceremonially inducted into the Alumni Campus Abroad—a program of studies that I strongly approve of on every college campus.

So why were we disappointed in Provence.

The biggest reason was the unimaginative food we were served at the hotel. That hotel was a significant disappointment, and the busses were boring. The narrow, cobblestone streets were hard to walk on, especially with traffic careening around corners, and dog shit surprising us every few yards. Old Town Aix' charms were mixed, mostly unremarkable.

And there was the Flea Market episode: A gypsy (we think) ripped off Barbara's billfold with cash and credit cards. The only time she and I are inclined to shop in stores seems to happen when we're without cash or credit cards. Surprisingly, the Mastercard people reissued new cards and they were delivered to us in Aix within two days after reporting them missing.

And I had a cold (I always blame my colds on plane trips and bad air), and Barbara was depressed because she'd had her billfold stolen, and—simply put—the two of us were not happy campers. There is no place in the world where unhappy campers can be made happy. Until—

We left Aix, returning to Nice, staying in an upscale hotel where we had an outstanding lunch. We napped and then, in the afternoon, we walked on the quay munching French-Fries with mayonnaise as is the custom in France (I got supersized Fries at a crowded MacDonald's). Delightful.

Then we strolled around Old Town, we had dinner at a highly recommended café, and we turned in for a good night's sleep.

The trip back was forgettable (not because it was bad, but because I don't remember it).

Hearsay's true! The lobsters are in abundance, and clams are sandy shellfish.

Yet Another Summer Vacation

✦

Boothbay Harbor, Maine
Summer, 2001

For the entire month of September, Barbara and I arranged to stay in a Booth Bay Harbor, Maine cottage. I was aware that many so-called "cottages" in New England are actually great castles—or large dwellings—and that's what we expected this cottage to be—sight unseen: a beautiful, well cared for, gorgeous palace. Or at least the really nice place our friends in Maine had located for us following their survellieance visit to that house.

So we packed up and drove all the way from Texas to Maine in three days, arriving in Boothbay Harbor late on a Saturday afternoon, tired and cranky. I was tired; she was cranky.

But we couldn't find the damned place because we couldn't read the hand-drawn map we had been given, and we kept looking for "a gray house with yellow trim."

After driving around in circles for over an hour, it occurred to me that perhaps it was the will of a higher power that we should never find it.

Suddenly. "Look." Barbara said, "There's a gray house with a yellow trim and that's the address. That's it."

I said, "But it can't be. It's a run down old shell of a building that obviously hasn't been lived in for years. It looks like the setting for a horror movie."

Barbara shot me a look of shock and dismay, the same look that Lana Turner shot John Garfield in *The Postman Always Rings Twice*. Just before the wreck. And I said, "This had better not be the place we're staying for a month."

Barbara brightened and said, "No, it's that big house over there. See? It's got to be. The one that needs painting, and the yard needs mowing, so let's turn around and go back to Texas."

I said (trying to console her), "Honey, we can't go back now. We're screwed."

So we parked the car and walked to the front door where there was a note posted—and although it was written in English, I could almost hear the voice of mad doctor Frankenstein dictating the note (German dialect added): "Dear Herr Docktor and Mrs. Carter: Come into zis house, and make yourselfs at home. I vill velcome you later on zis evening. Ha-ha-ha-ha-ha-ha-ha-ha-ha-ha."

We opened the door. It creaked. Creeeeeeeek. And we stepped inside. At first, it looked okay. In fact, I thought, "This is gonna be fine."

But then, Barbara began chattering. When I finally began to understand what she was saying through clenched teeth, it sounded like "This. place. has. not. been. cleaned. in. months." She looked at me (Lana Turner again) and said, "What are we going to do. (A rhetorical question, daring me to answer). She inspected the dirty house in earnest discovering that there were no linens, there was no laundry room, there was only one closet upstairs, and one bath upstairs and one down. Everything was old. But not nice old. The house was furnished with things one looks at and never thinks of stealing.

The wind began to blow, Whooooooo, and the shutters started creaking, and we began to smell something. Something strange and—unpleasant. It. Smelled. Like—No, it couldn't possibly be—But Barbara said, "The whole house smells of Pee."

I looked at her doing another impression of Lana Turner and said the only thing that occurred to me in an attempt to lighten the situation, "Well, at least it doesn't smell like shit." Lana was not amused.

In fact, she was so depressed she sat down in a wicker chair and stared out at lobster boats in the ocean and continued muttering, cursing, screaming, weeping, foaming at the mouth, tearing her hair, and generally behaving badly.

Our landlord arrived and apologized for the problems we had discovered, charmed Barbara, and during the weeks that followed, pretty much set the place to rights, hiring a cleaning woman, removing the doggy's urine-soaked rugs, and promising not to use the downstairs bathroom when we were in the house.

Yeah, that was another problem. He came and went at will, using a computer in the downstairs study.

Anyway, it ended up an okay vacation, and we ate lots of lobster & salmon & other seafood. We visited Vermont & New Hampshire & Nova Scotia on side trips, and our friends took us sailing around the islands. Life was blissful until—

Libba, our daughter, and a friend of hers came to Maine for a weekend visit. The following Monday, we drove them to the Portland airport and watched them pass through Security, waving bye-bye.

We took off for a weekend we had planned in Vermont at????. It was a great place to stay with good food and a great cabin and a lawn the Gods might have envied. But on the morning of the day after we arrived, Barbara awoke me from sleeping late and said, "You've got to come look at the TV. A plane's crashed into the World Trade Center."

I hopped up and arrived at the TV set just as the second plane crashed into the second tower. News reports were scrambled and confused, but we watched avidly for hours and days like everyone else in the US until there was a report that identified someone who was suspected of having been responsible for the crashes. The scene was rerun again and again, two men passing under the lens of an airport Security camera in Portland, Maine—

The same checkpoint our daughter had passed through en route to Boston the day before on Friday, September 10.

This grotesque statue was created using a lost wax (actually lost *human*) process.

Vesuvius and Naples

♦

Walking on the Edge
October 12–16, 2001

Before leaving for my walking tour of the Amalfi Coast of Italy in October, I prudently visited a podiatrist to complain of problems I was having walking. He suggested I buy hiking boots.

On **October 12th**, Barbara drove me down to the Austin airport, and I was idly staring out the Airport window when—Gulp. I saw a silver torpedo with wings, flying toward the airport, banking in the air, performing the same maneuver I had witnessed on 9/11. And for an unbelievable moment I feared the torpedo would crash just as it did into the World Trade Center. The plane straightened out, landed, and taxied to a standstill.

I arrived in Napoli on a Saturday, **Octobetr 13th**. The first sight one has of Vesuvius is a knockout. I heard myself saying aloud, "Lookit that mother of all volcanoes." But Naples, I decided, is ugly at the airport end of town. It wasn't until two days later that I saw the beautiful side of that city.

I stayed at the Santa Lucia hotel that had been billed as the New York Times "best in town" choice. The hotel reception folks had attitude problems, however, and if that place is truly the best, I'd recommend staying in some other town.

[Reader, you're about to read the word "great" over 10 times in the following paragraphs. So yes, I know I'm using it excessively.]

Next day, **October 14th**, I visited a great Archeological Museum with a great erotic collection of art objects from Pompeii.

Later I met the group I would be traveling with and walked with them through Cuma, a beautiful archeological site where the mythical cave of the ancient prophetess, Sibyl, is located: a long tunnel that ends in a rectangular room, an echo chamber. Cuma was uncrowded and I was impressed visiting the great cave of Medusa. That night I had a great supper with the group at the Nuevo Castile restaurant that wasn't unusual. It was just another great Italian restaurant.

On Monday, **October 15th**, I hiked with the group up, up, up to the top of Vesuvius and walked around the mouth of the volcano. The Russian playwright Chekhov wrote, after he made the same trek: "What a torture it is to climb Vesuvius. Ashes, mountains of lava, congealed waves of molten minerals, mounds and all sorts of nasty things. You take one step forward and fall a half step back. The soles of your feet hurt; you have trouble breathing...." I can testify it hasn't improved a whole Hell of a lot in over a century.

That was early in the day. Then we hiked for about two hours on a pine woodsy trail, my feet hurting. We had a great unpretentious lunch, and then we hiked through Herculaneum, a great archeological excavation. I thought, "This tour was supposed to be moderate hiking."

We ate a great unpretentious supper, and I went to bed happy, forcing myself to bear the pain of bad feet because the food, the company, the country, everything was so ... great.

But on Tuesday, **October 16th**, after we took a ferry to Procida (Proscheeda) and hiked over a mountain in the center of that village then up another mountain to a freakin' church, after a great lunch I decided to spend the afternoon resting while the others walked and boated. I napped until I was awakened by a throbbing pain in my ankle, and that's when I decided enough hurtin' is enough. I'm goin' home. I enjoyed a great supper with great company, but I didn't share my decision because I wasn't looking for sympathy.

We retraced our steps across the big hill through Procida on **October 17th**, returning to Naples by ferry. We had a great lunch of Margarita Pizza followed by a walking tour of beautiful Naples, and I made my announcement, short and sweet, said farewell to a great group whose company I really enjoyed, and I flew to Rome for an overnight at a bummer airport Hilton. My luggage took a side trip to Venice, but it returned the following morning, Thursday**, October 18ᵗʰ**, in time for my departure to the States.

Changing schedules and rerouting a trip is not easy, and it ain't cheap. I managed to make satisfactory arrangements, however, and I limped all the way home, greatly disappointed not to finish the trip as planned.

The insurance company denied my claim because I failed to declare the foot problem _on the day I made my reservation_ for the trip. Read the fine print.

I am so glad I hiked up Vesuvius. Damn. It was exquisite torture, but it's no small source of pride, knowing I'm the only one I know who's been up there. It was … grrrrrrrrrrreat.

Unique, fragile, undeveloped, and uncrowded. And it's not a tourist trap. Amazing!

Cappadocia, Turkey

❖

A Silverseas Cruise from Greece to Turkey
April 23–May 6, 2002

This is a fascinating account (If I do say so myself) of a trip to Athens by air, from there by cruise ship (the Silversea's *Whisper*) around the Aegean, thereafter a land tour from Istanbul to the Turkish region of Cappadocia that a surprising number of my acquaintances had never heard of. Hell, I didn't know it existed myself until I saw a remarkable photograph in an ad for tourism in Turkey. Tthree months later, I was there.

The landscape in Cappadocia is so unreal—even surreal—that I could never have dreamed up a description as extraordinary as it is. Truly. Hardly any Americans go there, and most of my readers will never know whether I'm telling the amazing truth or misstating facts. But trust me, it's all true.

Tuesday, April 23, 2002.

Barbara and I left home in Salado at 10am, and she dropped me off at 10:30 at the tiny Killeen, TX, airport and said something like, "Enjoy wherever it is you're going, Dear, and I hope your feet don't hurt again," then she kissed me goodbye. I stood on line at the check-in counter for about fifteen minutes, then I was directed to the aptly-named Waiting Room where I was processed by airport folks who don't quite have their security act together. Passengers checking in at the gate were cordoned off for an hour and a half in an area where there were neither restrooms nor water fountains (Clearly, there's a correlation), and no place for lunch.

We boarded at noon, left the ground thirty minutes later, flew for an hour to the D/FW airport with only pretzels to munch on, and then I spent an hour transferring from the American Eagle landing site to the Lufthansa departure gate for Frankfurt en route to Athens. Yes, that would make it 2:30 PM. I learned there would be no meal served aboard the plane until 5 PM, so I was forced by a burly check-in agent to bolt or throw away the remainder of a terrible barbecue beef sandwich before boarding. I eructated (Medical term for belching) barbecue sauce for the next five days. Then I boarded the plane bound for Greece at 3.

The big bird was airborne at 3:30. By my count, I had been five and a half hours en route—one quarter of my total travel time—and I had just left Dallas.

One of the compelling aspects of the trip was a free upgrade to business class on Lufthansa. That, plus no extra cost for traveling without a partner on the Whisper (Usually, there's a 110 percent to 200 percent penalty for traveling alone on cruises). Minus big discounts. These persuasive promotional concessions made the trip a package I couldn't refuse.

Flying Lufthansa, however, doesn't compete with American Airlines in small details. The German fabric "goody bag" for business class passengers has only a toothbrush, an eyeshade, socks, and no toiletries unlike American's imitation leather, zippered bag (suitable for reuse) with salves, balms, sprays, mists, creams, and a safety razor.

The German flight attendants rushed around efficiently, indifferent to my needs, serving drinks and spicy food; whereas, American's attendants usually satisfy my every need after I've called for them a couple of times, serving drinks and bland food. I'm being serious, but curiously, the Germans' inattention to details seemed more laid back than the way American micromanages passengers.

When I bounded to my feet to take a stroll every hour or so, the Germans didn't say "Das ist verboten." They gave me access to the whole plane, and considering that it was only about half full, that was a lot of plane. American attendants have refused to allow me to walk into the tourist cabin area. Walking helps enormously to relieve cramping.

I slept fitfully, I read sporadically, and I watched a movie I don't remember.

Wednesday, April 24.

At Frankfurt, early in the morning, I had a long walk and a long wait for the Lufthansa Athens plane to depart. Then I was seated in the front row (bulkhead) on the aisle, and I began to think the Germans were entirely too laid back, considering 9/11 cautions in place in the States. People kept coming and going out of the cockpit, flight attendants and staff, and an old man was welcomed into the cockpit with his grandson.

A tour agent for Silversea cruise line at the Athens airport didn't ask to see my passport, neither did the customs agent. They took the luggage I said was mine without double-checking for errors. Then they put my luggage on one bus and herded me onto another. I sat on the edge of my seat for the 2-hour trip from the airport through detours and traffic to our hotel in the center of Athens except when sleep deprivation knocked me out. I remember waking then passing out, only to awake then zonk out again and again. I was a zombie riding the Greyhound Dutchman. We rode the torn up 2-lane highways into town, taking back and side roads, speeding along at about 15 mph. When I wasn't sleeping, I was thinking, "They're putting a bomb in my luggage."

Everybody who's been there says, "Athens is an ugly town except for the antique stuff." So I looked over and addressed a fellow passenger sitting across the aisle: "It's not just an ugly town; it's one of the ugliest towns in the world. I can't remember seeing an uglier town in my travels. And today in the rain it seems even uglier than it did three years ago when my wife and I spent 3 days here."

The guy looked at me and responded with the comment I had obviously asked for: "So what did you expect?" He turned away, I struck him with a heavy metal object, and he bled to death on the floor of the bus, his body bumping spastically, the driver never missing a pothole.

When the bus came to a final stop, at 3:30PM, I reckoned I'd traveled from Killeen for about 22 hours straight with only fitful naps for breaks. That's a Hell of a long time to travel someplace without resting. I won't argue the point, but for me, naps aren't respite from tedium anymore than waiting to board a plane is relaxing.

Arriving at the Intercontinental Athenaeum Hotel at 3PM (not elegant but expensive; some hoteliers simply don't get it.), I searched for and spotted my luggage. I was assured it would be sent to my room by a guy who looked as if "It will be sent to your room" is the only English thing he says 1,000 times every day.

I said, "Where's my folding chair/walking stick?"

He said, "It will be sent to your room."

I said, "What are you gonna do with the bomb?"

He said, "It will be sent to your room."

I said, "I shouldn't have surrendered my carry-on bag, but I was sleep-deprived, and they took advantage of me. What have you done with it? Where is my carry-on."

You know what he said.

So. I walked around the hotel lobby for awhile, my arms hanging slightly forward (like the Frankenstein monster), my chin moving spastically from side to side, and by the time I finished strolling around and registering with the cruise ship agents and refusing to sign up for a $70 tour of the city, ("I've <u>seen</u> the Parthenon.") I was ready to sack out in my room. The luggage had been sent up, yeah, but it was still out in the hall where anybody could have put a bomb in it.

I thought, "What am I gonna tell the airlines ticket woman when she asks if it's ever been out of my sight? I'll have to lie like everybody else." I was really stressed out, so I dragged the damned luggage inside the damned room, looked out my damned window, and I thought, "Salado is prettier than Athens." Then I took the nap I badly needed.

I awoke at 8PM Greek Time (3PM my body clock time), ordered room service (Eggplant, lima beans, feta, olives, stuffed wine leaves, and a bowl of chicken soup), ate, and went back to sleep in earnest. I awoke at 2AM Greek time, tried to call Barbara at 6PM her time, missed her, went back to sleep, called again at my 5:30am, her 9:30PM, and told her "I bought you some ear rings, and I'm having a wonderful time." That seemed to reduce her anxieties considerably.

Thursday, April 25.

That morning, on my own steam, I took a taxi from the hotel to the Benaki Museum, recommended by the hotel's concierge, but when I got there, damn. It was closed by a strike of museum unions. Chagrinned, I walked to the nearby Cyclades Art Museum and discovered relics on display from the Cyclades islands in the Aegean whose art and artifacts look very unGreeklike, in fact, quite primitive. It wasn't until I visited Santorini several days later that I learned the connection between the primitive Cycladic society and Greek civilization had gotten disconnected.

From the museum, I took another taxi to the Agora (early Greek market place), wandered around, enjoying a lovely spring day with poppies blooming everywhere in the ruins, then I stopped a taxi and asked him to take me to the Theatre of Dionysus below the Parthenon. He said road repairs blocked the streets, and he assured me it was a short walk. So I stupidly decided to hike to the Theatre and, sure enough, the streets and sidewalks were torn up, causing me to walk for an hour like a mountain goat in a circular direction. I happened upon a restaurant I remembered from our last visit to Athens and stopped for lunch (Eggplant, lima beans, feta, olives, stuffed grape leaves, and a bowl of chicken soup).

Then I made a big, big mistake, I hailed a taxi because time was running short and I knew there wouldn't be enough time to walk to the Theatre since the hike and lunch had taken so long. We drove down dark, unoccupied streets, and he told me, "Taxi fares during afternoon cost 11 Euros from one district to next."

I said, "I didn't know that," but I was thinking, "He's trying to cheat me, but at the hotel I'll get the doorman to set him straight."

We rode for about ten more minutes, and as we neared the hotel, he came to a stop on a wide boulevard and said, "There is road construction so I must drop you here."

I said, "No, drop me over there—it must be six blocks away from here, the hotel."

He said, "Is too much trouble. That'll be twenty-two Euros, but you pay only twenty."

I thought, "I gotta get out of this cab. This guy's weird." I handed him two fives and a ten.

He said, "Wait." He held up the bills: "You just gave two fives and a one."

Confused, I fished out another ten and took back the one. He said, "No tip?"

I said, "Is too much trouble." Then I jumped out just as he sped off.

I had to go down a flight of stairs to walk through an underpass then across a street, then twenty-five thousand kilometers back to my hotel.

Checking my billfold, I discovered I had actually given him two tens and two fives. All I had left was the one. I asked the doorman at the hotel how much should I have paid for a ride from the Parthenon. He said, "Five Euros, tops." Shit.

I had been taken for a ride. *Again.* Even though I am convinced absolutely that every taxi driver in the universe is an incorrigible highwayman, out to cheat passengers. The only prudent policy is to get the fare in writing, notarized, before venturing anywhere by taxi. And then take the driver's photograph. No kidding. Absolutely no kidding.

Returning to the hotel's "Hospitality Room," I boarded the bus to Piraeus, seaport for Athens, an even uglier town than Athens—but what did I expect, right?

Standing on line to board the ship, two women passengers came on to me. Then they got distracted by a handsome ship's officer and they never saw me again the entire trip.

I boarded the ship and was shown to my very large suite (#537), about the same size as the Killeen Waiting Room, but it had a bathroom and a fridge and all sorts of gift stuff. It was clearly designed for handicapped passengers who need room to move around in wheelchairs, maybe do wheelies.

Biggest suite for that price on the ship, thanks to my travel agent, Fran Subar, who confirmed the reservation for me less than a month before the ship sailed. Fran got me discounts and a flight upgrade. The room was nicely appointed (first time in my life I've ever written "nicely appointed") with access to a deck (not a private area but one that only a few suite occupants were allowed to use, large enough for staging a movie musical (with a chorus of at least twenty singers and dancers).

The occupants in the next cabin were a psychiatrist and her father (an invalid) and her husband (a lawyer) in the second largest handicapped suite on that deck. They were cordial, and they were slow pushing that wheelchair around. I almost told the old man he was spoiling the trip for his daughter and her lawyer until I learned he had paid for the trip.

We had a fire drill, and I did everything wrong, arriving late at the wrong station wearing my life jacket wrong. But the ship's personnel acted amused and never once suggested I was stupid or drunk. And honestly, I had not drunk more than a half glass of champagne. I was simply happy to be aboard a big, beautiful ship, and as usual, I wasn't paying attention to instructions. Back in elementary school, I didn't pay attention, and a teacher called me stupid, and I thought, "She just doesn't know I'm just klutzy, not stupid."

I was constantly appreciative of the officers and crew for their patience, professional skills, and competence. Great staff. The ship was too big; but the staffers were grand.

That evening, I reserved dinner in the French café, took a nap, waking just in time for a special French menu, drank a great scotch, and sat with delightful company.

After one of the best dinners I've ever had aboard any ship, I retired to the computer room and checked out email that Barbara had forwarded to me, costing only $48....

I quickly responded, telling her not to send me any more email than we really needed to exchange. But at the close of the cruise, when I paid my email bill, I had to cough up about $70—now, that's truly expensive when one considers I don't pay much for it at home.

Then bed, a good book, and a good night's sleep.

We had smooth sailing every day and night on this trip and perfect weather, a bonus no amount of money could have purchased.

Friday, April 26 Santorini Island.

Wonderful, cool weather, and wonderful to stroll on deck sailing into the world's largest caldera (a lagoon created by implosion of a volcano) and to view several Greek villages perched high above the sea on the rim. It looked small, but it's a larger place than it looks.

We took a tender to the only commercial port where buses carried us switchbacking to the top, allowing us to look down and view the Whisper and her sister ship, The Shadow, toy vessels in a big rocky bathtub.

We toured the ruins of a two- to three-thousand year old civilization in an excavated town of Akrotiri, a Minoan city. Aha. This is where those statues and artifacts that I saw in that Athens Cycladic museum came from. Drawings of men in loincloths and women in antebellum dresses with bosoms exposed.

Evidentially, the city was destroyed by the volcano's big blast, and there was nothing remaining of residents of the doomed city because they probably left the island by boat only to be drowned at sea by a great tidal wave produced by the volcano, the same wave that destroyed ancient Crete.

We reboarded the bus and rode to Fira where a new archaeological museum houses Akrotiri pottery, wall decorations, etc., remarkably well-preserved.

Our guide gave us instructions on how to find our way through the streets of Fira, beginning on the Street of Gold, so-called because of the hundreds of jewelry stores lining the way, to the Funicular that descends to the sea, returning us to our ship. We could have walked down, but the donkeys that carry tourists up and down had littered the path, and nobody had cleaned it up since 1903.

The buffet lunch back aboard ship was not challenging. It was okay as were most of the lunches. It's dinners on Silversea ships that are special.

I napped for a couple of hours—too long a period for a guy trying to convince his body clock to adapt to another time zone. [My grandson, at two years old, enjoys saying, "Delicious," which comes out, "Duhlissus." Cute.] My daily naps were duhlissus.

Late afternoon is generally a time for reading and writing for me.

Then the long awaited dinner. Tonight an Italian dish and in the ship's Lounge afterward, a French-themed show, unimaginative but well-executed and designed for an upper middle class upscale, tired-out after a hard day's shopping and sight-seeing audience of retirees. I didn't like it, but I was entertained.

Then bed, a good book, and a good night's sleep.

Saturday, April 27.

I began the day with a brisk one-mile walk around the jogging track on the top deck with the ship's Phiz Ed Instructor. Then I watched the coast of Crete hove into view and continued walking around in the bay of Mirabello. We docked—late—at Aghios Nikolaos.

A ferry occupying our docking space threw the sightseeing schedule off, so we were plagued the entire day with traffic snarls—even on that small island. Even cruise ships have to negotiate with dock masters.

We went to the ruined temple at Knossos, fascinating, and tourists from our group and others listened to tour guides sporadically ramble on and on. Perhaps the most striking thing to happen while we were exploring the ruins was the appearance of a kitten, walking gingerly from one stone step down to another. The kitten upstaged the entire temple by virtue of being alive and vital; whereas, the temple seemed old stuff. We watched till the tiny cat turned a corner and disappeared into the scenery. We applauded.

Then we were transferred to the Museum where all artifacts from the temple ruins are stored and displayed elegantly.

We had lunch around 3PM at a large, charmless motel and returned to the ship scarcely fifteen minutes before it set sail.

After dinner, a lecture on the subject of mythology & democracy, titled: "Greeks Bearing Gifts." I'd had a drop too much wine and an ounce too much steak to appreciate an academic paper.

I went to bed with a good book, and I had a good night's sleep.

We had smooth sailing every day and night on this trip and perfect weather, a bonus that no amount of money could have purchased. Why am I repeating this? To offset my minor complaints with a major acknowledgement.

Sunday, April 28. Kusadasi, Turkey (Ancient Ephesus).

A thoroughly uneventful day, the one I had waited for so that I could do things like laundry, hot tub, email, non-productive stuff, etc. Highlight of the day was a massage by a German madchen who pummeled and poked me for half an hour, leaving me sore for three days.

In the evening, we went to a concert ashore at Ephesus, featuring a large string ensemble (about 20 pieces), "The Aegean Chamber Orchestra performing in the ruins of a small Roman theatre. It was charming; the music was not unfamiliar (Mozart's *Eine Kleine Nachtmusik*, etc.); the weather was perfect; the lighting was awful; the champagne was okay; and the audience was wowed.

Having produced about a thousand such shows and concerts in my lifetime, the best thing about the evening was watching people enjoy themselves. I love a happy audience even when I've had nothing to do with producing the show.

Monday, April 29

At Sea from the Aegean through the Dardenelles to the Marmara Sea through the Bosporus Strait to the Black Sea, sailing past Istanbul.

Awoke at 4, took a pill, read *Churchill*, went back to sleep till 8, dressed, walked a mile, then breakfast on the deck, while passing through the Dardenelles, the scene of Churchill's greatest defeat during WW1.

Attended a lecture, finished a four volume video set of Churchill's life, sailed right past Istanbul on the Bosporus Strait en route for Bulgaria, went to a crowded reception for folks who had been aboard Silversea vessels in the past, then dinner and an early turn-in.

Tuesday, April 30, Nesebur, Bulgaria.

The bus trip I took to a village about thirty miles from shore was like a trip to a neglected Third World, long before operettas characterized peasants as folksy and fun-loving. The only modern farming implement I saw all day was a giant John Deere tractor larger than our bus. Everything else was smaller than life.

Our tour guide, a swarthy, middle-aged cynic wearing an ill-fitting suit, lectured and I took notes, piecing the following monolog together afterward, 99 percent his words:

"Gut morning, Everybody sit. Now.

I am your guide, Christo Miro. Christo as in Christ. You know Jesus Christ? And Miro as in miro, miro on the wall, okay?

This is Nay-<u>Say</u>-ber, Bulgaria, so-called democracy and glorious tourist entrapment, okay?

And we shall trawel to a willage this morning where you will see church, farmhouse of awerage willager, and have drink of schnops.

Bulgaria is diwided nort and sout by Balkan mountains.

During first worlt war is Bulgaria on the side of Germans and loses war. But in second world war is Bulgaria on Germans' side again. And again loses war.

But then comes Russians and 46 years of corporation farms and everybody gives up homes to state and moves to city to make a liwing.

Then comes so-called democracy and state gives back farms to people who used to own farms and is like you get back something you didn't want to have because you don't remember how to farm, but you have to.

And you have to pay taxes on it, okay?

So much for so-called democracy.

Was before state-owned and controlled and no jobless because everybody obliged to work or not eat, and everybody old go to rest home and sick to sanitoria, but now is 30 percent jobless and nobody eats good except old communists who are now factory owners and become new capitalists, okay?

Everybody drink too much world famous dry white Bulgarian wine and world-popular red Bulgarian wine and smuggle drugs across Bosporus and Danube.

Only old people live in willages.

We stop now to look at willage eastern Catolik church, the true Catolik church. Everybody out of bus....

Now everybody back aboard bus.

Have you heard sound of peace and quiet and no machinery and not many cars but many horses and donkeys-drawn carts and smell of donkey poop and goats, and see spring tulips and white and purple lilacs and powerty in this so called democratic non-productive willage.

Now we stop for drinking free schnops and smelling ship and goats and chicken poop. Do not take deep breath. Everybody out of bus.

And now we get back aboard bus after drinking schnops.

You smell ship sheet?

On way back to Nay-<u>Say</u>-ber, you sit back and I read old legends and promotional information about Bulgaria and fertility rites.

Not much else to do in willage but fertility rite.

And I read discussion of interesting Christmas and Easter customs while you go to sleep all the way back to Nay-<u>Say</u>-ber.

And when you go back to America, you remember sights and sounds and smells of Bulgaria.

Okay? Okay."

And that was our tour and tour guide.

Later that day, I walked around Nay-<u>Say</u>-ber photographing one ruined Byzantine church after another, must have been eight in that tiny town, all with women willagers wearing rubber boots, selling souvenirs aggressively.

Why'd we dock here? Beats the Hell out of me.

Wednesday, May 1

We returned to Istanbul, clear, crisp, cool weather. Dodging seagull sheet on deck during my morning walk.

I got directions and a shuttle schedule, then I set out on my own, never nervous or anxious once. I headed for the Archeological Museum, but it was not easy to find. And my feet began to plague me after walking around in circles looking for it and then walking from one building to the next. It's a museum that presents many, many exhibits, notably the Alexander Sarcophagus, an enormous Trojan Horse replica for the children's' museum, and immense statuary from Persian and other early civilizations.

I decided not to push my luck walking. I hailed a taxi, and after requiring him to swear he would not mistreat me, I rode back to the shuttle bus stop, then bussed back to the ship.

I spent the afternoon loafing, reading about Istanbul, packing, and preparing to leave the ship the following morning.

In the evening I ate alone, not lonely, actually quite content to savor the good food and drinks without having to chat up new acquaintances.

May 2, Thursday.

After debarking in the morning and going through Customs, it occurred to me that I almost always get asked by Customs agents, "Business or Pleasure?" I tell them I always travel for pleasure. Liberal and right wing friends alike distrust pleasure, and some day, when we all arrive at the gates of Wherever, an angel will ask—before admitting us: "Business or Pleasure?" And to those who answer, "Business, right?" the angel will sadly shake his head and say, "Pity."

I went to the meeting place for the extended ITS (International Travel Services) tour of Istanbul and Cappadocia and met our tour guide, Kaan Gulcar, whom I liked at once, and who transferred us to the Istanbul Ritz Carlton (my kind of place). I discovered there would be only four of us on our land tour to Cappadocia. Wow.

There was a couple, Robert & Annett Hollo, she was from Paris, he was from Vienna. And a single woman from South Africa, Jill Rose. They regarded me, a naturalized Texan, as an exotic.

We began touring Istanbul early, first to the site of the Hippodrome, a gigantic sports arena, where Red Turks killed a stadium full of Blue Turks. (They were barbarians, you know.)

Then the Blue Mosque (Very big with distinctive architecture), Hagia Sophia (Enormous with unique architecture; pronounced A-ya Sof-ya), the underground Roman Cistern (Immense, a matchless engineering accomplishment—I'm running out of adjectives), and then lunch at a remote restaurant, the Beyti, with over forty different Turkish dishes.

That afternoon, after visiting the Grand Bazaar (Crowded and labyrinthine) we returned to the hotel, dazzled and exhausted.

There had been a room assignment mix-up, and I had been moved to an enormous suite with copious written apologies from the management plus a fruit bowl. Evidentially, the Ritz folks take their commitments to travel companies seriously. It's a great hotel.

Talked with Barbara by phone then went for a Turkish bath in the hotel, surprisingly boring and unerotic even though the guy pounded on me below my knees and above my waist for almost an hour. Hundreds of gallons of water poured out of the faucet, and I learned later that the Turks and Muslims believe in using only running water for ablutions and massages, never turning it off. Barbara said there was a drought going on in Texas, so I felt guilty. But not real guilty.

The four of us tourists ate together in the hotel's post-modern restaurant. The silverware was so unconventional I couldn't hold my fork steady. The knife and spoons were funny-looking, but the serving staff acted like they were special, so I played along and acted sophisticated.

Friday, May 3

Didn't sleep well (Who knows why?), but I had plenty of energy for a hard day's touring. Sensational hotel breakfast buffet. Then the Suliman Mosque (You seen one church/mosque/temple, you seen 'em all), then Topkapi Palace with its Harem and museum and an okay lunch buffet. Then the Chora Church, a little-heralded museum with the richest collection of mosaics and frescos imaginable.

Finally, the Spice Market (Yawn.) and return to the hotel where I had a great nap.

Met a friend of a friend for drinks, a personable guy who advised me never to call a Turk an Arab; they'll take exception.

That evening our small group had dinner in a ballroom at the Ciragnan Palace (& Hotel) that featured a disappointing "Sultan's Night" program and feast. The food was good, but the audience was listless, and the performers were indifferent. Virtually every song or dance lasted five times too long; result: colossal boredom. The shame is the performers were skilled and/or beautiful dancers and musicians—especially the solo belly dancer whose singular talent was interesting for the first twenty minutes she gyrated, but after that—

We left long before the show came to an end, one of the advantages of a tour group of only four folks. Producers of shows like that "Sultan's Night" always seem to misjudge their audiences' physical and mental endurance capacity.

Saturday, May 4.

Lovely weather as always on this trip.

After a short wait at the airport, we flew to Kayseri in a half full plane and drove for about 45 minutes to the Cappadocia region. The Turks had never built roads from Istanbul to the middle of their country until the 1950s because they didn't want to facilitate invasions from countries to their east. So the roads weren't in bad shape; they were pretty good. *Pretty* good means potholes.

Now, here's what's special about that part of the country. It's a terrain that had been leveled in centuries past by great—now defunct—volcanos that, erupting, scattered tufa—a permeable substance unlike lava, kind of like compressed dust. The volcanos also disgorged great boulders. Everywhere the boulders landed, the tufa was sheltered, and with the passage of time (centuries), the weather wore down the permeable tufa—except for mountains of tufa that remained covered by the rocks. In effect, all over that countryside, there were thousands of boulders perched on top of curious-looking tufa mountainettes with pointy shapes.

The touristy name for these hills is "Fairy Castles." No fairy I know would ever live in one, but that's where early Christian cults lived in carved-out caves that served as homes and churches inside these pointy mountains. They also dug downwards many stories underground, cutting into the tufa, gouging themselves passages to lodgings.

The first stop, the Goreme open air museum (an area where a commune of devout cultists, priests and nuns, had lived), was stunning. The hand-carved chapels with primitive frescoes had been vandalized easily during recent centuries because the tufa is crumbly. Even with old men guarding the rooms, visitors can't resist touching the walls.

Yes, I'm ashamed to say, I touched a wall, but I didn't deface a fresco, honest. Barely touching tufa produces dust. *I wonder how much longer the magic will last.*

Evidently, the country of Turkey is committed to increasing tourism, a non-polluting industry, and Cappadocia is a showplace of the first magnitude. But if those fragile caves are exhibited, they should also be protected from tourists, compelled like me to touch and feel the walls.

Discovering this curious world of caves was wonderful. I kept saying to myself, "This is wonderful." "Awesome" has been too much abused or I might have said "Woah, awesome.".

The "Kapadokya Country Club Lodge" was a surprising disappointment lodging. Why can't they all be five-star.

Lunch at the Lodge was super, however, with tomatoes, peppers, cucumbers, lentil soup, carrots, yellow potatoes, rice, and about thirty different eggplant casseroles. There was a bitter fruit served for dessert, but nobody ate it.

After lunch we drove around and around. I've never seen anything like Cappadocia in a lifetime of surprises and disappointment. Everywhere I looked I saw something imposing. It was as if the God of Tourism had said, "You want surprise and delight? Feast your eyes."

The Tour God said, "And here's a little something special." Upon reaching a mountain top with another knockout view, we were treated to an al fresco snack of champagne and cake with silver, crystal, and china at a skirted table especially transported to that location by our tour guide. When the waiter popped the cork, it sailed out over the edge of the ridge where we were standing, up and away like a golf ball, and then it dropped into the valley below.

Will I ever forget it? Never.

Dinner was superb that evening with what seemed like a hundred dishes of foods to sample. The place was crowded with tourists, only a few of whom were American.

Then to bed in my monk's cell in that poorly designed and maintained hotel.

Sunday, May 5

Chilly weather. Sensational breakfast buffet menu.

This morning a visit to Soganlik Valley. The Tour God whispered, "You thought yesterday was sensational? Check this out."

We were permitted to pass through a vehicle checkpoint where van and busses and donkey carts were scrutinized, and then we arrived at what looked to be an abandoned settlement without any old men guarding those fragile, impermanent ruined caves. Only wildflowers and children playing nearby. We studied complex storage rooms, including a wine-making room (The primitives who lived here were truly civilized).

By now, it was clear that every settlement had pigeon holes cut into the hill-sides with access to pigeon droppings below. That's how they induced those birds to fertilize their crops; they provided birdhouses.

We left that site and stopped for coffee at a wayside inn that had lots of trees blooming and buildings decaying. Old women with handmade dolls greeted us like long-lost grandchildren, smiling from tooth to tooth, laughing, holding up the dolls as if they were delicate treasures. We didn't buy. And the moment it became clear that we weren't in the market for dolls, the grandmothers muttered and scowled, "Argggg." One of them held up a doll by the leg and waved it at us in a threatening manner.

Looking back at the old women from the van, after waiting for a few minutes for our driver to finish refueling, I watched as they transformed themselves yet again back into sad, cheerless, weary old women, waiting for the next van and the next reconciliation with long-lost grandchildren.

We traveled from there to a small Greek village (Turkish only in the sense that it's inside Turkey's boundaries) where we had lunch at The Old Greek House in a room next to the dining room where the Princess of Liechtenstein and her entourage were eating. In an adjacent dining room, the Turkish Minister of Finance (Second in importance only to the Prime Minister) and his party of politicos were enjoying lunch. We were rubbing shoulders with people of no importance to us.

Following stops at photo ops along the road, we were locked for two hours inside a rug factory where I learned (as I had been taught in other rug-making countries) how wool is dyed and woven, and how rugs are singed and then scoured with soap, and finally how the wool is pulled over one's eyes. The Tour God whispered: "If you thought this trip was supposed to be merchandise-free, you've never traveled before. Tourism means 'Sales Opportunity'."

We were treated to a theatrical presentation of rugs being slapped down, one on to of another, then we were assigned personal sales reps.

I asked, "Do you have old rugs to sell?"

"Yes, indeed," my personal tradesman said, and he guided me down two flights into a great basement where he led me through vault doors.

I said, "How much is that one?"

He dickered with one of his coconspirators and said, "Special to you: Only $70,000."

"Um, no, thanks."

I left the building before I was given permission and waited outside while the rest of our gang of four went through the sales drill—but they didn't buy anything either.

Rug merchants are the pits, and I stopped liking our tour guide for conniving with those smarmy buzzards.

Tonight, after another excellent dinner with even more dishes to sample, we learned how to play Backgammon. First and last time for that.

Monday, May 6

Clear and chilly.

Another banquet buffet for breakfast, then a trip to another "open air museum" at Azur, underground caves at Derinkuyu, lunch at the touristy Hanedan restaurant, then a visit to a pottery shop where I made my first purchase of the entire trip, a single Turkish tile.

That afternoon we packed and checked out and took an hour-long trip on an uncrowded highway to the airport in Kayseri where I called and talked with Barbara to let her know I was beginning my descent.

I had picked up a cold with sniffles. Bummer.

The flight back to Istanbul was uneventful, and the overnight stay at an airport hotel was nothing to write home about.

Tuesday, May 7

An early departure at 6AM from Istanbul, and an afternoon return at 5PM to Killeen.

A Footnote: Cappadocia's hills and caves are as enchanted as the hieroglyphs I had traced with my fingers when I traveled in Egypt, and the stone table at the top of Machu Picchu, and the 24" high terra cotta figurines I held in my hands in China, and the crude 20,000 year old tools of primitives in the Dordogne. Sure, I'm dropping names of things and places, but the point is Cappadocia helped me define what I like most about traveling, and that's exploring worlds outside my experience. Nothing on this trip was surpassingly beautiful by any definition I have of beauty. But I've been thrilled again and again seeing and touching objects—especially forbidden ones.

You may think of me as a foreign forbidden fruit picker.

Imagine: A crotch shot of Oscar Wilde basking on rock in a Dublin city park!

Ireland

✦

An Adventure For Folks Over Fifty
June 16–30, 2002

Barbara and I traveled to Ireland on June 16th of this year, and returned on the 30th. No trip ever ends until all the charge card statements are in, so the trip took several months, virtually.

In brief, the best things about the trip were the Irish weather (No kidding.), the traveling companions including the tour director, the ala carte food at most places (The quality and presentation; not the slow service), gorgeous landscapes, several historical locales, and a chance to visit the beautiful part of Ireland.

The worst things were riding on winding roads day after day while sitting on a thinly-padded seat on a swaying, undulating, roller-coasting bus on two-lanes, dodging head-on traffic. The thing that was missing as we toured the countryside was music. Our tour guide's narratives on the loud speaker were appropriate but overlong. We might not have noticed (Fat chance.) the bumpy bus ride if recorded Irish folk music had been played.

The tour was long on bus ride and short of thrills and magic. The kind of tour you'd plan for old folks like....

Wait a minute. Wait a dadgummed minute. Those travel agents planned that tour of Ireland with folks over 50 like me in mind. Indeed.

Once you've seen the backsides of a thousand sheep, you've seen 'em all. And after you've seen 1,000,000 one-story farmhouses built with the same rectangular shape without a shed roof or gable or flower pot in the window, you've seen a million more than you ever wanted to see.

Sunday, June 16, 2002

Barbara and I left home in Salado, Texas, at 9:30am, intending to stay overnight in New York and then depart the next day for Ireland. We landed on time and took a car to the city and our upscale destination, the Essex Hotel, St. Regis Club, that turned out to be St. Regis in name only. Don't accept substitutes.

Their Security guards in the lobby appeared to have been hired to converse with backup Security guards. We conversed with them for about fifteen minutes until a desk clerk finally appeared. There were no bellmen on duty, so we showed ourselves to our room. The view from the dirty window in the room was New York's backside. The bed spread was old and dirty. The sheets were limp and pinched and wrinkled. Very disappointing.

I had planned for us to eat at a Michelin three-star restaurant adjacent to the hotel, but we discovered it's always closed on Sunday, so we ate dinner at a ground floor beanery, the Café Bulimia, whose food disappointed us and our guest, Buddy Smith, an actor who tried his best not to act disappointed.

Phooey. Don't start a NYC vacation on a Sunday night.

Monday, June 17

We had stopped overnight in NYC, hoping to break up the trip overseas into three units so that we wouldn't travel the entire distance—Austin to Dublin—in one day. But a stopover in Manhattan required us to transfer ourselves and luggage from airport to hotel and on the next morning, back to airport in heavy traffic to JFK via the Long Island Expressway (the single greatest argument in the world against urban traffic design) and—although the cost of air travel was no more or less than the long haul would have cost—the ground transportation round trip was expensive, the luggage transfers and crowded lounges were anxi-

ety-producing, and we were tired and grouchy when we arrived at our final destination. Traveling together is worse than traveling alone because one gets
grouchier somehow.

We flew for only five daytime hours to LHR (London, Heathrow) where we
were met by a car and zipped to the Lanesborough Hotel. We were lodged there
royally overnight.

Tuesday, June 18

We slept late, dressed, transferred to the airport for another dose of madness
(having to walk thirty minutes, no exaggeration, to an Aer Lingus departure
lounge), flew to Dublin, and took a car into town to the Merrion Hotel. We were
upgraded to a suite of rooms with Georgian ceiling stucco décor: 3D grapes and
flowers. (The upgrade was a bonus provided for folks who had traveled with
A&K before.) We had tea in the hotel Drawing Room, then we unpacked,
napped, and enjoyed a light supper in the hotel's Mornington Room.

In the evening we went to a show, *That Was Then*, at the Abbey Theatre, the
most distinguished theatre in the country with great oil paintings of 20th Century
Irish playwrights, Yeats, Gregory, Joyce, Synge, and O'Casey, wow. Also Wilde
& Shaw, but they weren't part of the movement that spawned that remarkable
theatre*****.

(I've placed * asterisks to indicate degrees of personal interest on a five asterisk
scale.)

Irish poetry and plays and folk songs are what most folks think of as Ireland,
but the land itself can't hold a candle to the language and music legends.

Wednesday, June 19

Arose early, then I went to the new Guinness Factory & Museum* for a self-tour
that explained barrel-making better than beer-making. It's an old building that
has been rebuilt cleverly to conform to post modern hands-on museum standards
with an admission charged and a reward of a glass of the manufacturer's boggy
brew at the end of the tour.

I headed back toward the hotel and tried to use my bankcard at a nearby
ATM, but the machine gobbled it up just as it had been eaten in China. I
retrieved it from the banker in charge of rescuing bankcards at the Bank of Ireland located just behind the ATM and went to meet Barbara. I didn't want to
keep her waiting for lunch.

We ate at an upscale café, Chapter One**, in north Dublin next door to the
Writers Museum. While waiting for our lunch to be served, I decided to go to a

close-by bank to get cash. But they wouldn't take my $100 bill because, the teller said, "There've been too many unique ones," translation: "forgeries."

I said, "But you're a bank."

And she said, "Sorry, Love. Next."

Hmmm.

The lunch was fine, and after we finished strolling through the Writers Museum****, we returned to the Merrion where I planned to go on a walking tour around the neighborhood with an A&K guide. I asked Barbara to go to the bank since she didn't relish a walking tour (She had broken a toe the day before we left town, and—although it had stopped hurting her—she didn't want to push it). So she went to the bank, and I went with the group for a walk (ignoring my chronic neuropathic foot problem—I wanted to see how far I could push it).

We walked around and through Merrion Park where Oscar Wilde's statue** reclines imperiously on a great boulder. We peeked into the National (Art) Gallery*** and the National (Archeological) Museum*** and then walked to Grafton Street where shoppers do serious shopping.

Returning to our room, Barbara told me she had had the same trouble cashing the $100 bill. I said, "I'll find some way to break into that bank, you hide and watch."

That evening, we had dinner with the entire A&K tour group in the Wellington Room at the Merrion with an amusing speaker, Dr. John Redmill. Struck up an acquaintance immediately with Charlie and Susan White, two folks from New Orleans whose company we enjoyed during the tour.

Some A&Kers had nightcaps at a basement bar.

But it had been a long day. We crashed.

Thursday, June 20

The morning tour of Dublin included St. Patrick's Cathedral*, Trinity College (The Book of Kells)**, and a great lunch at Browne's Brasserie*** after that Marianne Gorman, our tour director, kindly accompanied me to a bank where the teller said, "Of course we'll take your $100 bill. Why wouldn't we?"

In the afternoon, we bussed to the private *Helen Dillon's Gardens*, where we were given tea and a special showing around the grounds by Ms. Dillon's husband. Very civilized, don't you know.

Back at the hotel, we napped, freshened up, and that evening went for a Literary Pub Crawl* whose itinerary through four pubs was disappointing because the noise level in each pub was incredible. The actors performed scenes, shouting the works of Wilde, Joyce, and a contemporary (whose name we didn't recognize), but we couldn't hear the performances in any but the first pub. We skipped out on the last scenes to go to dinner at 10PM, still bright daylight.

At Shanahans Restaurant, our steaks were too salty, but our dinner companions (whose names we've forgotten) were a young Northern Irish couple from Belfast whose anecdotes were even saltier. We thoroughly enjoyed sharing a table with them in the restaurant bar called "The Oval Office**," where John F. Kennedy's rocking chair is on display.

Returned to the hotel at 2am. Golly.

Friday, June 21

We checked out of the Merrion Hotel and headed west on our motorcoach. The first leg of our tour had been scheduled for a cross-country train ride that, Marianne explained, had somehow gotten derailed, ending somewhere in a peat bog.

We had a rest stop at Locke's Whiskey Distillery (As noted above, Irish whiskey is spelled with an "-ey", not like Scotch whisky). It was a side trip that some of us skipped because having seen one distillery.... Instead, we had tea & scones with clotted cream.

Lunch of fish and chips** at a nondescript restaurant our tour guide recommended in Galway overlooking Galway Bay. Later, our bus driver, Joe, sang a sad song*** about a lass he loved who lived at Galway Bay. Ah, the sad laddie.

We arrived at Cong, our first stop on the tour, Ashford Castle, a creepy old Gothic revival edifice that our guidebook described as having impeccable service and excellent food. Yeah, but our room up and down staircases was uninviting—pretty much what you'd expect to find in a castle heedlessly renovated for tourists. The weather outside was cool and pleasant, but our room was warm and stuffy; so I placed an electric fan in one of the windows and called for housekeeping to bring us another fan for the remaining window. We were told there was a fan in our closet. I said one fan wasn't sufficient, "Please bring us another fan with an extension cord that will reach from the outlet to the window." The fan was sent up without a cord, so the porter had to make another trip down and up to complete the fan installation. Eventually, we cooled the room

That evening in the castle's Common Room*** was the first and only time on the tour that we dressed (that is., ties & jackets) for dinner. The food and service were both classy and appetizing with the maitre d' hovering about. We were five to a table since there were fifteen in our A&K group.

Saturday, June 22

We traveled all day, first to Westport House (and to tell the truth, neither Barbara nor I have the vaguest memory of it with only one snapshot to prove we were there. We attribute our amnesia to jetlag or disinterest).

On to Kylemore Castle*, another Gothic revival, built by two Americans a century and a half ago, currently owned and managed by nuns who have more square footage in their gift shop and café than castle space for tourists to traipse through.

We stopped for supper at Burke's Pub & Restaurant*** where we ate shepherd's pie with bowls of boiled potatoes and platters of chips (French-fries). The Irish sure do like their spuds. We listened to country western music with Irish lyrics played by a five-piece band, and we watched three little girls do folk dances; they appeared to be professionally trained. And we drank pints of Guinness and watched A&Kers dance.

We returned to our overwarm castle cell and discovered our notes to leave the fans on had been ignored. So we cranked up the fans and slept with only a sheet for cover.

Sunday, June 23

After breakfast, we escaped from the castle and had lunch at the Moran's Oyster Cottage whose food and service, we were told, would be great—especially the oysters. Nobody ordered oysters, and the food was not very good, and the service was definitely not great.

We drove through the barren Burren**, austere and awesome, and arrived at the Cliffs of Moher**** where every tourist in Ireland had convened. But Mither Nature triumphed with her sheer natural beauty. The cliffs and downdrafts and birds swooping & squalling and steep steps & ramps made it an exciting place.

Less than an hour later, after crossing the river Shannon by ferry, we arrived at our lodging for the night, Glin Castle****, another Gothic Revival country home redesigned impecably for tourists, whose rooms and gardens were impressive indeed. So was dinner*** and our suite*** for the night. This was the kind of lodging we'd hoped for but never dared expect.

Monday, June 24

After an early morning stroll in the Castle's walled garden, we boarded our private conveyance and rode to Killarney for lunch and shopping. From there we crowded into Jaunting Carts**, seven to a cart, and rode to Muckross House**, a larger-than-life Victorian-Elizabethan mansion. En route, we stopped to stroll around the crumbling walls of Muckross Abbey***, a ruined church & cemetery.

The Muckross estate is enormous. A perfect setting for a hunting lodge or manor house in an *Upstairs/Downstairs* genre film. Walking through the place and the adjoining gardens and gift shop/cafe was tiring, and for the first time since we arrived in Ireland, we got "walked out."

That evening we arrived at Sheen Falls Lodge****, a lovely, modern resort. Our room had a super view of the Falls. Dinner service was slow (3 hours) but the food was good. We were so tired we went to sleep while we were still conversing at dinner and then somehow got ourselves up to bed around 10PM.

Tuesday, June 25

We decided to skip the Ring of Kerry tour this morning, opting for a ride into the town of Kenmare for lunch at the Purple Heather*, shopping afterwards for our grandtwins. A nap after lunch was the highlight of the day.

I had been asked to do a twenty-minute one man show for the A&Kers, featuring monologs I've written in the past. So I wrote another monolog, satirizing our tour director (whose English is impeccable) by inventing a character with an Irish brogue leading a tour group in Texas:

"Ah, good. We're awl here abard the coach, now, so let's begin awr travel for today from Fart Worth with a hop dawn to Austin and a skip t' San Antonio and a stop on the coast at Soth Padre fer lawnch. Then, after lawnch, we'll continue zoomin' interminably acrawst the country ta El Paso with a detour to Monterray and a dip dawn to Mexico City, returnin' by 6 o'clock this evenin' to Fart Worth, dressin' for the dinner we'll be eatin' at the famous Mansion on Tartle Crick in Dall-ass. Our word for the day is the old Irish blessin' & curse: "May the wind be atchure back, and may it ahlso move yer ahrse."

I performed for the entire A&K tour group plus bus driver and luggage valet, and—Barbara will attest—I enjoyed myself enormously.

We also enjoyed dinner in one of the hotel's drawing rooms.

Wednesday, June 26

I arose early and strolled around the grounds then returned to pack and join the group at the front of the hotel. I hung my jacket on a hanger near the entrance and completely forgot about it. Miles down the road, our tour director got a call on her cell phone from our luggage valet saying he had the jacket, asking if it belonged to anyone in our group. Thank goodness for him and for the advantage of having someone to look after us.

Our first stop of the day was Blarney Castle* where we declined kissing the Blarney Stone and, instead, visited the huge Blarney Woolen Mills souvenir center*, purchasing two musical leprechauns for our grandtwins.

A highlight of the tour was the next stop at Kilshannig House*** (Princess Diana's ancestral home) undergoing restoration by the owners (whose names we forgot) who showed us around the place and served us a light lunch at a grand table in their dining room. The stucco ceilings were as old as the house, 1766.

The Rock of Cashel**, our next stop, is another ruined church, a curious but evocative architectural hodgepodge with a graveyard still being used for burial grounds by descendents of the original landowners of Cashel.

A long drive, and then the Mount Juliet Hotel****, the best lodging on the tour, opening onto a garden we shared with other A&K guests.

Dinner, however, took forever to be served, and I was surprised to be so annoyed by slow service. I never want to get served a good dinner too quickly. I just want service to be timely. I think Irish waiters are expected to handle more tables than American waiters handle.

Thursday, June 27

Slept late on our only morning to sleep in, then we explored the gardens on the grounds. Ate lunch in our semi-private garden with A&K guests.

That afternoon, we went on a trip to the Waterford Crystal Factory*** just to see what folks talk about when they come back from Ireland. Friends at home had let us know their prices are no lower in the States, so we determined that if we're gonna buy that stuff, we'll trade here in Salado. But the tour of the factory was interesting, watching glass blowers and shapers and all the other craft folks involved in the process of creating lead crystal objects. And we were presented with a lovely souvenir picture frame.

Returning, we had dinner at the Mount Juliet Golf Club Restaurant***.

Friday, June 28

We drove to the Russborough House*** a Palladian country manor, grand and glorious, open to the public. The stucco on walls and ceilings was stunning, but the carpets were huge, thick, and ugly. Lady Beit, the surviving owner of the house, (whose deceased husband, Sir Alfred Beit, bought and restored the old house, and hung priceless paintings on its walls, bequeathing the whole works to the National Gallery), lives in a wing of the mansion not open to the public.

We continued on to Dublin to Mahaffy House***, a charming Georgian private home rebuilt by the owner, an eccentric china and porcelain restorer. She showed us around and served lunch at tables on the ground floor. When I asked why was there no stucco ceiling ornamentation, she said, "Oh, my dear. Ceilings on ground floors never have stucco ornaments."

I said, "Why not?"

She said, "Because that's not how we do things here. How do you do it in America?"

I said, "Ummm, we don't have much stucco in the States."

"I see," she said, "Pity." Then she moved away to chat with others.

We returned to the Merrion for our final stay on the tour, and they crammed us in a small room with an enormous bed. I let them know I was disappointed, and I explained we had been upgraded to a suite with stucco fruit on the ceiling during our original stay. The management responded immediately: they sent us a bowl of fruit.

Since it was located just across the street from us, we checked out the Museum of Natural History*** (called the "Dead Museum"). Lotsa stuffed animals stuffed in that foreboding Victorian chamber.

That evening, we had our final get together, beginning with cocktails in a smoky, noisy bar at the hotel where everybody talked about the noise and smoke. Then we went to another of the hotel's private rooms for a banquet where almost everyone contributed original limericks.

My contribution was, unapologetically:

"A Tour Guide named Marianne Gorman

Expected her tourists to compose limericks.

     But she failed to insist

     That the limericks should scan perfectly

So this poet submits herewith an example of post modern verse that—to the uninitiated—may seem an excessively overlong unrhymed poem."

The prizewinning limerick, by an anonymous author (Not me, I swear.):

"There once was a girl from St. Louis

The wife of the pilot who flew us.

     She joined him in flight

     To Ireland one night,

And awoke with his fuckle in her clewis"

"Fuckle in one's clewis" is an Anglicized old Celtic expression meaning "to put a bug in someone's ear" as in "Let me tell you this about that." And that is the extent of my anonymous friend's command of the Celtic language.

We said goodbye to our new friends and several folks whom we hadn't gotten to know well, but all friendly tourists.

We had nightcaps, and the tour was officially over.

Saturday, June 29

Barbara and I had a farewell breakfast, then we did the National Gallery justice. We had lunch, then knocked off the Archaeological Museum again.

We napped, packed, went for dinner at Frere Jacques Restaurant***** for the best food I had on the entire trip.

Finally, coffee in the Hotel's Drawing Room.

Sunday, June 30

There was a big mix-up getting to the airport early in the morning: We thought our car was late, so we called a taxi and had our luggage loaded on. The driver of a car that had been standing by asked if we were the Carvers, and when I said, "Yes," said he'd been waiting for us. We tipped the taxi driver who helped transfer the luggage.

Our Aer Lingus plane from Dublin arrived late at Heathrow, so—after walking what seemed like miles to the American desk—we discovered we'd missed our plane.

It took me an hour to arrange for another flight, and to make a long story short, we made better arrangements than we had originally had, arriving in Austin two hours earlier.

Arriving early sometimes causes complications, but that's another story.

SUMMING UP:

For me, the A&K "Ireland" Tour was so delicately conceived and tweaked for travelers over age 50, it lacked vitality. There were no Leprechauns. Except some of the A&Kers.

We were well cared for. Our tour guide was a superior one. There were no problems with our bus or luggage or lodgings or food or scheduling. The sights are unique. Irish people are obliging and friendly. Quantitatively, we visited, toured, ate at, or stayed at over 25 different places under the A&K auspices.

But the bus riding was interminable, and nodding off a half dozen times daily left me feeling like a doddering old fool being bounced from one site to another.

After we arrived back home, the first time I was asked how I felt about the trip, I spontaneously replied: "Well, Ireland's like a great, wet, green museum, and I don't recommend it to anyone I know—unless, of course, you're wheel-chair-bound."

People don't want to believe I didn't think Ireland's stunning, so I've thought better of making tacky remarks like that. Now, I just say it was like almost falling in love.

My Pilgrimage to Lourdes, Minnesota

✦

The Mayo Clinic
September 14–21, 2002

There isn't a Lourdes, Minnesota, of course; it's Rochester. That's where the Mayo Clinic's shimmering, antiseptic towers are located. And the sick and halt and blind gather there in hopes of regaining health and strength and sight.

My specific destination was Mayo's Neurological Department where I hoped to find the cause and treatment for a problem of mine that had been diagnosed as *Peripheral Neuropathy,* but I didn't know for sure.

That's why Barbara and I went to Rochester in September, 2002, where I found myself on the next day after we arrived at 6:30 a.m., walking among the hordes of patients like religious penitents from hotels and entryways through subways and skyways on foot, or in wheelchairs, or using walkers, or sitting at the wheel of battery-powered mopeds, converging on—Ta-da.—The Clinic.

But have you ever tried to overtake and walk around a person in a wheelchair accompanied by his entire family, all of them eating breakfast afoot, blocking the path?

I could attach (but I won't) a long history detailing how I came upon a diagnosis of Neuropathy after consulting with nine medical practitioners (ten, if you count Barbara, the house physician) who determined that my condition was "idiopathic" that means they didn't know the cause, therefore, they couldn't advise treatment accordingly. Nor relief from pain.

My appointment with Dr. Dyck (pronounced "dick")—the Doctor who wrote the definitive book on the subject of Neuropathy—was scheduled for 7 AM on that September morning, so we sat with hundreds of other patients and their spouses, all of us waiting for a thorough diagnostic examination from various doctors who shared the same waiting room. I was asked to fill out a comprehensive questionnaire (a redundancy because it duplicated the information I had sent to Dr. Dyck's office months before making the appointment). Questions like "Are you a diabetic?" No. "Do you have any problems other than those already noted?" Yes, I threw in a smallpox complaint, hoping to get attention.

When I was at last admitted to the inner sanctum of Dr. Dyck, he was most cordial, a kindly old practitioner, who laughed when he asked if I really had smallpox. I said no, but there were blanks to be filled in, so I had allowed my imagination to invent that attention getter. Then he was gone, leaving me with his assistant, Dr. Somebody with an East Indian name I was never able to pronounce or retain who scheduled me for examinations lasting two full days.

I reported to the dispensery and was issued two plastic jugs. And when I asked what for, I was told to carry them around with me for the next two days to collect my urine. Not satisfied with urine samples, they wanted every drop.

I underwent all manner of exams, from the kind that would be inappropriate to mention in this journal to the kind that my readers would find boring, boring, boring.

At the conclusion of the two-day exams, I was readmitted to Dr. Dyck's chamber where he and his assistant assured me that I do indeed have an idiopathic case of Peripheral Neuropathy in my feet and only in my feet.

The treatment, he said, varies from individual to individual, but he suggested I try several medications [Like Neurontin that I have found efficacious] or—I got the distinct impression—I might consider prayer and/or psychic healing methodologies. He said, "Too bad it wasn't Smallpox. We can prevent Smallpox, but we can neither prevent nor cure Neuropathies. If you're lucky like some, you might outgrow the condition or have a kind of remission. Good luck finding a palliative, and have a good life."

He showed me to the door.

We had traveled to Lourdes, seeking the Great Oz, but he was not helpful, at best he was only reassuring. So what does one who has an infirmity do who loves to travel?

One keeps on traveling.

Aboard the *Sea Cloud I* for a sail around Sicily and a swim in the Mediterranean.

The West Coast of Italy

✦

With Yale Exes Aboard Sea Cloud I
August 15–September 1, 2003

I returned to Austin at the close of my fantastic *Sea Cloud I* yacht adventure on September 1st, 2003, Labor Day, four p.m. And would you believe the weather in Texas had been ten degrees cooler than the week-long heat wave I had just endured in Europe. Texas was chillin'.

I waited outside the airport terminal for an hour or so, wondering why my wife hadn't yet picked me up. My cell phone was dead. I didn't have any change except for a 5 Euro bill that nobody was willing to cash, so I finally asked a stranger to loan me fifty cents to call Barbara long distance on her cell phone (I've got a phone card with over 1,000 minutes, so I knew that if I could just get access to a phone, I could ask Barbara what's up). The stranger waited to make sure I wasn't going to stiff him for fifty cents, and he seemed relieved when I returned the coins and thanked him excessively.

I dialed. Barbara answered. I said (affecting a casual tone), "What's goin' on, Honey?"

She said, "I had a wreck about an hour ago, and the car's a friggin' mess, but other than that, I'm fine."

"WHAT! (Please note caps indicating both shock and compassion) Why didn't you call me? I could have come to get you, Sweetheart. Are you really, truly okay?"

"I'm the one who was coming to get you at the airport, Dear. I'm fine."

There followed a conversation that, for the most part, consisted of me asking if she were really, truly fine and her assurances that, yes, she was as fine as she could expect to be after bending the fender of her Mercedes. At least, that's the impression she gave me, dear Reader, so keep in mind that I believed the fender just needed a little work.

I'll report the truth later in this journal.

Steve, my son-in-law, picked Barbara up, and I rented a car and drove to the home of my daughter, son-in-law, and their two four-year-olds, and we all commiserated with Barbara. (The grandtwins contributed more confusion than commiseration.)

Suddenly thought to ask me, "How was your trip?"

Instinctively I knew it would be inappropriate for me to tell my family what a gloriously fantastic trip I had just returned from because we were all still focussed on Barbara. But I lost my head and—Wow. I began describing my adventures, sailing on the world's largest four-masted yacht, from Rome down the Coast to Malta, around Sicily, sails flapping in the breeze—

They were all looking at me as if to say, "How nice for you."

The boy grandtwin used his dinosaur to bite my leg. It's a 1½ foot high T-Rex.

I said, "But my trip can wait till later. I'm so glad Barbara's really, truly all right. You *are* okay aren't you, Honey? I mean really."

Again she said yes, and I stopped conversing, longing for my next cue.

About an hour later, we all sat down to supper at a Mexican restaurant where the kids performed without cease.

There was a brief lull in the storm, and someone said, "Tell us some more about your trip. And pass the salsa."

Again, I mistakenly took that as a cue for passion to begin the narrative I had been rehearsing from Valletta to Rome to London to Dallas to Austin. However,

I hadn't quite finished talking about my flight from Austin to Dallas when I heard someone say, "Let's get some more queso & chips, and I'm ready for another Corona. How about you, Barbara?"

Clearly, I did not have their full attention, only their forbearance.

So I said, "No, *later*. I'll type up a travel journal and send it to you by email so you can read it at your leisure."

No one objected. And my four-year-old grandson smiled up at me, letting me know I had made the right choice.

So that's what follows, my Sea Cloud Journal, a tome I finished composing after filling out the friggin' insurance claims, etc.

Thursday, August 21. I fly to Rome

Arrived in Rome at 8 AM and waited around for a bus to Hotel Excelsior (A four out of five stars hotel—a nice place, but one star missing is like a front tooth missing). I was travelling alone because Barbara had opted out of this trip. She and I will be traveling together in October to Spain.

The bus didn't depart until 1 PM following the arrival of all the other Yale Exes embarking on the Sea Cloud I adventure. The heat & humidity was intense, so I sat alone, and avoided conversing with anyone because Mark Twain was right: nobody ever knows how smart or dumb you are until you open your mouth.

I ate lunch alone at Le Paris across the street from the hotel, conversing with myself ("Did you enjoy your lunch, Ramon?" "Yes, indeed, I did." "What did you eat?" "A sensational egg plant casserole with a buffalo mozzarella & tomato salad and a dynamite glass of red vino." "I'll bet it was great." "It was fantastic.").

I returned to the hotel and napped. Afterwards, I had a massage in the hotel's health spa, but it was just an okay massage.

I dressed for a reception scheduled to begin at 7 PM in the hotel lobby bar, and I resumed my conversation with Number Uno.

"Uh-oh, that tie doesn't go with your shirt."

"Too bad."

"Your belt looks like it cost all of $3.98."

"You think?"

"And your socks don't match your trousers."

"Change socks."

"Will people think you're a bozo wearing this ubiquitous blue jacket?"

"Of course not. Don't be silly."

"Right, they'll just think it's conventional and unimaginative."

"Yeah? Well, that's tough shit."

"Relax. The room will be full of folks who think they're looking great, but they won't look any better than you. Honest, Ramon, you look really…. Okay."

At that moment, I recalled dialogs I've had with myself alone on the first leg of several journeys in the past. I've had two Yale Exes trips, and on each opening night, I've had stage fright. As a rational human being, I'm aware that most intelligent people fear looking stupid in front of strangers. I am not stupid. Repeat: I am not stupid. I knew that all I had to do was keep my mouth shut and act cool. I said aloud, "I can do that."

"Oh?"

I winked at myself in the mirror, rolled my eyes, and headed for the door. "It's showtime."

Leaving the room, I entered the crowded elevator and descended with six tight-lipped Yalie-looking people. And sure enough, when we reached the ground floor, we all headed for the same noisy lounge where strangers were chatting up strangers.

I stood alone holding a glass of club soda, and I'm sure I appeared to be an intelligent-looking guy with a knowing smile, the ultimate outsider onlooker, silent as a tomb, until a handsome woman approached me and said, "Good evening."

I said, "Oh, thank God. I thought nobody was ever gonna talk to me. The only reason I'm wearing this jacket is because my mother made me, and I'm sweatin' like a pig, and you're looking sweatier than me. No shit."

Actually, I didn't say anything so stupid. I don't remember what I said, but I thought, "She's thinking I'm extremely clever."

That's when she said something like "Excuse me. I've got to go find somebody intelligent to talk with."

I assured myself, "She likes me. Everybody will like me." And I persuaded myself that everybody in that room that night thought the same thing. Or, at least, those of us who gave a damn about how well we'd be perceived.

The faculty who would be lecturing aboard ship were introduced, and they each spoke a bit more than they needed to, short lecturettes. That was the entertainment.

I didn't eat a single hors d'ouevre because I kept tasting egg plant from lunch.

I chitchatted with about 200 of the 20 people at the reception. Then, I said my good-byes to no one in particular, left the reception, and went up to bed.

I had just about dropped off to sleep when a maid appeared at the door and, startled, said, "You don't want a chocoletto?"

I said no, thanks, and good night.

Friday, August 21.

I enjoyed breakfast in a relaxed atmosphere, folks talking unself-consciously. The morning excursion to the Roman Forum was fun, too, because we all seemed to be glad the reception was over with. Now we could loosen up.

The tourguide was not good. She was cute, however, and she used cute expressions like "Afterwards we will toilet," and "It is dirty for pollution reasons," and "Gladiators tried to avoid that they died."

Guides get carried away with themselves. They should be forbidden to volunteer any and all information. They should speak only when asked questions like, "What's that ugly stuff that looks like doodoo over there?" They should always say, "Now, that's a good question." And their answers should never last more than 30 seconds. And sometimes that's too long.

The Forum tour was similar to the one I had taken almost thirty years ago when I shepherded a flock of 30 college students through the ruins. Hadn't changed a bit, of course, but it was hotter than I remembered it. Not as many cats this time around.

I rated the excursion A+.

Lunch at the hotel was followed by an afternoon lecture by Mr. Kennedy, Yale Professor of History, on the subject of Imperialism, positing the question: "Is the United States an empire in the tradition of the Romans and Great Britain?"

I asked, "Has the US become an accidental empire?"

He said, "A nation becomes an empire only by design."

Hmmmm.

That evening, we were given a special tour of the Vatican museum and Sistine Chapel. We were incredibly hot throughout the tour (except for the Chapel and air-conditioned bookstore) but after hours, the place was mercifully quiet, allowing us to study the paintings without the sound of tourguides competing for attention. I lay on some seats on my back and stared up at the chapel ceiling until a museum guard roused me. Great way to study that ceiling.

After about a thirty-minute visit, we were ushered out. I lingered, and two guards followed me, urging me to keep moving down those halls whose decorations were o-t-t (over-the-top). Question: Why have they stored so much of that stuff in the Vatican? Answer: Who else could afford it and where else would they put it?

So much *stuff.* I dragged my heels and succeeded in being the last tourist in the Vatican for the day. Gave me a real sense of accomplishment and achievement. Another A+.

For dinner, Sheila Cook, the Yale rep, and John & Marge Winter and I went to an inexpensive restaurant across town. Hot but charming, we had good food and great fun. The A plusses were beginning to multiply exponentially.

Later, in my room, I called Barbara and listened to her chat about our grand-kids. She asked, "Did you enjoy the Forum & Vatican?"

I said yes, but I was hot. Over 100 degrees Fahrenheit.

She said it wasn't that high in Texas.

I ate the melted chocoletto on my pillow, and said good night to Barbara.

Saturday, August 23.

We toured Rome.

Breakfasted with a downright convivial crowd, then I set out alone for the nearby Spanish Steps that I had never visited before. There's not so many steps as they appear in photographs. Then I returned to the hotel for lunch in the bar of the Excelsior and an endless wait for the bus to transfer us to the Borghese Museum.

The tour of the statue-stuffed Borghese Palace was another A plusser because of a few truly remarkable pieces of sculpture amid all the o-t-t stuff there.

The bus continued on to Civitavecchia by the sea and to the dock where Sea Cloud I was waiting. Then, Shazam. There it is. Looka there. Oh, my gosh, what a grand sight to see. A+. It was more than I had expected and my expectations are always absurdly high. I've been aboard lots of large and small ships and boats, but this one—to quote Goldilocks—looked just right.

Its overall length is 360 feet, making it the world's largest yacht with 4 masts. It's 50 feet wide with 32 cabins (new and refurbished since 2002). The height of the main mast is 178 feet, and there are 30 sails.

The passenger to crew ratio is about 1:1.

Under sail, we cruised at 4.5 knots maximum speed, but the ship has been clocked at 14.5 knots.

Phone & Fax communication is expensive, but email is free.

According to the published ship information, "Sporty, casual clothing is appropriate onboard. For the Captain's Welcome and Farewell receptions and dinners we recommend more formal attire for women and a jacket and tie for men." But once we were seated in the dining hall, on both occasions, men were allowed to shed jackets because of the heat.

My immediate impression of the vessel was best expressed by an old Salt, many years ago: "Only some ships are truly yare." The Sea Cloud turned out to be way yare. And I never changed my mind.

Upon embarkation, we were greeted by officers and staff with glasses of champagne & cakes. Then, one at a time, we were led to our cabins. Mine, #29, was highly satisfactory, small but efficiently designed with polished woods and marble and some original-looking trim and a large window. And there was a bottle of champagne with the Sea Cloud imprint, and fruit and flowers. It was a great cabin for one person—if only the air conditioning had performed adequately. The room stayed hot and stuffy every day until late at night. I really needed a fan, but that might have suggested the ship's owners truly believed the cabin needed a fan (if you take my meaning). I went to sleep sweating each night. No A+ for my cabin, but 4 out of 5 stars.

I had a quick shower and then we all had dinner in a lovely dining room, paneled with bookcases. Around 10 PM, I returned to my cabin and, tired out, fell asleep.

Sunday, August 24.

We spent the day At Sea.

I arose, hastily dressed because I didn't want to miss anything, and went to the Bridge where four of us talked with the First Mate, charting our journey. Then I had breakfast with companions whose company I was beginning to enjoy.

This feeling of camaraderie increased considerably during the voyage. I quickly developed and maintained three kinds of relationships: close, cordial, or as sometimes in life, distant. I particularly liked the Texans aboard ship.

Just before lunch, I attended another illuminating history lecture by Mr. Kennedy on the subject of the Mediterranean Sea and battles fought there.

That afternoon, one of the most A+ things on the whole trip happened: a chance to swim out into the middle of the salty Mediterranean Sea. Hoorah. Most of us aboard, including staff and crew, walked down the lowered gangplank and stepped into the sea to swim happily, cavorting, having great, great fun. I've never seen so many people smiling and splashing without being prompted for a photograph. And considering the diminished beauty of some of our bodies, not many asked for photographs.

From time to time, small and large motor boats on Sunday outings approached the ship to ogle us. We ogled back at some topless sun worshippers.

Lunch, a nap, then a talk by Charles Ellis about "Winning and Losing" in the stock market. He performed well and I applauded

Later, drinks and a Welcome Aboard dinner with coat & tie and good company in the dining room. The most interesting thing about dinners aboard ship—aside from the excellent food—was the two to three hours we spent at table conversing each evening. Who needs TV.

Monday, August 25. Positano.

I has some simple thrills.

After a morning rendezvous with the first mate on the Bridge, I joined the group who opted not to go to Pompeii and Herculaneum preferring a visit to the seacoast village of Positano.

Arriving by tender from the ship, we went separate ways to explore the village and shops, walking up stairs and streets and sidewalks to Hotel Sirena. En route, I passed dozens of kids wailing and/or whining, and I thought, "What is it about beaches all over the world that turns children into screaming little monsters."

Of greater interest to me was the current Italian style affected by women with particularly large boobs who appeared bra-less, wearing filmy, flimsy blouses revealing all but their nipples as their breasts bobbled and bounced about, kaboom, kabop.

It was Bazoom City.

I saw two unfortunate women who, I'm sure, didn't know that their areolas were showing. Whoa, mamma.

Then one of the most memorable events on the trip occurred: I joined four of the ladies from the ship having tea on the terrace of the Sirena Hotel, looking out at a view that appears on most of the postcards of the village. We enjoyed a vista that made us all feel perfectly content to stay there on that terrace always—or at least for that three-quarters of an hour. Viewing the world from exotic terraces is justification enough for travelling around the world. A+

Golly, it was beautiful. I had no idea rooftops could be so sexy. Or maybe I was still reacting from all the kaboombas still bouncing around in my short-term memory.

Later, we were herded by a local tourguide like poor little lambs aboard a bus to return to the ship. One little lamb, late arriving, had lost her way. So we waited. The bus was hot as hell, so I said, "Lord have mercy on such as we. I'm gonna have heat stroke."

The tourguide used the "uh" ending on his words, a habit that some Italians affect, and insisted that we should "Wait-uh aboard-uh the bus-uh."

But I said no-uh, and I led a revolt-uh and we all got off—uh.

I said, "When that damned oven isn't being used to haul tourists, you probably use it to bake pizzas."

We pretended to shop as we went from one tourist trap to another, huddling around ineffectual window unit air conditioners. Finally, the prodigal tourista returned and we took off, steaming back to the ship, the bus dodging Vespas and Hondas.

Back aboard, I had lunch seated across from Jim Binger and Jane Mauer from Minneapolis who asked me the questions everybody always asks universally when making my acquaintance: "Where are you from and what do you do?"

I say "Salado, above Austin. I'm retired from teaching drama, but I'm still a playwright."

Everybody says, "Oh? Have you ever had anything produced?"

And I say, "I've had some plays produced off-Broadway and in Hollywood, San Francisco, Atlanta, yeah."

And they say, "Gosh." Then they stop asking.

But Jane Mauer asked, "Where in New York?"

And I said, "A theatre on 42nd Street, I've forgotten the name. Why? Nobody ever asks for names of theatres."

And she said, "Because my husband owns five Broadway theatres."

Then I, a playwright who has spent his entire professional life looking for a theatre owner, said—in the most offhand manner I could pretend as I dropped my jaw to the floor: "No shit."

Jane and Jim laughed.

And I said, "Jujancyn?"

Jim looked surprised and said, "Only one in a million people would know that I named my company for my three children." Then we started talking about things other than theatre.

And I thought, "Yeah, and now they'll think I'm a ringer who got on this ship just to cozy up next to them."

And for the rest of the cruise, until my last night in Malta, I acted weird around them, trying to find some way of saying, "Oh, by the way, if you think I inveigled my way onto this ship just to meet a theatre owner, you're wrong. Okay?"

That afternoon, after a nap, I went ashore alone, took a bus into Salerno, kicked around for half an hour, then returned to the ship, thinking, "Salerno may look like a nowhere burg, but this little dot on the map was where the first decisive battle of the Allied assault forces who landed on Europe took place in 1943."

There were no scars on the land that I could see. Nor comments made by any of my peers aboard ship. Hell, it's been 60 years.

At dinner that evening, somebody gave me a cue to perform, and I dazzled my table mates with songs and recitations—everything but a dance on the table top—and the seven of us stayed until every other table in the dining room was deserted. I have an extensive repertoire, and I had a great time. So A+, of course.

Tuesday, August 26. Stromboli and Lipari.

I watched a volcano erupt.

There was a stunning electrical storm in the night with winds & waves rocking the boat, and my cabin cooled down to the lower 80s.

In the very early morning, I arose and went up on deck to the Bridge to watch Stromboli, the volcano, erupt. Hot dog. Lots of smoke and a glowing coal at the pinnacle. Wow. A+.

Others on the ship arose late and missed it.

We ate breakfast, then a trip by tender to Lapari where a bus took us around that craggy island. We stopped first at an herb stand. A what? Well, there were these ladies, perched at an overlook on the mountainside, selling herbs they'd ground up and packaged with postcards. I bought some, and worried that I hadn't bought enough for gifts. Later, after tasting one of the packets, I realized the peppers in it were too sizzling hot for me, therefore probably too hot for gifts.

We continued driving around and saw lots of rugged mountains & sea, olive trees & grape vines.

And pumice. Tons of pumice. And it takes a lot of pumice to make a ton of this volcanic stuff.

We stopped at a volcanic ash beach and a grungy little seaside café to purchase postcards and use the toilet. Not a tourist stop I'd recommend for folks who ain't much impressed with pumice.

I took the tender back to the ship, showered, ate lunch, and—another busy day—sacked out. Or, at least, dozed intermittently.

A problem I've discovered is the muffled "booms" of what must be a rudder located beneath my cabin. I consulted the ship's engineer who said there's nothing anybody can do about it. I said, "But it wakes me up."

And he said, "Suck it in, Jack," but he said it in a nice way.

I went up on deck in time to watch our ship's young sailors climb the masts and rigging, untying the ship's sails. Golly, what an amazing thrill. Up until that afternoon, there hadn't been enough wind to justify using the sails. Then, when the sails were raised, I cried aloud, "A+."

I didn't have to explain myself to anyone.

There followed another talk by Charles Ellis. Very entertaining. He fended Q&A expertly. Afterwards, I asked him to sign a copy of his book, and he was very gracious.

Early that evening, while I was having libations with my new best friends, there was a squall with heavy rains and winds. It was a special feature, Mother Nature dazzling us. A+

The rains slacked to a sprinkle, and we went up on deck (and I climbed up above the Bridge) to view the strait of Messina between Italy & Sicily, only a few miles wide, the legendary passage between Scylla & Charybdis. Cynthia Farrar, Yale professor of political Science, stood on the Bridge deck and read aloud from Thucydides' account of Odyssus passing through this narrow strait, lashed to the mast of his ship to avoid being seduced by the two female sea monsters. A+.

After unlashing myself from the top deck, I joined my new acquaintances for dinner.

Wednesday, August 27. Taormini, Sicily.

I ate eggplant again.

I began the day on the Bridge, making sure the First Mate was staying the course.

Went on an excursion to Taormini and enjoyed the Greek Theatre and particularly enjoyed an eggplant and shrimp dish at The Baronessa Restaurant in the company of Yale Rep Sheila Cook who, with Karen Levy (the Gohagan Travel Company Rep), effortlessly manage to run as tight a ship on as smooth a trip as I have ever taken. A+.

Several of us boarded a zodiac to return to the ship, but when I heard a young sailor speaking on his two-way radio in French, I said, "Just a minute. We're not going to that French ship anchored out there; we're on the Sea Cloud. Just drop us off there, d'accord?"

But the young sailor stopped the zodiac on a dime, turned around, and took us back to shore, evidently afraid he would be charged with Shanghaiing Sea Cloud passengers. Minutes later, our tender picked us up and took us to the ship in time for tea.

I nodded off during the afternoon lecture by Ms. Farrar. She was fine, but I was drowsy. And drowsy trumps fine.

From this point on, I wasn't greatly impressed with the academic program for the cruise. It seemed culled from too many old lecture notes.

I returned to my cabin around 5:30 and planned to nap for an hour. Nope. I overslept three hours, missing the first course at dinner.

After chow, I went ashore expecting to attend a street fair, but it was just itinerant street venders selling stuff I wasn't interested in, so I retired to a café for iced tea.

Then I returned to the ship—on the correct tender.

Thursday, August 28. Syracusa.

Today's breakfast had an interesting lecture by Cynthia Farrar on the subject of the tragic end of the Peloponnesian Wars to prepare us for the scheduled sightseeing.

Ashore, I boarded an uncrowded bus and sat alone—the way I usually prefer to sit—until another passenger, a Texan, Corky Hilliard, asked to sit in the seat beside me. Corky's good company, so no problem. Funny, but I view being able to spread out over two seats on uncrowded busses a real luxury. But I also enjoy folks who like to talk, especially when the scenery gets dull.

Syracuse is loaded with archeological sites including a Greco-Roman Theatre (the largest in the world), Roman amphitheater ruins, and a stadium. The place must have been an entertainment Mecca.

We stopped near the ruins noted above to view the rock quarry where 7,000 Athenians were left to die at the end of the Peloponnesian Wars. Sobering.

Then we started off on what was represented as a thirty-minute walking tour to the Cathedral of Syracuse, every archeological-architect's dream-come-true, a Christian church utilizing the walls of an old temple, achieving utility and beauty. Thereafter, we were given 15 minutes to shop around with instructions to reboard the bus several blocks away.

I chose a wayward path and walked along the edge of the sea on a lovely avenue lined with great Ficus trees. All was well until I ran out of trees and had to use unshaded city streets & sidewalks to wind my way in the Sun back to the ship.

I arrived, pooped. I bolted my lunch. Then I snagged a nap and awoke to go up on deck to lie on my back watching sailors hoist sails as we set out to sea again. Spiders weaving webs. Wow. A+ again.

Two shots of Stoly's later, and four sheets to the wind, I went up on the Lido Deck where Bar-B-Que was being served, and I went around, table-hopping, enjoying the company of virtual strangers, most of us behaving like long-term friends.

When I went to bed, I lay awake, my face burning from too much sun. There was nothing to do but use a cool washcloth to ease the discomfort.

Sometimes, two Stoly's are not quite enough.

I learned the next day that the crew had sung, as promised, sea chanteys and bawdy songs just after I left the party. For many Yalies, it was a highlight of the trip.

Friday, August 29. Agriento, Sicily.

I tasted salt in the air.

I skipped the tour of this island and stayed aboard because my face was still warm and because I read in our shipboard newspaper: "You will be in the sun more than any other site. This is a dusty place of scant charm." *Scant charm?* What a promise of disappointment.

Those of us who remained aboaard watched about thirty double-axle trucks laden with salt pass by en route to another dock. There was so much salt in the air, we could stick out our tongues and taste it, and it wasn't the mild taste of sea water.

Those who took the tour came back raving about the remarkable "Valley of Temples" and a fantastic tour guide. That makes two highlights I missed.

After a buffet lunch portside, we sailed for an hour or so until the captain announced it was time for swimming again. Almost all of us who took to the water were well over 50, most of us over 60, but we didn't have any embarrassment laughing and splashing like sea gods and goddesses. I sang, "O Joy, O Rapture Unforeseen."

Again, A+.

That afternoon, I missed Mr. Kennedy's final lecture, but the truth is I was lectured out.

This was our last full day aboard the ship, so I paid my bill at the Purser's and packed most of my clothes.

In the evening there was a reception on the Lido Deck followed by a banquet. Afterwards, I finished packing and slept very well.

Saturday, August 30. Valetta, Malta.

We disembarked.

Valetta's harbor is just about the most beautiful harbor in the world, and sailing into that seaport is unforgettable.

I saluted the first mate on the Bridge. A+.

We recovered our passports, checked out of the Sea Cloud, and checked into the Malta Meridien Phoenician whose sofas in the cavernous lounge looked like five shades of sherbet.

My room was nice, but the water wasn't potable.

The weather continued extremely hot, so I went only halfway through a walking tour to the Co-Cathedral, the Grand Masters Palace, and wherever the Hell else my group walked. Our guide was both informed and boring, but my shoes were rubbing blisters on my feet, so I said, "Skooza. I'm outta here."

Back at the hotel, after a so-so lunch in good company, I napped, and then I asked the hotel concierge for directions to a shopping area where I might buy some toys and clothes for my grandtwins. He steered me wrong. Nothing was open that afternoon. So I came back to the hotel, showered, and dressed for a casual dinner, missing a panel discussion of Yale's current standing.

From comments I heard later, I felt I hadn't missed much.

A reception followed, and—thinking back to the first reception I had so dreaded—I truly enjoyed this one except that saying goodbye to my new best friends was like paying final respects at a cheerful wake. Remarkably, there had been no serious mishaps on the trip, no significant disappointments, and the trip had far exceeded expectations—at least all mine. I have the greatest admiration for the Yale staff and the tour staff who made it all work out so beautifully.

A group photograph was taken and then—Oh, wow, A+—the group sang Yale's Alma Mater.

Some of the gang were bona fide Yalies, some of us were ex-grad drudges, and some were connected to the school only by proxy, but all of us were caught up in the magic of their singing of the song they love so well.

"Bright College Years, with pleasure rife,
The shortest, gladdest years of life,
How swiftly are ye gliding by,
O, why doth time so quickly fly?
The seasons come the seasons go,
The Earth is green or white with snow;
But time and change shall naught avail
To break the friendships formed at Yale.
In after-years, should troubles rise
To cloud the blue of sunny skies,
How bright will seem, through mem'ry's haze,
Those happy, golden by-gone days.
So let us strive that ever we

May let these words our watch-cry be,
Where'ere upon life's sea we sail:
"For god, for Country, and for Yale."
Then it was goodbye.

I was invited by Jane Mauer and Jim Binger to join them for a final dinner with Sheila Cook at a seaside café. Beach umbrellas, waves lapping the shore, theatrical lighting: a picture postcard locale. We ate Lumpuki fish (that run only a couple months each year), and we had a great time.

I remembered, "My play was produced at the Samuel Beckett Theatre on 42nd St."

Too late. If you're gonna drop a name, timing is critical.

Returning to the Phoenician, we had drinks, a few laughs, then we retired early.

Sunday, August 31. Valetta—Rome—London.

I was up at 6, said goodbye to Sheila & Karen—two world-class managers—then off for the airport at 7, taking a flight to London for an overnight since I couldn't get a good connection from Malta straight to the States.

I transferred to the Gatwick Meridien, reconnoitered the airport shops for gifts for the grandkids and settled on a princess costume for Quinn and a book on dinosaurs for Carver.

I met up with a couple who had been in our group and who were staying overnight at the hotel, and we had supper together. Good company.

At this point my journal ends where I began, but there's a sequel:

Wednesday, September 3, Austin.

Several days after my return to Austin, I went with Barbara to the Collision Center where the Mercedes was being held hostage until our insurance claims could be processed and we examined the damage.

Fender-bender, indeed. The car was a total mess if not a total wreck. It looked as if Barbara had entered and lost a demolition derby. And most regrettably, her bruises were beginning to show up in places where she didn't know she'd been damaged, and the bruises had transmigrated all over her dear little body.

I had been misled on the day I returned because she acted like the accident was no big deal.

But it a *colossal* deal.

Surely a trip to Spain would make everythng all better.

I visited Gehry's art museum at Bilboa on an earlier trip to Spain. Wish I'd returned.

Spain

◆

Hold Onto Your Passport In Madrid.
October 11–28, 2003

I really didn't know how to begin telling what happened on our trip to (and our cruise around) Spain during October of 2003 because the trip was a snore one day and a shock the next.

Barbara was recovering from a car wreck and suffering from Shingles. We had hoped the trip would be a time and place for her to convalesce, and it was, sort of.

Our friend, Joyce Mayer, was coming with us for her first cruise ever, and we wanted it to be perfect for her. And it was, pretty much.

In many ways, the trip was like Kurt Vonnegut's book, *Something Happened,* a novel in that almost nothing happens until the next-to-last chapter when Pow.

Nothing much happened to us and then, Whammo. Something happened, and Kablam. Look out. Kapow. It was Batman Redux.

Attempting to record all the minor triumphs and tragedies that beset us, I decided there is only one word for the medium I chose for my message. And that word is "melodrama," a dramatic form that keeps asking: "And then what happened?"

I've never used so many punctuation marks in a narrative before.

Prelude to the Melodrama

We had scheduled the Spain adventure for spring of 2003 when suddenly it was wartime. The airlines and the cruise line allowed us to postpone the trip until fall, thank goodness, when Barbara and I and Joyce took off from our home bases and commenced the journey together from Dallas.

Joyce's home is San Angelo, but her flight schedule allowed her a restful three hours between her arrival at D/FW and departure for Spain; whereas our flight was late, and the connection was tight and that made us tense. We almost didn't make transfer, but we boarded a cart intended for old and infirm folks, and I tipped the driver excessively. He put the pedal to the metal, and Whoosh., we arrived at our gate and boarded just as they closed the door to the plane. Slam.

October 11, 2003, Saturday, Dallas to Madrid.

If you fly American Airlines to Spain from Dallas, you have to go via Miami, and there you have to have to change planes. The Miami airport was sweltering inside and outside with long lines for Security inspections and a three-hour layover. Our flight to Madrid was delayed an additional two hours, and then—all of a sudden—"Immediate Boarding." Grab your belongings, and move smartly aboard, fasten your seatbelt, sit back, and ignore the safety procedure drill as usual.

(Every time the flight attendants start up that routine, I think of the grim joke somebody once told me that the instructions they're *really* giving is "In the event of a crash, bend over, put your head between your legs, and kiss your ass goodbye.")

October 12, Sunday, Madrid.

It was an uneventful flight (if you accept headaches, leg cramps, and stomach distress as inconsequential) until we arrived at Madrid and transferred to our hotel, the Palace, for a total of 18 hours traveling.

Then we took another 2 hours for an ill-advised nap.

We woke up refreshed (actually, we were stressed but we couldn't tell the difference at the time). We hastened downstairs to the lobby and walked across the street to the fabulous Thyssen-Bornemisza Museum. Golly. I had no idea it held so many, many pictures. Hundreds. Still life and landscapes and portraits of people with bad teeth.

Look. There's another picture of Christ crucified *and another and another and another*. Change the subject for Heaven's sake. Why isn't there a shot of Jesus smiling? And there's his mother Mary suffering, praying for an end to her agony. It was agonizing to look at the poor woman. Yeah, I know, that's what the artist intended.

I urged the girls to move faster or we wouldn't be able to see everything before the museum closed. The best you can ever do in a museum is give the collection a once-over; hardly anybody ever returns to spend the day actually *studying* the art objects. The benches aren't intended as places to contemplate art; they're rest stops. Museums are (usually) beautiful places that don't require a lot of time to visit, and that's why they attract so many people. "Y'all come on, or we'll never get to the damned impressionists. And I'm hungry."

All too soon it was 7 PM, closing time. Talk about mixed emotions; my mind told me I would never—in all probability—see those masterpieces again (Oh, no.), and my stomach told me it was suppertime (Hoorah.)

But wait a minute. Wait a dadgummed minute—

The Spanish don't eat dinner until ten PM.

Awwwww, no.

Yeah, but most of our hotel clientele are Americans, so chow's on at 7:30.

(Reader, be aware I'll leap in this narrative from future to past tense, shift abruptly from 1st person to 3rd, and use lots of parenthetical editorial comments. I'm doing it intentionally as a stylistic device to illustrate the difficulty of moving from the US to Spain and from one time dimension to another, and if reading it makes you dizzy, sorry but that's what I was then, dizzy, and that's what my prose is now.)

That evening after dinner we went to bed and slept soundly without incident until the middle of the night when—Bammo.

Asleep, I slugged Barbara. On the right side of her chin. I actually clobbered my wife, bruised the skin, and an infection set in, but we didn't know it until a week later. (See below.)

The following morning she said, "I know you would never have done it intentionally, but sometimes you flail about wildly in bed and last night you clobbered me. But it's no big deal. It doesn't hurt."

I protested. "I couldn't possibly have hit you. You're just imagining that enormous swelling in your jaw."

She gave me the look she's perfected during the years she spent teaching in kindergarten, "Right." And she assured me that if, for one moment, she suspected I had done it on purpose, she would have returned the favor. She said, "It's nothing to be concerned about."

(If only she had been able to "See below.")

October 12, Monday. Madrid to Barcelona

After an early breakfast, I strolled over to the Ritz Hotel a block away to check out the prices and look at a room in case we should find something to prefer over the Palace on our return to Madrid at the end of our trip. Neither the prices nor the rooms convinced me we would be better off, but the restaurant looked impressive.

The Prado museum was closed so we weren't able to go through it, but I hoped we'd have time on our return. Actually, I hadn't looked at our tickets closely, and I didn't realize that there would be no time for the Prado on this trip.

Back at the Palace, we packed, checked out, and left for the airport with plenty of time to spare before boarding an afternoon flight for Barcelona. Our luggage met flight standards, but the big suitcases were *too* big. Why do I say that? Because the 36" Samsonite suitcases we had bought for half price allowed us to pack too much in them. By the time I had hefted and schlepped them, unpacked and repacked them, I understood why the Samsonite people had given customers discounts to take those heavy loads off their inventories.

("Heavy Load" was the red tag that the airlines people had hung on our luggage at our first check-in, and—getting ahead of my story—when we returned home, those red tags became permanent display items in the Carver's baggage museum.)

The smiling, nodding agent at the Iberia Air counter didn't speak English, but that didn't matter. He processed our tickets, returned them with seat assignments and passports to me, and I passed them onto Les Girls. En route to the security checkpoint, we congratulated ourselves for having arrived and departed Madrid without incident. We were laughing at the way some people use the Castilian pronunciation of Bar*th*elona and some don't when suddenly—

Eeeek.

Somebody screamed with mounting terror.

Eeeeeeeek.

It was Barbara. The same Barbara who had displayed such equanimity when forgiving me for slugging her the night before.

Eeeeeeeeeeeeeeeeeeeeeeek. I've lost my passport. Somebody's stolen my passport. I don't have it. You didn't give it back to me."

I said, stupidly, "Yes, I think I did;" whereas I *should* have said, "Oh, no, Sweetheart, I'm *sure* I did."

She said, "No, you didn't, did you?"

And I said, "I'm sure I *think* I did."

She said, "Well, I don't have my passport."

Joyce said, "Ramon gave me mine." Thank you so much, Joyce

I said, "And I gave you yours, Honey."

Barbara said firmly (in a way only Barbara can say firmly), "I don't *have* it, and that's what matters, right?"

I should have said, "Right. *You* don't have it," but she was greatly distressed; so all I could manage was "Okay, okay, okay, stay here, and stay calm. I'll go back to the counter and accuse the agent of stealing it."

I returned to the smiling agent who, of course, was still unable to converse in English. All he could do was smile, nod, and say, "No problem," the universal expression that means: "If I say 'no problem' enough times, and smile and nod fatuously you'll give up and go away."

A superintendent appeared and—I thought—she's gonna say something I can't understand in Spanish, and even though I've studied Russian, German, and Latin, she'll think I'm another ignorant American. But she surprised me and said, in the purest Castilian English: "Ith there a problem?"

I said, "Yeth—I mean yes." And I told her that the smiling agent had slugged my wife on her chin and had stolen her passport. Actually, I didn't accuse him. I simply explained—using a lot of incomprehensible sign language—that my wife's passport was missing from the packet she wears around her neck and she's next to tears and afraid she'll never see her grandchildren again.

The superintendent said, "Let me help you report your loth to the polith."

"My loth?"

"Your loss."

"Oh, yeah. Yeah. Where's the police station?"

She said, "Just there. About a mile down that way."

"*How* far did you say?"

She said, "You want me to tell you in meters?"

I said, "No, what I'm thinking is if I have to walk a mile there and back, I'll miss the plane."

She said, "Yeth. I'm tho thorry."

I thaid—I mean, I *said*, "If I send my wife and friend on ahead to Barthelona, will I be able to catch a flight out today?"

She said, "Yeth, of courth. I'll insure that you get on the nexth plane."

"You can do that?"

"Yeth, of courth I can," she said, "I'm the thuperintendent."

I said, "Yeah, well try asking 'em over at the American Airlines desk to change a schedule and they'll charge big money."

She said, "Tell your wife and friend to go ahead. I'll take care of you. Go, go. Go, go.

So I went, went back to insist that the Girls head on out, assuring them a car would meet them as scheduled, and I would join them at the hotel soon after I reported the loss of the passport. I half expected them to protest, but they only paused and wavered for an obligatory nanosecond and then took off.

For the next hour I walked from one end of that airport to another talking with information booth employees in TexMex at best, thrusting a photocopy of the first page of my wife's passport in the face of a policeman who was determined to ignore me until I stood my ground without stepping aside. He finally sent me to another policeman who could say 'no prob' in perfect English, but that was all. He photocopied my photocopy and pinned it on the wall behind his desk and dismissed me with an imperious wave of his hand.

I returned to my new best thuperintendent friend, and she—true to her word—issued me a ticket on a flight that departed one hour behind my wife's flight. An hour and a half later, I arrived in Barthelona, took a taxi to the ARTS Hotel, driving in traffic that was winding down from rush hour. Amazingly, my driver arrived ten minutes after Barbara and Joyce checked in. I greeted them in the lobby and noticed they seemed calm, no longer distraught. Joyce was averting her gaze, and Barbara was looking coy, blinking at me like a little girl, the way she did the night we got married over forty years ago.

I said, "Does this mean you're gonna sleep with me tonight?" She said "Heavens, no. It means I found the passport hidden in one of the many pockets in the thingy I wear around my neck." She said, "I'm so sorry."

I nodded, smiled, and said (as many different ways as I could say it), "No prob. No prob. No prob. No prob. No prob."

We went to our rooms and the view from our windows was spectacular, easily the best in the hotel. I can't help but think it's because our travel agent listed me as a travel writer. We looked down on the colossal golden Phoenix statue Frank Gehry designed (Long before his work caught on in Bilbao).

The food was okay. The twin beds were better than the food.

Tuesday, October 13. Barcelona

We awoke late, ate breakfast, checked out, stored our three big suitcases in the hotel luggage room, and took a private car for a three-hour tour around Barthelona. The driver stored our three carry-on suitcases in his trunk for security.

Our first stop was Gaudi's architectural masterpiece, *La Sagreda Familia*, where crowds standing on line discouraged us from walking around inside that great unfinished church. Then we went to Parc Guell (pronounced Gweyl), a park that Gaudi designed with serpentine benches, "Modernista" columns and ceilings, and a fountain with an enormous ceramic lizard covered with scales made of tiles. The park's design elements are difficult to describe but fascinating to take in.

Finally, we went to the Palace of Catalan Music (Palau de la Musica Catalana) that was the most arresting architectural stop for me, absolutely unique, a genre of Spanish art nouveau. We missed the one tour of the day offered in English [If only we had known to reserve a place on the tour] so we had to be content with a slow stroll inside the building's lobby and an unhurried amble around the building's ornate façade. Three "must-see" places for tourists, but we didn't get to see much of them during the three-hour tour. Our driver dropped us off for lunch at a restaurant that I had read about in a travel article in the *NY Times*: "Passadis del Pep." We had two bottles of Torello cava (a Catalonian sparkling wine) and over a dozen tapas, mostly shellfish. We ate *Pan amb tomaquet* (bread rubbed with tomato, garlic, batter-fried baby sardines, Palamos prawns, and grilled squid). Sensational. Probably the most original presentation of food we ate during the entire trip.

Returning to the hotel, I had our oversized, overweight luggage loaded onto the taxi and discovered—Uh-oh.—the three carry-ons were missing.

The porter said, "Senor, these are the only three bags stored in your name."

Of course. They had been placed by our driver in his trunk that morning, and he had gone on to another client.

So.

How to get in touch with him without alarming the girls?

I went to the Concierge's desk and asked him to track the driver down. He called and located the driver on the other side of the city; so I said, "Ask him to bring our carry-ons back to the hotel."

The Concierge said, "Oh, you want your carry-ons?"

I said, "Yes. With all my heart."

He said, "They're downstairs in the luggage room stored in your friend's name, Mayer, right?" He paused. "Right?"

Rather than explode, I smiled, nodded and said, "Right. No problem."

The bags were found and loaded up. Barbara said, "What took so long in there?"

I said, "Nothin'. Are you ready to rock and roll?"

Yes and yes and awwwwwll right.

We three wayfarers headed out for the ship and got out at the terminal, turning our luggage over to a proper deckhand. Finally. Welcome aboard.

The Silver *Wind* had been reconditioned top to bottom, and 285 passengers were booked for this sailing, near capacity.

The personnel aboard the *Wind* have charm and grace in abundance. Our chamber maid showed us to our midship suite and private veranda, then we went with Joyce to her suite to make sure she was happy. She was.

We returned to our suite, and alone with a bottle of champagne and two stems, we hugged and enjoyed ourselves enormously.

Our luggage arrived, we unpacked, napped briefly, and then we went up on deck for a fire drill, everyone aboard wearing life preservers. What a funny sight—old folks with orange boobies.

Afterwards, we registered for a few land tours, went to supper, and sacked out for a good night's sleep at sea. That's what we needed.

Ah, but it was not to be.

The sea was choppy at first; then it got really bad. Not rough; terrible. It was a tempest.

We tossed and flipped and twisted and flopped all over the suite, and—after a couple of hours—I called Joyce to tell her this was not how it was supposed to be on her first night out. Barbara and I couldn't sleep for fear she might be getting seasick.

We didn't give her credit for stamina. She laughed and told me she was okay and urged us to get some sleep.

I said, "You're okay? Honest?"

She said, "I wouldn't know how to be anything else."

What a nice person. She might even have been telling the truth.

After that call, however, the storm *may* have continued for hours, but we didn't notice. We slept well.

Wednesday, October 15 Mallorca

Barbara's jaw continued swollen; I must have really let her have it.

The storm abated until we were safely ashore on the island of Mallorca, our first land tour. The bus was comfortable, but our guide was unsophisticated and yet, condescending. Have you ever had to hang out with an ignorant person who acted as if *you* were the ignorant one?

Joyce had the good sense to stay aboard the bus while Barbara and I stepped out into a gentle sprinkle following our snobby guide to the local cathedral that promised to have some art work by Gaudi. The bus pulled away, and Boooooooooom. The tempest returned, hurricane strength, drenching us. We hastened through puddles up to our ankles for about 100 feet, and then we turned a corner and saw the cathedral—two blocks away. There was no turning back. I kept saying to Barbara: "This will build our character if we don't drown." She kept saying, "Don't say that again."

Finally. We arrived at the wrong door. Damn. We had to go around the block to the right door.

Like dogs shaking themselves, we toweled ourselves dry with Kleenex, squeezed them out and used them again.

The guide stood on line for tickets. We waited. We entered the first area. The guide began a boring recitation memorized for tourists. Barbara and I wandered ahead. The guide chided us. We acted as if we couldn't understand her. She led us into the second area where her second speech was more boring than her first speech. We left her behind and adventured into the church sanctuary. It looked like yet another church, and we weren't particularly interested in seeing another Gothic church. We discovered that the back wall of the chancel was composed of inlays of tiles. That looked like Gaudi's work, but was that it? I asked a church warden standing by the entrance: "Is that all there is?"

He was very helpful. He replied, "Que?"

I asked somebody else's tour guide.

He said, "Yeah, Gaudi did that back wall then he and the bishop had a fight, and Gaudi left Mallorca and never came back."

Ahhhhh.

We were ready to leave, but our guide wasn't, and we didn't know where the bus was parked, so we were stuck. And that, boys and girls, is what's wrong with tour guides—they hold you hostage.

Later, we made two other stops, a fortress and a castle, both jazzed up for the tourist trade. We passed by the oldest olive tree in Mallorca, and I picked up a fallen olive.

The deluge continued intermittently, and the best thing that happened all morning was saying goodbye to that guide.

Back aboard, we had lunch, we had a siesta, we dressed up for an Italian dinner that lasted almost four hours, we went back to our suites, and then we went to bed. The storm at sea was a repeat, if not quite as boisterous.

Thursday, October 16 Alicante

Barbara didn't sleep well. Shingles plagued her. Her jaw is still swollen, but she says her makeup hides it. Sure it does.

We docked at Alicante. I went ashore to buy a cheap watch for Barbara whose watch was broken. She didn't want an expensive watch, and she didn't like the one I got, so I took it back to Spain's ubiquitous department store chain, El corte Englise before lunch.

We ate, we napped, we read, we sat on the veranda and meditated; we enjoyed ourselves.

That evening, drinks, dinner, and sleep.

It rained some, but the sea wasn't up to its old tricks.

Friday, October 17 At Sea

Neither one of us slept well. All those naps I guess. Plus Shingles plaguing her and a sore shoulder hurting me. Funny, even with all that luxury, pain had a schedule of its own.

I saw dolphins leaping out of the water following the boat. From our veranda I leaned over the rail and looked down at the textured carpet of foam created by the ship cutting through the blue, blue sea. Nothing but a horizon to separate the sea from the sky. No sight of land. What would happen if I jumped overboard?

Wait. Where did that scarey thought come from?

I had asked a ship's hostess what would happen. She said, "You'd drown absolutely." I said nobody would save me? She said, "Very hard to do."

I asked, "How many people die on a ship this size during a cruise?"

She said, "One or two tops. I mean the average age on this ship is around 65. I used to work the QE2. Lots more die on that ship."

I said, "How did you get to be a ship's hostess?"

She said, "I've got the body for it, and I speak four languages, and I'm a liar in all four."

I said, "You mean not all that many people die aboard ships?"

"Naaaaa," she said, "only the ones who jump overboard. Don't ask me any more; you're depressing me." And with that she winked and I watched her walk away. She had great sea legs.

Late that afternoon, massive volcanic-shaped mountains came into view, and there was a vast sky with a riot of cloud formations: Cirrus, Cirro cumulus, Cirrostratus, Stratus, Cumulus, and even a hint of Cumulo nimbus.

Drinks, supper, sleepy time. I stretched out on a chaise on the veranda and sacked out for hours. I dreamed of jumping overboard—and jumping right back in.

Saturday, October 18 Malaga

Barbara's chin was looking bad with a scab she was still trying to hide with makeup. I insisted that she go see the ship's doctor. She resisted. I said, "I'll call him for you," and I did. So she made an appointment for late in the day.

Having traveled to Grenada from Malaga on another trip, I decided to stay in Malaga and shop with the girls and to eat in a local restaurant.

We walked ashore and went from shop to shop, buying little.

Afterwards we hired a hack and horse to drive us to the fort. He agreed to do it, but when he started going in another direction, we pointed to the fort, and he said, "Es impossible."

We threatened to get down from the wagon, but he held us hostage, clipping along at about 20 miles an hour. He returned us to the ship and asked for his money and a tip. I said, "Here's your tip: don't say you'll take us somewhere you can't go."

Back aboard, Barbara insisted on going to see the doctor alone. When she returned I got the report I had feared: the doctor had had to lance the infection on her chin, prescribing an aggressive antibiotic treatment. Evidently the Shingles had caused her natural antibodies to diminish, and that's why the infection had spread. The doctor was confident the treatment would work, and he assured her he would change her dressings daily, checking her progress. Her prognosis was positive, and after a couple of days, so was her attitude, but it was a truly disturbing issue. It's only a half step from "laid back" to "depressed," especially since the Shingles didn't seem to be letting up. But she made the best of it and wore a patch on her broken chin even when dressing up for dinner.

Sunday, October 19 Cadiz

We went forward with our plans to travel to Seville after docking in Cadiz. We had a great bus ride with a chance to see most of the beautiful buildings in Seville, even the church of the Macarena, Virgin of Seville, whose 17th Century statue of the virgin is regarded by worshippers as a big deal. All I could think of was the Macarena dance that evidently originated there.

We went from there to the Alcazar, a royal palace modeled on the Alhambra in Granada, a highlight of the trip. I got lost from the group immediately after coming out of the building, and I spent about thirty minutes searching for the restaurant where lunch was being served. [Another problem with group tours: the guides don't want to tell you the itinerary and schedules for fear you'll venture out on your own.] I found the restaurant by fluke and—as I anticipated—Barbara had saved me a seat. The long table where we were situated, however, was half occupied by a private party from L. A. who had somehow gotten estranged from their friends.

Usually people aboard the ship were open and welcoming to folks seated at their tables. These folks, however, were downright hostile and refused to speak with us, a neat trick since the food had to be passed around the table. The only reason for mentioning this unpleasant event is to note that it was the only time anything like it happened on the cruise.

The Andalusian tapas served for lunch were a mix of fish and pork dishes that didn't seem an exciting and exotic mix, but it was as good as other curious dishes.

We left that place to visit the Seville Cathedral, a grim, poorly lighted, gigantic (third largest in Europe) repository for one of one or more of Columbus' body parts. His is a great elaborate tomb with four large statues that pretends to hold more than it probably does considering the several other tombs in other churches around Spain where Columbus is said to be interred.

The church courtyard with its gorgeous trees does not disappoint, however—except for the portapotties located in one corner. You'd think by now, after so many centuries (The church was begun in the 1400s), the church fathers would have provided something better for tourists and pilgrims to use than those smelly units.

The visit to Seville concluded with a stop at the Plaza de Espana—a 1929 World's Fair relic designed for photo ops—in need of much repair. The weather was hot, so I bought Barbara a lacy plastic fan souvenir of Spain.

We napped all the way back to the ship.

That evening, we had to dress up, and we watched Flamenco dancers perform at cocktails. Afterwards, we had a lovely meal with truly impeccable service as usual. [I've failed to remark upon the superior quality of the service. It was always high, and the servers were consistently efficient and cordial.]

Monday, October 20 Casablanca.

We stayed aboard ship rather than visit Casablanca rug shops and fight off venders who are customarily described as aggressive.

Several commonplace events struck me as extraordinary:

From the deck, I watched 18 enormous derricks transferring containers of goods to or from the holds of merchant ships. Hmmm. I wonder what was going out to sea besides rugs.

I saw a massive accumulation of sea birds following a fishing trawler into port, fighting for fish being thrown overboard. The birds almost hid the boat from sight.

Then I spotted a thick trail of trash and effluent—almost solid enough to walk on—that had been jettisoned from some ship entering the harbor. A policeman stationed on the dock stared down at the garbage. I could almost hear him say, dismissively, "Hey, it's not _my_ job."

The rest of the day we spent "at leisure," a term that requires no amplification.

Tuesday, October 21 At Sea

I looked down from our veranda and watch a gorgeous explosion of bubbles, indescribably beautiful, mushrooming at the side of the ship as it cuts through the water. The sea was full of trash yesterday, but today I stare at the lacework so delicate and three-dimensional it mesmerizes. I want to sail the sea forever. Ahhh, water. Next best thing to air.

We had sandwiches in our room for lunch, a novelty.

Barbara's condition had improved, and our friend, Joyce, helped keep our spirits up.

There was a formal farewell reception on the ship in the evening even though we had two more ports before the end of the trip. The captain was genial and as a master of ceremonies, he introduced an enormous number of uniformed personnel: maids, laundry men, and a lot of invisible laborers who materialized for the first time.

Then we went to a formal dinner and enjoyed ourselves as usual.

Items we enjoyed not listed above: Strolling on deck, conversing with strangers, emailing, using drapes to divide our suite into two private areas, complimentary vodka in the fridge, all the bottled water we can drink, fruit & flowers (usually fresh), and the courtesy of staff. We weren't nickeled & dimed to death for drinks. And we simply signed for all our shipboard purchases, charged to our credit cards with a $300 bonus gift from Silversea lines.

Items we didn't enjoy: Creaking doors & walls during storms, uncomfortable mattresses, land tour guides, air conditioning thermostats difficult to control, unfinished remodeling in our bathroom (that is, rust and need for paint).

The enjoyment far exceeded the minor discomforts, but lumpy mattresses weren't an insignificant problem.

Thursday, October 23 Arrecife

I took a shuttle bus into town and rode around this overcrowded little Canary Island in the rain. Lots of volcanic lava rock looking pretty harmless wet.

Once around was enough.

Our last dinner aboard ship: a French Tour de Force in the Terrace Cafe. After dinner, Barbara and I finished packing and sat together on the veranda forever.

Friday, October 24 Tenerife, our final port

All we saw of this largest of Canary Islands was the new symphony hall, an architectural wonderment designed by Calatrava to look like a great wave from the ocean, washing ashore. (On the Sunday we returned to the US, the building was featured on the front page of the Arts and Leisure section of the NY Times.) The driver who had been hired to take us to the Tenerife Airport refused to stop long enough for us to walk into the building, so—when he pulled to a stop—en route, I stepped out of the car and studied the building for several minutes. It's a marvel.

The airport, on the other hand, is new, built to handle many more airlines and services than those that are housed there now. We had a sandwich, an expresso, an ice cream, and waited to board the plane.

When we left Tenerife for Madrid, we sensed the best part of the trip was over. We were so right.

Arriving in Madrid airport, I took a look at those heavyweight bags in the carousel and decided to opt for a hotel closer to the airport than the Palace. At a Lodging kiosk, I called to cancel our original reservations and signed us into the Auditorium Hotel, the largest hotel in Europe, and the soon-to-be scene of our only actual travel catastrophe.

The Auditorium was indeed located nearby, and at first, the omens looked good. The rooms were respectable and the hotel restaurant opened its doors at 7:30. We had a good enough supper, and we retired for the night with no inkling of what lay in store for us the next day.

THE MELODRAMA COMMENCES

Saturday, October 25 Madrid

I was the first one dressed so I collected the big bags and took them one at a time down to the hotel baggage room. I left my carry-on in the room, ate breakfast in the cavernous and crowded cafeteria, and checked us out of the hotel.

Joyce came downstairs and waited at a table for Barbara to join her for breakfast. I rolled the last of the three mongo suitcases to the baggage room and went to the cafeteria to join the ladies.

But the ladies weren't there. In their places were two extremely frightened and angry women whose purses had been snatched. And Joyce's carry-on containing all her jewelry & makeup had been stolen.

Evidently Barbara had been jostled by a man passing in the crowd behind her and when she turned to stare him down, he smiled, and she looked back across the table to see that Joyce's stuff was no longer in view. She turned back around and discovered her purse was missing. Just them Joyce arrived with her plate of food, and the girls started trying to figure out what had happened.

When I arrived on the scene, the woman in charge of the cafeteria was trying to calm down the two women by saying the worst thing she could have said to them: "No problem."

Barbara and Joyce were incensed. How dare the woman shush them and say, "No problem." But then they lowered their voices to avoid embarrassing the woman.

[Later, Barbara said that if she learned anything from that experience, it's to scream aloud, "I've been robbed." every time you get robbed.

I said, "But no one in that place would have understood you."

"Oh, yes," she said, "If I had screamed they would have understood me perfectly." And she's right, so next time....]

Soon, a delegation of hotel employees and security personnel gathered to stare at the two foreign women making a racket. Only one of them, a woman who identified herself as Beatriz Palomo, the Conventions Manager of the Auditorium Hotel, appeared to be sympathizing, listening, questioning, speaking English.

The hotel security men were absolutely nonplussed when neither Barbara nor Joyce showed any signs of crying or weakness. In fact, those tough cookies got more and more angry as time passed.

I insisted that someone from the hotel accompany us to the Madrid airport where—we were told—"the police would commiserate provide a document that would serve as permission to leave the country."

I said, "Bullshit. The last time I talked with the police at that airport, I got no commiseration and no help whatsoever. Come," I said firmly to the young woman, "and go with us to translate."

She demurred. "But why do you want someone from the hotel to report your missing passports?"

I said, "*Stolen* passports," I said, but she didn't nod or act as if *stolen* were the correct word. "I need you to accompany us because it was your hotel where the crime occurred."

She didn't respond at first, and then she said, "No problem," whereupon my wife and Joyce raged, and I told her, "Never say 'no problem.' again to us."

We boarded the shuttle bus to the airport, we three, Ms. Palomo, and our big luggage. "Why couldn't they have stolen the heavy stuff?" I joked. Nobody laughed, not even me.

At the airport, I reported to the American Airlines desk while the three women went in search of a commiserating policeman.

The agents and management personnel at American were extremely kind, but they explained that absolutely nobody leaves Spain or arrives in the USA without a passport—unless, of course, he is somebody way important.

"We can put you on the plane tomorrow," the manager said, "but today you'll have to go to the American Embassy and get a replacement for your stolen passports."

I said, "If you're saying you'll give us new tickets—"

He said, "Done."

I said, "You're gonna charge me big money?"

"No," he said, And tickets are the least of your worries. Here, use our phones to cancel your missing credit cards."

Ohhhhhh, wow.

"Then," he said, "get in a taxi and go to the Embassy before it closes at one o'clock."

I asked, "Won't we have time to get there?"

He said, "It's ten a.m., the average time it takes to get a new passport is three hours. And today, I need to remind you, is Friday, and they'll be closed for the weekend."

I said, "Caramba."

Just then, the three women appeared, Joyce & Barbara waving the notarized certificates like winning Bingo cards, assuming they would allow them to return to the US without passports. The looks on their faces when I, very slowly, very gently, broke the news that they would have to get new passports was the closest they ever got to crying. Close, but they turned away so I never got to see how close they got.

There was no help for it.

Ms. Palomo said, "Does this mean you're staying?"

I said, "Yes, and the hotel will take care of us tonight?" I presumed?

She said, "Of course." the way Europeans make those two words sound like, "Of course, you stupid idiot."

"And will you see that our luggage—that is, what's left of our luggage—gets back to the hotel baggage room?"

"But of course."

I turned to Joyce. "Here's the phone number from the back of my Mastercard. You'll need to call them on that phone over there while I call them on this phone to report the missing credit cards. Just give them your name. They'll have your number on file."

Joyce called and got a sympathetic operator who gave her the number for American Express, and she cancelled that card, too. My American Express card is different from Barbara's so her loss wasn't my loss. And that was important became my card became our one source for financing the return to the US. Credit cards are important when one is in a foreign country. I repeat.... No, I don't need to repeat.

Cancellations completed, we walked outside where Ms. Palomo was waiting for the shuttle to take our luggage back to the hotel. She was gracious. She was always gracious. But the more I was around her the less I trusted her motives. I became convinced she felt obliged to save the hotel's reputation for any damage we might cause.

Then we went to gate of the Unamerican Embassy. Un-because the guards we met there weren't American, and their command of English was basic. They were Madridians (or whatever they're called). I tried to explain to the guy and woman who were guards that my wife and friend had lost their passports. They dismissed me immediately, but not without me protesting.

That's when the guy guard took me by the shoulder and walked me from the building's entrance to the edge of the sidewalk where he looked at me—'if looks could kill'—and said, "Stay," the way a person tells a dog to 'stay.'

He allowed Barbara and Joyce into the building, and just before the door closed, I yelled, "But you don't have any money."

Slam.

I waited over thirty minutes out in the cold—and it was quite cold—until the guard reappeared and signaled for me to follow him into the building. "Come."

I said, "Are you worried I'm gonna get even colder? Because I'm as cold now as I'm gonna get today." The sarcasm was lost on him.

He smiled and pointed into the bowels of the Embassy and said, "Fetch." No, he didn't, but that was his subtext when he said, "Go in there."

I went in there. I was buzzed through. I'm certain somebody was tracking me on the video equipment. I walked past a receptionist who waved me toward a door to the room where I found Barbara and Joyce working on their biographies with the same seriousness of purpose our grandtwins use when putting crayons to paper.

But they were so pissed, they didn't even greet me.

I said, "Why do you think they let me in?"

Barbara said (without looking up from her work), "Because each passport is going to cost $85 and we don't have any money. That clerk over there gave us a hard time. He said we would need to pay for a photograph, too."

"Oh," I said, "I'm important because my credit card is important."

That was the wrong thing to say. Again. (It was true, but it was inappropriate.)

So I just shut up and started looking at "Wanted" posters.

(Actually, there weren't any such posters in the Embassy; there was nothing even mildly interesting on those walls.)

Suddenly, the door opened and the guard entered, looked around the room. He spotted Barbara—

(Dear Reader: You're not gonna believe this, and if you can guess the rest of the story, you'll say, "No, that couldn't have happened.")

The guard spotted Barbara and walked over to her, holding a woman's purse—

(Naaaaa, you don't believe this, right?)

And said, "Here."

Barbara took the purse and said with astonishment: "That's—That's *my* purse."

The guard turned and walked away, and that's the moment when we should have had the presence of mind to say, "Where did you get this?" but, sadly, that's not what happened.

What happened was Barbara reached into the purse and pulled out—

(I told you you wouldn't believe it.)

Her passport.

(Right?)

And—

(If you didn't believe that, you sure as hell won't believe this:)

Joyce's passport.

(Unbelievable.)

And all we could do at that moment was cheer. Hurrah. Three cheers. Hurrah. Hurrah.

The girls marched over to the mean clerk and turned in their written assignment and said, "We won't be needing your help, thankyouverymuch."

And we walked out of that Unamerican Embassy, happy as clams, and we never thought to ask anybody where the hell the purse came from.

Damn.

Missed opportunity. But this isn't where the mystery ends.

Our spirits were high, but I knew it wouldn't last, so I said, "Hey, while we're feeling good, let's go to that ubiquitous Spanish department store and get Joyce some new makeup and stuff."

That's all it took to depress them. Having to replace makeup and stuff.

So I said, "Okay, then let's go to the Prado. We thought we weren't going to be able to visit it, but we will now, okay?"

That went over like a lead balloon, too. But we went there anyway because we knew how embarrassing it would be to say we had been to Madrid, but we hadn't been to the <u>Museo Nacional del Prado</u>, the House of Velasquez.

So we enjoyed walking miles and miles through the Prado. Finally, we had lunch in the museum's dismal cafeteria, and we bought souvenirs.

Afterwards, we went to a department store and got makeup and stuff, but before I gave the girls my credit card, I called the hotel and asked for Ms. Palomo. I thanked her for sending the purse with the passports down to the Embassy. And I asked if Joyce's purse and carry-on had been recovered with Barbara's.

She was quiet for a moment then said something like, "Que?"

I repeated myself, and I waited for an acknowledgement but she said, "I don't know what you're talking about. We didn't find anything belonging to your wife and friend. No purse. No carry-on. Nothing."

I said, "Wha—?" I was taken aback. "Then, who—?" I was alarmed. I said, "Are you saying you don't know how that purse with those passports got dropped off at the Embassy precisely at the moment the girls finished drafting their bios?"

"I don't have any idea," she said.

Now it was my turn to be silent. And I was for the longest time. Then I said, "This is absolutely unbelievable." I don't remember the rest of the conversation because I was so completely bumfoozled. I said good-bye and hung up. And I staggered back to tell the girls the news.

They didn't know what to make of it either. But here's where a "conspiracy theory" was born: Somebody we'll call "they" was fooling around with us. *They* stole our stuff; *they* returned the passports; therefore *they want us to leave the country.*

We all three agreed that this theory and these events don't make plausible fiction.

Hell, this story doesn't even make a good lie. But that's it. I swear.

DENOUEMENT

Sunday, October 26 Spain and Texas

Joyce was a joy. We three had great times together on the ship and on land in Spain, and we thoroughly enjoyed ourselves, doing nothing well.

We returned home retracing our Miami routing, but everything that happened en route seems woefully anticlimactic, so I'm not including it here except for....

Here it comes.

The plot thickens as I am sure my reader will deduce from the final two entries below. That is, I *think* they'll be the final entries....

Two days later: October 28, Tuesday morning, 5 AM

I'm asleep and I get a call from a bookkeeper at the Auditorium Hotel, Madrid. Without apology for calling early in the day, the woman informs me that I owe the hotel 333.84 Euros for our stay on Friday, the 24th. She speaks in broken English.

I respond in incomprehensible English: "I, what, uh, who, what are you, I, is there something wrong?"

She explains that I stiffed the check-out person. She doesn't say 'stiffed,' but I get the message.

I babble: "Okay, I think, just a minute, you mean I didn't pay the charges that I was not supposed to pay because I was told we could stay another night at the hotel free?"

There was a long pause, and then she said again, "You must pay 333.84 Euros for yourself and Mrs. Mayer, not the room, do you understand?"

I go, "Yes, I understand, but I don't understand why you're calling me in the middle of the night because we were given to understand the second night's stay would be free."

"Mr. Carver, you must understand that you must pay for the cost of the rooms. You understand?"

"Listen. I *do* understand and sincerely disagree. The free rooms were authorized by Ms. Palomo."

"No, Mr. Carver, she says you must pay."

"She does?"

"Yes."

"Then let me speak with her. Is she there?"

"Yes, I'll connect you. One moment, please—"

Suddenly I hear loud recorded music, a country western ensemble playing *You Always Hurt the One You Love....*"

Then I hear: "Mr. Carver?"

I say, "Right, okay."

"This is Beatriz Palomo. Did you have a safe trip home?"

"Yes, thank you, uh, do you know what time it is here?"

"I'm sorry. Shall I call again?"

"No, no, now's as bad a time as any. You said the hotel would pay for our second night."

"No, I never said that. You must understand I am not authorized to provide you with a courtesy room."

"Why not?"

"You must understand the hotel is not responsible for your wife's and Mrs. Mayer's purses."

"Then what we have here is a failure to commiserate. I honestly understood you to say we would have a courtesy room—if that's what you call it when that's what you do for a guest."

"Did I tell you it would be a free room?"

"No, but I understood you to say the hotel would take care of things."

"No, I only authorized an upgrade; *you* must pay for the rooms."

"Did you tell me you were going to authorize an upgrade?"

"No, but I assumed that's what you understood."

There was an awesome silence as we both realized how absurd we both sounded, then I burst out with "Okayokayokay. I got it. But this is a rude awakening. In fact, it's the first rude awakening I can remember ever having in my life, okay? Have you prepared the paperwork that reports that a purse-snatching occurred on your premises?"

"No. Because—you must understand—the hotel cannot assume responsibility for the purses. We have studied the video tapes, and we see you and your wife and Mrs. Mayer enter the cafeteria with the purses, but we do not see them get stolen."

I started to laugh. Then I realized she wasn't joking.

"Wait a minute. You're saying you've looked at security tapes aimed at over 100 people eating breakfast, and you can't see the purse-snatching event occur?"

"That is right, and you must understand—"

"You're saying you can't see it; therefore it must *not* have happened, and you can't accept our words and our loss as tangible evidence that it happened."

"The hotel cannot assume the responsibility for whatever happened."

"Waitwaitwaitwait. You think this is some kind of scam we've run so that we could stay over another night—free—at your hotel, doing everything we had to do, that is, get new plane tickets, stand on line at the Unamerican Embassy, pay for taxis all over town—"

"Mr. Carver, you must understand the hotel is not responsible."

"You couldn't say it more clearly. You are irresponsible. When I first met you that morning and explained what had happened, you said that it was possible somebody picked up their purses and luggage by mistake, and I said that's non-sense, then you said then maybe they lost them somehow. I protested they were *stolen*. You spoke with my wife, and at that moment I am sure you believed it was possible that a theft might have occurred, but from that moment on, you sought to defend the hotel's reputation. You tried to prove the hotel was not guilty. You agreed to assist us with our airport and police transactions. You even supervised the transfer of our luggage—"

"You must understand—"

"Stop already. Don't say 'you must understand' again. Holy Crap. Listen to me. You are impugning my integrity with your continued denial that your hotel hasn't any responsibility."

"But—"

"No. And now I'm going to hang up, then I'll type this up, then I'll email you a copy, and I'll send American Express a copy, and I'll publish it so all the world will read about this occurrence as if it were a big international incident. I'll antic-ipate your response, but the only response I will welcome is an official statement that the theft did indeed occur in the hotel cafeteria as my wife and Mrs. Mayer testified. If the hotel assumes that responsibility, I will assume the responsibility of paying an additional 333 Euros. Have a nice day. Bye-bye."

I made a copy of this journal, emailed it to all parties involved, and waited for a reply.

A week later: Tuesday, November 4

I received a letter from the Hotel Auditorium, the first contact since October 28, my email notwithstanding. It was a statement identical to the one that I signed on the 24th, checking out of the Auditorium the first time.

Only this time it's stapled to an unsigned receipt charged against my American Express card.

Grrrrrr. (The sound of teeth grinding.)

I called American Express, contesting the claim.

Weeks Later: *The Final Curtain*

American Express disallowed the claim of the Hotel Auditorium.

There was no curtain call.

Oxford and Cambridge

✦

Second Person, Present Tense
July 11–19, 2003

So you decide to enroll in Oxford University for a one-week-long summer school program entitled "Fiction: Eight Creative Essentials." Why Oxford? Because you've never been to there, you want to explore that legendary bastion of academe, the price is right (for a week of classes, lodging, and meals), and—of course—a class in fiction writing might be nice for a travel writer knowing how travel challenges fiction.

So, on **July 10, 2003**, you travel from Austin to London to Oxford, and it takes you eleven and a half-hours. Add another half-hour to traipse to your hotel for a two night stay. Then four hours for a reconstitutional nap. Finally, 16 hours after you've begun your journey, you wake up and feel you've arrived.

You take a sight-seeing bus with a live guide (Who'd want a dead one?) rather than the recorded narration offered on other busses. The bus is virtually empty, but the young guide is animated and amusing as we ride atop the open air double-decker. He spins yarns and guarantees pronunciations that will save you from embarrassment (for example: Magdalen is pronounced Maudlin, etc.)

Afterwards, you stroll over to "The Oxford Story" where you're the last customer of the day to purchase a ticket for this Disneyish tourist attraction. You board an antique desk replica on wheels that slowly (excruciatingly slowly) tracks up and around a great loft displaying artifacts of early Oxford (the town) and Oxford (the university). It's sort of a loveless tunnel because you don't have a partner to kibitz with. Your wife chose to remain in Texas for the week.

Returning to your hotel, you ask the concierge for a recommendation for a light supper, and you take his advice to Zizi's, and it's a crowded tourist trough, but it's okay.

You stop at an email café and receive no email, so you go back to your room to sack out, but it's unseasonably hot, and there's no air-conditioning, and a 12 inch electric fan just doesn't do the job.

Finally, with the help of a sleeping pill, you go to sleep, happy that you've avoided caffeine and liquor for the two days prior to the trip so you've absolutely escaped jet lag.

The next morning, **July 11,** you board a bus for Cambridge, you read a book and ride for three hours, transfer to another live tour-guide bus exploring the town and university, and you stop at the Cam river bridge (Cam-bridge, get it?) where you and several other tourists take a flat-bottomed boat tour with a college student "punting" (actually, pushing us down river with a pole), narrating a pro-grammed monolog, interrupted only once when a French mother says her little boy has to peepee. The punter, unabashed, says, "Have him pee in the river, s'il vous plaît," and continues his narrative as the child performs without incident.

You enjoy the boating non-event.

You resume the sight-seeing bus tour, then you transfer to a bus returning to Oxford. After another three hours, you arrive, walk to your hotel nearby, and dress for dinner (jacket & tie) at the posh Randolph Hotel restaurant whose menu isn't anything to rave about, and there's nobody else in the place wearing a damn jacket & tie.

The next day, **Saturday, July 12**, you enroll in summer school at the Oxford Rewley House complex, and receive directions to your room: "It's just there."

You set out to find it and—with the help of a porter—you take your belong-ings to 37 Wellington Square and up to a 4th floor room *en suite* (meaning "bath-room adjacent") located, and after passing through three fire doors (Three?) at the end of a narrow corridor, you discover there is no fire escape. Furthermore, there is no air moving in that complex of rooms and hallways and the lodg-ing—probably designed by Christopher Wren in his early teens—has no air cir-culation. The heat is stifling, and the standard electric fan doesn't help much, but hey, you're in Oxford. Chill out.

There's a reception in the Lecture Theatre of Rewley House, then an intro-duction to your tutor, and then a visit to the House Library (and a reintroduction to the ancient Dewey Decimal System in use there). Tea is served, the first semi-nar commences, and you hear your tutor say, "I'm Lorna Fergusson, and I prefer lecturing without student interaction unless it's absolutely necessary, right?"

Some of the students in your class begin a muted growl of resentment that increases in volume during the week to follow, but you don't mind lectures with-out discussions *if* the lecturer proves to be interesting.

And yes, she does, so no, you don't.

During the first meeting, the class is allowed to sign up for tutorials, that is, each student is allowed to plan on 30 minutes with the tutor on Monday, discussing the 1,000 word essay assigned in early May that has been graded by the tutor.

Dinner is served in the common room, a good dinner with potatoes. You haven't had potatoes in weeks because it's just not part of your diet, so you enjoy them for a change. Jolly good.

Wine is served following dinner, and it's not very good wine, in fact—to use an old English expression—it's frightful. Therefore, you put your glass down unobtrusively, and you say good night to no one in particular.

You retire to your room across the street, up four flights of stairs, through the fire doors, down the corridor, fishing in the dark for the correct one of three color-coded keys (The light's burned out so you'll ask that it be replaced tomorrow). Finally you open the door to your oven. Temperature 350 degrees Fahrenheit. In Centigrade that's 350,000 degrees, surely.

By morning, **July 13**, you're done to a crisp, so you shower, perform your customary ablutions, and prepare for a Sunday at Oxford.

Breakfast of sausages, eggs, and potatoes is good, especially the sausages, and you strike up an acquaintance with an old fellow whom you never see again the entire week. It doesn't immediately occur to you that the old fellow, Major Somebody, may have matriculated and died.

In short order it becomes clear that many students (especially those in their seventies and eighties) have returned after many summers spent at Rewley House.

At the desk, you ask that the light outside your room be replaced, then you spend some time futilely trying to email your wife. It's not until the end of the week that you learn a phone call using a phone card to the states costs only five cents a minute (Wow.); so why waste time emailing.

After classes and self-imposed silence, you are so hungry for conversation with your peers, you brashly speak with classmates before being spoken to. The Brits seem a bit wary of you. After all, you *are* an American, but after making acquaintances, they seem eager to put in a bad word for Tony Blair and George Bush. You never meet anyone who admits to liking or trusting either one. Evidently, the Gulf War is very unpopular.

Your relationship with your peers improves immeasurably when they suggest you start using their word, "Bollocks," instead of the word you brought with you, "Bullshit."

You go for a long walk to Magdalen college and the Botanical Gardens where you sit on a bank of the river and watch people punting and pedaling in several kinds of boats. What an agreeable place to spend a Sunday afternoon.

At drinks-before-dinner, you learn you're going to be served potatoes at every meal for the entire week. It's a good thing you like potatoes.

Monday morning, **July 14**, you ask the maids to replace the lamp in the light fixture outside your room. One of them cheerily says, "Naught a bloomin' chance." And the other says something like "Niver gonna happen, Boyo." They are both toothless, so you may have misunderstood them.

Your private tutorial goes well with your tutor complimenting you "for being clever—if initially rather confusing—with an excellent use of idiom." You learn later from classmates that she has not been so sparing of their feelings.

Sliced potatoes with lunch.

Then a nap, but it's too hot to sleep, so you take in the Ashmolean Museum (an amusing name coined from the donor, Elias Ashmole, and one of the world's oldest museums with a history beginning in 1683 when use of the term 'Museum' was a novelty in English The term did not gain general usage nor was it defined in a dictionary until 1706 as 'a Publick Place for the Resort of Learned Men).

You enjoy an exhibit of impressionists' work as well as modern Chinese paintings. The place is fascinating, you don't remember whether it's air conditioned or not.

After a fish dinner with chips that evening, you spend some time preparing another 2,000 word essay to submit to your tutor, then you return to your furnace, take a pill, and hug the fan to your chest until you fall asleep.

Next day, Tuesday, **July 14**, you leave a note for the housekeeper: "Please replace the burned out light bulb in the hallway outside my room."

After potatofast, You enjoy the morning lectures followed by coffee and the pleasure of developing an acquaintance with classmates.

You satisfy your urge to participate when you say something that amuses your tutor and new acquaintances; then lunch in the company of young and ancient graduates of Oxford who wonder why on Earth an American would want to attend summer school with Brits and why there are so many Yanks attending short courses in other colleges at the University. Apparently, summer rent is a major source of income to the colleges; that, and admission fees of 1 to 5 pounds just to check out the gardens.

That afternoon, with directions from a classmate, "It's just there," you hike for a mile or more to visit the University Museum for a look at the remains of a Dodo Bird on permanent display in that hilariously Victorian architectural improbability. The Museum has dozens of statues depicting English scientists, explorers and discoverers as handsome giants. There's not an ugly face on a single larger-than-life statue. Remarkable.

Adjacent to the University Museum is the air-cooled Pitt Rivers Museum displaying archaeological and ethnographic objects from all parts of the world, founded in 1884 when General Pitt Rivers bequeathed his collection of archaeological eccentricities to Oxford.

You return to enjoy dinner with your new friends and—after sharing potatoes—you go up to the computer sweatbox to hack out your 2,000 word paper.

You postpone your exit until late, then you reluctantly inch your way back-up-over-down-through and into your room for the night, pausing only to take a sleeping pill before throwing yourself in the path of the fan, panting from the heat and gasping for breath (You never do anything in a small way), praying for sleep.

But sleep does not come. You take another pill. Still can't sleep. Delirious, you fantasize that your dearly departed father, a refrigeration engineer, is speaking to you as he did when you were a child at a time when you weren't interested in anything he had to say until now when when you remember, "I said, turn that fan around and blow hot air out of the room and you'll pull cool air in. All you're doing right now with that fan is moving hot air around."

You say, "What?"

He says, "You heard me, kiddo. Just do it, son."

So you do it....

And wonder of wonders, you push hot air out and cool air rushes in, and you begin to breathe normally, and you look around to thank your father, but by now you're asleep, and he's gone, and you dream about him, happy at last in Heaven knowing that you've finally listened to him.

Wednesday morning, **July 16**, you tell the director of the school you need to have the light bulb replaced. Now. Today. Immediately.

She says something like "Straight away," or it might have been, "Go away."

Breakfast au gratin. Lecture. Coffee. Lecture. Lunch with spuds. Afternoon at liberty.

You're told where to find the nearest bus stop ("It's just there."), and you wait for the bus to Blenheim Palace in Woodstock, about a half hour north of Oxford. You wait. The skies darken. It begins to sprinkle, and you figure rain might keep you from enjoying the gardens at the Palace, so you do the right thing and go to a pub—The Eagle and Baby, called by the locals, "The Bird and the Bastard"—for ambience. C. S. Lewis imbibed there, making your visit a historical pilgrimage, so you drink to his memory.

You've never had hard cider before. Tastes great, but it doesn't taste alcoholic so you have another half pint. Wonnerful, wonnerful, so you half another punt for the rood. By now, you're talkin' Irish-Cockney, an archaic neverland language, and you're swaggering doon Jarge Street all th' way t' Wellington Squar, singin' in th' rain. Fortunately, no one can tell you're snockered because you've put you head up into your umbrolly because your voice resonates better. "Whadawonerful feelin', just singin' in the rain."

You sober up at supper upon seeing your boiled potato rations. You mutter, "Bollocks," but your classmates think you've said something complimentary. They can't understand much of what you're saying ("Pardon?") because they've been swilling that awful wine. Doesn't anybody understand what anybody else is saying in English here? ("Pardon?")

Your room that night is tolerable because the heavy sprinkle has reduced the hotness to less than 2,000 degrees Farenheit (That's two billion degrees centigrade), and you pass out—doubtless because you've eaten too many potatoes.

First part of the next day, Thursday, **July 17**, is the same again, and then, first thing in the afternoon, you get another 30 minute tutorial. You jest, and you enjoy your tutor's sense of humor. She's fun, and she's exhausted from so many tutorials, so she allows you to talk and amuse her. You bond. And on your final Student Assessment Form, she says, "You've been the star of our show, contributing salient comments, interesting questions, and above all witty and imaginative ideas. Thank you for being such a great participant and good luck in the future." In truth, you never said much, but what you said must have been cherce.

But you're not through with school yet. You have one more day, and after that, who cares if they never replace the goddamned sonovabitch bulb.

Early that evening you attend a performance of a bunch of serious-looking musicians performing Vivaldi, Bach, and Handel in the Sheldonian Theatre (an early oddity designed by Christopher Wren—after he built the furnace room where you're staying. Wren designed the Sheldonian as an early multipurpose (therefore no purpose) facility to serve artistic and scholastic and ceremonial functions. Badly. Obviously, he listened to too many voices on his building committee).

The orchestral conductor announces that the program will last three hours. It may have, but you enjoy only one hour of it, bolting at intermission to stroll at dusk past college gardens where four different plays by Shakespeare are being performed in Oxford during that week. You pass by a garden, backstage of a performance in progress, just as an actor shouts, "Which way ran he who killed Mercutio?" You don't give away Tybalt's hiding place. You simply walk on by rather than assume any responsibility for the death of poor R&J. They always die, killed by coincidence every time.

Friday, the final day, **July 18**, forget the friggin' lightbulb.

The weather's fine, your classes are fine and dandy, the morning potatoes are fine, even the weather is fine. It's a grand day for a trip to Blenheim Palace so you trek to the bus stop and board the bus just as rain begins in torrents.

No problem; you've brought along the umbrella and windbreaker you've been carrying around every cloudy day since you arrived. At last, the weather you expected.

The bus deposits you at a stop outside one of the gates leading to the Palace. "It's just there," the driver says. Uh-oh. By now, you know that "Just there" means a great distance. You cross to the gate and, sure enough, there's the Palace about a mile from where you've been deposited. You lean into the wind that has turned into a gale. The rain is only drizzling. You put away the umbrella and pull the hood of your plastic windbreaker up over your head and—turtle-like—you alternately sweat and freeze en route to the Palace. You say, "Bollocks." a lot.

When—two hours later—you arrive, you're the only person not in a group, so all the docents look at you suspiciously, expecting you to make off with Winston Churchill's christening gown or nip a priceless crystal tumbler.

What a marvelous place—if a bit overdone.

Program note: The name Blenheim derives from a decisive battle that took place on the 13th of August 1704 on the north bank of the river Danube, near a small village called Blindheim or Blenheim, where John Churchill, the first Duke of Marlborough, won a great allied victory over the forces of Louis XIV, thus saving Europe from French domination. In reward for his services defending Holland and Austria from invasion by the French, a grateful Queen Anne signified that she would build him, at her own expense, a house to be called Blenheim.

The rain clears up mostly, and the wind stops blowing. You walk back to the bus stop, catch one, and get off "just here," not far from your destination, "just there," Rewley House, where you enjoy a last gathering with your classmates and tutor.

You let everyone know that as a playwright, it's been fascinating studying methods that are properly epic rather than dramatic, to cite Aristotle. You admit that you will probably *never* write a novel. No one acts disappointed to learn you haven't been converted to novelty; in fact, a couple of them are yawning. Exhausted from the intense study, doubtless.

At dinner, you make a "Mr. Potatohead" out of your favorite veggie, then you mutilate it.

Afterwards, you perform in a talent show at the Lecture Theatre, reading a short monolog. The rest of the evening is long on performers and short on entertainment, but it's okay. You're in a forgiving mood. You've truly enjoyed the company of your classmates.

The following morning, Saturday, **July 19**, you check out of your lodgings and say goodbye to the few classmates who remain. Then you return to London by bus, staying at the Sloane Club, a private hotel. You've received a special offer of a reduced price room rate, but the catch is it's a tiny, Spartan room, without a/c. That's all right because you place the 12" fan on the window ledge and aim it outwards.

You take in a matinee performance of ABBA's *Mama Mia.* that you thoroughly enjoy because you know all the tunes. And an evening performance of *Hitchcock Blonde*, a mystery comedy that has a great first act but a thoroughly implausible second act.

You and one other guy are the only ones wearing ties & jackets in the theatre. So much for London dress-up theatre customs.

Dinner at a smart Italian restaurant across from your hotel, then return to your cool (by now) closet-sized room *en suite.* Would you ever recommend the place? Bollocks, no.

You rise early in the morning, **July 20**, transfer by taxi to Victoria Station; thence to Gatwick and an uneventful return home.

You don't eat another potato for a month. But you say "Bollocks" at every possible opportunity.

Turning the tables on Japanese tourists, Americans flood their temples and parks.

A Cruise To Japan

✦

Notes from the RSSC Voyager
March 11–29, 2004

In March of 2004 I sailed on the Radisson Seven Seas Cruises ship, the Voyager, the newest ship in their fleet, launched in 2003. The word on the street was positive although I had not heard of any accolades or PR laurel wreaths being thrown by travel publications.

Attracted by the idea of a cruise on a state-of-the-art ship with an Asian itinerary, I left a message at the line's headquarters that, Gosh, I would be willing to give Radisson a Media Trade in exchange for free passage. I was put in contact with a company agent, who—after reviewing my pitch—made me an offer that I considered reasonable and a 320 square foot penthouse suite with a 50 square foot balcony, and a butler to sweeten it up. Wow. Who could refuse?

What follows is a description of the trip from beginning to end, acknowledging the RSSC special rate with thanks, but making no concessions evaluating the quality of the trip.

~PRIOR TO BOARDING THE SHIP~

Wednesday, Thursday, March 11, 12, 2004

Travel by air took over 24 hours (including transfer time) from Austin to Hong Kong. Landing at the Chek Lap Kok airport, all passengers walked through an infrared-screening device designed to detain persons with fevers entering the country. The scanning of passengers occurred each time we entered a port in China as a diagnostic precaution against SARS and Bird Flu and, I imagine, any other illness producing a fever or generating heat by any other means.

Moving through Customs was easy and efficient. That airport's a truly elegant facility, lots of light and space, and the architecture's useful & beautiful.

I passed through turnstiles of the Airport Express and my first thought was "Where do they get all these courteous people?" Then I realized, "Of course they act courteously; they're Chinese."

There were no crowds at 8 am, but there were dozens of workers standing idly around with nothing to do but act courteous.

After a wait of very few minutes, I boarded the express train, fast and slick. It cost $13 USD from the Airport, and I arrived at the Kowloon station in about 15 minutes. A free bus shuttle from the station to Kowloon hotels was available, so I was able to ride to a stop near the Intercontinental Hotel. But construction in the streets made the going rough, damn it; and when I left the damn bus, I had to roll my damn luggage through a damn maze of obstacles including a goddamn shopping mall. I hate transfers, and I hate getting lost. Thank goodness I'm an unflappable guy.

At the Intercontinental, I got a great room overlooking the harbor with a window ten feet wide and five feet high. I sat, leaned forward with my hands on my chin, and watched ships, boats, junks, sampans, and all manner of craft, at least thirty in view at a time, plying the water. I napped, awoke in time for complimentary tea with sandwiches, then browsed in several hotel shops for presents for—Guess.

Right, my grandkids.

I had supper at Spoon in the Intercontinental, the Alain Ducass restaurant. "Spoon" because Ducass believes spoons are the essential eating implement for good food—and that's what the food was good, great quality, unpretentious, but the presentation was superb. Afterwards, I went to bed and awoke refreshed the next day, sans jet lag.

I looked across to Hong Kong as the fog lifted slowly and then I watched as it dropped again, enveloping the entire city, with only outlines of buildings showing, a Great Wall of skyscrapers, materializing, disappearing, then reappearing. Fascinating.

I showered for almost half an hour, taking the kind of time I never allow myself at home, followed by a slow, close shave. I toweled off, and suddenly, I noticed, staring back at me in the full-length bathroom mirror, a naked Buddha. And it was me.

Covering my chubby tummy with my hands and wearing nothing but a happy smile, I wondered "Why is this fat old man smiling?"

I thought, "Of course. Because I'm beginning a journey in a land where I've traveled before, but this time I'll take a transcendental route like the Buddha."

~BOARDING THE SHIP~

Saturday, March 13—Hong Kong

Before checking out of the Intercontinental that morning, I asked the hotel concierge for a copy of printed directions to the baggage loading location at the Ocean Center embarkation terminal so that I would be sure not to have to drag my suitcase around again. The concierge warned me that he would give me a map, but the embarkation building was under construction, and I might have trouble finding my way. My taxi driver took one look at the map and told me in Chinglish that he would drop me at the spot marked on the map, but I would be lucky if anyone was there to help me up the three levels to the ship.

And it was true. He dropped me at the side entrance, and I entered the lower-level hallway of a building under construction with hard-hatted workers carrying wallboard and aluminum studs, and there was no one and nothing to help me but direction signs: "Embark Here," "Now Go There," and my favorite, "Escalator is Out Of Order." There was no elevator in sight, so I schlepped my damn suitcases up three flights of that out of order escalator. There had to be a better way.

I had begun my trip as Buddha resurrected, but now I was transformed into the Mad Hatter, scurrying like a damn squirrel through Wonderland.

Eventually, I heaved my stuff up onto the loading dock and across the gang-way to board the ship, checking in. I was welcomed on deck and given a receipt and instructions to follow a crew member. I complained mildly at the Registra-tion Desk of my ascent up the inoperative escalator, but the clerk and I both knew that after that inauspicious beginning, there was no way to begin again and do it right. I chalked it up to my accustomed "transfer distress."

Waiting for the crew member to usher me to my room, I looked around the main lobby, surveying the scene. It's a beautiful ship, and I realized immediately it would have staff and services comparable to Silver Sea and Cunard ships. And I was right.

The embarkation building will be noteworthy at some time in the future, but it wasn't ready for the RSSC Voyager. The ship was posh. My suite was first class, and my butler, Ryan, a young man from India, was outstanding from day one—even though he tended 11 other penthouse suites. During the voyage he made every effort to accommodate me, always serious of purpose with a droll sense of humor.

Oh, boy, was I pleased with my upscale penthouse suite and veranda. The design of the suite reminded me of accommodations on the Princess Sun, but the clientele was classier—for the most part. More about that below.

At lunch in the handsome Compass Rose restaurant, I asked to sit with any-one seeking a lunch companion, but the maitre d' told me it might be a long wait. He seated me, and I waited a long while then ordered lunch and ate alone. I did *not* want to eat alone with no one to confide my recent adventures to, poor damn me.

Afterwards, I unpacked, strolled about, then went ashore to survey what has to be one of the world's largest malls (as one might expect in Hong Kong) adjacent to the dock. Returning, I met a woman and her daughter pulling their suitcases from the escalator onto the third level. They were exhausted, so I helped them to the ship, saving them a few wrong turns.

At dinner, I asked to sit with anyone seeking a companion, but the maitre d' told me it might be a long wait again. I imagined him saying, "You poor guy, you're going to have to eat all by yourself again," but he didn't. I waited awhile, thinking, "I *am* a poor guy;" then just as I had given up hope and placed my order, a couple was seated at my table. I acted pleased to be with them, but I found it a stretch. The wife was loquacious and kept apologizing for her hus-band's infirmity that she attributed to Parkinson's Disease, but I'm pretty sure he had Alzheimer's, too, poor guy. Now *he* was truly a poor guy. I never felt sorry for myself again the entire trip.

After dinner, I took in a delightful one-woman show featured Sally Jones, a real class act. Funny with a style ranging from "Don't cry for me, Argentina" to "I'm a Broadway Baby."

Sunday March 14—Hong Kong

The sailing was postponed one day. We sailed that night. The change was never explained to me, but I didn't mind.

I did stretching exercises with a trainer at the Fitness Center, and for the remainder of the trip I stretched whether I felt like it or not. I was determined not to gain weight.

Quite sincerely, I liked the way the guys running the ship seemed professional and personable, the Captain, the Cruise Director, the Hotel Director, Tour people, and the two or three other managers I met, notably the Club.Com manager who supervised a big, handsomely-equipped computer room, busy night and day. I appreciated the loan of a computer in my suite—a generous gesture by the Hotel Director.

At the Captain's cocktail party that evening, I chatted up Sally Jones, and we arranged to hang out with a group I'll call "Les Girls:" Sally and three other young women, Dianna Streak, Shirley Ganse (a lecturer), and Kirstin Spencer (a performer). Lively conversation, great fun, and at last, a gang to hang with.

Monday, March 15—Kaoshiung, Taiwan.

After docking, we boarded busses for two local temples (both remarkably designed and maintained) and a Buddhist Cultural Museum in a remote town called Fokuanghshan. The "Museum" appeared to me to be a front for a sect, followers of Master Hsing Yun whose image is all posted all over the place in photographs and statuary. The place had all the trappings of a religious studies program with hundreds of clerics, children to adults, almost all with shaved heads wearing monks' attire.

There were many large multi-story buildings with oversize Chinese architectural facades, enormous gardens of blooming orchids and other flowers mixed with artificial (plastic & fabric) greenery, and plaster statues of the Buddha. Atop one five-story building was a larger-than-life, three-dimensional display of horses and gods that seem to be jumping over the building.

The fake crown jewel of the place was a tall building with a dining hall, devoid of ornamentation, the length and width of a football field. We were invited to walk into the dining room and watch about five hundred young men and women, chanting hymns in unison, serving and being served a simple lunch of rice and vegetables. The servers were wearing surgical masks and rubber gloves, and they went about their work while the young monks chanted, and then the signal was given and they all ate together without a whisper. Amazing. All those shaven-headed teen-agers, not talking aloud together in a lunchroom. It was obviously intended to appear as an act of religious devotion, but it looked to me like a staged performance, timed to coincide with our entrance into the building.

I got cold chills. I hated it.

Our next stop was supposed to be a village where paper umbrellas were manu-factured and where aboriginal arts and crafts were sold. We arrived after a long, dusty drive, and it was closed. So we went to an *objet junk* store in a nearby town. My first impression of Taiwan was a poor one.

After returning to the ship, I had dinner in the shipboard Signatures Restau-rant with new acquaintances. Then we went to a performance by the ship's "Peter Gray Terhune Singers & Dancers," all capable performers with professional skills and talent. I had learned that's not always the case on ships.

Late that evening I made a little prayer to whatever gods may be that I would never again have to listen to the tour guide we had that day screaming into her microphone.

Tuesday, March 16

As luck would have it, the same tour guide chaperoned us to the Taiwan National Museum. I approached and told her that she needed to adjust the volume on her microphone a few notches down, and she did, and it was okay. It was just … okay.

The Museum is enormous, well-designed, clean, and well-lighted, everything a national museum should be. I had been told that Chiang Kai-shek had ripped off most of the relics of the Forbidden City in Beijing when he left the country for Taiwan, and it sure looked like a Chinese national treasure chest was being housed there in Taipei. All those trappings from the Mainland transplanted to that small island. I photographed dozens of art objects and artifacts. There were no restrictions on photographs at that museum or any of the Chinese temples and museums we visited. Dazzling. My impression of Taiwan improved.

Upon our return, we set sail for Shanghai, skipping the port at Okinawa where there was only a two-hour stop scheduled.

I had dinner in Signatures again with a young couple and an old couple. We enjoyed laughing together, the youngsters on their first trip abroad, and the old-sters on their 45th trip around the states and overseas.

The concert for the evening was Stephen Fischer-King, a young man with a powerful voice and a stage personality I couldn't connect with. But offstage, we developed a cordial relationship.

Wednesday, March 17 (St. Patrick's Day)—At Sea

I enjoy being at sea or on a train almost as much as I dislike being airborne or car borne.

Today I attended three lectures by good speakers. First, Stephen Bauer, head of the White House Social Staff for four US Presidents. He made gossip sound like serious talk about protocol. Then William Webster, the only guy who's ever served as both head of the FBI and CIA sounding more sage than secretive. Lastly, Shirley Ganse, with whom I enjoyed discussions on the subject of Chinese pottery & porcelain, her area of expertise, a subject that interested me because I own a piece of China that looks like antique porcelain. Shirley helped me appreciate that my stuff may not be genuine antique, but it may be a genuine original. Which would be better?

I had dinner that evening with Les Girls followed by another show featuring the Terhune Singers and Dancers.

Thursday, March 18—Shanghai

Ah, so *that's* why the ship had scheduled a stop in Okinawa—so we could say we hadn't just come from Taiwan. At least, that was the rumor circulated around the ship when we learned the Chinese officials in Shanghai were unhappy with our itinerary. We were told we would be allowed to stay in Shanghai only one of the two planned days.

Customs officials came aboard and inspected us for fever, poking our ears with ear thermometers (or whatever they're called). Then they insisted on examining our passports before we left the ship, checking us off, room number by room number.

Although I had traveled to Shanghai before, I wanted to see that city again with a group rather than venture out alone. So I took a "Best of Shanghai" tour to the Shanghai Museum where I got some great shots of porcelain & pottery art, then to the Old Town area where I got lost in the Yuyuan Garden, and finally, to lunch at a local hotel that was—believe it or not—the same hotel where I had lunch five years ago (Largest city in China and I ate lunch at the same hotel).

We went to a so-called Friendship Store (The word "friendship" means "Americans will buy this stuff") where I bought some old hand-painted saucers, and we finished the tour at the Children's Palace, a school where kids are taught (with their parents required to attend lessons) how to play old music on old instruments and dance old folk dances. They were charming.

Each of these stops came with a sales opportunity. Land tour companies are shameless, and most tourists seem to eat it up.

That evening, exhausted, I returned to my suite where I ate dinner alone and sacked out early.

Friday, March 19—At Sea

We cruised on a day when we had expected to be in port and headed for Tientsin, a city of six million people with access to Beijing (but more on that later).

I spent the day writing.

There was a show that evening featuring a comic who reportedly insults people, but I don't need that shit.

Saturday, March 20—At Sea

I washed underwear and socks in the ship's laundry, and I packed for the overnight trip to Beijing. Then I spent the rest of the day writing, rewriting, and editing this piece and others.

That evening I attended Kirstin Spencer's concert, unlike any other cello recital I've ever heard. Great fun with "Strings Electric," an acoustical cello and a large electric cello (She played her instruments expertly, and she played with her audience the way a cat plays with a mouse).

Sunday & Monday, March 21, 22—Beijing

Off for a "Grand Voyage Event Program," a free land tour and overnight stay in Beijing.

We left a little after 8 AM on a bus, arriving in Beijing around noon. We ate something that passed for lunch at the Royal Friendship Restaurant (Here the word "Friendship" means "Americans will eat anything"), a really second-rate restaurant located in the Chinese History Museum across from Tiananmen Square. I note my disappointment with this restaurant (a crowded dump that Shirley Ganse said she marked off her Smithsonian Society Tour List years ago) because I hope it won't become a fixed stop for tourists the way my Shanghai lunch restaurant became, improbable but true.

Next, we visited Tiananmen Square where I walked years ago. I've described that occasion elsewhere in these journals, but this time it wasn't awesome as I remembered it.

Later, when we visited the Forbidden City, I had the same truly déjà vu experience. There were no surprises.

The next day at the Great Wall, the "Been there, done that" feeling persisted even though it was not the section of the wall that I visited in 1999. I determined that five years ago I expected mystery, and today there was none. I was no longer exploring the unknown.

The only portion of the tour that I had not seen before was the last stop, the Ming Tombs. They're not much to look at, just another big photo op of a place modeled on Forbidden City architecture. I don't know exactly why, but as I walked around those grounds, strangely, my strength faded. Up until that stop, I had felt energized and able to climb up and down Forbidden City Steps and the Great Wall, and walk around Tiananmen Square, but at the Tombs, my feet gave out. I didn't feel infirm, just tired of walking. I was enjoying myself and the tour and the company, but I was glad to start back to the ship on the bus.

I've got to say that I regard the opportunity to revisit those sites a real privilege in the old-fashioned sense: I was treated like a person who—courtesy of Radisson—was given special considerations, and I think most of the passengers felt the same way. We had a superior stay and dinner at the Shangri-La Beijing Hotel on Sunday night, and a good lunch and shoportunity at the Beijing Friendship Store on Saturday.

The bus driver drove back to the ship like a bat out of Hell, and I was convinced on two occasions that we were gonna die. But we didn't.

Back aboard, after dinner with Les Girls, we went to a performance by Sally Jones that sparkled and delighted. Afterwards, I went with the group for a late night drink, and when Sally joined us, we gave her another round of applause.

Tuesday, March 23—At Sea

I awoke spaced out with my joints creaking, and I thought I've got the flu or I had too much to drink last night or perhaps it was climbing that Great Wall.

I'm sure it was the wall.

At stretch exercises I felt I was pulling and stretching myself to pieces. But I did it, and I limped away feeling proud of myself.

I spent the entire day revising my journals, and at dinner I sat with Les Girls. After a concert featuring Kirstin, I went back to my room to write.

Wednesday, March 24—At Sea

I rebounded at "stretchercise," feeling good again. The weather improved, so I walked the deck, several laps. Then I returned to my suite to work through the rest of the morning.

Karla & her mother—the woman and her daughter whom I had helped up the Hong Kong out-of-commission escalator—joined me on my veranda for lunch; we were hungry for hamburgers and beer.

At dinner, I had another enjoyable visit with Les Girls. By now we had a virtual comradeship. Afterwards, I stayed up late, not to party, but to write.

Thursday, March 25—Hiroshima & Kyoto, a special excursion

The Tour: "Kyoto at Leisure." (Who names these tours?) An overnight trip to Kyoto

The Itinerary: 1) The Peace Memorial Museum & Park in Hiroshima, 2) a trip on the Shinkan-sen (Bullet train) to Kyoto, 3) lunch at a local restaurant, 4) the Kinkakuji Temple (The Golden Temple), 5) The Ryoanji Temple (The Rock Garden), 5) our lodging for the night: the Hiiragiya Ryokan; then on Friday, 6) The Heian Shrine & Garden, 7) Nijo Castle (The Shogun Residence), 8) the Sanju Sangendo Temple, and finally, 8) another trip on a bullet train to Kobe and a transfer back to the ship docked there.

We're off.

A little after 8 am, on a cold, overcast morning, we were transferred by bus to the Peace Memorial Museum & Park in Hiroshima with a brief stop at the Atomic Bomb Dome (A warped and twisted outline in metal, the city's only remaining bomb-damaged building, a UNESCO World Heritage Site).

Our tour guide told us to call her "Tsugi" and said we would have an hour to visit the Peace Museum that commemorates the atomic bomb blast over Tokyo in 1945. Tsugi is a Japanese woman whose English was quite hard to understand for the first few hours, but I must have learned her language because by the end of the tour, I understood her clearly. She laughed when she said neither Chinese nor Japanese can hear the difference in English R & L sounds.

At first, I thought it's a shame to have to attach temporal dimensions to our visits, but after stopping at seven historical sites during the two days of our tour, I didn't feel cheated.

In fact, it was in the Peace Museum that I felt the repeated message to abolish nuclear weapons and promote world peace was reduced to propaganda. The artifacts from the bombing and other kinds of materials reiterated the tragic events of that day, but the Museum program failed to attribute the cause of the blast to the villains who deliberately caused WW II.

I believe the reason for dropping the bomb in the first place was to shorten the war and prevent the loss of countless Japanese and American lives that would have followed an invasion. What stuck in my craw was the stinging accusation posted on a placard in the first room of the Museum that Hiroshima was selected as a site for the bomb to be dropped because the Americans wanted to see how extensive the damage would be, and Hiroshima was chosen because it had received minimal damage from bombing up to that time. To make sure I hadn't read the placard wrong, after touring the entire Museum, I went back and read it again. I had come into the building, expecting to be moved to tears because I was already persuaded that the Museum exists for all the right reasons, but I was extremely distressed to note that the Americans had *arbitrarily* experimented at Hiroshima—like mad scientists. I prefer believing that bomb was dropped for a substantive reason—however ill advised.

I left the Museum, and as I walked alone in that park that honors the Hiroshima dead, I remembered my travels to Omaha Beach in France, and I recalled walking alone in the US cemetery there.

Leaving Hiroshima, we were told that at present there are over a million people living in Hiroshima and over 127 million people living in Japan. We headed for another town, Kyoto.

It may be that the best way to travel within Japan is by rail on the fabled Shinkan-sen or "Bullet Trains." They've been around for over 30 years, originally built for the Tokyo Olympics, and they've been refined; sexier than ever. Our ride was fast (reputedly over 180 mph), safe, comfortable (wide, reclinable seats), and smooth (hardly a bump), a sleek operation. And quiet. We could converse without raising our voices. I loved it as much as anyone can love a train. I bought a bottle of green tea from a train attendant, and chatted happily with passengers from the ship across the aisle throughout the trip.

Arriving in Kyoto a little after noon, we transferred across the Hozu River to a restaurant whose name I never got where we cooked some of our lunch, drank beer or sake, and used the facilities.

Kyoto is Japan's historic capital and a center for traditional culture, but at first sight (in fact, most of the time) I thought the principle streets were boring and cluttered. It wasn't until we visited the first of our objectives, gardens of a temple called the Golden Pavilion, or Kinkaku-ji, that I thought well, okay. This is more like it. Originally built at the end of the 14th Century as the shogun's retirement villa, it was later converted into a temple. In 1950, it was destroyed by fire and reconstructed in 1955 following the original blueprints.

We had a lovely stroll admiring the gold-leafed pavilion, and the flowering plums. At a nearby worship site—a kind of Shinto prayer-op—there's a large incense pot. Adjacent to the pot, there's a place to write down your secret wishes on special papers. One may also fold and knot the wishes and hang them on lines nearby. It's also possible to purchase a small "message board" for about $2 to write your own wish for good luck or a message to an ancestor that will rise to heaven with the smoke when the wishes are burned ceremonially.

Not far from the Golden Pavilion is the Ryoan-ji Temple, a simple rock garden. We removed our shoes and went inside a souvenir shop and out onto a veranda where we contemplated this world-famous garden of 15 rocks. It's not possible to count all the rocks in the garden from any one position except directly overhead. We sat on a wooden-planked tier of seats overlooking a sea of perfectly raked white pebbles surrounding the rocks, and I wondered how long it would take me (Definitely not within the hour we were given to view it) to get to a place in my mind and psyche where I could appreciate this garden, sometimes called the quintessence of Zen.

"Time's up."

We reboarded our bus and passed through the center of town to within a rock's throw of the "Kyoto Tower", a candle-looking structure built for the 1964 Olympics. We were told it offers panoramic views of Kyoto and the surrounding mountains on a clear day. We were also told to be prepared for a cheesy cultural display on the way out of the observation area and bad food for sale. We passed on those options.

That evening we discovered my real reason for wanting to visit Kyoto: the prospect of staying at a Japanese ryokan (ree-o-kan) or inn. A friend had told me that if ever I were to visit Japan, the most Japanese thing I could do would be to stay at one of many ryokans in Kyoto. Historically, these ancient inns were stopping places for Samurai warriors and the old ruling class of Japan. Old temples and palaces still exist in Japan, but the ryokans are guest houses where people lived out a gracious, long-gone way of life, and I was going to stay overnight at one.

The inn that was part of the "Kyoto at Leisure" tour, the Hiiragiya (Hir-ra-gi-ya) Ryokan in central Kyoto, is arguably the most famous old inn in Japan. Since 1861 six generations of owners have entertained travelers there. I was looking forward to it, and it did not disappoint.

We drove up in a light rain shower and, at first sight, I wasn't impressed by the simple clay exterior, located in a narrow busy street just a block away from a central Kyoto shopping area. But as we entered the Hiiragiya inn, we smelled a trace of incense, and stepping into that vestibule, I stopped thinking we were anywhere near downtown Kyoto.

There was a chair provided for us to remove our shoes and put on leather slippers. There was lots of bowing, and then each of us was shown to his/her room by a "room maid." (The first time Tsugi, our tour guide, used the term I thought she was saying "roommate" and I protested.)

The inn has 33 rooms connected by long narrow winding halls. I was shown to number 16, and I followed the room maid through the two sliding doors, shucking my slippers, and we entered an elegant series of small rooms: a central location, then a tiny hall with access to the toilet room, lavatory room, and bath room. There was also an indoor veranda with sliding rice paper-covered doors to close it off from the central room and—on the outside wall—sliding glass doors that opened onto a tiny private garden.

There was a painted screen and a Japanese flower arrangement in a tiny alcove. I learned that the stained glass window was one of the oldest to be found in Japan.

In the veranda, the floor had lots of tightly fitted tatami mats with a low table and two low chairs with backs. There was yet another low, decorative red-lacquered table in a central location with a cushion and separate arm rest next to it. As a concession to the 21st Century, there was also a small TV in the room and a telephone draped decorously with a cloth.

The room maid left me alone briefly to get acclimated, then she returned for a simple tea service, proffering a frothy bright green tea (godawful tasting), followed by roasted green tea and a paper-thin fruit-stuffed cookie. She bowed, I bowed, she bowed, I bowed—Then I realized she wasn't going to leave until she had the last bow. So I waited, and she bowed out.

There was yet another set of leather slippers in the heated toilet room for use on the tile floor. It was a western-style toilet (meaning not just a hole in the floor), and it had a heated seat with a warm-water spritzer for cleaning body parts.

I sat and pushed a button that turned the spritzer on, and I thoroughly enjoyed its function for awhile. I waited for it to turn itself off.

And I waited.

The warm water started to get cold after awhile, and I started to panic. What if I touched the wrong button while trying to shut the dadgummed thing off.

Tiny diagrams right next to each button suggesting anatomical applications, but they weren't clear; they just looked like funny pornography.

I raised myself up, placing my hand over the spritz, hoping to block it, but that isn't how it works. Water started going everywhere.

I sat back down on top of the cold, cold water, oh, my.

I studied the buttons again and finally decided on button number 3. Right. It worked. It stopped. For a moment.

Then water began spraying again from another, unfamiliar direction. Woahh-hhh.

I pressed button number 1, the only choice left to me. And that did it. Thank goodness.

Gosh. What if it had started spraying from some other direction.

Ummmmm.

Before supper, I learned that after tea time, one is supposed to bathe, soaking in a private o-furo bath, a tiny hot tub about 3'x3'x3' made of shaved cedar. (There was an option to schedule a half hour in one of the inn's larger communal o-furos; but I opted out.)

I had received instructions from Tsubi that—before I could use the o-furo—I would be expected to perform my ablutions the way samurai did for centuries, sitting on a tiny wooden stool, using a wash cloth, dipping water from a half-gallon hand-made wooden bucket. I was told that only after I was totally clean could I get into the hot tub. When I satisfied myself that I wasn't going to get any cleaner, I climbed into that boiling hot water and instantly peeled off a superficial layer of skin.

I soaked for as long as I dared and then I got out, red as a beet.

After rubbing lotion all over my scalded body, I changed into a crisp cotton robe (a yukata) and a short sleeveless jacket. I tied a belt around me but it wouldn't stay, so I had to ask for help from my room maid. She didn't understand a word I was saying, but she knew how to tie me into that outfit so that it stayed tied on.

I joined other guests from the ship for dinner, served in a room large enough to accommodate five of us at low tables. We ate a traditional Keiseki meal that turned out to be beautifully presented—mostly raw fish—one course after another. After 10 courses, we stopped counting, but we ate enough to feel we'd eaten quite enough raw fish.

Returning to my room, I discovered that the low red lacquered table had been moved and two futon two mattresses with a down-filled duvet had been arranged on the floor for me.

I'm surprised how well I slept, and I was also surprised the next morning to learn that some folks hadn't slept well. One said he heard a samurai ghost laugh.

Friday, March 26

I awoke before my 7 AM wake-up call, made some notes, read the *Herald-Trib,* dressed, and I was ready for breakfast when it arrived. I was served at the table next to the garden glass screen. I slid the screen back to expose myself to the morning air, gobbled up my western omelet, toast and juice, and welcomed the cold, sunny day into my room from the garden. Golly, what a joy.

We all were packed and ready to leave when the bus arrived. The room maids insisted on carrying our luggage out to the front of the inn, and the current owner, her mother, the desk clerk, seven room maids and another employee stood on the street, smiling, waving, and bowing.

What a great stay.

As we were driving off, Tsugi asked if I had enjoyed my room. I said, "Of course. How could I not?"

She said (and I paraphrase rather than use her English) that she was pleased because she had learned that I am a writer, and so she had assigned me to room number 16 because that is where Kenzaburo Oe, Japan's Nobel laureate author, always stays when he visits Kyoto. She said that maybe one day I will become an American Nobel laureate.

I thanked her profusely, but I said, "I'll never be a Nobel prizewinner, my dear. Hell, I can't even figure out how to turn off a dadgummed toilet spritzer."

We boarded the bus.

First stop was the yellow and bright orange Heian Shinto Shrine with its great Torii Gate. We started walking through the garden and lo and behold, weeping cherry trees. I said, "Nobody's gonna believe this at home. I come to Japan, and the cherry trees are in full bloom." So for proof, I asked one of our group to take my photograph with my camera. He tried and then said the camera wasn't working. I said, "But it's a brand new digital camera. You've got to be joking." But it wasn't and he wasn't. The battery had gone dead. I wasn't able to photograph the cherry trees blooming in that lovely garden that morning. What a disappointment.

As soon as we returned to the bus, parked blocks away, I put in a new battery, but after that the cherry blossoms were few and far between.

We visited the Residence of Shogun Ieyasu, completed in 1626, next on our itinerary. It was a large and extremely imposing building, and photographs were not permitted inside, but I got some terrific exterior shots of this so-called Ninomaru Palace and Gardens (Nijo-jo).

There are both original and restored walls and screens inside the building with scenes of pine trees painted on gold-leaf. The most distinguishing hallmark of the place, however, is its squeaky floors that sing like nightingales when walked upon. The floors were designed and constructed to squeak so that the shogun would be able to tell if someone were sneaking up on him for any reason in that event his guards could leap out from behind tasseled doors and dispatch intruders. Haiiii.

Last stop. Sanju Sangendo Temple.

There were exactly 1001 statues of Kannon the Buddhist god in Sanju-san-gen-do (meaning "a hall with 33 spaces between columns").

1001, but you seen one, you seen 'em all.

Garish and grotesque, most of those original gold-leafed wooden statues were burned in a fire, but 130 have survived from the 12th and13th Centuries. Each figure has dozens of hands out raised so as to be able to "lend a hand" to worshippers in need.

Somebody in our group made a disparaging remark about these ugly images, and someone else asked if such remarks are sacrilegious. The response was "Not unless it's *my* religion."

Hmmm. I never thought of it that way.

We returned to the ship via the bullet train, boarded, and I went straight to my suite and stayed there the rest of the afternoon and evening, entering these notes into my journal.

I enjoyed the ryokan visit enormously. It's not just the comfort and design of rooms where I like to stay. It's knowing my wellbeing has been taken into account in design of the facility. An elegantly-maintained Japanese inn makes the point clearly and attaches historical significance to it; and, a handsome suite onboard a cruise ship makes a similar contemporary statement.

Saturday, March 27—Kobe

On my own, I took a ride on a shuttle train from the ship to the center of town and strolled through a department store and a busy outdoor arcade. It's a much more modern-looking town than either Hiroshima or Kyoto, considering it's been rebuilt since a devastating earthquake hit in 1995.

It's also a very expensive town. I walked around and returned to the ship within an hour. There's lots of stuff, but nothing in Kobe for me.

The ship sailed around 5, the Captain's final reception for departing Tokyo passengers commenced at 6:30, and seven of us sat down to dinner at 7:30.

Kirstin & Sally had already left the ship, ending their two-week stint. The Terhune singers & dancers were to stay aboard a few more weeks for their term of contract. They performed a Sondheim show late that night.

Sunday, March 28—Tokyo

I spent the morning typing and packing and occasionally, I walked the deck. A beautiful day.

When we docked and the ship was cleared for a tour of Tokyo, I got aboard a bus that took us all for a tour around town at a time midday when traffic was slow. Later we got stuck in traffic, and the tour guide said, "This is more like it." We drove through the Ginsa district's crowds, narrowly avoiding bikers and walkers who challenged us in the streets. We continued around the Imperial Palace (Open only two days a year), and then through an area where about 100 young girls were dressed up in modern *haut couture* costumes, extreme to the max, parading around, studying each other.

Most city tour guides I've heard talk fast as if the faster the talk and more words, the better the description. No, the greater the confusion. And this tour guide repeated herself: "Look there, look there, and over there, no, there, and over there, no, there."

We stopped at two Shinto Shrines, one named for Emperor Meiji who opened Japan to the outside world, and we witnessed a costumed wedding recessional, allowing us to take countless pictures. The other shrine was closed for the day, but there were still people standing on line at the entrance, a congested conglomeration of temples evidently dedicated to commerce, for tourists as well as locals crowded at souvenir shops that stretched several city blocks. Cherry trees were in full bloom, but the crowds were buying Mickey Mouse dolls.

I returned on the bus, late for a party to that I had invited about 15 guests. I opened my suite door, and they were all inside, having a good time. They greeted me with a "Surprise." as if I had arranged a surprise for myself. What a great party.

Ryan, my butler, had saved the day, greeting guests and providing them with all the refreshments they needed from my freebie liquor cabinet. I said, "May I have your attention so that I may thank you for your camaraderie."

Toward the end of the party, a guest said, "Don't you think most passengers on this ship are old or senile? Most of 'em are boring and fat or ugly, or they really belong in a nursing home."

And another guest said "And they're mostly nouveau riche and poor taste. They buy those tacky paintings on sale on the fifth floor of the ship. And have you ever watched them fight with each other in the self-laundry room, using the washer and dryer rather than pay a few bucks for the ship's laundry to do it?"

And I said, "Stop, stop. Tell me where you fit in so I won't step on *your* toes?"

It's easy when you're young, beautiful and rude to denigrate others. I was tempted to tell them something obvious that they'll be old sooner than they think, but instead I said, "Hell's bells, we're all in the same boat."

We laughed because it was true.

The Voyager is as good as a cruise ship gets. The administration of the RSSC Line is outstanding and the staff & crew of the ship are courteous and willing to work with real people—even when they act like real pissants.

Even those passengers paying top dollar got *much* more than they paid for.

I had a extraordinary time. Especially in Kyoto.

Monday, March 29—En route to Austin

I awoke early the next day, left the ship around 9:30, traveled by taxi for an hour and a half in heavy Tokyo traffic to a small town, Narita, where the major airport is located, and I expected to whiz bang right through to customs. Yeah, well I didn't.

The American Airline desk person said, "Your luggage is overweight; you'll have to repack some of your stuff into your carry-on." No nonsense.

So I opened up my suitcase and took out my books (three hardback books is three too many) and booze (I couldn't just leave those two full bottles they gave me on the ship), and I said "Okay, now?"

And she said, "Take out a couple of dirty shirts and that pair of trousers," so I did, and she said, "Fine." And she started doing whatever it is that they do, and while she wasn't looking, I put the shirts and trousers back into the suitcase and shut the lid.

My carry-on weighed about 200,000 pounds by this time, and I discovered how easily a carry-on converts into a drag-on. (Never again use a carry-on, never, never, never.)

I waited six hours for my plane to depart, spending a couple of hours with my friends departing from the elegant United Airlines lounge (super elegant, never seen anything like it), then an hour with at a short-order café, then I spent the rest of the time waiting between the American Airlines and Cathay Pacific lounges, boarding the plane around 5 PM.

The Bowing 777 was nowhere near as comfortable as the Airbus to Hong Kong had been but the flight attendants were superior.

The San Jose Customs area was a dream, a short walk, a cart for my carry-on, courteous Customs people, and a table for me to transfer my books and booze back into my big suitcase.

I waited for three hours, then the plane to Austin took less than four hours.

Barbara was waiting for me. We drove to Salado, and I began the only truly tough part of the trip, coming up for air. Recovering from jetlag and long distance travel is a Herculean task for me. Fatigue and weariness are my unwanted companions for days.

Resurfacing and decompressing—Boy, do I get the Bends.

Each Great Lake looks like the other, and all retirement-age tourists look alike.

The Great Lakes

◆

Aboard the Orion with Yale Exes
Sept 16–24, 2005

Saturday, September 16

Hulda Horton, our driver from Salado to Austin, saved the day of our departure by escaping a traffic bottleneck en route to the new Austin airport, leaving us with just enough time to skirt through Security. The flight—with one stop in Dallas—to Montreal was uneventful (if you call leaving a cell phone aboard the Austin to Dallas flight uneventful. Hoping to retrieve it, I sprinted about a mile back to our Dallas arrival gate—an unappreciated constitutional—where a flight attendant searched, found and recovered it for me.) The happy return to Barbara was the uneventful part, that is, until I learned we were about to miss boarding for Montreal. The narrow squeak you just heard was the door to the plane closing behind us.

We might have gotten confused if we had rented a car in Montreal, a city whose street and directional signs are all in French (Not unusual when one considers that it's the second largest French-speaking city in the world), but our taxi driver was bi-lingual (He was bi-polar, too, but that didn't matter. He was an excellent driver, and only his mood swings were deadly). We survived the trip from the airport and checked into the Ritz-Carlton, meeting a relative-by-marriage for a delightful five-hour dinner. We had a great time.

Friday, September 17

We joined Yale Exes at breakfast, checked out of the hotel, and boarded busses for a city tour, embarking in the pouring rain onto the cruise ship, The *Orion,* after a lengthy Security check of all luggage (an absurd and arbitrary search for contraband and weapons). The embarkation port was a loading platform for asphalt and gypsum with tons of salt stored under a football field-sized tarp, and that dock had nothing to recommend it as a waiting station.

We finally checked into our cabin, small but satisfactory, and we went to an interminable welcoming lecture, a ceremony that compounded the inconvenience of having waited for the better part of the afternoon for Security clearance.

Dinner was great, restoring our good nature in time for bed.

Saturday, September 18

We were rewarded with a surprise trip to Boldt Castle on Heart Island while sailing through the "1,000 Islands Settlement" in the middle of the St. Lawrence River. The river is populated with hundreds of summer houses on islands—some less than an acre in square footage—and some valued at over 25 million dollars.

Boldt Castle is a restored six-story mansion in great shape on the exterior but in disrepair on the insides, modeled after 16th Century architectural styles. It's a monument to great imagination as well as decay and vandalism. Never completed, the owner built the castle for his wife, but he stopped construction on the day she died, and it was never resumed.

Our passage to and from Heart Island via zodiacs was over choppy waters, lots of salty sea spray. Debarking was precarious, but life-threatening maneuvers make travel exciting.

We had lunch, then a massage, then a lecture, then a nap, then another lecture, then announcements, then it was time to dress for dinner. (I'm always amused to see men on cruises wearing what their wives allow them to wear. If the wife isn't dressed well, then the husband isn't, never the other way around.) Then a late movie on TV, then bed.

Sunday, September 19, 2005

Having seen Niagara Falls from both the American and Canadian sides on another trip, Barbara and I opted not to take a scheduled excursion of the falls and sailed instead with the ship on the Welland Canal where there are eight locks. I'm an inveterate lock-watcher, and I continue to be impressed by 40 foot (or more) high gates opening into watertight chambers, allowing a ship to be lifted or lowered from one level to another. We read books and watched traffic on the locks.

Monday, Sept. 20

We arose early for a full-day excursion to the Henry Ford Museum and Greenfield Village in Dearborn, Michigan. Because we docked in Winsor, Ontario, we had about a 45-minute drive from the Canadian border to the Museum.

At the Ford Museum we saw the original Montgomery, Alabama, city bus (obviously manufactured by the Ford Motor Company) on which Rosa Parks ("The mother of the Civil Rights Movement") had been riding when she was asked to give up her seat and to move to the rear. Almost everyone who passes by that seat reaches out to touch it. And so did I.

When the incident occurred, we were told that she had actually been sitting with "Coloreds," as required by city ordinance "to be seated from the rear to the front of the bus." Evidently the bus had picked up some Whites, accustomed to sitting from the front to the rear, who expected Coloreds to relinquish their seats to them. When Rosa Parks refused to move, the bus driver had her arrested, and she was tried and convicted of violating the local ordinance, thereby causing a non-violent protest tipping point for equality in the South. Her arrest sparked a citywide boycott by blacks of the bus system, lasting more than a year. The boycott raised Martin Luther King, Jr. to national prominence and resulted in the U.S. Supreme Court decision outlawing segregation on city buses nationwide.

Years later she said she really had no intention of making a grand statement by refusing to go to the rear of the bus; she was "just too darn tired to stand." Amazing what can happen when one person breaks a law without waiting for nine members of the Supreme Court to declare it unconstitutional.

We rode a train around the Greenfield Village, a reconstructed settlement that seeks to show what life was like in the years just before the turn of the 20th Century. Then we walked to a cabin relocated from the original site where George

Washington Carver had conducted his experiments with peanuts. There were lots of artifacts and memorabilia there, and a Black man and woman asked if I would take their picture in front of a bronze cast of Carver's hand. I obliged and then I told them my name is also Carver. They acted much impressed and a little confused because I'm obviously White. To add to the awkwardness of the moment, I said, "But what's in a name? A rose by any other name would smell as sweet."

After a moment's hesitation, the Black woman said, "Sure enough, Dr. Carver and Rosa Parks were two gorgeous roses." And I said she was right.

Tuesday, Sept. 21

An Indian Pow-wow was scheduled to be performed for tourists at the Manitoulin island, followed by a "champagne, orange juice, and Manitoulin gourmet snack" and a reception accompanied by a local musician on the pier.

We passed.

Wednesday, Sept. 22

We disembarked for a full-day excursion to Whitefish Point and Newberry, touring Michigan's upper peninsula, featuring stops at the Great lakes Shipwreck Historical Museum (with an exhibit of the *Edmund Fitzgerald* bell) and a logging museum at Newberry, reboarding the ship at Sault Ste. Marie.

The only special thing about the day for me was the chance at Sault Ste. Marie to peer out over a dam at the one Great Lake that we would not see otherwise, Superior.

We sailed on all the others in the following order from the St. Lawrence River: Ontario, Erie, Huron, and Michigan.

Thursday, Sept. 23

Disembarkation for a morning excursion on Mackinac Island began at 8:20. We were ensconced on horse-drawn carriages for an hour long tour. Afterwards, Barbara and I explored the Fort and walked down to the pier where we shopped around and bought nothing for about an hour; then we boarded the ship.

That evening we attended a crowded Captain's Farewell Cocktail Party and Dinner and met the first congenial couple (whose names aren't important here because I can't remember them) whom we met the entire trip. It simply wasn't one of those Yale trips that leant itself to conviviality. Stuffy little boatload.

But the *Orion* was great, the unhurried time spent with Barbara was great, and the Lakes, of course, were Great.

Friday, Sept 17

We took an early morning stroll around the ship and watched the city of Chicago grow larger on the horizon. Disembarking at Navy Pier, Barbara and I had a pre-arranged meeting with an old friend, Reese Elledge, from my days living in Germany (while I was in the US Signal Corps), and we had a snack while visiting the new Gehry-designed amphitheatre and the "Bean," a clever and massive piece of sculpture.

With little time to spare before our plane was to depart, we said goodbye to my friend, to Chicago, and to the Yale Exes Adventure on the Great Lakes.

Only my friend hugged back.

Germany's Christmas Markets

◆

A Cruise Down The Rhine
November 21–December 1, 2004

Having been stationed in Germany from 1956 to 58, I've always wanted to return for a visit, but I've never quite trusted that impulse. Nor did I want to spend big bucks. After all, I had been innocent (comparatively) back then and impressionable. I loved my visits courtesy of Uncle Sam's inexpensive travel clubs to the Black Forest & the Zugspitze, Ludwig's fantastic castles, Wagner's Festspielhouse at Beyreuth, East & west Berlin, and I really didn't want to travel at 100 mph on an autobahn through an industrialized, modernized Germany.

I had pretty much decided not to mess with my memories. Then one night while surfing the web I discovered that "Vantage Deluxe World Travel Company" promises Rhine River cruises to romantic old Deutschland on trips that don't cost an arm and a leg.

Actually, the feature that snagged my attention was the "Christmas Markets" theme available in November, cruising from one scenic German town to another, visiting holiday markets aboard a ship less than two years old.

Why Christmas Markets? Read on.

The entire cost of the ten-day trip was advertised at a reasonable price, less than $3,000, including all international air travel (Texas/Germany), river and land transportation, all meals, all excursions and tours, insurance, and a single cabin—a sensational all-inclusive price, especially when one considers current international dollar exchange rates (1 Euro = $.75).

"If you have to ask how much a Euro costs, you can't afford one."

I was seduced by the advertisement and skipping to the bottom line: After making the trip, I can heartily recommend the Vantage cruise for the cost alone.

So I sent in an application for the trip, and I was pleased that the paperwork progressed without a hitch, a good omen. Right up to my departure I was provided with updates on the Vantage web site, and so, naturally, I pushed my luck. I informed the Vantage sales persons that I'm a card-carrying member of the

International Food, Wine, and Travel Writers Association, and I said I would be delighted if I could receive a reduced rate.

No response.

A week before I left, I emailed the management to ask if I was going to be given any kind of upgrade—not because I required it, but because when I'm writing journals for publication, I like to know if I'm being singled out for special attention.

I was not informed that I was being singled out for special attention. So that answers that question. I wasn't.

Barbara, my bride of 45 years, doesn't enjoy traveling more than once or twice a year, and since she had reached her quota for 2004, she suggested I go alone, so I did.

But as usual, one pays a tariff for traveling alone. One has no one to confide in. Or disagree with. Or see the sights with. Or wonder what to wear with. Or eat lunch with. Only strangers. Some of whom are stranger than fiction.

New acquaintances can be delightful, but *boring* new acquaintances make loneliness seem a blissful option. I always resist the impulse to flee screaming from someone with whom I've spent an interminable three hours during the first three minutes of an encounter, but I make sure I *never* spend time with them again. Underscore <u>never</u>.

During the Rhine cruise I encountered only six passengers who bored me witless, all of whom I describe below [No names, please] because my reader will be anxious to learn what factors vex me most during social intercourse.

The First & Second Days, Sunday & Monday, Nov. 21, 22

The trip by air from Salado to Austin to Chicago was okay, but overnight to Frankfurt was exhausting. I napped several times during the flight then bounced aboard the bus for Cologne surprising myself with—I thought—my newfound ability to escape the curse of Jet Lag. En route, I chatted up folks from Minnesota, California, and Maine, and I held up manfully until I checked into my cabin aboard ship, the *MS River Explorer*. I began to unpack, decided to lie down for a brief nap, and slept for four hours.

I awoke, afraid—Ohmygod.—I'd missed lunch.

I hadn't, but I wasn't pleased when I sat down in the ship's dining room to a plate of curled-up white bread & cold cuts at a table with a couple of Hawaiian natives who informed me (before I had occasion to inquire) that not all Hawaiian women wear grass skirts, and the Golden Gate Bridge in San Francisco does not stretch to Honolulu.

The food was awful and that couple were unaware they were being weighed in the balance and found wanting. They said, Aloha, and I thought, "You have no idea how Aloha."

I found my way back to my cabin and sat on my bed in shock, fearing the food *and* the passengers might range from bad to worse. I decided to continue my nap rather than jump to conclusions—or jump ship.

Several hours later, I awoke from a bad dream in which someone who sounded very much like my wife was telling me, "You *don't* get what you *don't* pay for, Sweetheart."

I showered, dressed casually and went to the lounge for an interminable hour-long indoctrination conducted by the ship's 19 year-old (Well, he *looked* 19) First Mate and a blonde Purser whose appearance and performance style reminded me of Ellen Degeneras doing an impression of a German submarine commander saying things like "You *vill* return to zee ship by midnight, or vee *vill* sail vidoutchoo, okay?"

Then, thank God, things turned around.

At dinner, I sat with an engaging couple from Arlington, TX, and I was greatly impressed with them. And both food and service were above average for the remainder of the trip—except when white bread periodically appeared because, believe it or not, some Americans prefer Miz Baird's Bread to German hard rolls.

Afterwards, I strolled for about an hour offshore, a short distance to the Cologne bahnhof (an enormous train depot/shopping center where it seemed thousands of people were darting about. The noise of trains and crowds was over-powering, and it was all in German. Even the trains growled in German.), then I returned to the ship, detouring to explore the insides of a big, blue, balloon-shaped concert hall where Queen's *I Will Rock You* was showing that evening. I passed up that performance opportunity, climbed aboard ship, took a pill and slept for twelve hours straight, resolving my eastbound jetlag problems for good.

The Third Day, Tuesday, Nov. 23

After my favorite European breakfast of toast, bacon & scrambled eggs (the American version of a European breakfast), I joined an excursion led by a sensational docent at Cologne's remarkable Roman History Museum. The Museum has a collection of artifacts detailing the origins of the city ("Cologne" derives from the Latin word for "colony"—not a perfume by-product). The relics and antiques were extraordinary.

Then I walked to my first Christmas Market located in a square next to the famous cathedral. That market—like most on the trip—contained a handsome collection of vendors' booths with legends on the roofs identifying the various sellers' wares. I was looking for hand-made wooden Christmas ornaments.

Why? Read on.

But wait. What's this?

Surprise. On my walk back to the ship, I discovered a park designed in a gorgeous geometric arrangement of sloping, undulating cobblestones with blocks made of some kind of stone or concrete. I marveled at this simple but stunning public art plot composed of cobblestone berms. I haven't the vaguest idea who designed these units or why, but I found them beautiful.

I had lunch back aboard ship with three elementary school teachers. Conversation was pretty elementary. You can take a teacher out of the classroom, ...

For the rest of the afternoon I read a novel in my cabin until time for martinis. Then dinner with a couple from Nawth Carolina. She works for a county tax assessor-collector in the "Garnishing Wages" Department. She protested that she thoroughly enjoys her work. I enjoyed her Southern Accent.

After dinner, I skipped a concert by a local men's chorale singing sea chanteys in German. Instead, I went for a stroll ashore and enjoyed the lights.

Simple pleasures.

The Fourth Day, Wednesday, Nov. 24

I was awakened early by the sound of the ship underway in the Rhine, and I discovered an email from Barbara delivered under the door of my cabin:

"I'm okay but Pete Jennings died this morning. None of us expected his Alzheimer's would take him out so suddenly, but he hadn't eaten a thing in days, and the Hospice people said it could happen at any time. How could we have known? Jo Ann said she wanted me to come to dinner and Paul and Mary Chris insisted several times, and I suppose they'll need me to help with the phone, registering things like food from neighbors, or whatever. So I said fine.... Connie's cooking. Maybe I can help. Jo Ann is numb. Mary Chris is crying. And Paul is working on the program. It's all so very sad. The rain finally stopped this morning. It's been awful and very threatening with tornado watches, hail and dreary dark days. I forgot to say the memorial service is Saturday with a private family burial beforehand. It will probably get down to freezing tonight. I'll cover plants outside.

"I love you."

What a shocking, sad message. I couldn't respond by calling home immediately for fear I'd wake her up. So I went up on deck where the wind was icy. That allowed me to feel I was somehow sharing the same cold wind with Barbara and the Jennings family.

After a bit, I went to the ship's only computer available for passengers and sent a tribute to be used at the memorial service:

"It's impossible to write about Pete Jennings without acknowledging Jo Ann. He once said to me while we were walking together, "Jo Ann's my partner for life; I could never get along without her." Considering that she devotedly ministered to him for six years while his health declined, I can only guess that when he said that about her, he must have known something the rest of us didn't.

"Pete & Joann threw a party for Barbara and me within months after we moved in as neighbors, giving us a head start meeting folks in Salado. For years, we went with them to all points of the compass, and we had adventures—the kind friends take together, discovering new places with old friends. "Now, Pete," Joann would say when he would launch into one of his tall tales or one of his stories from life in Africa, England, or Iran. To this traveler, his stories never disappointed. Pete & Joann gave us great joy because they made the verb "to love" resonate. I am very, very proud to have known a great friend, Pete Jennings."

That afternoon I called and talked with Barbara, and she described in detail the somber events of that day. News of my travels didn't seem appropriate to share with her at that moment, and she didn't ask, so I said I'll call tomorrow, and I did.

I've included this sobering account in my journal because it took me by surprise, or rather shock, and I was reminded that one never travels from home and loved ones.

During the remainder of the trip, I kept in touch with Barbara and my daughter by email, but communications with them don't belong here.

After breakfast that same day, I went back on deck to view the cold Rhine countryside, but alas, it was all shrouded in fog.

A voice from the public address system in the Heavens described castles and landmarks along the Rhine, but no one could see anything. Not a damn thing.

It was laughable.

"And now on port side" (And everyone in the lounge rocked the boat over to the left side, pushing heavy chairs out of the way, stretching their necks in vain to see what was being described), "you'll see the oldest and most photographable—

"And now, look. Look on the starboard side." (And everyone rushed to the right side of the boat and rubbed the windows to clear the condensation away.) "There is the most charming, most delightful—

And up ahead, there. Look. See? There is the famous rock celebrated in song and legend, the Lorelei. Listen closely, Shhh. Listen and you can hear the wicked Siren's song."

There was pandemonium, passengers crashing from one side of the ship to the other, not knowing which side—neither port nor starboard or both—that the celebrated legendary rock might be located on, unable to hear the wicked Siren's song for all the commotion.

I stayed on port side during the entire time, and I squinted and—sure enough, there.—visible through the heavy fog was a sign that read, "Loreley."

"Will you look," someone said. "Whoever painted that sign misspelled Lorelei."

And a voice from the PA System said, "That's how we Germans spell it."

Almost everyone aboard could be heard saying, "Ohhhhh."

And then "Ahhhhh" as the fog began to lift and, coincidentally, the scenery disappeared, revealing an uninteresting part of the Rhine that nobody has ever celebrated in song and legend. "Awwwww."

The tiny voice of a 100 year old woman standing nearby said to no one in particular, "I got some great pictures of the fog with my digital, see? I used a flash. It looks like real fog."

The ship sailed on.

We docked at Ruedescheim, went ashore, and strolled to the Drosselgasse, a narrow alleyway that passes between gasthauses & souvenir shops, arriving at the entrance to "Siegfried's Mechanical Musical Haus" featuring 350 astonishing examples of music boxes, calliopes, and self-playing musical instruments. I hadn't expected the place to be much more than a tourist trap, but it was wunderbar. And my small group was conducted on a tour of the place by Siegfried himself, a great bearded figure who resembled a fat Bach wearing an imposing costume.

But he was a music box lover with a great sense of humor who has dedicated most of his life to collecting rare and euphonious instruments. It was a delightful treat, among the most unexpectedly remarkable things I witnessed on the cruise.

Afterwards, we were given entirely too long a period for shopping at the sprawling Christmas Market; then there was a dinner in a crowded but colorful gasthaus, "Winzerkeller." Live music, passable food and wine were served by costumed waiters.

The Fifth Day, Thursday, Nov. 25, *Thanksgiving*

After docking overnight at Ruedesheim, the ship cruised to Mainz, and arrived about 8 am.

I elected to take an optional full-day bus and walking tour of old Heidelberg, an imposing university town surrounded by mountains with vineyards descending sharply to the Neckar River.

The higher our bus climbed up into the oldest section of town, the more impressive the architecture. Tumbledown walls looked as if stage scenery designers had worked for centuries to dress up the vistas. Gorgeous.

We arrived at Heidelberg Castle, a romantic ruin dating back to the Middle Ages, destroyed for the most part by the canons of Louis XIV and only partially restored as a tourist attraction.

At the time I was stationed in Germany, there were lots of buildings and monuments in ruins all over the country. Towns like Heidelberg were being rebuilt, and as a young romantic, I imagined I could smell the dust and ashes of war in the air when I walked on guard duty at night. But even then, in the late 1950s, there wasn't much evidence remaining that there had been a second world war less than fifteen years before. Just lingering, smoldering resentment.

Heidelberg Castle's ruins today reminded me more of a grand opera setting than a centuries-old battleground. No dust. No ashes. It's a positively elegant ruin. Mark Twain called it "the last possibility of the beautiful and terrible," an apt turn of phrase.

Down below in the modern city, the Christmas Market was located in front of Heidelberg University where beautiful young Germans and international students hung around wearing shabby genteel sweatshirts & clothes emblazoned with American logos.

What war? One has to shrug off remembering a generation-old war and centuries-old battles. Shrug it off. We're got other wars to fight.

I shrugged and ambled about searching for Christmas tree ornaments.

I had hoped to have lunch in "Zum Roten Ochsen," the Red Ox café, the town's oldest café, but our group didn't get to go there. Instead, we enjoyed a meal in an exquisitely restored hotel dining room adjacent to the Heiliggeist-kirche (Church of the Holy Spirit).

That evening, after returning to the ship, we had a Thanksgiving Dinner featuring turkey stuffed with chestnut-apple bread "on sellery [sic], carotts [sic] and peas." Spelling of English words on the ship's dinner menus were okassionally inkorreckt. Evidently their word processor didn't have a spelchk.

The Sixth Day, Fri., Nov. 26

We arrived in Wertheim, "former capital of the counts of Wertheim" (as if that historical footnote has any significance in the grand scheme of things for travelers from anywhere but Germany). The day's walking tour featured "Daily life in Wertheim," a day probably like any other unexciting day in Wertheim. I realized how boring that walking tour was when our group looked across a canal at another group from our ship listening to a lecturer drone on. Everybody in that group looked as bored stiff to us as we must have to them.

There was a castle, "the famed old castle of Wertheim"—but there wasn't time to visit it, and that was okay because it couldn't have compared favorably with Heidelburg's.

Back aboard ship, lunch was served just as we departed at 1 PM, followed by a glassblowing demonstration in the ship's lounge at 2:30, and a Christmas Cookie baking demonstration at 4:30. Too much excitement, so I spent the afternoon reading and napping.

Martinis at 6 PM and supper following at 7 with an old Frenchman and a couple from South Carolina. The Frenchman couldn't understand anything the couple had to say in their dialect, and he kept asking them to repeat themselves almost as often as they asked him to repeat himself. I was no help, y'all.

I skipped dessert.

I also skipped Bingo in the lounge.

Perhaps I don't need to note that this day was the low point of the trip.

The Seventh Day, Saturday, Nov. 27

Rothenburg. On the Romantic Road.

The best preserved example of a medieval town in Germany, Rothenburg ob der Tauber; only 12,000 people live within the old town's battlements, half-timbered houses, narrow lanes, and picture book churches.

And at least twice the number of tourists as residents.

The weather was cold and rainy, but I felt great while snapping pictures, slipping and stumbling over wet cobblestones, strolling alone in Wunderland.

The entire town of Rothenberg, indoors and out was a Christmas Marketplace.

(Coincidentally, I live in a village, Salado, Texas, and I know what it's like during our annual Christmas "Stroll" when—during a two weekend period—merchants and townspeople endure incredible crowds. One of my greatest pleasures that day in Rothenburg was knowing that I don't have to live there year-round.)

I ate lunch with my group in a restored antique of a restaurant; then I milled about, bought a sweatshirt souvenir, and watched vendors prepare a bratwurst & brotchen with mustard that I gobbled down for supper. Ohhhh, Heaven. Best memories of Germany: the food & beer.

Then a wonderful thing happened. I found the tiny wooden Christmas tree ornaments I had been searching for—at every stop along the way—to replace some old, damaged ones I've used to decorate a little artificial Christmas tree every year for over 45 years. The ornaments were as original-looking as the ones I bought when I was a soldier stationed in Boeblingen, near Stuttgart, but my new acquisitions are made of olive wood. Gosh, they'll last for a hundred more years.

"But," you say, "You could have gotten Chinese imitations at Hobby Lobby." Yeah, but I knew I'd find real ones in Germany.

But that's not all. I got a music box that plays "O Tannenbaum" with a cut-out Christmas tree for my granddaughter. [And she loved it.]

And I found a little plastic house with a thermometer and a little plastic Damen und Herren who move in and out of two little plastic door openings as atmospheric pressures change. I'm sure kitschy objects like that will appeal to my 5-year-old grandson (Not the scientific part; rather, the plastic parts). He's wild about everything plastic: plastic monsters & plastic superhumans.

I also discovered some plastic cowboys & Indians, perhaps too politically incorrect to be distributed in the US. So I bought them for my grandson, too. [He enjoyed playing with them for awhile, so mission accomplished.]

My objective, returning to Germany, was complete. I could go home happy and successful with tree decorations and presents for my grandchildren.

As we returned that evening with our trophies, everybody showed me their presents, and I showed them mine. It was an ecstasy of exhibitionism. But *good* exhibitionism.

Dinner was gemuglich with my comrades, and I toddled off to bed where I finished reading my novel, and I slept well.

The Eighth Day, Sunday, Nov. 28

We had docked the day before at Wurzburg, taking a bus to Rothenburg, and today we were spending the morning visiting Wurzburg's "Residenz" whose claim to fame was a splendid Baroque interior with giant frescos by Tiepolo being restored after centuries of neglect.

It's always amusing to me that scholars always lecture crowds herded into historical edifices (like the Residenz) as if we really want to hear that the buildings were damaged by "Allied Bombs."

Sunday was a slow day and there was little traffic. We strolled around on our own, avoided churches—except for one that had a choir singing—then we had coffee and pastry at a bakerei. Afterwards, we returned to the ship, leaving Wurzburg behind in our wake.

That afternoon, there was a lecture on "Christmas Traditions in Germany" that filled the lounge. And there was an optional tour of the ship's galley. I preferred going up on deck to watch the ship's first mate negotiate locks.

Ashore, the Germans were doing what they do on Sundays, hiking through the countryside in all directions. After awhile, I chose doing what I do best: napping.

High tea was served in the lounge; I passed, and when I awoke, it was time for Martinis.

[Dear reader, do I give you the idea that programming of events aboard the ship was low on a ten scale? How about a 4?]

I enjoy Martinis periodically, but aboard ship I seemed to enjoy them with greater frequency than I ever have in my life—even though the barkeeps were stingy with their vodka, and the drinks were pricey. (That's where the ship makes additional income: They charge a flat fee for basics I've identified above, plus fees for drinks, extras and tips.)

Afterwards, there was a "Crew Show" in the lounge. Seen one, y' seen 'em all.

I went to bed instead and read.

The Ninth Day, Monday, Nov 29

Bamberg has a beautiful old city center "Am Kranen" whose distinctive public buildings are painted on the exteriors with saints & dignitaries. Since Bamberg survived World War II without damage, many of the original buildings still stand, notably the old city hall (Rathaus) built in 1744–56 and situated on an island in the middle of the rushing Regnitz River—a remarkable sight to behold in a neighborhood that was defined centuries ago in a style called Franconian.

Back aboard ship, there was a Bavarian Buffet featuring Sauerkraut, Bratwurst, Dumplings, Spatzle, and other dishes that had only been dished up as samples until that evening. We might have enjoyed them more frequently, but of course, that might have characterized the ship for what the chef did best: "Deutscher essen." The "International food" was not quite as good as the German.

I returned to "Am Kronen" searching for an email internet café, waiting in vain for a computer almost an hour in a public library, then another I spent another half hour in a Whataburgerish email café.

I went back to the ship and called on the single AT&T cell phone that was available to those of us who had purchased AT&T calling cards. I confirmed with Barbara my arrival on Wednesday. I also let her know she would have loved the Bavarian Buffet Sauerkraut.

At 6 PM, the Captain's Farewell Reception was held in the lounge with one of the captain's rare appearances. His eyes were glazed over by the time I arrived, and there was nothing memorable about our brief encounter. I told him I had enjoyed the trip, and he nodded, "Okay, okay," and passed me on to the next guy.

Obviously I didn't think highly of that ceremonial event. All that was free at the reception was warm mulled wine.

I sat at a crowded table for the Captain's Farewell Dinner with people whose company I enjoyed. Then I skipped whatever nonsense was planned for after dinner.

The Tenth Day, Tuesday, Nov. 30

Nuremberg artifacts are gruesome.

We visited the stadium grounds where Hitler convened his massive outdoor gatherings that I remember vividly from film clips of the era. I saw the grandstand and a portion of the wall where a great swastika I had seen destroyed in newsreels, a symbol blown to smithereens by Allied Forces.

One could imagine the location as a potential rallying ground for today's neo-Nazis, so assembly on those grounds is verboten. It's a huge, empty, forbidding, windswept space.

Next, our bus parked in front of the nondescript courtroom where "Judgement at Nuremberg" trials were held on the top floor with the prison adjacent. We weren't admitted to the courtroom because, we were told, court was in session all day.

The mood changed with the weather as the sky cleared, and we were transported to the oldest Christmas Market in Germany, specializing in children's items. What a country of contrasts.

At lunch, our tour guide sat across the table from me and explained that every tour group has problems appreciating Nuremberg. And yet, tourists want to see it. It's one of many cities in Germany that continue to be associated with Hitler's rise to power. The guide confessed that it is only the current generation in Germany that has begun to confront in public schools the grisly Nazi atrocities. He said they're just now getting around to dealing with their pernicious history. I wondered that he might be telling me that simply because I'm an American tourist, and Germans know Americans tend to distrust them for their proclivity to making war. He was by far the best tour guide we had on the trip.

One last Martini in the lounge; then, table hopping, I said goodbyes. Then dinner. Then packing. Then an early bed.

The Eleventh Day, Wednesday, Dec. 1

Disembarking at Nuremberg around 9 am, I was transferred to the new airport at Munich in a little less than two hours, chatting all the way with a couple whom I recognized as we were departing the ship as people I had known as a student at Baylor, a pleasant last minute surprise.

The airport was peopled with annoying security personnel and an airline lounge attendant who asked me why Americans are so rude. I told her I thought that was a rude question. In truth, I never perceived any of the Americans I was with as rude. On the contrary, I could identify (but I won't) only a few couples whom I would not want to travel with ever again.

When asked to fill out an evaluation questionnaire regarding my attitudes toward Vantage and the ship's staff, etc., I indicated I thought the overall quality of the cruise was high—as was the value. Would I travel on Vantage again and would I recommend Vantage to others? Yes and yes.

What were my favorite parts of the tour? Ranking from top downward, I indicated "almost every place we visited," then "interaction with passengers," then the ship, then the cruise itinerary, then the staff, and least of all travel to and from Germany (specifically air travel).

The flight home was crowded and stuffy, but I slept. When we arrived at Dulles Airport in Washington, hurtling down from the sky in rough weather, I discovered my flight to Austin had been cancelled. The luggage & customs inspections were slow and impeded by crowds from five other international flights that landed at just about the same time we arrived.

I stayed at a less than adequate motel overnight and then flew to Austin the next day on a poorer than average airplane whose flight attendants were sub-human. A sissyboy and giggly girl told us to "get seated or this plane will never take off, okay?" They thought they were being clever with "Once this soft drink cart starts down the aisle, you're stuck like chuck, so if you're going to the bathroom, go now." Nobody laughed.

I wrapped blankets around my legs and froze from the toes up. The girl said, "We can't do anything about it."

The boy said, "The truth is we don't know how, okay?"

What a bummer end to a very nice trip.

Was it a great trip? No, it was nice. "Nice" ain't great. I've been on as many one-stop tours as I ever want to go on. Do I recommend the trip for others? No. It <u>was</u> worth the money, and I had a good time, but I missed a great funeral. That's a grim joke, but it's probably true.

I've read *1000 Places to See Before You Die* [Patricia Schultz, Workman, NY], and I've determined that (for me) the only way to travel is to go someplace and stay long enough to get a feel for it. And avoid long-duration air travel as much as possible. Will I take my own advice? I dunno.

I enjoy the people I travel with. They're not incidental or irrelevant. But I don't travel to meet people; Hell, people are everywhere. Travel is about places. Like the places Jo Ann & Pete & Barbara & I used to visit. Places where old friends store new memories.

Romania

◆

Three Weeks With Global Volunteers
May 6–29, 2005

The Prequel

In the moonless dark of early morning on April 21, 2005, I left Austin, TX, for my latest trip to Europe, en route to the airport from my daughter's house where I had stayed the night before, when I realized—

"Stop. Stop and pull over."

I had forgotten my passport. And my camera. And my cell phone.

With no time to spare driving in considerable traffic, my wife, Barbara (serving as a chauffeur), and I turned back toward my daughter's house and reviewed aloud the various places where I might have left those three items. "Reviewed aloud" means comments which incited anger and apologies and recriminations—and that primarily from me. For the most part, Barbara remained silent as a steaming clam.

I vaguely recalled that the phone had been clipped to the passport. So as we approached the house, I asked her to wait in the car and to dial my cell phone number the minute I entered the house, taking a chance all three items would be located in the same nest, and the ring of the phone would guide me. Whereupon I would grab up all three objects into my arms and rush back to the car, and we would speed back to the airport in time to make my plane.

And that's exactly what happened—

Except for the part about arriving at the airport in time to make the plane.

That bird had flown away. I wasn't worried however, because I knew I would be all right. Hell, life and planes go on with or without me. So I unloaded my luggage and kissed my wife goodbye. It was no small comfort to hear her say in parting, "Be safe, Sweetheart. I love you." And this from the woman whom I'd greatly inconvenienced.

Disaster was averted because I'm a Platinum level frequent flyer with American, and the woman at the ticketing desk scrawled notes on my old ticket, scheduling me on the next flight out, and as a courtesy she gave me access to the first class waiting area.

I couldn't make heads or tails out of her scrawl, but the individuals who examined the tickets seemed to understand what she had written (Probably, "Help this half-witted person get aboard.") So I got good seats on new flights, departing an hour and fifteen minutes later than I had been scheduled to leave. Curiously, I arrived in NYC less than a half-hour after the plane I had been ticketed for.

Go figure.

New York City.

I bussed from La Guardia to Midtown, took a generic hotel bus from Grand Central to my lodging at the Yale Club, and within an hour after I landed, I set out in search of a theatre—any theatre—where I could get a good seat in the orchestra. I would have been happy to see any of five shows, but I got a desirable seat at a performance that evening of *The Putnam County Spelling Bee,* music & lyrics by William Finn, directed by James Lapine (the team which had put together *March of the Falsettos* years ago). You can always get a seat at a Broadway show; all it takes is chutzpah & cash.

I stopped at Brooks Brothers and bought a sweater, realizing it's still cold in New York, the same latitude as Romania where I'll be working. Then I went to a deli for a sandwich & cheesecake, returned to the theatre for the show, enjoyed it a lot, went back to the hotel, called Barbara, then retired for the night. Zonk.

The following morning, I slept late, then I tried on the sweater I had purchased. It was too small, so I put it back in the shopping bag, dressed, and took the elevator to the restaurant on the 22nd floor of the Yale Club for breakfast. I presented myself to the maître d', a fellow many years my junior who proved to have more "attitude" than the current President of the United States. He gave me a look which I shall always remember as effing condescending, then he looked above and beyond me, frozen, only his lips & jaw moving, searching for words.

I waited a bit, then I suggested, "Am I dressed inappropriately?"

He whispered, "You're wearing sneakers."

I said, "Yes?"

He looked at me as if to say, "The ball's in your court."

I stuck out my chin and said, "Other than that?"

He said, "And we prefer jackets to windbreakers."

I said, "We do?"

He waited. He was obviously accustomed to outwaiting ill-attired Yalies.

I sighed and capitulated, turned and took the elevator to the ground floor and out the front door.

I got a bagel & schmere with coffee at the nearest Starbucks, returned the sweater to Brooks Brothers, then went back to my room and waited until Randy Barbee, my good friend and lunch date, called to say he was waiting for me in the lobby. I rushed down, took him to the registration desk where I asked the clerk to recommend a place to eat. He paused ever so briefly and said, "I think you'll enjoy our tap room, sir. You won't have to dress."

I thanked him, took a look at Randy and as I expected, he whispered, "We won't have to *dress?*" And sure enough, we didn't, and we did enjoy the tap room's buffet lunch.

After lunch, I checked out of the Yale Club for the final time ever in my life. Randy insisted on helping me with my luggage to the pier, pulling my duffel bag into the busy street. He noted that one of the wheels was broken.

"Damn," I said, "That's a new duffel bag. What else can go wrong."

We tried for the better part of an hour to find a cabbie who would agree to brave cross town traffic. Finally, a hack materialized and zipped us to the ship.

Embarkation at the pier was scheduled for 2 PM. We arrived around 3 as I had intended, expecting to board the ship following the crush of early arrivals. But no. It took two more hours, standing on line, to get aboard because there was a Union screwup which even the *QM2* Administration couldn't manage.

Randy stayed with me for the first hour, and we had a great time talking. (He's one of my former students, and I am very proud of him.) Then he left me the duffel bag with the broken wheel which I had to drag with my carryon for the length of a football field. And it was painful. Sweet Jesus. I was worn out by the time I schlepped that dead body up the ramp onto the ship and into to my 6th deck cabin.

An inventory of good things that had happened in transit: A narrowly-averted departure disaster, a "Be safe, I love you" benediction from my wife, a delicious deli sandwich & cheese cake, a performance of a highly-amusing musical comedy, a visit with a very dear friend, and a large bed to collapse upon. I was having a good time. Really.

I. The Ship.

Years ago, Barbara and I went transatlantic on the sad old *QE2* in 1st class, and this year I sailed alone in 3rd class on the *QM2*. Two gay guys we met on the Queen Elizabeth were fond of saying of that ship, "This tatty old queen should be put down." It was a memorable trip, but not the once-in-a-lifetime experience I had hoped for.

The Queen Mary—on the other hand—is brand spanking new, and that in itself is an attractive recommendation. The crowds in the Britannia Dining Room make the ship seem less exclusive than traveling in 1st or 2nd, but when one considers how few of us there are who sail her majesty, one is properly awestruck and appreciative of the opportunity. It's a *stunning* and accommodating ship.

There is no end to information available on WWW describing the Cunard shipline's provenance and the history of events which led to designing and building the *QM2*. Also there are videos widely available featuring royalty, politicians, and movie stars endorsing the ship. The monitor in my cabin featured *QM2* retrospectives every hour on the hour. All the hoorah was inordinately self-congratulatory, so I stopped reading and viewing details about the size of this and the reason for that. I figure my reader can get it elsewhere, almost anywhere, so I dispense with statistics.

Rather, I'll detail my first and lasting impressions, good and ill.

Here's some bad stuff first:

Cabin 6132: My cabin was attractive. I had been upgraded* to a "hull veranda" cabin, the kind I had read about in travel blogs whose writers complained they really aren't verandas, just holes cut in the side of the ship allowing just enough floor space for a couple of plastic chaise lounges and a plastic table. One cannot see the ocean when reclining on the chaise, only the sky; so that kinda reduces the charm of that space to the off-putting appeal of a steel <u>outbuilding. A porthole would do as well. Or better—since portholes have no pretensions.</u>

*"Upgrade" is a term currently used to suggest to the buyer that he's getting something at a bargain rate. Actually, it's a ruse. The list price is the inflated virtual price; the upgrade is the actual price. Got that?

But I didn't dislike the hull veranda; I just didn't like it much. I had heard that the ship's architects—when updating plans after they had already begun building the ship—tried to adapt to the trend for verandas in cruise ships. Thus, the steely "hull holes" seem a ship builder's unloved afterthought.

I didn't spend much time on the veranda for two reasons which have nothing to do with design: I stayed indoors because the deck wasn't ever cleaned during the entire time I was aboard, and there were cigarette and cigar butts & ashes and somebody's old slipper on the always wet, slick, dirty floor.

The other compelling reason for staying indoors was the weather (Most days it was too cold for comfort). Hastily, I must add that the cabin's interior was very, *very* comfortable and cozy and always clean, thanks to Maggie, my stewardess. Evidently, cigar butts weren't on her checklist.

There was a keyboard for sending emails located at my desk, but its current software has limited editing capabilities, so I used it to send only one message for $2.50 to several recipients. I preferred using my net address at computers in the Cyber Center on Deck 2 because the computers there were easier to edit messages on—if less private and proximate.

Everything else in my cabin was super, especially the modular walls & wall trim, fabrics, and the things that gave that ship its "look." The entire ship for that matter has a brand-new now-and-forever feel, and it's gorgeously-designed and executed throughout. I enjoyed being aboard at *almost* every turn. (The hull veranda was the only Achilles heel, and I wouldn't have noted it if I hadn't paid for it.)

Programs on the cruise were many and varied.

Performers: The singers and dancers showcased in the Royal Court Theatre (with a very fine orchestra) are simply superb. They're stunningly disciplined. And the productions are full of surprise and delight. The corps de ballet has amazing talent, skill, and incredible endurance. Although the shows were long, they were well-paced and never boring, and the dancers were stalwart & athletic & fit to the task with leaps and lifts and extensions and poise. They were marvelous (Maybe their eyes were a little glazed-over during final curtain calls, but no wonder. They had to be near collapse, but never once did I see any of that troupe reveal their true exhaustion. They displayed not a whit of self-pity.). Bravo.

Other Performers and Lecturers: There were lectures, notably a series by Terry Waite, the abducted author, whose self-effacing style seemed absolutely right for the QM2. And there were lectures. I listened to one by one of the fellows on the Oxford University faculty series. He didn't snag my interest. Yawn. So I read my book rather than attend that series. I did attend a cocktail party honoring the scholars and got stuck listening to the leader of the Royal Academy of Dramatic Art troupe who allowed me to feed him cues to his packaged speeches explaining Shakespeare and Chekhov to me. I never interrupted with "Hey, Buddy, I know all that stuff. And I saw the show you performed, and it was only okay. Save your promotional talk for the uninitiated."

That would have been rude for me to say that. And pointless. He never would have believed me.

Soft drinks: On the first day of the trip I bought a $25 "Soft Drinks Package," paying in advance for all the Diet-Cokes I would consume during the cruise. But even with a "paid in full" sticker affixed to my shipboard pass, the payment transactions for drinks took forever to process, and on more than one occasion, I asked, "Whom does one have to screw to get a Coke around here." No one was amused.

The Casino: Impulse obliged me to gamble in the ship's Empire Casino. I lost a total sum of $10 in two minutes. It all happened so quickly I thought it was *my* fault.

Shoportunities: I skipped all art auctions, cruise sales, "Mayfair Shops" sales, and photo shop and op sales (Opportunism.). And I avoided wine tastings, afternoon teas, as well as appearances at bars (except on special occasions—every day), the cigar lounge, and social dances (including line-dances) aboard ship. I just don't hang with those crowds.

Food Service: I had a problem with the food service emporiums aboard ship, but that problem was directly related to my entirely subjective social class-consciousness. So here's a divertissement justifying my attitude toward some people:

The *QM2* PR boasts "Elegance" as a descriptive adjective for the ship. The brochures and catalogs promote and promise elegance. Thus, passengers are urged to follow dress codes and behave like ladies & gents. The truth, however, is codes of dress and behavior are lost on folks who ain't got no suavity nor probity.

I am not the kind of guy who goes around dissing passengers who are dressed inappropriately (It's obvious that I don't know sneakers from windbreakers), but really. We're talkin' bad clothing choices for fat people with ugly faces. (True, I *am* a bit overweight; but my features are quite regular, and on some occasions, I'm the most handsome ogre in attendance.)

My quarrel with the *QM2* promoters is the ship surrenders its authority as arbiters of elegance when admitting aboard anybody who can afford passage. There ought to be a test to insure that doofusses are kept off the ship, so that I don't have to sit next to them when I'm eating—which brings me back to Food Service.

One has no choice as to the table where one is seated in the Britannia Restaurant because they hold to that old-fashioned policy of not providing for open seating for evening meals during the voyage. You're on your own during the day.

I enjoyed meeting the people whom I was assigned to sit with at table 293; in fact, they were three of the five most agreeable people I met. But I wanted freedom of choice; I paid for it.

Quite literally, I paid cash for three meals in Todd English, a restaurant named for an imaginative chef who has a justly deserved international reputation. The food was grand, every bite (Except for the after dinner card stock cookies). The meals produced in me a rare effect of feeling guiltless after having gotten stuffed. I was *glad* I gorged myself to near bursting, knowing I shall probably not pass this way again.

The buffet lunches in the Kings Court are simply glorified mall food court options. There were no signs of Grandy's, McDonald's, or KFC, but the concept was unmistakable. The food was satisfactory, but the crowds. Oh. I had to dart in and out of line to get what I wanted avoiding people who rudely darted in and out of line, grabbing, stabbing, and using their hands to pick up food. Their germy, filthy hands.

I asked a blessing on my food that I wouldn't contract some gastrointestinal virus. And I helped myself to ounce upon ounce of the alcohol installed in dispensers at the head of most lines where food servers instructed us to "Have a wash." The smell of alcohol was strong, but I felt safe even as I was buffeted on my backside by the crowds. Aha, that's where the word "buffet" comes from.

It's worthy of note that I never got stuffed at those Kings Court buffets.

I had two lunches at the Golden Lion Pub, a crowded watering hole which served Fish & Chips and Bangers & Mash. Lovely.

Food service was very, very good overall. I enjoyed myself.

Sailing: The weather was good and chilly, and the roll of the ship was barely noticeable. None of the pitching and tossing I remembered from the *QE2*. From time to time I could feel semi-quaver quivers, and I could hear an intermittent hum in different locations on the ship. Nothing alarming, simply a trifle annoying.

My Worst and Best Experience on the Trip: When filling out an interactive internet application to travel on the ship, I was never asked for my elegance status. That should have tipped me off. As I suggested above, they take anybody who can dial their 800 number.

I had great difficulty explaining on the net to an agent that I have a Press card, and I'm writing a book. Eventually, I gave up trying 1) to request permission for me 2) to have access 3) to a computer 4) on board ship 5) so that I might edit documents 6) which I would carry aboard 7) on a disk. Too many ideas for one sentence. I couldn't seem to cut the requests down to one simple sentence. The agent kept saying that whatever I was asking, the answer was, "Quite impossible."

I said, "Nonsense, I don't believe in impossible."

So I wrote to the Cunard Public Relations Manager who responded with a courteous note explaining that "while I am not able to secure a personal computer for you [to edit your book], … I will let our cruise hostess, Amanda Reid, know that you will be on board."

That gave me a name to drop, and so once aboard ship I made an appointment with Ms. Reid, and we had a pleasant but nonproductive chat. She referred me to "Mitch" in ConneXions where banks of computers are provided for instruction and for sending emails. All the computers are reserved for those purposes only, not to be used for word processing and editing journals.

Mitch at first advised me to go to the Purser's office, but then he said "Wait. They'll just tell you it's impossible."

I laughed (exuding confidence) and said, "Impossible just takes time, right?"

He said, "I'll get back with you."

When I ran into him later that afternoon, he said, "I'll let you know something tonight or tomorrow."

I considered approaching the Hotel Manager next, remembering that it was that officer on a recent voyage with Radisson who gave me approval for the same request.

By the third day, however, I had lost steam and I resolved that when next I saw Mitch, if he told me "It's impossible," I'd just give up. There were only three more days remaining on the trip.

I hung around the computer center on the off chance Mitch would actually appear and provide me with word processor access.

And that's precisely what happened. Wow.

But it was not easy. Permission from Higher-Ups had to be obtained and one of his dedicated computers had to be reprogrammed for my use. And that, in brief, is what Mitch had done, spending a lot of time programming and writing instructions for my use of the computer. He handed me the instructions, talked me through them, and I inserted my disc into the CD Drive, assuming that because I had brought the disc in a box with a plastic cover labeled "Best&Worst-TravelsDocs," that's what it would be.

We waited and waited for the text to appear.

Nothing.

After much fooling around, we confirmed—Oh, Nooooo.—that I had brought with me a blank fergodsake disc.

What does one say when one learns one will not be able to edit one's documents because one has left them at home on a disc on one's desk. One says, "***** ****** ** **** ***** ** ******* ** **** * *****". (Asterisks indicate strong language).

But wait. It would still be possible for me to record my impressions of traveling on the *QM2* while I was still aboard ship, and I could do that with my only restrictions being class times. No problem. In fact, that's all I had time to do in the three days remaining.

I was pleased with myself for having gone as far as I could go by dint of my unflagging, nagging persistence and Mitch's persuasive politics & generous programming. What a nice guy.

Alls well that ends well, to coin a phrase.

What I Liked Best: The *QM2* cuts through the water—zoop.—in the greatest haste: "Gotta get to port, gotta speed home, go, go, go."

Leaning over the side of the ship on a low deck, I liked staring at waves kicked up by the turbulence of the ship's prow as it slices through the water, churning the sea into frothy blankets of foam. And then ripping the blankets apart in threads. I have seldom ever watched those lacy blankets dancing that I haven't said, "Incredible."

At the stern, I've watched the same kind of frenzied foamy blanket seem to dance and chase the ship, leaping, lapping, skipping, alive.

All that soapy-looking lather has an irresistible fascination for me.

And studying that kind of turbulence is what I enjoy doing most while sailing on the sea. And when there's nothing out there but water, it's as if that's the way it's 'sposed to be. No poem intended.

On the last morning of the voyage, we docked at Southampton and disembarked as scheduled. Nothing very ceremonious.

There was no one to say farewell to but Mitch.

II. The Isle of Wight

Nobody I know seemed to know what or where the Isle of Wight is except for Chuck Wilson, a former student and my host on that 23-mile wide island just below Southampton off the southern coast of England. It's pronounced like "white" without the "h" sound.

I transferred from the QM2 via taxis and a ferry to the middle school where Chuck's an instructor, arriving in a drizzling rain like an abandoned orphan at the door of the school with my broken luggage. Chuck, hospitable as ever, stashed my luggage and offered me lunch at the school cafeteria consisting of mashed potatoes, French fries, and escalloped potatoes with a thin wafer of beef. Generous portions, but oh, my. What does one do with a plate of three kinds of potatoes and a piece of boiled papiere mache.

Chuck showed me around the school, locating me at a computer where I got my email using his access code. (Obviously, use of the net is restricted to middle school kids. Only teachers can surf with impunity.)

After meeting and chatting with the school's loquacious principal, the school let out, and I met David Moorse, a teacher—and coincidentally, Chuck's landlord, who put my luggage in the boot (trunk) of his car. Double-speak began almost immediately, meaning I was expected to translate British/American expressions from one language to another—not a difficult task except when the speaker mumbles or mutters words in an undecipherable dialect; then one is permitted to say, "Pardon?" But only twice. Thereafter, the speaker virtually shouts the word, assuming the listener is deaf. There's lots of shouting when using double-speak. IF ONLY THE BRITISH WEREN'T SO DEAF.

Whizzing from the village of East Cowes and dazzlingly bright yellow fields of Rape seed (Canola Oil is a product) to the larger village of Newport in David's car, we arrived at their very large bachelor's pad, roomy (5 bedrooms) & cheerful. Chuck had prepared a room for me with a fat, fleecy comforter on the bed. I have never been able to sleep under a comforter; the damned things attack and smother and heat me up to roast at about 105 degrees Fahrenheit. So I thanked him profusely, stripped the duvet off the comforter, added a light blanket, and settled in.

That evening we went to a nice family pub for dinner, and Chuck surreptitiously picked up the tab. I insisted that from that moment on I would be paying for dinners out as well as admissions, passes, transfers, and fares to offset his and David's generosity as hosts. It seemed only fair.

The next morning I was left to recover from my trip and to explore Newport on my own. I followed directions down to the town's centre (spelled "centre" because the spell-check on this computer rejects the American spelling) where a Friday-only farmer's market was set up. Busy and crowded, it held nothing remarkable. I was drawn to a nearby building which housed a meals-for-the-elderly tearoom featuring coffee and biscuits for sale. I got my meagre (Again, my guardian spell-check) cuppa cawfee and sat down at one of the several long tables beside two persons older than me, an ancient mariner and his good wife. I couldn't leverage the conversation to any level which interested me, so I returned to the counter, held out my cup and with a wry smile said, "Please, ma'am, may I have some more?" expecting a mock-indignant reply from Dickens' *Oliver Twist*: "MORE.????"

Instead, while refilling my cup, the ma'am said, "We don't find that amusing, young man."

"Young man?" I haven't been called that in a generation. I looked around the half-filled room and discovered I was at least twenty years younger than anyone there. I simply didn't belong. So I left.

I went to the Island Historical Museum where I was welcomed to view dinosaur bones, photographs of historical persons, costumes, and the stuff one always sees in historical museums. The dinosaur artifacts were unique if not awe-inspiring.

"That's it." I said to myself as I left the building, "That's what I want to experience. Something awe-inspiring, damn it"

For the remainder of the morning, seeking awe-inspiring damn it experiences, I was greatly disappointed. So I settled for a lunch of asparagus soup at a friendly pub, then returned to the bachelor's pad, number 71 Oak Grove (Easy to remember because there wasn't an oak growing on the street). Instead, there was one of England's ubiquitous hedgerows on one side of the road and on the other a line-up of houses which are described, categorically, as *attached, semi-detached,* or *detached* from one another. I made the mistake of calling them "row houses," and I was advised that that's a pejorative term used to describe dwellings which house po' folks.

The interesting (if not awe-inspiring) characteristic about this line-up is the garden spaces in front of each house—virtually every occupant has one. But not one resembles another. There's obviously an imperative for each homeowner to have vegetation different from adjacent neighbours (Okay, neighbors). If I've planted tulips, then you must plant iris or anything which differs in every way from my flora and foliage.

Each house front is architecturally different from the neighbours'. And it would appear that if a building's original architectural design is not distinctive enough, then porticoes, foyers, even vestibules must be added in competition for uniqueness. There is no virtue in unique, however; so the differences appear as more arbitrary than distinctive. And those are the most exciting observations I made all day, noting not-very-remarkable details which are seldom described in serious works of literature, but which may be found in Victorian novels as well as erudite journals of this kind.

That evening I persuaded the lads to join me for dinner at a pub. I felt I was becoming assimilated.

On the next day, Saturday, Chuck took me for a trip exploring the island villages by bus. We rode in the top level of double-decker busses, transferring from one to another, visiting historical sites and gardens. The only town which I liked was Godshill which we didn't come upon until late in the day. We stopped for a Cream Tea event which we enjoyed.

That evening back at 71, David prepared a lamb roast using a recipe which he picked up on a trip to Athens; and it was lovely (a term which the English use excesssively to describe anything and everything).

On Sunday, I explored Carisbrooke Castle by myself and found it, at last, awe-inspiring. Featured as the last dwelling-place for Charles I before he was hauled away and beheaded, the character of the buildings—both old and new—was grand.

I walked up and around the castle's ramparts, hundreds of feet above the dry moat, hazardous because some of the railings were low and the flooring was uneven. And I climbed and descended steep stairs. Centuries olde (No, the spell-check didn't do that, I did).

I admire the current administration who maintains the buildings because they must care mightily to have such a gorgeous palace. From now on, when I hear the word "castle," I'll remember Carisbrooke—mostly for the danger of toddling around the tops of those outer walls.

After that two-hour adventure, I descended the castle hill and went for lunch at a pub, enjoying the best food in the world, a cold beer and a very hot Irish potato with butter. There's nothing better after a castle adventure.

I returned to 71 to visit with David's guest, June WhosenameInevergot, and we went out to dinner at a lovely restaurant with a grand garden and enjoyed pheasant, a bird they have a lot of on the Island.

The next day, Chuck and I traveled by David's car to a ferry to a train, transferring two times to Brighton. The town is ugly-at-first-sight and seems a Mecca for hostile-looking teenagers and obnoxious women with unbelievably big boobs and pierced navels accompanied by their biker blokes who have more hair than God intended.

I said to Chuck, "Have you noticed that I'm the oldest person in this crowd?"

He said, "No, I saw a guy a *little* older."

"Obviously," I said, "I don't belong here."

We followed the crowd, thinking we were all going to the same destination, the palace which George I had remodeled and remodeled, egregiously spending millions upon millions to create a hideous, colossal self-indulgence of a castle.

But the crowd trooped to the seawall and thence to the Brighton Beach & Pier. Of course. *That's* where those animals were going. We had assumed the Queen's Pavilion, and we thought it would be facing the beach.

But no, after traipsing through what seemed like miles of "Do NOT Cross Here." "Nor Here." "Wait." "Now, Cross Here Quickly at Your Own Peril." we came upon that gigantic curiosity of a palace, walked miles around it to the entrance, then—irritated beyond measure—entered that abomination. I'm admitting I was irritated before beginning our tour of the building because I'm sure that accounted in part for my unenthusiastic appreciation of that oedifice (Hmmm. Is that a slip of the pen?).

A gracious docent took us in a large group from one inexcusably costly room to the next, explaining how George, Victoria's son, would have dinners with over 100 items served in 36 courses. As a result the shameless glutton grew to weigh well over 350 pounds and had to have a bedroom built for him on the bottom floor because he couldn't climb to his upstairs bedroom.

We left the tour at a complete loss to understand how a monarch could be so capricious as to build such an ugly building. I, however, was more stunned by the hideousness than the costly extravagance of the building. It's a great, shamelessly ugly place to visit.

Awful-inspiring.

Dinner al fresco at a charming restaurant. Then we returned to the Isle of Wight, content that David's *semi-detached* domicile was practical and cost-effective, unattractive but not hideous.

May 3rd was my last full day in Newport.

I hitched a ride with David to the East Cowes school, took over a computer with school kids sitting on both sides as I typed and saved my journals to date.

Then I walked about a mile to Osborne House, one of Queen Victoria's hangouts, and walked into the gardens—the wrong entrance, it turned out—and strolled around the buildings to the castle's restaurant where I had a great lunch. Then, continuing on my way around, I found the entrance and went in.

A smiling guard greeted me with "May I have your ticket, please?"

I took out my billfold, intending to buy a ticket, and the guard backed away, startled, as if I had reached for a gun.

"Oh, no. You must put your money away, sir." (Evidently she thought I was trying to bribe her.) "You should have purchased a ticket at the reception area where you entered."

I confessed I had entered through the camellia bushes, and horrified, she shamed me with "Sir. That is not an entrance. You cannot possibly enter there."

Rather than debate the matter, I asked where to find the ticket booth.

She began explaining in the most condescending manner how I must go just there and then just there and not to return until I had paid full admission, atoning for my sins. She actually shook her finger at me and said, "Really, sir, there are right ways and wrong ways to do things."

I resisted saying, "You're acting like you just caught me masturbating, ma'am." Instead, I hung my head and slunk away and promised never to do it again.

But she wouldn't let up. She called, "You should know better, a grown man, indeed."

I can laugh while recalling the event, but at the time I felt like shouting obscenities at that unenlightened guard. Instead, I stopped, turned, smiled and said, "Thank you so much for your kindness, Bitch."

Ahhh. She turned to ice.

At the ticket booth/gift shop, I examined a book containing photographs of all the rooms in the castle, and I determined there is nothing in that Victorian chockablock building that would interest me, so I walked out the front of the gift shop, exiting the wrong way, never again to accost the Ice Maiden.

From Osbourne House I took a bus to Newport for a haircut and groceries from a Safeway Supermarket to replace David's larder. I found a "charity shop" [second-hand store] where I bought a duffel bag to replace the one with a broken wheel which was giving me fits. At a bank I withdrew cash but not until I negotiated *for over an hour* with the bankers and on the phone with Master Card security persons. No easy matter.

I chatted with Barbara on the phone, then Chuck joined me at a tourists' pub for a dinner of oily fish and soggy chips (nothing to rave about). Back at the digs, I packed and prepared for an early departure the next morning.

May 4th, Wednesday, was overcast and windy.

I imposed on David to take me to the ferry landing, took the ferry, transferred by shuttle to the train station where I boarded a train for Salisbury. Arriving I met a "Tourist Helper," a jolly woman named Anne, who helped me choose the White Hart Hotel with a rate of 70 pounds and proximity to the Cathedral.

I strolled around Salisbury Cathedral and its "close" and took a tour of that impressive, upbeat building, highly recommended by Bill Bryson in *Notes from a Small Island,* and I agree with him. But it's just one more cathedral, and if you've seen one....

Then I spent a couple hours in the nearby Salisbury (& South Wiltshire) Museum, really enjoying a trip from ancient to present time. A flyer describing the museum cites Bryson saying "Salisbury Museum is outstanding and I urge you to go there at once." Clearly, Bryson has a justifiable prejudice for that town.

I had lunch in the museum's tearoom, eavesdropping on two Brit matrons. Veddy chic shabby genteel.

That evening I had a great dinner at the Venison Café and saw a show at the Salisbury Playhouse, *Map of the Heart,* by William Nicholson, author of the C. S. Lewis play, *Shadowlands.* The play had something to do with wives forgiving husbands for infidelity if the husbands apologize because we all need each other, okay? It was a drawing room comedy played like a melodrama. Bad choice of styles.

I wasted most of the following morning in the local tourism office trying to arrange for accommodations in Dorchester. I took pictures of the cathedral and later erased them because I simply couldn't capture that monolith on film (Okay, digital camera).

After lunch at an outdoor restaurant shooing away invasive effing Grackles, I took a pleasant two-hour bus trip to Dorchester, searched forever to find their tourism office, couldn't locate a four-star lodging, so I just popped into a pub and took a room with bath. As if I hadn't had enough walking around aimlessly for the day, I hiked from the town pump down the right hand side of East High Street following the green dotted line on the Town & River walk map and phooey. It was another waste of time and energy.

So. I took a chance that the Dorset County Museum, boasting the world's greatest collection of Thomas Hardy's original manuscripts, would be interesting and it was indeed. As always, museums exhibit too much for the eye to take in, and this one was no exception, and the presentation was excellent. Hardy, author of books featuring local landmarks, was the major attraction as expected, and his study and desk had been relocated to the museum, and there was a celestial voice narrating passages from his work. Neato.

That evening I dined alone in the Michelin-listed Sienna restaurant. It did not disappoint.

The next day, Friday, May 6, I took a train to Woking, a station where I had to transfer by bus to Heathrow. I had the good fortune to sit beside a 75-year-old widow who travels the world with her 73-year old boy toy. She said, "I'm spendin' all me money travelin' the world and leavin' m' kids with th' memory that their mither had a grand time before she pissed away."

At Heathrow, one of the world's most colossal nightmare air terminals, I booked a room at the Renaissance and called and talked with my wife & daughter. After a light supper, I hopped on a bus to the Underground, thence to Victoria Station where I enjoyed a performance of a great new musical drama, music by Elton John, *Billy Elliott,* and afterward, I returned to the hotel. Great, great, great evening.

On Saturday, May 7, I arose early & transferred to Terminal 1 at Heathrow where I stood in a long line of passengers and spies getting ticketed for Eastern Europe & Russia. Eventually I went from that line to the Security line, arriving at the departure gate just in time to stand on line there. Non-events, hardly worth mentioning in a journal if they hadn't taken over three effing hours of my life. The trip from London to Bucharest took less time than that.

III. Barlad, Romania With The Global Volunteers

Information about Global Volunteers

Why did I want to go to Romania? Most reasons will appear in this text; however, I confess I like to see countries off the beaten path, and Romania qualifies as more off-the-path than most I've visited. Also it's a place where I felt I could do some good teaching conversational English. And I wanted to work with Global Volunteers again after my three weeks in Xian.

Why Do I Believe in Global Volunteers?

Each time I go with GV, I marvel at what can (and can't) be accomplished, volunteers working with children.

What are Global Volunteers? [*The following information may seem dry as dust to anyone who doesn't really care what GV's all about*]

GV is a non-profit organization benefiting Volunteers & Communities around the world. Here are some GV objectives 1) to work only where specifically invited, 2) to cooperate with hosts, 3) to further community-driven human & economic development, 4) to recognize that locals *must* be in charge, 5) to work under the direction of local leaders on community-based projects, treasuring what is learned from locals, 6) to perform whatever services are asked, 7) to avoid offering unsolicited advice (the most difficult task), 8) to send teams several times each year, returning year after year, 9) to stay in the community while in-country, 10) to provide modest financial support for community-based projects, 11) pay for items like meals, lodging, water, local transportation, cooks, etc., and 12) to have no hidden agendas.

Information about Romania from the *CIA World Factbook*

A Brief [135 words] History of Romania: Wallachia & Moldavia were united in 1856, were designated Romania in 1859, and were given full independence from the Turks as a monarchy in 1878.

Skip to World War 1 when they allied their country with the Allied Powers, fighting against Germany. However, in WW2 they allied with Axis Powers and, losing the war with the Soviets, surrendered in 1944.

From that time to the end of Ceausescu's reign (1965–1989, the year that dictator was executed) the country was dominated by Communists (actually till 1996 because the Communist Party was more influential than others); thereafter, for eight years, by fractious coalitions of parties.

As recently as December 2004, a center-right alliance of the Democratic Party and National Liberal Party scored a surprise victory, electing Traian Basescu as President who appointed Prime Minister Calin Popescu Tariceanu.

<u>Noteworthy Information about Romania</u>

Geographic area: Slightly smaller than the state of Oregon with 237,500 square Kilometers.

Climate: Temperate; cold winters with snow & fog, hot summers with frequent rain.

Natural Hazards: Earthquakes, severe in the south & southwest, and landslides.

Population: 22,355,500 est., with declining growth ratios

Health: HIV/AIDS, less than .1 percent with 6,500 living with HIV/AIDS

Ethnic Groups: Romanian 90 percent

Religions: Eastern Orthodox 87 percent

Literacy: Total population 94 percent

Government & Legal system: Based on the constitution of France's Fifth Republic with universal suffrage and Executive, Legislative (bicameral Parliament), and Judicial branches

Economy: 45 percent below poverty line

National Debt: $18 billion est.

Transportation: Highways, 198,603 kilometers, most unpaved; Ports & harbors on the Black Sea; Airports, 62 with 36 of them unpaved runways; Heliports, 1

Military: Compulsory at 20 years of age for 12 months; manpower fit for service: 5,000 est.

Illicit Drugs: Romania is the major transshipment point for Southwest Asian heroin and small amounts of Latin American cocaine bound for Western Europe with vulnerability for money laundering in casinos, banks, and currency exchange houses.

"The Consular Info Sheet" distributed by the US State Department notes that most tourist facilities in Romania have not yet reached Western European standards (A *major* understatement). A passport is required for Americans; whereas,

Romanians traveling to the US must have a visa, sometimes waiting years for permission to travel. Medical care is generally not up to Western standards and basic supplies are limited—especially outside major cities. Most crimes are non-violent with organized pick-pocketing and confidence schemes. Credit card & Internet fraud are the most common crimes affecting foreigners. Romania is a "cash only" economy because of credit card fraud.

At Last: My Trip to Romaia

For a week, I traveled a slow, circuitous (albeit pleasurable) route aboard the new QM2 from the US to Southhampton, by ferry to the Isle of Wight, then British Rail around Southern England, then by air to Bucharest, Romania.

When I Arrived in Bucharest, **Saturday, May 7, 2005,** my first encounter at the Bucharest Airport with the 67th Global Volunteer team was positive. I liked our group leader, Michela Cirjontu, on sight. Most of us, 3 men and 12 women, bonded almost immediately with minimal self-consciousness.

The cast of characters: Sabrina Adamson, Sarah Butler (both entirely too young for the job, and that's as unkind as I'll get), and Patti Thomas, their guarantor, from Alaska; Debi Phillips, Peggy Poirier and Sarah Urton from Canada; and the rest of us from the States: Mary Vitalich, Nancy Anderson, Cathy Johnson, Tiffany Bartlett, Linda Baker, Pat Donahue, Sam Soseos, Ken Severn, and me.

After settling in at Bucharest Hotel Cape that reminded me of an upscale Mexican motel, we went to dinner at La Mama (Romanian, not Italian food) and had the first of many great meals: schnitzels and kabobs and dozens of kind of chickens and veal dishes.

That evening, I had a problem with the A/C in my room because I didn't understand the directions on the remote control, but when I woke up sweating (and swearing) in the night, I realized I had to take the damned thing seriously and learn how to program it. I did and afterwards, I slept.

The next morning, **Sunday, May 8,** we began our 7-hour trek stopping at the "Metro," a Romanian kind of Wal-Mart big box, then we headed north to Barlad, the town in northeast Romania where I would be teaching for the next weeks. Our ugly Mercedes-Benz "macrobus" was full, every seat used, and a trailer was attached to carry our luggage. We stopped for lunch at the only MacDonald's (same ole, same ole) between Bucharest and Barlad. Afterwards, we continued on our way until we were stopped at a police barrier and informed that a bridge en route had been washed out by floods. That detour added two hours to a trip we had expected to take only five, but spirits remained high, a good omen.

Arriving at Banca, the village where we would be housed near Barlad, my heart sank lower than at any other time during the entire trip. The living quarters were unfinished and they *looked* unfinished. Every day thereafter, the builders would add another feature to our rooms and apartments. I liked my room immediately, but the builders hadn't cleaned up, and I started out with a punch list of no heater, no TV set, no phone, no desk lamp, no bathroom mirror, no bath mat, no soap.... And the mattress wasn't anything to rave about.

The weather when we dragged in from Bucharest was drizzly/gloomy. The ground was muddy/boggy. And I was depressed/dismayed. Oh, dear God, I've made a big mistake.

I'm sure I was having a reaction to an overlong trip because later that same evening when I went for a walk with my new comrades, the sky cleared, my heart leapt up, and I was glad I was in Romania.

After dinner, following a brief introduction, our leader asked the group, "Is there anything else you need or want?"

There was silence for a few seconds, then Sam Soseos spoke up: "Yeah, a pony."

That non sequitur loses its punch on the printed page, but at that moment we were all ready for a big laugh and that produced a howl. Hilarious. "I want a pony" became a running gag.

So what could we agree that we had all come to Romania for?

Briefly, my colleague, Cathy Johnson, and I wanted to work in tutorials with kids who had studied English for at least four years. I planned to emphasize pronunciation, use of vernacular, and extemporaneous conversation. I had lesson plans borrowed from my GV trip to China about Texas and my home and family; I expected to prompt improvisational responses with questions revealing personal attitudes and opinions; and I planned to have them read from Ex pat Romanian Eugene Ionescu's *The Bald Soprano*, an absurdist drama milestone.

We were told that two Romanian teachers on the staff of the Elena Bibescu Middle School, formerly Scoala #5 (an indifferent designation), would assist us, providing students & materials: Mihai Boholteanu and Carmen Ouatu.

Manuela Ivas, a high school biology teacher would arrange for English-speaking students to come to #5 from their high school.

The rest of my comrades expected to work with children in the clinic (orphanage) at Tutova, a nearby village, adjacent to a hospital under the supervision of Dr. Delia Asoltanei. Their objective was to play with and interact with about 36 children, most of whom had been orphaned, some of whom had disabilities. "No sickness," I was told. "Some sniffles, maybe." Oh, yeah.

During the course of the next weeks I learned from the clinic workers that there were mostly girls who had been abandoned and a significant number of twins & triplets. Of course. Two and three babies would be even more difficult for poor folks to take care of than single infants. I learned that the current governmental policy is for children to remain in the clinic for three years before they are promoted to the "placement center" for adoption. No formal adoption is possible for the first three years; and thereafter, only Romanians may apply, or Americans of Romanian descent. Evidently, the government resented international accusations that Romania had become a haven for black market baby farmers, so they took them off the market, and that's why children languish in clinics and placement centers. Yes, foster parents may take babies on a trial basis, but no formal adoption until after the third birthday.

Over 90 percent of all the infants & toddlers in the orphanage had been abandoned, but that's not common knowledge. And although persons in charge would never deny that fact, they'd say, "We just don't know. You Americans want to know everything, but you just can't"

The stuff (ie, diapers, medicines, foodstuffs) provided by Global Volunteers and other contributors is stored in closets & cabinets as is the custom of Romanians who say there's no point in using new diapers until the old ones are worn out. Local customs are as hard to deal with as old diapers are sometimes hard to fold. But why don't they use fabric softener? It's not the custom.

It wasn't all playing with and teaching the kids and no travel, however. We all worked as directed on weekdays and we took weekends off to travel around Romania on trips I'll discuss below.

Monday, May 9, nice weather [I indicate the daily weather because bad weather often requires an attitude or mood adjustment].

Overall spring in Romania was cool, breezy, and pleasant, but there were warm, humid, breezeless mornings giving me an idea of what summer's gonna be like without a/c almost everywhere.]. At first, I was freezing in my room because the heating hadn't been properly installed, and I couldn't keep warm under one blanket. So I asked for and got one more.

I opened my second-floor apartment window that first morning, and there below me, was a worker cutting the grass with a *scythe*, forgoshsake. The tool that the Old Year carries on his shoulder.

At breakfast, we had a "team-building" exercise allowing us to agree on objectives: 1) To care for children, 2) To see the country, 3) To pay back society for our own good fortune [And most of us were well-off and able to afford to travel without pinching pennies].

We piled on that awful bus with an entertaining If unsafe driver (Nicku Panait) and took our first tour of the school. We ate lunch at an upscale restaurant. Then we toured the clinic.

The first look into the eyes of kids abandoned by their parents is inescapably heartbreaking. God damn. Fifteen minutes later, sitting on the floor with three kiddos, I felt good for being there. I got them laughing, playing peekaboo. And I _absolutely_ understood the importance of work by volunteers. I admired those Volunteers, spending around five hours a day with those kids. They bonded with the children quickly, and the kids became attached to all of them. It was clear that the kids were needful because they could be soothed by any and all of the Volunteers.

That evening, on our return to the motel, driving from the tiny village of Tutova, I studied the landscape and saw fences everywhere. Every home owner has fences, front, sides, back. A synonym for Romania must be "fences." There were Lilac bushes in bloom behind fences. Chickens and cattle in front of fences. The wheat fields and pastures were fence-less, but the houses were all fenced in.

Horse-drawn wagons with loads of green stuff trotted at a fast 1 mph. Fat & skinny old folks sat in chairs, or squatted on the ground, or strolled perilously close to the highway. [I don't know how they grew to be so old walking that close to that busy highway.]

Sheep and cattle munched grass in open fields with shepherds & cattle herders (Thousands of cattle herders in that country, and I had never used the term, "cattle herder," before).

Vineyards were located everywhere there was a hill difficult for plowing. And throughout cities and country, there were miles of graceless insulated pipelines of enormous proportions through which hot water was pumped.

I saw men and women hoeing weeds in open fields *by hand*, no tractors. Row crops were emerging, and there was lots of rape seed. And not a sound of modern farm machinery. Maybe they hauled it in after we left.

My first impressions were permanent, and my reactions were mixed. Everywhere I looked there were stern, grim faces that I attributed to hard lives. Then, oops, upon my return to the States, my wife and I went to a local ice cream parlor and watched people enter and leave with generous servings of ice cream on their cones, and their faces were stern and grim. I guess what's on your mind is what shows on your face, internationally.

But Romania has the feel of rural USA before WWII. The cities are cluttered with tall, chunky apartment houses. Evidently, the dictator Ceausescu ordered that homes in cities should be torn down to provide stacks of living space, destroying much of the indigenous architecture—an act not unlike the destruction of historical dwellings by Chairman Mao during his reign in China.

The majority of apartment houses in Romanian cities are Russian Cement Blockhouse in design, and they had cracks in the surface that stretched up several stories. I never saw one of those badly-neglected buildings that I liked much; however, I found many distinctive old buildings with character that I greatly admired.

Tuesday, May 10th, was the first day of school, rainy.

I had a morning session with five bright 10th grade girls. In the afternoon, I met with five middle-school boys, two very bright, three very slow. At first, I thought it might have something to do with the mental capabilities of the students; later I learned that they were simply friends of the bright students, accompanying them to class as buddies following the promise that their bright buddies would prompt them. Whole lot of prompting going on.

At lunchtime, I used a nearby internet café to communicate with Barbara and respond to emails from the states. Wonderful thing, email. A lifeline?

Wednesday, May 11th, was clear and cold at first, later rainy.

Silly me, I had expected the same students who came to class Monday to appear on Tuesday. I was surprised by 5 bright, new high school students. The guys who showed up in the afternoon were another cast of middle-school characters, 4 indifferent, bored and boring students. Oh, well, I thought, that's a fluke. The morning had been great, as good as it gets.

That evening I performed scenes from *Texassity* for my comrades—a great audience. Life is all ups and down.

Thursday, May 12th, another rainy day.

5 more bright, new high school students. Wow. Only 2 bored boys in the PM, worse & worse.

Today we signed up for a tour to Transylvania costing $140 for lodging, and breakfasts with an additional $50 for travel. Not bad.

Took a walk toward Banca as the Sun was setting. Ran into a flock of Grackles fighting and shitting from the treetops. Encountered natives, one of whom nagged me to pay him to take his picture.

Friday, the 13th of May, clear

Ken visited my morning class as a consultant/kibitzer. No PM class.

We returned to the motel for lunch and to pack for our weekend trip to Braslov with our tour guide, Alex Grebeci.

We left at 3 and arrived at 7:30, settling in at a so-so motel (Three stars means don't bring any expectations with you.) Dinner at the New York Café that evening was disappointing.

Afterwards, Alex and I went in a taxi with Debbie to the emergency room of the Braslov hospital to determine if she had broken her foot. In no time at all, the hospital staff examined and x-rayed and consulted with her and put her leg in a cast and charged her only $10. What? Moral: if you're gonna break a foot, it's cheaper in Romania than the US to get medical help.

We were back to the motel by midnight.

Saturday, May 14, sunshiny & cool.

We toured the Black Church whose tour guide made the place *seem* interesting. The guide's performance was more engaging than the looks of that Lutheran church. It was built in the 14th & 15th Centuries, but in 1689 the city and church were burned, leaving only the blackened walls and a few icons. After it was rebuilt, a custom was establish by traders who trekked China's Silk Road, bringing Asian rugs and Muslim prayer rugs as an offering of thanksgiving for having their lives spared. When their lives weren't spared, no rug. The current collection, draped all over the place, is reputed to be the most valuable in the world.

Then we danced to the oom-pah-pah music of a town band and shopped around aimlessly. Skip the *Star Department Store*. Linda & Sarah from Canada bought international cell phones, and I bought a useless phone card. We ate pizza at the Doma Restaurant featuring corn & chicken as toppings.

Then we went to Bran Castle, supposed haunt of Count Dracula [The source of the fictitious Dracula legend is Bram Stoker], but the castle is actually a fortress where Vlad Dracul stayed briefly. Vlad was a ruler of Romania known as "the Impaler" because he executed prisoners by impaling them on poles like kabobs, very, very painfully. He's regarded as a folk hero by the kids I taught in school.

Ascending the ramps and steps of the castle was difficult for me because I've got some foot issues, but I appreciated the view from the top and the architectural design. There was a ratty souvenir marketplace adjacent and a Coke café where I passed the time with Debbie & Nancy while others shopped.

We took the bus to Busteni in the stunning Carpathian mountains. Our dinners that evening were paid for by Peggy, Nancy, and Debbie. Generous to a fault.

From my so-so motel room, I could hear birds twittering and dogs barking—all goddamn night long.

Sunday, May 15, clear.

We toured the 105 room Peles Castle that King Carol I had designed and built at the end of the 19th century, with an elevator and a built-in vacuum cleaner as well as eclectic design features rivaling Queen Victoria's taste for the bizarre and King Ludwig of Germany's madness. Appearing to be a cross between a Bavarian schloss with formal English landscaping, the interior has a lavish display of cabinetry and furnishings, glass and massive mirrors from Murano, armor and weaponry from every civilized country in the world (Note the clever irony, weapons/civilized), and a secret door in the library. King Carol had a Hohenzollern bloodline with the sensibilities of a theatrical producer because the stuff he stuffed in that place belongs on a stage, not in a home.

Of course, his home was his castle.

We had lunch at Marlene's, a kind of Swedish chalet, then—since the scenic cable car wasn't functioning—we had time to stop at an internet café. Funny how the trade-off seemed a better option.

We started back for Barlad when—kaboom. A blowout. One of the tires was ripped to shreds. But it took only 15 minutes for our driver to fix it with the help of our tour leader. No one could speak Romanian, and incomprehensible language for anyone in an emergency situation; so when the tour leader wasn't available to converse with Nicku, I was the only American who commanded enough German phrases to let him know what we wanted from him, mostly *langsam. Go slow dammit.* I was also able to use four-lettered German words to punctuate our demands.

We finished repairing the tire. Then there was another [Can you believe it.] washed-out bridge and countless, hazardous pot holes that caused us to spend six hours on the road, zigging, zagging, swerving, braking, racing to pass other vehicles, avoiding demented drivers trying to pass oncoming cars. Somehow, after the first couple of hours, because of our driver's self-confidence ("In over 50 years driving, I have never accident"), we felt safe but only because we have never accident—yet.

Returned to Banca in time for chow. Good chow.

Monday, May 15, clear.

Slept soundly, arose early. Washed socks & underwear, hanging them on the newly-functioning wall heater to dry.

In class at school with the high school girls, I learned how proud the kids are of their Roman heritage, their Romanian language, and their nation. Regrettably, they have little confidence that economic, education, health, and other social conditions will improve in the near or foreseeable future. One student volunteered: "Our worst problem is corruption in government and in everyday life. If you want to see a dentist, you have to bribe him with a gift of coffee or something like that or he won't see you. That's a holdover from the old Communist regime." Candid students.

One of my boys in the afternoon class shocked me when he said, out of the blue, "I did not sleep with that woman, Miss Wolinsky." Out of the mouths of babes, a testimony to the gravity of Clinton's tragic flaw, a world away and over six years ago.

Time to find thank you cards—required writing. But where's a Hallmark card shop? How do you shop for such things in a land where the language and customs baffle you? Easy. You persuade a student (who speaks English) to take you in a taxi to a Graphics shop where you browse through a card catalog, and the student translates, "Happy Christmas," "Best Wishes for Graduation," but no thank you cards. So you select 5 copies of a blank card that has a hunting lodge fireplace and a dead partridge on it rather than the other blank card that has flowers and a lace lady's glove, and the clerk rummages through drawers and produces the cards and envelopes. Then, like a blind man, you depend on the student to help you wend your way back to school.

As you become more and more familiar with the town and locations of drug stores, money exchanges, and market places, it's possible to make educated guesses, but language is a constant problem especially when you're trying to find a battery charger for a Kodak camera.

Tuesday, May 17, clear. A disturbing night's sleep.

Good class of high school students as usual in the morning, but only one middle-school student in the afternoon, really frustrating. So I talk with the school's English teachers who tell me they're frustrated, too, and they blame the other teachers for keeping their best students (who—coincidentally—are the ones who speak English) in extra class sessions to insure they'll pass tests in their areas.

What we have here is a political situation in a third world microcosm. The English teachers simply don't have clout. Or money, no share in the school budget. So all they can do is complain that there is no cooperation between teachers within the school or between schools. One teacher told me, "It's hopeless."

I said, "So tell me how am I supposed to get students who can speak passable English in tutorials in the afternoons. Forgive me for being rhetorical, but what are we volunteers doing here? We've come to your country to work with students who, presumably, want to work with us. Where the heck are they?"

Response: "It can't be helped."

Conclusion: Be happy, Ramon, that you've got bright high school students every morning. Rejoice that you may spend your afternoons writing this journal unless students drop in. Adapt to the situation. You don't have the ability or prerogative to solve this political problem. And that's the answer. The only political answer.

That evening, a sensational feast at the home of our motel hosts, celebrating the first birthday of their 3rd daughter. There was a folk musical ensemble with esoteric instruments and eight dancers in costumes and a soloist crooning folk songs. Wow.

They know how to treat their guests.

Wednesday, May 18. Clear

The early bird gets to use the new computer just installed in the motel. There is such great demand for emailing, I'm sure there will be a line.

There's no regularity in the constitution of my morning classes so I have to ask, "Have I already given you 'Cowboys and Longhorns' to read?"

My co-worker, Cathy, had her hands full this morning trying to maintain decorum in a class with seven eighth grade boys in it, so I traded my class with her. Then I had to kick two of them out of class. If they can't speak English, I can't coach them in pronunciation. This job assignment is not supposed to be babysitting.

I didn't bother asking myself if I were being too tough on the kids. Why not? Because I had heard the principal screaming at kids running in the halls, and I saw her cuff one kid twice on the back of the neck as punishment. They still do corporal punishment in Romania.

I had three of the same indifferent boys again at 2 PM, so I let them go early. Around 3:30 I hiked with one of my high school students over to one of the town's four high schools to watch performances of six plays competing for a prize. I lasted through three of the shows with the help of that student sitting next to me, translating the lines. Imagine: Watching inexpert high school performers directed by amateur directors perform poorly produced plays in a foreign language.

Almost all of the Global Volunteers get to contribute a page to the team's Journal. Here's an entry by Sam Soseos for today, May 18, that was written from the perspective of one of the clinic workers.

"Sam's Journal entry, May 18
It's 10 AM and all hell is breaking loose.

The toddlers are all screaming simultaneously—except for Ionut. He's probably screaming, too, but he and Ken aren't here at the moment. No one knows exactly where they went; maybe they made a break for the Bulgarian border.

30 minutes late and everyone has quieted down. Tiffany goes off to change the nastiest diaper in the world. She's gone a long, long time.

11 am. Andréea just ate the tag off a Beanie Baby. Just another typical day in the toddler room.

It didn't start like this. Breakfast was fairly normal with tureens of warm milk and cold cereal and the usual array of goofball antics and smartass remarks, punctuated by brief periods of silence while everyone fuels up with caffeinated beverages.

The bus ride is as smooth as it ever gets, meaning there aren't any "Oh, my god. We're all going to die." moments

On the way to the clinic, we stop at the school, losing a pair of teachers and gaining a pharmacist. An even exchange.

Fast forward to lunch. Looks like steak and lobster again. No, wait. It's chicken and tomato and cucumber salad. Again. But it's good so it's okay.

After lunch, a Coke-run to the store down the street, then we head back to the clinic. The afternoon goes quickly, part of it spent outdoors in the play yard getting some sun, the rest inside getting peed and puked on.

On the bus ride back to the motel, we stop at a new tech appliance store, and we all buy the same CD, Ozone singing, "Love Me, Love Me, Love Me, Feel Me, Touch Me, Hold me, La, La, La, La," that none of us has ever heard of before. Impulse buying.

Dinner time. It's chicken, of course. It's actually very good. It could have been far worse. It could have had Crap (the Romanian name for the fish, Carp).

Ramon went to a play this afternoon, and he's late for dinner, and we decide that if he can't be bothered to be on time, we'll just go ahead and eat our soup. Then he joins us and all is well.

After dinner, he and I and Ken go for a walk toward Banca where we discover that a 9-year-old Romanian child is a far better soccer player than Ken is.

Now it's 10 PM. For some of the team members, our time here grows short. We don't have to think about that now, though. Not until tomorrow night.

Time to sleep. Tomorrow we get to wake up and do it all over again—Except maybe not have to change the nastiest diaper in the world."

Thursday, May 19, Clear

Switched classes again with Cathy. It's like trying to keep a lid on a can of clowns.

Paid in advance for lodging and breakfasts for our weekend to see the famous monasteries, Number One on my travel list, and to visit Iasi (pronounced *Yosh* as in *gosh*): $162 for two nights' lodging & breakfasts, $50 for transportation. Not bad.

That evening we expected something sentimental and ceremonial to occur at our last supper with the Volunteers who would be returning to the States on Saturday. Nothing special happened, but it was a nice occasion as usual with good company.

I had my television set installed in my room, but I couldn't get CNN or any reputable news agency in English, only sports, soap opera, and something called the "spice Channel" that featured the most graphic sex I've ever seen. Only I and the teen age girls got that hook-up.

Friday, May 20, Clear

I did a poor job of copying names & addresses of our team because Scoala #5's copier is in poor shape. I handed them out to the Volunteers and said, "Don't thank me." They didn't.

Hugged the girls goodbye, Sarah, Nancy, Peggy, Debbie, and Tiffany. Sam settled for a handshake. Then we (Linda, Pat, Ken, and the two teen-agers) boarded the bus for our weekend excursion with Alex accompanying us again as tourguide.

I don't care how interesting scenery may be (and it wasn't), five hours on a bus whose shocks are shot is no fun. And the tortuous bed at Villa Alice that night was not amusing either. The camaraderie of the six travelers at dinner *was* great, however. Good times.

May 22, Sunday.

Okay. The monasteries in the region of Bucovina. Hot dog. The prospect of visiting those monasteries is what had hooked me on traveling to Romania. I had seen photographs in travel magazines. And I wanted to touch the walls of those churches with my bare fingertips like an idolatrous pilgrim just as I've touched petraglyphs in Egypt and the high altar at Machu Picchu.

Usually I dislike visits to churches; I view them as tombs where God is buried. But these monasteries' churches looked as if they might be different—and they were. Absolutely.

Briefly, they have wide roofs, and the walls have Byzantine/Gothic shapes, but the distinctive features àre the frescoes painted inside and outside on the walls and ceiling, almost like strip cartoons, depicting Biblical and apocryphal religious scenes. All three churches' decorations are masses of angels & devils & symbols & colors & gold & textures, and my eyes couldn't stop moving from one image to the next to the entire wall. The frescoes are intended to dazzle the beholder. And they do.

That Sunday, from the moment I woke up I was ready & raring to see them.

But first, we stopped at a shop where pottery was fired *black* (I can't imagine why anybody would buy that ugly stuff). Black pottery is a local product (of absolutely no interest to me).

Then we visited the first of three monasteries, the largest, Sucevita. I loved it. It's surrounded by a fortress with four towers. Thousands of pictures decorate the walls of the church, outnumbering the pictures on churches at *all* the other monasteries.

Alex described the allegories in the largest depiction of Judgement Day, representing a cruel God damning sinners into a burning river of hellfire. Wow.

En route to the next stop, seated in the front of the bus, I couldn't look at any *one* thing; the entire landscape was awesome, all of one piece. I was blown away by the vast panorama of hills upon hills and the *incredible* beauty of white-flowering trees and the rich shades of springtime greens. Other regions of Romania cannot possibly be more beautiful, and this area cannot be more beautiful at any other time of the year. It was stunning and I was duly stunned.

We arrived at a village outside the unfunny "Humor" church (1530) monastery, a small but exquisite one, and we stopped at a farmhouse where we were fed the best meal of the entire trip by a woman who also sold us souvenirs of some merit. I got three hand-painted eggs. (That's the extent of my entire souvenir shopping during the visit to Romania. Hell, at 72-years-old, I can resist almost all shopportunities.)

Following our visit, as we strolled back to the bus, we joined a funeral procession headed for a nearby cemetery. The body of the deceased was carried by pallbearers on a flat board that allowed viewers to see his entire corpse. Damn.

Lastly, we saw Voronet, the "Sistine Chapel of the East" (1488, its frescoes were added later). It's not near as grand as Rome's, but it's remarkable for the frescoes' vivid colors. Standing below the dome and staring upward, I thought, "God. How glorious." I think that's the intended response.

Several in our group spent more time shopping at the stalls outside the monastery than at the church, and I had to wait. All alone. By that ratty bus. So how many mothers does it take to change a lightbulb? None. "I'll just sit here, all alone, waiting in the dark."

The journey to Iasi (Yosh by gosh) was three or four or five or fifty hours long—Hell, I don't know the difference anymore when riding on that damned shuttle bus. It's the same kind of bus the Barlad transit system uses. I've tried to justify using these skinny buses with their bad suspension systems. They can shimmy on down the road, weaving in and out of traffic (unlike larger buses), passing other vehicles within inches, and that's good because there aren't many inches to spare. They're probably fuel efficient, too. But comfort was never a consideration in the design of these16 seaters. And it's not just that Americans are slightly overlarge in the rear seat department. As if some Romanians don't have big butts.

Houses in northern Romania don't have a whole lot in common with western Romanian houses. There is more space between houses, some are two-story as opposed to a uniform one-size-fits-all-families in the west of Romania. The north has more tile than tin roofs. And property lines are defined by unique and original (but not necessarily interesting) fences instead of the factory-produced fences between Barlad & Tutova.

During this leg of the trip, our driver made several wrong turns because (he said) he's accustomed to driving a different route. I think thumping this buggy over hundreds of thousands of pot holes has left him confused; he keeps looking for an exit and can't find the way out.

We couldn't persuade him to stop and allow us to photograph a stork in her nest atop an electric pole until suddenly—He came to a jolting and abrupt stop, having selected just the right stork for us to photograph. Somehow it seemed like the only way it *should* have happened.

May 23, Monday, Clear

Walking is something Americans do for exercise. For Romanians it's a mode of transportation; it's how they get where they're going. Kings of the road are people who share their cars, pickups with campers, and minivans. BMW & Mercedes drivers don't stop for God.

There was some disconcerting news at the motel. The maids had quit because the departing team members had left tips for them, and the maids assumed the management was testing them to see if they would "steal" the money. So no maids at breakfast.

Then I had the only disappointing morning since my arrival when my high school contingent didn't appear. Neither did the afternoon junior high school after lunch bunch; so I spent the day mostly typing on this journal and editing the journal entries of my colleagues.

May 24, Tuesday Clear

I awoke early, around 5, and went down to the computer to email Barbara. On top of a tall reception desk, there was an opened bag of "Joes (a chocolate snack/cracker)," and an unopened bag. I assumed the departing team members had placed the Joes on the desk as a gift rather than stuff & crush them in suitcases; so I helped myself to the opened package of about ten crackers, scarfing 'em all down as I typed the email message.

Later, at breakfast, Patti regaled us with the story of her midnight visit from a mouse. She said she heard a rustling sound and traced it to an opened bag of Joes; so she picked up the bag and discovered Mr. Mouse in it. She shooed him out of her room and, for no clear reason, set the opened and unopened bags on the desk by the computer then went back to bed.

I wondered … Could that bag I consumed be the one the mouse rummaged around in? You think?

I didn't tell Patti that I was the one who nabbed her snacks because I wouldn't want her to worry about my health. There should be no consequences—unless I die, of course. In which event, will someone please tell Patti I absolve her for putting me in harm's way. She never would have eaten those Joes, I'm sure, but what's more important, she never meant for me to get snared in that mouse's trap.

I had a great day in another high school tutorial. And that afternoon, the boys who had been in my first afternoon class returned and said they were ready to meet with me again. I said okay, and I'm glad I did because as I listened to them read, mispronouncing words, and I realized they have virtually no grasp of phonics. Astounding. I should have spotted the primary reason for their lack of pronunciation skills weeks ago. I should have given them ear-training exercises primarily. A native speaker can provide instruction that their teachers can't. [I wonder if I'll take this insight to the GV administration. They may have heard all this before and don't want to change a policy of allowing teachers to muddle through. But I feel I should because in some ways I feel I've wasted 3 weeks of those kids' development of their ears.]

On the next day, for the final QV Team Journal entry on **May 27, Friday noon,** I wrote:

"Pat did a great and loving job in her journal entry the other day describing and thanking us for being members of this GV Team, so I'll add her name to that same list for her laughter & strength of character; and Manuela Ivas from the high school for her kindness and patience and Niku (Nikoo), our driver, for his skill avoiding sure death on the highway.

I hope that takes care of everybody.

Now let us praise Global Volunteers, Inc., that has made it possible for us to be a team of wayward saints, enjoying the company of one another, working with children who need the kind of love we can give them. And GV be praised for giving us an excuse to explore Romania. And allowing us to work with children who need the kind of help we're eager to give.

Global Volunteers is truly a remarkable institution, working a <u>major</u> miracle: organizing and facilitating the efforts of volunteers and providing material support—for example, here in Romania, GV has donated wooden cribs, mattresses, sheets, tiles, water heaters, heat for the building, a washer and dryer for diapers, and food and medicine for the children in the Tutova clinic. And in the school, a computer with all the trimmings, a CD player, and a library of books and materials for studying English. And of great importance, a salary to provide for one of the best managers of people I know of, Michaela Cirjontu.

Yes.

Bless Global Volunteers. Bless Romania. Bless the children. Bless the people who've looked after us. Bless their hearts.

And God bless us everyone."

I had no sooner finished than Linda asked if she could read something.

Well, of course.

She had written the first of our Team Journal entries, noting that our mission was to give children hugs, snuggles, and "songs we have yet to sing," so it was appropriate for her to have the last word, and here's what she read:

"Everything I Needed to Know About Life I Learned in Romania

Joy really did seek us out in Romania. Everything goes better with "unt," one of the five basic food groups. Four different desserts for lunch are a right, not a privilege. Including whipped cream cake.

Orange Fanta—another of the basic food groups—and Gianni's homemade wine are "bun."

The words "friendship, family, babies, and love" are interchangeable in English & Romanian.

Strudel is one of the five basic food groups. That and tomato & cucumber salad. No one can take care of our babies like we can—at least we've convinced ourselves we're right.

"Joes" are yet another of the five basic food groups. And Polenta. And chocolate crépes.

Tears of separation are agony. Not even Ursus Beer helps. Anything can be schnitzeled. Schnitzel is the fifth and final of the five basic food groups.

Andréea, the Predator

Andréea is a large child for her 20 months who was chronicled in her personal journal by previous volunteers as "The Predator." "She drinks from her bottle lying on the floor, sucking out the last drops of formula like most infants, but then she crawls around the playroom, scrambling over anything and anyone in her way, snatching bottles away from weaker babies."

Sure enough, we found her to be a tiny drama queen who collapsed into loud sobs, covering her face with her forearm like a faded movie star if any other baby got picked up before she was.

Every toy was hers. And every adult's lap was her personal property, and she knocked other babies out of the way to prove it. Even empty bottles she spotted from across the room were hers, and she barreled over to make sure they were drained dry, and then she moved on—like a tiny Romanian army tank.

This last week, however, we all agreed she appeared to be acting differently. Dare we say she's become a softer, gentler predator?

We watched as she was on the bottle prowl—but now she was looking for discarded ones rather than snatching the nipples out of other kids' mouths. And she actually, agreeably shared my lap with little Octavion, having a tough day because of his terrible diaper rash. And she knew she was sharing.

Nearing the end of our final day, Pat was sitting in a chair crying (Poor sad Pat, hating to leave the babies to return home), and I was propped up against the wall sobbing (Poor me for the same reason). And I could swear Andréea looked at both of us like, "What's happening to you ladies." And then she picked up a plastic baby spoon left on the floor and handed it to me. I'm absolutely sure it was a loving gesture meant to soothe and comfort me. Then she crawled to Pat, climbed up into her lap, and tried to cuddle and console her.

There was no mistaking her intentions.

Willa Cather once said: 'Where there is great love, miracles will follow.'"

The Sequel

I left Barlad that evening on the Blue Train, the "best train in Romania," and one of the best I've ever traveled on, no rock and roll, no neck-wrenching braking. The ride was smooth as silk.

Mihaela insisted on meeting me at the train station for the 6 PM departure to insure I would have no trouble finding the tracks & train. I think she wanted to make sure I left Barlad. She had purchased the ticket ahead of time just as she had bought all the meals I'd eaten and paid for lodging and transportation using the fee I had sent GV to participate in the Romania Service Program. Three weeks' room, board, and transportation for $2,865, or $136 a day to travel and experience what I did and to learn more than I taught. "They're only children."

As I took my seat on the train, I looked back through the window toward the station, and there was Mihaela looking in to insure I was okay. I waved; she waved, and the train started for Bucharest.

Mihaela was and is a superior manager, sweetheart, and scout mother. We all fell under her spell during our stay; she *knew* we'd love her. I'd quote her for looking deep into the eyes of each team member and hypnotizing with her husky Romanian accent: "You vill *luf* me."—except she didn't have much accent.

It was an intense summer intellectual romance.

In Bucharest I got ripped-off, overpaying a taxi driver (Taxi drivers are almost all thieves universally.—No offence intended) from the train station to the Marriott, and I under-tipped the bellman who took my bags to my room [I never did quite grasp the US Dollar equivalent for that Romanian Lei].

The next morning, **Saturday, May 28,** hot, I employed a guide whose English was poorer than any of my students', her car was filthy with a door I couldn't open from the inside without kicking my way out, and it was hot as blazing hell without a/c. So I didn't much enjoy being with her touring to the House of the People (Ceausescu's Palace), the second largest building in the world (second only to the US Pentagon). However, the Village Museum of old homes and buildings located in a park on a lake near the Danube was interesting, but I'll enjoy it more if there's a next time I visit Bucharest.

I took an a/c cab to the airport where I caught up with Ken Severn, a prince of a fellow, and we traveled as far as London aboard the same plane, then we went our separate ways.

I left Romania with the fondest memories possible. Who knows, having been there once, I may return.

Ostuni, Italy

✦

Two Weeks with Global Volunteers
October 2–21, 2006

In October of 2006, I traveled to Italy to work as a classroom teacher of Conversational English with Global Volunteers. Actually, I went to see a part of Italy I had never seen before, Puglia (pronounced <u>Pool</u>-ya), and I agreed to work while enjoying Italy during the first days of fall. The weather was glorious during my stay, and I was lucky that it rained only on the morning of my departure. The two weeks I spent in that darlin' village went by with a whoosh.

Ostuni, known as the White Queen for its whitewashed buildings, was my destination. It had been established as a Greco-Roman settlement in the first century AD, with an Old Town spread over three hills, a confusing riot of cobblestone alleys and streets. My greatest dilemma getting to and from and around town was the high cost of taxis for transportation. Taxis became a necessity after I wore out my feet during the first week I was there, walking from our lodging outside town to the center of Old Ostuni. I should have invested in a rental car.

And I should have taken a language study course to prepare me for transactions with townspeople who acted as if English were Martian. I don't speak Italian? *Non.* And when one of the supervising teachers learned that most of us Volunteers *non parlo Italiano*, she said, "*Perfecto.* The students won't be possible to converse with you in Italian. Only the English will they speak." Her language skills weren't perfecto, but we never let on.

Most of the Global Volunteers on my team were friendly and a pleasure to work with; notably Jan Bush, Angela Bellante, Joan Engelhaupt, Jane & Don Holkestad, Mel & Barbara Shapiro, David & Connie Pursley, and Jean Wilkinson. But two Volunteers (whom I'll just call Nelda& Zelda) were extremely high-maintenance. Also, I had great difficulty liking one of our group's co-leaders (whom I shall not discuss except to say she and I shared a mutual dislike at first sight. Too bad for both of us.

I've opened this report with a critique of my peers because one's comfort level is always influenced by the company one keeps. And of all the things that can go wrong on a trip, getting stuck with people who you don't like (or who don't like you). I liked every other Italian and American I met.

I was assigned to teach in classes with the head mistress of Ostuni's *Classico* school, *Professa Isabella Ayroldi*, and I also got to work with the school's drama director, *Allesandro Fiorella*, winner of a competitive play contest.

I got to know only one other teacher at the school, *Isa*, a woman whose last name I never got, who transported me daily in her car along with two other Volunteers to and from school. At the close of our time in Italy, she graciously invited us three Volunteers to enjoy a luncheon of Gnocchi, boiled beef, bread, salad, cheese, and fat persimmons in her home.

Before class on my first day, Isabella said, "In a few minutes, we will discuss William Wordsworth. Do you know his work?"

I responded by saying "Sure, but the only poem of his I remember is about wandering lonely as a cloud."

She said, "Great. That's the one poem of his we study. Today you will teach it."

Gulp.

"Piece uh cake," I said, and it was pleasurable because, talking about the poem line by line, metaphor by simile, watching the students sit silently, looking rapt or smiling as I spoke, I thought, "I'm doing such a good job. They understand the metaphysics of this poem." Later, I learned they didn't understand a friggin' word I was saying. They were doing what I always did as a student, keeping quiet for fear of being called on to perform. That was the only class reluctant to interact with me.

Most of the rest of the school kids I taught were loud, rowdy, loud, rude, and loud in the extreme, and they bullied their teachers, but somehow I managed to entertain and amuse them. Perhaps that's because I'm primarily an entertainer. I'm a teacher after the fact. They liked me enough to give me an expensive fountain pen and six other gifts at a party on my last day in class.

But some days, when I was teaching, they threatened to get out of hand like incipient Mafiosi, so I found out who was the student *don* or *prima donna*, and I got his or her help in keeping them in check. I'd say, "Please tell them to be quiet."

"*Basta.*" was all my young honcho would have to shout; and—*Subito.*—they'd hush.

One especially obstreperous class I taught had a *prima donna* who listened to me attentively, but she ignored her peers, allowing them to chatter until she could no longer hear me, and then she'd lay into them with expressions which can be translated roughly as "godalmightydamn, yousonsabitches, shaddup." Then they'd behave. After a few minutes however, they'd start acting up again. She would yell, and they would get quiet, and then they'd get noisy, she'd yell again, then quiet again, noisy/quiet/*Basta.* until the bell signaled close of the class. One day, a math teacher entered and heard me mutter to myself, "Buncha animals."

The following evening, while returning from a dinner in the old town, a friend and I discovered ourselves walking into a crowd of lemming-like students, and I said to the friend, "These kids all look alike to me except—You know? These look a lot like that boisterous class I told you about."

And lo, it was indeed that very class. I hadn't recognized their faces until they turned toward me and shouted, "Ramon. *Buona sera*, baby. Whas happnin'."

I laughed with them and returned their greetings with "Yo. *Come sta?* Goodta-seeya."

But then I heard the unmistakable voice of my *prima donna* silencing the group with "Ramon. Why did you tell our math teacher that we're a bunch of animals."

The crowded street fell silent and I said, "Right. I did say animals. Like pussy cats. All bouncing out of a basket, going in different directions. You're my—Pussycats."

My *prima donna* paused, turned her head sideways, and I could tell she liked being called a pussy cat. She said, "*Poosicot?*"

I said, "Yeah, and you're my *prima donna poosicot.*"

There are times in life when you luck out and say the right thing at the right time. This was one of those times, and the term I chose for the group and for her in particular was absolutely correct. So correct that I could hear—I swear I could hear her purr.

After a few more exchanges she and the group moved away. But one baby-faced lad turned back to me and said, "That math teacher is an asshole."

What the hell was I doing, trying to teach conversational English. They already understood vernacular.

Learning to drink two or three cups of heavily caffinated cappuccino every day helped me to understand the Italians I worked with. I bonded with students, teachers, and Volunteers except, of course, for the three aforementioned Volunteers who were a minor irritation periodically.

My mattress irritated me, too. It was lumpy. And that's about the sum total of my complaints: three volunteers and a mattress.

Lodgings for Volunteers at Hotel Incanto were quite adequate, however. Sheets were changed every other day; towels were fresh every day; hot water was hot; and cleanliness was uncompromised.

There was a window in my room overlooking the entrance to the hotel from which I could look at the moon, a <u>full</u> moon during my stay, and at a distance I could view the old city perched on mountains, illuminated at night like a fairy kingdom. *O Joy, O Rapture Unforeseen.* And every morning, there was the Adriatic sea filling the horizon. Also, I could watch passers-by from the window.

People-watching is a national pastime for Italians. I thoroughly enjoyed myself looking out at people, unseen, an omniscient demigod. But one day while I was observing the behavior of both tourists & Italians, uh-oh, I discovered I was being watched by a man at a higher-up window about twenty feet away on my right side. Disconcerted at first, I looked away, and then I bravely returned his stare and began playing the game. We stared inexpressively at each other, our eyes locked in combat, neither willing to capitulate until—Gotcha. He blinked, looked away, and after a few seconds looked back to see if I were still staring at him. Yes, I was. Only now I was smiling, enjoying my triumph. He turned away from the window and disappeared from sight, the loser in an ancient contest of wills. After a moment I shifted my gaze to my left, and there was a woman whose toothless grin let me know that she had been watching the game, an unseen spectator.

Discovered, she laughed aloud, reached around and grabbed the curtains on either side of her and drew them together in a silent whammo. She was like an actor disappearing behind a grand drape. Seconds later, she opened the curtains, reappeared, and looked at me with—"Hee-hee-hee"—her Halloween Witch cackle. Then zip. She was gone.

I slowly backed away from my window and side-stepped out of sight having participated in a voyeuristic vignette complete from beginning to end. I closed the curtain, turned to my right, and yikes. I was shocked to see another man looking at me, looking <u>back</u> at me from my mirror, shocked, but only for a moment.

Narrowing my eyes to stare at myself, I assumed the look I rarely project, that of an unflappable, world-weary, sophisticated Uhmuricun tuhrist.

American tourists abound in Ostuni, a small out-of-the-way village. And there reside mostly Italians, but English and French people have invested heavily in real estate owing to current low exchange rates. The English don't lease apartments for sunny vacation digs; they buy condos outright against the day they'll be able to sell them at higher rates.

On one particularly sunny day, riding in a van with a friend, Jan, and two of the vexatious Volunteers cited above (Nelda & Zelda), I ventured across country to visit the one town I truly wanted to see in the region of Puglia. Our driver was Giovanni (his real name), and he was great fun to be with until Nelda & Zelda pissed him off.

We traveled on backroads of flatlands viewing olive trees (some ancient, over five hundred years old) and almond trees in orchards delineated by stacked limestone rock fences which stretched as far as the eye could see. *Bella.* Unforgettably beautiful. Oh, yes.

We made a stop at a cavern which had no interest for me. Nelda & Zelda and Jan took a walking tour, and I read a book, saving my energies and ankles for later in the day. After a couple hours, the three women emerged assuring me that they had walked quite enough and were ready to continue driving across country to Alberobello. When we arrived there, Giovanni allowed us to buy his lunch. Then we went walking off independently with a mutual understanding (Never trust a mutual understanding.) to return to the van within a reasonable period of time (There is no such thing as a reasonable period of time.).

I walked and photographed to my heart's content the famous *trulli* (plural of *trullo*) which are located in Alberobello. *Trulli* are indigenous houses, whitewashed stone buildings with round conical (beehive-shaped) roofs composed of flagstones without mortar. Some *trulli* have been renovated with modern amenities (which must comply with the region's zoning laws) to attract tourists. I was hoping to find precisely what I found: beautiful, unique, and a bit other-worldly hobbit houses.

After about an hour wandering about, I returned to our meeting place where Giovanni asked if I had seen Zelda. Jan & Nelda were eager to move on to the final stop on our itinerary. "No," I said I hadn't seen Zelda except once when we crossed paths, and she told me she was looking for a *Trullo* church. I had advised her to return to the fold soon (Soon is a meaningless word in English as well as every other language in the world).

We waited for about fifteen minutes, and then Giovanni set out in search of Zelda. Nelda waxed indignant that she was being forced to cool her heels because she said Zelda was taking unfair advantage of our patience and good will. Another fifteen minutes passed and Giovanni reappeared to say, "*Maledizione.* [Damnation.]" he couldn't find Zelda. He took off again. Another fifteen minutes passed, and Nelda decided we should go off in the three directions not taken by Giovanni to search for Zelda.

I said, "No, there's no point in all four of us getting lost."

Nelda looked at me as if I weren't following directions and then pointed to a table where she told me to "Stay here, then."

I said, "I intend to. And I wish you'd stay, but if you insist, promise you'll return within fifteen minutes." They agreed and took off. My reader may have already guessed what happened next: Suddenly, I felt someone tapping on my shoulder, scaring the bejesus out of me, and I heard a petulant baby's voice say, "Has everybody but you gone to look for me?"

I turned around, laughed, and blurted out: "Wow. Are *you* in deep doo-doo. Where the hell have you been, Zelda?"

Zelda, a 75 year old woman with modest tattoos, trembled, then burst into tears, fell into my arms, and began hugging me as if I were her friend. I said, "Wait. I'm the enemy."

She wailed, "I've ruined everything for everybody, and I've made an ass out of myself, and everybody's gonna hate me. It's because I'm old."

I said, "You're old enough to know you shouldn't be throwing your arms around a man on a street corner and crying like a school girl."

No, I didn't say that, but I did say "Unhug me, Lady, and stop crying. People will think I'm abusing you. Where have you been?"

Zelda said, "I wasn't thinking, I guess. But now,"—and the tears began again—"I've ruined everything for everybody."

Just then I looked over her heaving shoulder and saw Nelda & Jan returning. Jan was smiling. Nelda was steaming.

I said to Zelda, "Lady, if I were you I'd say you got lost so they'll pity you; otherwise, they'll wanna murder you."

She said, "Oh, I couldn't lie, I'd be so ashamed."

Just then, Jan came upon us, and Zelda shreiked: "I got lost. I got losted." (I thought the 'losted' was a bit over the top.)

Jan bought her story and allowed her to hug her and get her shoulder all wet, and I walked over to Nelda who was still fuming, ready to explode. Hoping to defuse her anger, I said, "She's taking this very badly; she's very apologetic. She says she got losted."

Nelda refused to sympathize. "'Losted' is an absurd thing for an old woman to say."

I started to say something when she said, "What did you do to make her cry."

"Wha—" I was taken aback, and I responded accordingly: "Now, you wait just a minute. That lady is crying of her own accord. You're out of line to say I provoked her."

Nelda said, "I'm sorry. I am <u>so</u> sorry. I apologize, okay?"

She reached out to touch me, but I had reached my touch quota for the day, so I backed away. I said. "Get your sweet ass over there and tell her everything's gonna be all right. She won't stop crying until you go hug her."

"She's a *manipulative* old woman," Nelda said as she started in B's direction. Then she stopped and returned to whisper, "I want you to know I'll just be pretending to forgive this neurotic old crybaby. I'll just <u>act</u> sincere so she'll stop sniveling." Then she went to B, squeezing her breathless the way an accordion player squeezes his instrument, cutting her sobs short. Wah. Whump. Wah. Whump

After a few minutes, following reassurances from Nelda & Jan, Zelda's crying stopped

Then Giovanni returned, angry. Zelda rushed to his arms and began caterwauling, but he—an Italian stallion—would have none of it. He pushed her away and said, "*Va bene. Zitto.* Now, we go." That triggered more tears, but there was no one left to comfort her. She took the back seat in the van and punished us for miles down the road, simpering and whimpering. What a performance, deserving of an award for bad acting. I include it here because it was unrivaled by any other travel nightmare of its kind I've ever had. <u>Age-inappropriate</u> may not be a conventional term, but it applies here.

Eight Volunteers took another trip the following weekend in the same van to Napoli where we visited Pompeii. We drove three and a half hours each way, and quarters were close on the van but we had a delightful time together. Pompeii, however, was not delightful, nor did I really expect it to be.

Ancient Pompeii is a city (which only an archeologist could love) composed of ruins of buildings and avenues destroyed by a lava flow after an eruption from Vesuvius in 79 AD. That same eruption suffocated a neighboring city, Herculaneum, which I had enjoyed visiting years ago.

When Pompeii was rediscovered after centuries, it was dug up and preserved for posterity (That means tourists primarily). It's huge and mostly boring except for grotesque artifacts and three modern toilets in little round houses which automatically clean themselves following every visit. The toilets were the only fun part, the rest of the visit was history at its least interesting.

Herculaneum, on the other hand, has fewer visitors, greater beauty, and it's smaller in size. I walked miles (literally) through Pompeii's wagon wheel-rutted streets, but I saw very little of its remaining and reconstructed gardens and walls and frescos to compare it with the well-preserved beauty of Herculaneum. A superficial judgement, perhaps, but it's a <u>genuinely</u> superficial one.

Reader, if you ever have a choice, choose beautiful Herculaneum.

On the afternoon before my last day in Italy, I took a train ride by myself to visit Lecce, a town less than an hour from Ostuni. I got lost at once and discovered a theatre which I entered uninvited. There was an acting class on stage with a movement instructor showing teenagers ways and means of moving onstage using tiny as well as grand gestures.

I sat down in the back row of the orchestra and watched, able to understand every move, every acting exercise, without understanding a single Italian word. As an acting teacher I had taught my students all the same moves, particularly Italian *Commedia dell Arte* techniques. I stayed slumped down in the opera seat until someone came to tell me I was not welcome. I nodded, arose, walked like a deposed prince to the curtained entrance to the theatre, took hold of the curtain, bowed grandly to the young actors, turned, and waving the back of my hand in a princely fashion, I made a proud exit.

One of the chief joys of Italy is it invites leisurely strolling. In Lecce particularly, but also Pompeii & Ostuni & Alberobello & almost any other Italian town you name.

While waiting to return from Lecce to Ostuni, I ordered my last cappuccino at the railway station, and I sat on a bench at my platform. Holding my tiny cup & saucer, I crossed my legs at the knees the way most male Americans do. I mused that I'm the luckiest traveler on earth as I watched trains rush headlong into the station, stopping precisely without screeching where travelers were waiting. I listened for a conductor's whistle and watched each train begin moving, quickly, more quickly, fast, faster, whoosh.

Each train raced away and out of sight, and after a minute or two, there was no sound to reveal that the train had ever been there.

I thought, "That's what this trip to Italy will have been for me, my peers, and my students when I leave. A whoosh into town, a brief stop, and then a whoosh out of town."

But a delightful whoosh.

Ciao e *ciao*. [Hello & goodbye.]

An Afterword

To reiterate: In all my adventures and misadventures, I've seldom gone anywhere just to discover new or old worlds. They're always there. What I'm looking for is places and people I can enjoy. So how do I get from here to there?

Well, my best and worst travels so far have ocurred while negotiating basics like comfort, safety, good weather, good company, good food, means of controlling heat & cold, and shelter for the night.

And as the journal entry of my most recent trip to Italy will attest, I hope to whoosh away again very soon to some exotic land (exotic for me, commonplace for the natives) where I can enjoy myself and have the great pleasure of enjoying others.

Why else would anyone want to travel?

To get there?

Naaaaaa.

978-0-595-42453-5
0-595-42453-8

Printed in Great Britain
by Amazon.co.uk, Ltd.,
Marston Gate.